As a troubled teenager, Maggie Young left her hometown of [illegible] States Navy. Stationed on the USS Higgins out of San Diego, [illegible] worthy shenanigans. After a platonic, financially driven marriage, an NCIS investigation, a few wild port visits, and some turbulent affairs, she traded the Navy's ranks for UC Berkeley. After graduation, she backpacked Europe, was a television reporter in Alaska, and eventually hit a quarter-life crisis that will be documented in her next book, *My Dilemma*. Maggie has been published several times in the *San Diego Weekly Reader,* including two cover stories. Her mission is to expose corruption through a memoir's emotional authenticity. Although she's an avid world traveler, Maggie is currently based in Seattle.

Just
Another
Number

Maggie Young

BAD REPUTATION PUBLICATIONS

BAD REPUTATION PUBLICATIONS

Copyright © by Maggie Young
All right reserved. No part of this book may be reproduced, scanned, or distributed in any printed or electronic form without permission. Please do not participate in or encourage piracy of copyrighted materials in violation of the author's rights. Purchase only authorized editions.

JACKET DESIGN BY COLE SWEETON
EDITED BY ASHLEY TABORSKY

ISBN: 978-0692388129

Printed in the United States of America

To Kevin Foster Cox:
Thanks for being such a badass teacher.

"With enough courage, you can do without a reputation."

Margaret Mitchel, *Gone with the Wind*

Synopsis

I used to think that women were equal to men.

I was delusional.

After thousands of years of being pinched, painted, corseted, negotiated and sold by our daddies as the decorated broodmares they called "wives," we wear pants. We vote. We own property. And with a twenty percent pussy pay cut, we can even hold a job. We should be grateful, right?

Like most of us, I danced the independent woman charade. I played sailor with the boys. I worked. I traveled. I fucked bachelors and paraded the bars with artificial liberation. I got into a prestigious school. I was allowed in Corporate America. But like my mother, grandmother, and all the women before, I was incarcerated. My shackles were just a bit lighter.

Incarceration is the yank of hot wax ripping pubic hair from my throbbing vagina. It's the swollen blisters from the stilettos that elevate my rump to the supple, fuckable shape men like. It's the itch of a black lace thong flossing my ass cheeks. It was the pressure to join the Navy boys in their cackles of sexist gossip as if I was rushing into an elite fraternity. Incarceration is every female magazine being a recycled instruction manual for molding myself to be the perfect balance of sex kitten and angelic bride. Incarceration was being told to preserve my hymen as the ideal clean, unsullied marital livestock. Incarceration is the deprivation of chivalry, manners, friendship, intimacy, and romance that is replaced with a dick down my throat, slap on my ass, and cum on my tits followed by passive aggressive criticism about my sexual track record when I refuse to water myself down and plaster on an innocent, delirious, girlish mask. Incarceration is the way men dangle their fictitious respect for us as treats for our proper, ladylike behavior. Incarceration is the embraced and digested idioms of "boys will be boys." Incarceration is a man saying he respects a woman who doesn't prematurely spread her legs for him. Incarceration is the way a woman is expected to date like a soccer goalie-shuffling back and forth to block the balls constantly flying in her direction and shamed the moment she lets one slip in her net. Incarceration was wondering what *I* did wrong every time my lovers disappeared. Incarceration is when nobody writes a happy ending for a woman without a man.

My wakeup call wasn't some light switch of empowerment. From as early as preschool I feared that if I didn't grow up to be the pretty princess men fawned over, I was a failure. That mentality was my disease. It got me raped. It made me feel dirty and devalued because my cherry wasn't popped on a bed of rose petals. It fueled an adolescence juggling starvation and vomiting until my throat bled out and my stomach acid burned through the plumbing. It made me snort coke, smoke meth, and routinely gulp down narcotic petri dishes in hopes of obtaining hallucinogenic intimacy with junkie boyfriends. But most of all, it made me waste my youth chasing, obsessing over, fighting for, worshipping, clinging to, and crying over one after another loser. At some point, I just quit giving a fuck.

Men have ruled the majority of our history. Rarely could women get jobs, education, property, and political rights. Women had to devote their lives to beauty, virginity, and reproduction. They had to be skilled in patience, loyalty, and male ego nourishment. They had to tolerate mistresses, tempers, beatings, and belittling for the roof over their head. That has all changed. But what has happened is that emotional evolution has not caught up with our economics. We are still haunted by the outdated myth that women need men.

This book isn't about burning bras, shaving heads, or growing bush between our thighs. This book is not meant to be an exorcism of femininity, sexuality, or romance. This book isn't about disowning all of our gender roles. This book isn't meant to bash men, but to address the detrimental ways all genders have been told to act. This book is my rigorous trek to emotional freedom.

Introduction

I didn't write this book with honorable intentions. I had no plans of connecting with my readers, treading the rugged path towards gender equality, or exploiting myself for the greater good. I was just venting.

At twenty-two, I was recovering from the most recent of my slew of failed relationships. When my college professor suggested I write a book, tales of my romances and sexcapades began vomiting through my keyboard.

I was emerging my four-year and barely honorable military enlistment. Since my teens, I'd been playing roles much bigger than my combat boots.

I had been one of the many harlots repeatedly accused of contaminating America's armed forces. At eighteen, I was the thirteenth female aboard the freshly integrated USS Higgins crew. Suddenly, the glorious boys in blue were forced to serve their country without their precious nude pinup posters hung in the open. They had to walk on eggshells and learn the ropes of political correction. Affairs began, drama spread, and traditional, good-old-boy camaraderie was tainted by the temptresses who represented the inconvenience of feminism.

Less than a year out of high school, I was one of many girls planted in a steel box of men. Spotlighted in unfamiliar territory and carrying a mix of teenage insecurity, homesickness, curiosity, and hormones, we certainly rocked our boat.

Predictably, I slept around.

The females showed their vulnerability by caving into the comforting arms of their shipmates. The males put us in our place through a cat and mouse game of wooing and slut shaming.

Only the most fluent in military language dodged the bullets of heartbreak, unplanned pregnancies, mistress roles, and the wrath of jealous Navy wives.

Four months into legal drinking age, I evolved from a naive Tennessee teen to a criminal. A year into the Navy, I entered a platonic marriage for a housing allowance and off base living quarters. With a six-month NCIS investigation, interrogation, and threats of embezzlement charges, the Navy set their sights on making an example out of me. A year later, I made an example out of the Navy. Thanks to the salvation of my JAG lawyer, I escaped legally unscathed. One day into civilian freedom, I submitted my *San Diego Weekly Reader* cover story, *Confessions of a Phony Navy Wife*.

The college final paper turned smash expose' spilled the beans on the fraudulent marriages and infidelity that still run rampant in services. I told a brutally honest tale of my own reasons for entering convenient matrimony and addressed the forbidden. I targeted the flaws in America's blessed military, an establishment meant to be unconditionally honored, respected, and cherished by any decent patriot. I was referred to as both an anti-American whore and a brave truth teller. Whether condemned or praised, I got a ton of attention.

Although I could decorate *Confessions of a Phony Navy Wife* with a mission to address corruption and improve life for single sailors, my heart was vengeful. I left the Navy bruised and embittered. My words were my kick to the military's groin.

I embarked on *Just Another Number* with that emotion. I didn't understand my urge to dive into my sexual encounters. But it only took a few paragraphs to realize that I was haunted.

As an author, I became an internal pioneer. I explored the foundation of my sexuality, from my childhood discovery of self-induced orgasms, to a fifteen-year-old's road rash after shaving her southern borders. I dipped into the darkness of my adolescent drug use, eating disorders, and rape. I even had fun, gulping red wine as I splattered filthy words and my gritty episodes of intimacy clashing with bodily functions. Throughout my stories, only one message was consistent. Every grave I dug for myself was in the name of a man.

Although I left a man to enlist, ironically, the unexplainable urge to please them only amplified. Loaning my soul to the government was more intense than simply stumbling into 'bros before hoes' territory. When I enlisted, the military was rapidly changing. Technology had altered everything. Suddenly, the brave warriors parading to combat with bugles and bayonets were replaced by the push of a button. The combination of the War on Terrorism and the declining economy damaged my generation's patriotism. The Navy seemed to push old school rituals like marching, uniform inspections, and military bearing like a parent demanding their children ditch their smart phones at dinner. Once brains became more powerful than brawn in wartime, females flooded the military's ranks. The Navy began with staffing women safely ashore, but we inevitably leaked into aircraft carriers and then smaller ships. I was one of the first on my destroyer.

Like any player in tumultuous change, life wasn't easy. We were in the heart of all gossip, from our whereabouts the previous night to the ten pounds of post boot camp weight gain. Ship women were constantly accused of interrupting a crew that once functioned peacefully. We were sexual targets, marked as eternal sluts for exploring the desires only acceptable in men.

Every female handled herself differently. Many remained discreet about their personal lives. Some put on an air of meek innocence, granting them more likeability than the rest. Those who were able to pull it off rocked their tough bitch personas. My strategy was to become one of the boys. I developed the mouth of a trucker and pursued men as sexual objects. I spent four years loud-mouthed and full of fury, only to suffer the consequences of stepping out of bounds.

As I told my tales of boot camp body criticism, screaming chiefs, and affairs with married men, I emailed drafts to voluntary readers. Although I knew that I was not the only Navy woman who'd been ditched for a Thai prostitute or dubbed one of the ship's most infamous hussies, I was in awe with the level of connection they felt.

"Somehow I feel less alone and broken," they told me. "I wish I had known that somebody was going through the same thing."

Outpourings reached beyond soul sister connections. Once women caught wind of my confessional memoir, they responded with experiences far more intense than my black sheep status.

From eighteenth birthdays celebrated with threats of getting kicked out of the Navy if she dared to "fuck one of his Seamen," to rape kits mysteriously lost in the abyss of NCIS documents, I learned that my worst military horror stories were merely a taste. Aghast at how good I had it, I initially wondered why they remained so hush-hush.

"I have kids," they told me. "I'm an officer's wife. I will ruin his career if I talk about this stuff."

Then, the end of one confession never left me.

"Thank you for being so bold and brave," she wrote. "I know I could never put myself out there for the sake of my children, but I truly love you for it."

I do not claim to be a martyr or anything holier than an articulate attention whore. But despite my original intentions, my writing suddenly has a purpose beyond my understanding.

Number 1

Moccasin Bend.

"Ugh, even the name creeps me out," I thought.

I pictured a dark lake full of snarling water moccasins, eager to bite the toes off of those who dared to dabble their feet within reach. I hated snakes.

I should have been spending my winter break viewing Christmas lights with my parents or drinking peppermint milkshakes in diners with my friends. I should have been spending movie nights with girls who have skittle fights and smoke weed out of their bedroom window while profusely squirting Bath & Body Works Country Apple spray in half-assed attempts to smother each hit.

But, by my junior year, I strayed far from all squeaky clean suburban sixteen-year-old clichés.

My date that night would not end with a high school boy fumbling around my bra hook on a park bench.

I was headed to Moccasin Bend Mental Health Institute to see, not a boy, but a twenty-one-year-old man. Just as the date was unconventional, so was my preparation for it. I didn't spend hours giddily humming to music as my shaky fingers dabbed foundation on my cheeks. I wasn't daydreaming about the taste of his kiss or the scent of his cologne.

I *was* nervous, but not the cutesy kind.

It was a brisk January night. It must have been cloudy because there were no stars to decorate the sky. During the Tennessee winter, no crickets were chirping. No lightning bugs that I used to toss in mason jars as a child flew through the trees.

I drove down a long, straight road with no streetlights. Thick woods swallowed me. The distant glow of downtown Chattanooga disappeared once I turned onto that creepy road. I was all alone driving my 1994 Grand Am with the eerie, electronic sounds of Radiohead's KID-A blasting through my cheap, crackled speakers.

"Does this road ever end?" I thought, impatiently.

My chest tightened when I realized that I had been holding my breath. Despite my car's chilly interior, I felt the perspiration on my palms tightly gripping my steering wheel.

No, I wasn't eager to see this man with swollen eyes and bandaged wrists. But I was on a mission. I wanted answers to the question gnawing at my brain.

"Am I still a virgin?"

"Sex really isn't all that great," my mom, Annie, repeatedly told me as I approached puberty.

Having the limited sexual experience of an acceptable southern woman, she may have truly meant that. Or she could have been paranoid that her daughter's curiosity would lead to a repeat of her own teen pregnancy. If she had been worried about me at all, she had damn good reason.

As I shuffled through high school, I heard about the cherries of my peers popping off like fish in a barrel. Some strategized the big night with their boyfriends. Others guzzled Cuervo and spread their legs for the nearest erection. Whether romantically suited for a nostalgic *Dawson's Creek* episode or a cautionary man-hating *Lifetime* tragedy, there were always intriguing whispers between lockers.

I had no solid plans for the fate of my own flower, but as I climbed the high school ladder, the pressure to get picked only intensified.

I was already finding men to be a pathetic disappointment.

From my earliest memories, ideas of romance were imbedded into my brain through *Sleeping Beauty*, *Cinderella*, and *The Little Mermaid*. Believing that winning the heart of a man would lead me to a happy life, I kept my eyes out for that prince. But for the most part, boys were hyperactive assholes who ripped heads off the Barbie dolls I idolized. As I got older, my male expectations continued to build through *NSYNC ballads and TV shows where boys threw rocks at windows and held stereos over their heads in grand displays of affection.

My mother's romantic history wasn't exactly Hollywood magic either. The birth of her sex life quickly led to the birth of me, leaving a twenty-year-old single mom with a daughter who possessed the face of the man who chose the college life over her.

Fatherless and raised in a female dominated family, men were mysterious to me. All of my cousins, who were my best playmates, were girls. My childhood was littered with estrogen, sparkles, and My Little Ponies.

Mom and I lived with my grandparents in a tall, four-story house in the little town of Easley, South Carolina. Their digs resembled a large log cabin in the woods. Life was comfortable before my stepfather. Because of its rarity, I got a rush from male approval.

The first man in my life was my granddaddy, Everett Young. I was terrified of him. When I played too loudly, he'd shout, "Stop that noise! Hush!" Granddaddy was not comfortable around kids. He didn't read me stories or tell jokes. His voice did not raise an octave as most do when speaking to young children.

Although only 5'8", he was masculine with a sharp nose, dark eyes, and a thick, grey beard. When I was little, I was timid when having to go places with him alone. He intimidated me so much that I could not hold his hand like I held my mother's and grandmother's. Instead, I wrapped my palm around his large thumb. Holding his hand felt like too much physical closeness.

I pulled under a lamppost in the dark Moccasin Bend parking lot, relieved that it was full of cars. Appreciating a bit of company, I sat with my thoughts. My memories of Christmas break were hazy.

Since school let out, not a day went by where I didn't pop at least one kind of pill, smoke, or snort something. The popular trend among my acquaintances were prescription downers: Xanax, Klonopin, Vicodin, Lithium, and if we got lucky, the occasional Oxycodone.

Ironically, I wasn't a fan of drugs. Getting high made me paranoid. I was a bulimic teenager and already uncomfortable in my own skin. Weed only amplified that self-consciousness. The classic case of the munchies didn't help either. Every time I took Xanax, I blacked out, cried, and babbled my most intimate secrets. Oxycodone made me sick. Vicodin made me drowsy. But I took everything offered to me. Drugs were a normal social activity. I never paid a dime for them. Whatever random, unidentified pills someone managed to snag from their grandma's medicine cabinet were generously distributed at every gathering. Someone's dirt-crusted palm was always our community petri dish. I used, not because I liked or needed it, but because it was my way to bond with boys.

I got out of my car and grabbed a white plastic bag of things I brought to entertain Number 1 in rehab. He liked to draw, so I brought him a set of colored pencils, pens, and a sketchbook. I also included candy and bubble gum. I glanced at my dashboard where I kept a rubber duck I stole from a small shop in downtown Chattanooga. By then, I had become quite the kleptomaniac. I usually smuggled clothes and CDs, but the black devil horned rubber ducky was my first theft. I kept it for good luck.

"Good luck my ass," I thought, rolling my eyes.

I snatched my Satan duck and threw it in Number 1's rehab goody bag.

Once again, I asked myself the same questions.

"What happened that night? Was I raped? Is that what I'm supposed to call it?"

Beyond my confusion, I didn't feel a lot of anything. I wasn't traumatized, heartbroken, or depressed. I didn't feel violated or victimized. I just wanted to remember.

The fiasco began with an innocent visit to my friend Marshall's apartment.

It was a box-sized dump with stained, mud-brown carpet and off-white walls that were clouded with bong smoke. The neighborhood was infested with low-budget crack heads. But nineteen-year-old Marshall took pride in his "crib" after leaving his parents' suburban nest.

"You know, your boyfriend was here last night," Marshall remarked with the sly smirk, his trademark expression.

"*Ex*, Marshall. Ex-boyfriend," I scowled.

Marshall was a feisty kid who loved to provoke people, especially me. He was no different than the seven-year-old who throws rocks at the girl he likes.

Marshall was quite aware that I was still bitter about the ending of my first legitimate relationship.

"You're still in love with him!" he nagged.

"Shut the fuck up, Marshall. I am so done with him," I snapped.

"You're full of shit, Maggie," he replied nonchalantly. He kept laughing at me as I rolled my eyes.

"What is it about him anyway?" he continued. "That dude is dumb."

"Why are you even friends with him?" I asked him, trying to turn his attention away from my uneasiness.

Marshall combusted in laughter, squinting at me as if I just asked him where babies came from.

"I'm not his friend," he said. "That guy is easy as fuck to use. He just lets me smoke all his weed and take all his pills."

I began laughing with Marshall. I was always happy to hear others bash the boy who rejected me.

"Anyway," Marshall continued his trash talking, "*I'm* better looking than him."

Marshall sounded confident, but I saw him glance at me from the corner of his eye for my approval.

Marshall wasn't ugly. I just wasn't into him. He was short, without an ounce of extra fat on his body. His bleach blonde hair was buzzed. His best physical feature was his baby blue eyes that complimented his fair skin. Marshall idolized the white rapper, Eminem. He even imitated his facial features from music videos and emulated his "I don't give a fuck" persona like a gospel.

I knew Marshall from what I called "the Nightfall crowd." Nightfall was weekly Friday evening concert in downtown Chattanooga every summer. A busy road separated two sides of the park. The bands played on one side of the street, crowded with parent-aged patrons toting lawn chairs and coolers packed with boxed wine and locally brewed beer. On the other side of the street, teens sprawled out over small grass hills and clustered tightly in attempts to form discreet weed smoking burrows.

Nightfall kids were the youth who had slipped through the cracks of southern convention. Some scurried to the group as a fortress from the social ostracism chucked at them throughout childhood because of their poor families, oddball personalities, intimidating intellect, closeted homo or bisexuality, inept athletic abilities, or nerdy fetishism in video games, theatre, poetry, anime, or Internet hacking. Others willingly committed social suicide. They flaunted their rebellion with electric blue Mohawks, charcoal-smeared eyelids, baggy JNCO Jeans with marijuana leaf patches flimsily stitched on the back pockets, and jingling metal chains connecting wallets to belt loops like a dog to a leash.

Occasionally, I could spot a private school trust fund baby in Birkenstock flip-flops, a pastel Polo, and a khaki visor that sat as a crown atop thick mop of ash brown curls. They didn't linger long though. They were shoppers while the Nightfall kids were their vendors. However, most Nightfallers were the type of kids Bible Belt parents prayed their children didn't bring home.

The irony was that, with their forced diversity, they created their own cliché. Whether they donned rainbow pajamas, shredded tank tops, or bubble wrap skirts, they made great efforts to appear predictably unpredictable. It was my long blonde mane, baby pink cheeks, and fitted Gap denim that made me look like a foreigner. However, beneath my flesh, I was just like them. We were all animals trapped in a cage of Mega Churches, Tennessee Vols, and the Republican Party. Without understanding how sheltered our southern micro city bubble was or exactly why so few of us could relate to our parents, our frustrations festered into angst. We craved any substance to escape our reality. We smoked, snorted, drank, and pill popped. We hid in our rooms, locked our doors, blared songs of strung out or deceased musicians and searched for gloomy lyrics we could identify with. We scribbled them on our bodies, walls, and notebooks to accompany our own poetry of demented fantasies and chronic despair. Without understanding why, we were aimlessly broken.

Months after my breakup with my boyfriend, we were still spending every weekend together. It never occurred to me to ask myself if I had been happy in the relationship. If anyone had asked, I would not have been able to pinpoint what I liked or missed about him. I only knew that I had been dumped. For one reason or another, I wasn't good enough. Something was wrong with *me* and I had to fix it immediately.

He wasn't a catch. His looks plummeted from drugs. He had been kicked out of two high schools. Although he was highly intelligent, he lacked the social grace to project it. His transparent eagerness to be loved by everyone and anyone made him easy, vulnerable prey to even the clumsiest predators. He was the kind of guy who paid twenty-five bucks for a dime of Catnip and would snort lines of expired Aspirin if somebody asked him to.

However, his aloofness only led to my harsher self-crucifixion.

Whenever I had the gall to face my own image in a mirror, I would stand full-frontal, lift my shirt, and squeeze my lower stomach flesh with both hands. Sometimes I would hysterically sob. On the days I felt stronger, I used my sharp critiques as fuel to brace the scratches of my nails in the pit of my throat, tasting the sour burn of stomach acid and regurgitated food.

I didn't exactly adore Marshall. His companionship drained me from our constant tango along the boundaries of humor and hatred. But, I went along with our gritty banter in hopes of sparking some jealousy from my first flame.

"Your ex was fucking around with some fat skank right there," Marshall nodded his head to my lap.

His light blue eyes lit with amusement.

I let out a quick gasp as if Marshall had just pounded a hammer into my chest. Just as he intended, I was dumbstruck by not only what he said, but how casually he said it. My first boyfriend had officially moved forward and he handled the news like a chat about the weather.

"Oh, that was your boyfriend?" Marshall's roommate, my Number 1, pierced the silent corner of their den.

In the thick of the tension, I had hardly noticed him.

The three of us had been gulping hits from Marshall's bong, but he was mute besides an occasional smoker's hack.

I looked at him a bit more intensely. Number 1 was a familiar face from the Nightfall circles, but I mostly knew about him through gossip among girls. I was certain that I was alone in not feeling flustered when he greeted me with a hug. As a

Venezuelan who'd recently moved from New York City, he was certainly an exotic bird in our sheltered reality. He was reasonably handsome with jet-black hair, dark-tan skin, and charcoal eyes that widened when he smiled. His warmth and charisma made him magnetic. But for some reason, his sweetness felt a bit like a lie.

I removed myself from the seat that my old boyfriend had, according to Marshall, received a blowjob on the night before. I scooted down to the floor and snatched Marshall's bong out of his hands.

"You're really over him?" Marshall asked me, arching his eyebrows in artificial shock.

Suddenly, his expression went blank.

"I don't believe you," he said flatly. "I bet you haven't even kissed anyone since him."

My chest tightened. It was true. My ex and I had been broken up for four months and I had yet to touch another boy.

"I bet you won't let him lick your pussy," he stated, glancing at Number 1.

Number 1's eyes widened, but he kept quiet.

It took me a few seconds to process our dialogue.

"Are you fucking serious, Marshall?" I asked.

My reaction was a bit delayed from the weed.

"Look at you," he taunted. "You're scared!"

"I'm not just going to let just any guy's tongue inside of me!"

With the exception of my sloppy first truth or dare kiss with a boy who'd jumped in a pool of Axe body spray and swapped gum with me mid tongue thrust, my old boyfriend was the only person I had been physically involved with. For the first time that night, I truly took notice that I was the only girl, high, and in an apartment with two men. Nobody knew that I was there. I briefly considered bolting out the door with my purse and keys when Marshall said just the thing to grasp complete control.

"Imagine how pissed off your ex would be if he found out."

Suddenly, my fury cut through my fear. I looked at Number 1, who stared straight back at me, still silent. Without a thought, I took his hand and pulled him into his bedroom. I shut the door behind me. I was relieved to be in the dark, silent room away from Marshall.

"I'm a virgin," I blurted.

I must have looked like the child in my yellow hoodie, frightened blue eyes, and wavy blond hair that frizzed over my round cheeks.

"That's okay," he said soothingly.

"I don't want to lead you on," I explained. "So, before we do anything, I'm telling you now that sex isn't happening."

"No worries," he reassured me. "There's no pressure to do anything."

I realized what bothered me about him. It wasn't his bright and constant smile, or his exaggerated happiness. It was his voice. When he spoke, he was neutral of any accent. He didn't possess the nasal, bold tone of New York and also lacked a southern twang. It was his pitch. It was too feminine. I was suddenly turned off by any hint of attraction I may have had for him.

I stood motionless in the dark room with Number 1 inches away from me.

"He's going to kiss me," I thought. I was nervous, but there were no gleeful jumps in my stomach. Having kissed only two boys in my life, I was curious to see what Number 1's kiss felt like, but nothing about what was happening thrilled me.

I felt the warmth of his body press up against mine. His tongue was quickly inside my mouth. His lips were soft. His kisses were gentle, with no aggression. It was obvious that Number 1 was more experienced than his predecessor. He lacked the awkward teenage tendencies of choking me with his tongue or salivating on the side of my face.

We continued to make out and stumbled to his small, single bed in the corner of his messy room, tripping over piles of clothes on the floor. The clutter quickly escaped my mind as I sat on his bed with Number 1 climbing in with me.

"This can't be happening," I told myself, high enough for every rustle to repeatedly echo in my ears. I thought of my ex-boyfriend again.

"Why doesn't he want me?" I thought. "His friends want me, but not him." Once again, I felt tears rise into my eyes and blinked them away.

Then a faint optimistic sensation approached me.

"But everyone's going to know about this tomorrow," I thought, brightening up. "Of course Marshall's going to run his big mouth about what happened tonight."

I lied back in the bed, still smiling. Thinking I was smiling because I was enjoying myself, Number 1 returned my gaze with his bright, fake grin and unzipped my jeans. I resisted the urge to squirm away from him. I dreaded revealing any skin my clothes covered.

"And here comes Marshall's dare," I thought, forcing my eyes not to roll.

I had only experimented with oral sex once before in an awkward attempt to try it for the first time with my ex. We snuck under the pool table in my parents' game room on the 4th of July before my uncle barged in.

"Am I even wearing cute underwear?" I wondered, nervously. "When did I last shave?"

From my first stab at second base, I became obsessively concerned for my vaginal upkeep. I began shaving the day after I felt my first tongue down my throat. The first buzz was a disaster, causing horrifically itchy dull razor breakout that made me look like I made love to a poison ivy bush. Whenever I thought there was a chance of unveiling my privates, I smothered every breakout with the same foundation I used for the occasional teenage acne face breakouts. Because of the spontaneity of my first night with Number 1, I was not baby-smooth. But since I didn't even like him, I didn't give a shit about what he would find beneath my cotton bikini panties.

"Off they go," I thought as Number 1 pulled off my jeans and underwear, tossing them on the floor by the bed.

I lay back on his bed and closed my eyes. He slid his tongue inside of me. I shut my eyes tighter and tried to relax and enjoy the experience.

His tongue was slender, moving around my clit too quickly. His hands were as soft as his lips. As he felt up my snatch, I became very afraid that sex was *terribly* overrated.

Although Number 1's tongue did not cause me to scream out in pleasure or claw the skin on his back, it still succeeded in heating things up between us. My skin grew balmy as he began to lightly suck on my neck, rubbing himself up against me.

I noticed that Number 1 had taken his pants off and was in nothing but his boxers. He was on top of me as I sat upright against the wall his bed rested on. My legs were spread, Number 1's torso against mine. I realized that only two thin layers of cloth separated his baby maker and mine. What had been excitement turned to fear. Getting the sudden urge to open my eyes, I looked down in shock.

"Oh my God! His dick is out!" I thought, furious with his attempt to slip it inside of me as if I wouldn't notice.

I quickly put my hand down, blocking his reach of anything between my legs.

"No!" I scolded him as if he was a dog about to piss on the carpet.

"What?" he asked innocently. "Relax, Maggie, I wasn't going to actually put it in." His face looked hurt.

I was annoyed with him, but assumed that maybe I was jumping to conclusions. I was sixteen and he was twenty-one. I didn't want to seem immature. What my virginity couldn't assist me in had to be replaced by my attitude.

"Sorry, " I told him, trying to sound sincere. "This is just moving too fast. I'm going to put my jeans on."

BANG! BANG! BANG! came from the door out of nowhere.

"GET THE FUCK OUT OF MY ROOM!" Marshall shouted at his roommate. "I'm tired. You horny little bitches can fuck around in the living room!"

Number 1 ended up unconscious and snoring with his body wrapped around mine like a burrito. I was exhausted, but my claustrophobia kept me awake.

"I didn't see this coming," he mumbled as the sun began to rise.

"Neither did I," I robotically replied.

"But I'm glad it happened," he continued, softly kissing me on the cheek.

"Is this guy kidding?" I wondered.

I assumed that we were just following Marshall's dare. Did he actually interpret it as something more?

"I need to go," I said the moment I knew that I could get away with going home without my parents getting suspicious of my excursions.

I wanted to escape the grasp of Number 1 and hide inside my own bed. I didn't even realize that I had just spent my first full night with a boy.

I squirmed out of his grasp and walked out the door. The screen slammed behind me.

It was 7 am by the time I pulled into Flagstone Drive. I lived in a picture perfect subdivision with color coordinated houses and mailboxes, yellow labs prancing within the borders of invisible electric fences, and balding dads on riding lawn mowers. It was the type of community where housewives spent their summers tanning by the pool, half-heartedly watching their Ritalin pumped brat beat another brat with a foam noodle while rehashing Sunday's Bible study between whispers of Susie's weight gain and Dan's canoodling with the babysitter.

I foggily drove through the rolling hills. My neck was sore from being crammed in a moldy loveseat with Number 1. Approaching my driveway, I was relieved that my mom's mobile dog grooming van was gone.

My relationship with my stepfather, Carl, had always been complicated. He came into my life when I was six years old. My mother met and married him in four months, igniting my temper tantrums at the news of their engagement. Despite going through the motions of legal adoption, Carl never developed the "I'll kill you if you lay a hand on my princess," protectiveness stereotyped in southern daddies. When my mom wasn't watching, Carl didn't flinch on the nights I stumbled into our front door slurring my speech and practically drooling out the corners of my lips.

My teenage sex talk was as simple as, "Yer sixteen. If yer not fuckin' now, you will be soon. Let's getcha on tha pill." In Mom's absence, Carl played good cop, making it easy to for me to sneak gulps of Grey Goose from his garage liquor cabinet while he lounged on our large back deck and entertained his belligerent buddies with his vibrating, ten-thousand-dollar stereo system. However, in Mom's presence, Carl was the domineering, temperamental disciplinary who barked orders, sentenced groundings, and demanded the title, "Sir."

"This is nuthin' compared to what ma parents woulda done," was his go-to justification for every outburst of belittlement. "Yer just lucky I haven't beat tha tar outta ya like ma old man."

Carl constantly told horror stories of cursing and beatings from his father and the twenty-four-hour blackout screaming of his alcoholic, pill-popping mother. He used his trauma like a caution sign for what he could do if I didn't silence my backtalk.

As a child, I ate up the image Carl strived to portray: An inspirational rags-to-riches tale of a go-getter emerging the hell of his sulfur-scented, Podunk Texas upbringing. With a community college dropout education, Carl managed to reach six figures as a mobile home lot manager when the trailer park industry boomed in the early nineties. He decorated his accomplishments with a large house, yachts, and weekly morale shindigs for his salesmen bursting with open bars and filet mignon. However, my mother was by far his prettiest accessory. When they met, she was the prized, sparkly-eyed-twenty-six-year-old, platinum blonde daughter of the wealthy chiropractor who owned the land his lot stood on.

Even into middle age, Annie emulated the innocence of a six-year-old girl because she never had to face responsibilities beyond that maturity level. As a child, her four siblings would be elbow deep in yard work beneath a layer of grimy sweat within the scorching South Carolina summers while Annie lollygagged in the bathroom, claiming that she could not so much as touch a pine cone until her golden locks were curled to perfection. However, Annie was far too adorable to be scolded for laziness. She grew up without discipline or even obligations to hold humbling service jobs as a roller skate waitress or greasy fast food cashier. Although my grandparents lived like the depression babies they were and almost relished faking poverty, their bank accounts were mysteriously bottomless. Annie was cheery, charming, and universally likeable. Her interests were too cluttered with beauty products, baking, and cute, fluffy animals to allow room for controversy. The first true crack in her yellow brick road was my out-of-wedlock birth. Even though it was considered one of the greatest sins within my staunchly religious family, my conception was shrugged off as a brief slip from a girl swept away with her first love.

"I would have followed him to the end of the world," Annie always said of my biological father.

My mother's true appeal went beyond the clash of the beautiful trust fund darling as the arm candy of an overweight trailer salesman. Carl grew up in harsh, chaotic poverty. His escape was the alcoholism that was conceived during puberty and flourished throughout adulthood. His initial career was a diesel mechanic wearing faded coveralls with oil up his nails and sweat on his brow. His earliest homes were the dingy trailers he would later profit from. His first marriage was doused with benders, acid trips, and sex crazed parties packed with orgies with a first wife who'd lost track of number of dicks shoved down her throat in the midst of intoxication. I don't know what sparked his revelation, but at some point, Carl decided to fiercely pursue the world he envied. He wanted a life of starched, white shirts, ties, SUVs, and picket fences. He ached for the scent of steaks grilling on his sunny patio. He dreamed of white-collar southern beauty and my mother, in all her naïve innocence, was the loveliest possession he could ever obtain.

Once Carl charmed my grandparents, I stood as his only obstacle. Six-year-olds just aren't old enough to be swayed by sales tactics.

After his honeymoon, Carl was welcomed home with mail fraud accusations. The three of us moved to Chattanooga, Tennessee, which was four hours away from my grandparents. That's when my problems began.

One would have thought that my grandparents resented me for the negative attention my conception drew around their religious Easley Baha'i community. Although gossip and backbiting is considered the Baha'i Faith's most detrimental sin, southerners have mastered picking, choosing, and rationalizing religious texts to fit their social agenda better than their own mother's fried chicken recipe.

"*Psst! Don't sit on the toilet seats*," Grandmother would hiss to her children before entering the Baha'i gathering at the home of Osie Jones. "Her daughter, Rhonda has *herpes.*"
I can only imagine what they said about my mother. Parenting had never been Grandmother Adele Young's forte. At seventeen, Adele boarded a bus from her dusty, cotton factory farm town, Thomaston, Georgia, to Palmer Chiropractic

College in Davenport, Iowa. She socially and academically fought her way through chiropractic school as one of just two or three women in her graduating class. I don't know if my granddaddy put her in her place, or that she just gave up, but Adele surrendered her path as a female medical pioneer for the life of a privileged housewife. Far too intellectual for her role, she busied herself with spa retreats, pottery camps, pilot school, and acquiring college art degrees she would never use. To this day, her children claim she was both physically and emotionally absent, suspecting she popped out five of them out of pure boredom.

But by the time I came around, Grandmother softened into her fifties and her maternal instincts finally developed. My mother and I lived under my grandparents' roof. They funded each and every one of Mom's flighty, short-lived goals towards incomplete college educations, beauty school, and finally pet grooming. While Annie played mommy here and there, Grandmother handled the grunt work, getting me into Greenville's most prestigious Montessori preschool and flaunting me around the southeast for Baha'i retreats like her beloved doll. To my grandparents, I was much more than a granddaughter. I was their do-it-right-this-time prize they finally had the maturity to mold into their pristine human being.

"You weren't an accident," Grandmother repeatedly told me. "God put you on this earth for a reason. *You,* Miss Maggie, are destined to change the world."

It wasn't really a loud-mouthed, hyperactive little pig-tailed blonde that made Carl cringe. It was what I represented. While his upbringing was battered humiliation, I was spoiled, doted on, and spoon-fed by the world. I don't think he was even aware of his intentions to reduce that child to his own state of self-loathing, but he was truly brilliant at it. Carl never crossed the line of abuse. He just crept up to it and lingered there. He never hit me. He never touched me. He only played subtle, but potent mind games as fluid as the air he breathed.

My mother, forever a child herself, remained at her back seat parenting. She just watched, numb and empty headed. At seven years old, Carl felt that I wasn't eating enough vegetables. He spent hours forcing me to swallow the chalky, adult-sized pills that were too big for my throat. I wailed like a prisoner unaware of the crime I committed. I thought I would die right there in the kitchen chair I was confined to, choking to death. Then I figured I could chew that pill to freedom. I remember breaking open the gel cap between my baby teeth and feeling the bitter, dirt paste seep into my mouth. I struggled to collect enough saliva in the crevice of my gums to wash away the taste until my stomach jolted uncontrollably. My throat felt like floodgates pried open by a tsunami as vomit exploded out of my mouth. I was so embarrassed. I just cried as Carl demanded I clean my mess, rolled his eyes, and stormed away.

I quit sleeping when we moved to Tennessee. I didn't understand the cause of my insomnia. I only knew that sleep meant surrendering control of my body. That terrified me.

It wasn't that every day was hell with Carl. Before we moved away, he was actually an attentive new stepdad. I ate up the masculine activities he introduced to me, like fishing and camping. Since Carl wasn't a Baha'i, he brought the Christmas rituals I'd been deprived of. We ventured into the woods and chopped down a flimsy, malnourished pine tree to layer with plastic red and green balls and Wal-Mart candy canes. He loaded my stockings with toys and even bought the massive, Pepto-Bismol pink Barbie Dream House I'd been drooling over. I can only imagine how endearing he seemed to my mother as he knelt over to drill his Mega Pro screwdriver into the glitter sunroom. In his earliest daddy days, he sat through Disney movies, fastened hair bows, and gracefully accepted F's when we played school. That's why I spent my childhood in denial of the relief I felt when he was gone.

When I was nine, our patio talks began. Carl would lean back on a cushioned deck chair, his gut toppling over his belt. He held a teal, plastic liter mug filled with iced Jack and Coke in his right hand and a cigarette in his left. We would banter back and forth about society, human nature, and life goals. To an outsider, the interaction between the middle-aged southern salesman and a child may have seemed bizarre, but it provided a philosophical outlet Carl couldn't find with my mom. Annie lived to please others. She was raised by Granddaddy at the height of his male domineering ferocity. She grew up around Granddaddy's frustrated scowls at my retaliating Grandmother, Adele, questioned him. She challenged him. She outwitted him. She was the better chiropractor and the tougher fighter. Time and time again, he kicked her out of his office, knocked her up, and restricted her chiropractic adjustments to kitchen tables and living room floors. In the end, he preferred a bubbly housewife who knew when to marinate her pot roast and shut her trap.

"I just wanted my dad to like me," Mom often told me.

Although I've known Mom my entire life, she's a stranger to me because she is a stranger to herself. She had nothing to teach me beyond scouting discount facials and manicures. There was no denying that Mom dumbed herself down to please the men in her life, but I still can't figure out whether it has been an act all this time or permanent damage. I just know that she blossomed from the perfect daddy's girl to the ideal wife. She cooked Carl's chicken fried steak, laughed at his jokes, and adopted his opinions. When they argued, she pouted, but never defied him. Although she was the puppet he cherished far more than the rest of his toys, the oblivion that made their marriage work was also its void. Carl saw me as a little girl precocious enough to entertain him, but naïve enough to nourish his ego. I could spout feedback to keep the banter alive, but he would always be the father of all knowledge. Carl saw the immediate impacts of our talks, like nods, grins, and arguments but the premonitions stopped there. Our chats occurred during my construction. A child is like a soft lump of clay. Carl was my artist. My life views on sex, men, dating, and self-worth were sculpted by the unfiltered ramblings of a drunken misogynist.

"The last thing ya wanna do is get fat," Carl mentioned.

I was eleven and on the brink of a prepubescent chubby phase.

"Now yer not bad now. Only bout fav' er ten pounds overweight. But you don't wanna lose control. The worlda' treat ya differently. You'll have less opportunities and it'll be harder ta landa man with a good payin' job."

Starvation was the first indication of my self-discipline. I was devoted to anorexia. I went the distance of memorizing the calorie content within every bite of food while calculating the exact amount of exercise I needed to burn double my consumption. I was luckily young enough to mask my excessive exercise with juvenile hyperactivity. Nobody thought twice about the fact that I was constantly rollerblading, biking, and running for hours in stifling summer humidity. I learned to cut my food into tiny bites and move it around my plate. I read that standing burned more calories than sitting, so I refused to watch television without doing crunches, leg lifts, or at least walking in place. When socially forced to soldier through a movie, I tapped my foot in desperation to knock out about seventy-five extra calories. From age eleven to twelve, I dropped forty pounds and halted the one period I'd had.

"I'm proud of ya. You look great!" Carl told me.

But I couldn't let my guard down. I knew that Carl's eye was watchful because my puberty progression was a constant conversation topic. Carl liked to talk about the female form. Once I lost weight, he elevated my status above my cousins because they were getting chubby into puberty. He praised my genetic lottery by telling me, "You look exactly like your mother," he told me when I was about twelve. "Cept' you got tha ass. I have no idea what tha hell happened to hers."

Carl often spat out advice for my future dating life. He never described the type of man I should go for beyond one that makes a good bit of cash. He never taught me to seek intelligence, education, or respect. He never cautioned me to look for chivalry, door openings, dinner payments, or flowers on the right occasions. It wasn't about how he would earn me, but how I would earn him.

"Every man wants sex and nuthin' more," Carl told me. "So, if ya give 'em what he wants right away, he'll think you're a whore, stick his dick in ya, and move on. String 'em along for 'bout a month. Get 'em investin' his time. Play hard to get. Give 'em blue balls."

"But once ya get 'em," he told me one night when I was about fourteen. His face was bloated and flushed from his third liter of Jack and Coke. "Don't be a prude lak your muther."

Carl discreetly turned his head to the left and then the right to make sure Mom wasn't within hearing range.

"I tried to stick it in er ass once and she didn't speak to me for a week," he nearly whispered before belting out a slur of loose chuckles. "And gettin' 'er to do ya on top? Forget about it!"

In ways, I morphed into Carl's description of the ideal woman. Like Mom, physical beauty was my ultimate priority. I spent hours on end stripped naked, posing in front of my full length bedroom mirror at every angle so that each wrinkle, roll, and pinch of fat could receive sharp scrutiny before I strived for complete self annihilation. I made it a habit of studying every *Teen* magazine model and the skinniest cheerleaders in my middle school yearbook. I observed their arms, legs, and hips. I held their images against mine with a goal for my bones to protrude further and calves spread further apart when standing straight. However, I saw the way Carl bent his head down and lowered his voice when he spoke about Mom, as if it was our job to keep a feisty, barking puppy believing that it was our guard dog.

"Ure mom can't help she got half ure I-Q," Carl would chuckle.

I took pride in our superiority. I made valiant efforts to be Mom's opposite. I rebelled against her smiley, likeable character. I grew into a confrontational, brooding teenager. I learned to push buttons and to make snide, inappropriate remarks in front of their friends. While Mom was a blonde ball of sunshine, I wore despair like a fashionable cloak. Bulimia was flattering apparel.

After three years of anorexia, I was hungry. I was at war with my body, desperately fighting its natural progression to womanhood. I couldn't focus in class because I was thinking about food more than a nymphomaniac thinks about sex. I caught myself digging in our household garbage cans to nibble half eaten burgers like a malnourished Holocaust prisoner.

At fifteen, I went on a month long Baha'i youth retreat to Dallas. It was the longest stint away from home I'd ever had. Although I never felt homesickness, I couldn't shake the fear of gaining weight and Carl noticing. It only took a socially mandatory pizza party to send me hiding in the bathroom to hack up the half slice with the cheese scraped off.

"Well, looks like ya lost a few pounds," Carl remarked.

I had just gotten back that morning. I was in my parents' bathroom treating myself to my mom's fancy beauty products and curling iron when Carl walked in. His first response to my arrival wasn't to rush over and hug me or to ask me about the friends I made. Before even saying hello, his eyes shot to my toes, up my legs, my body, and all the way to my eyes like he was waiting for me to drop something I'd stolen.

After a long silence, he said, "You look good."

He nodded in approval and walked away.

"Did you have fun last night?" Carl asked me.

He was six feet tall and a hefty three hundred pounds. He had slightly salty, hazelnut, feathered crew cut with goatee to match. He always wore slacks, loafers, and a white dress shirt to work held together with a black leather belt that, when hung up, was nearly as tall as me. Despite his physique, he never ate breakfast. He was preparing his morning coffee when I came home from my night with Number 1. Carl always knew when I was out partying, but a parental interrogation was always more effort than he ever felt like making.

"You're home awful early," he commented casually. "Well, I'm off. Have a good day," Carl said, before heading out into the garage to start up his truck.

I felt relief when he was finally gone.

"Thank God," I thought. "I'm starving."

I could finally binge without judgment. I hated that my parents closely eyed every morsel of food I consumed, knowing that I intended to hurl it all up minutes later.

I would be home alone all day. I wouldn't have to turn on the shower to muffle my gagging sounds with running water. That was one of my best bulimia hiding tricks. I used to unscrew the shower drain and vomit when I was actually in the shower. It worked well because the running water smothered my purging sounds. The water also cleaned up my vomit. I hated scraping regurgitated food splattered on the side of the toilet seat. But after several months of my shower tactic, my stomach acid burned through the pipes. My parents were furious with the damage costs. They saw my knuckles scarred with tooth marks. They knew my taste buds were impaired from stomach acid when I complained about the water tasting funny.

"We know what you're doing, Maggie," they said. "We've already wasted a thousand dollars on that psychiatrist that's not doin' a damn thing to change ya. We're sick of throwin' money at the treatment you just blow off."

I knew I was sick. There was something extremely fucked up about a girl vomiting in Tupperware and hiding it in her closet. There was nothing normal about a sixteen-year-old who stole junk food from grocery stores, only to quickly gulp it down and drive to random public restrooms to throw it all back up.

At night, I'd lie in bed with my throat burning and heart racing, wondering how much longer I would keep it up. But the next day, my stomach would growl. I would tell myself, "Just one more time. This is the last time. I swear. I'll stop after I eat this." I would desperately devour the food, hating myself more and more with every bite. Once the belly growling ceased, I loathed the full feeling of food digesting in my stomach. I had to get rid of that horrible food that had the power to make me fat and ugly. Each time, I fled to the bathroom, closed my eyes, practically shoved my entire fist down my throat, and heaved up every warm, burning clump I could force. The more empty my stomach became, the greater my success.

I pulled out some leftover meat lover's pizza Carl ordered the night before. I ate a few slices, went to the bathroom, and freely gagged and coughed as loudly as I needed to. I felt dirty from the stench of smoke clinging to my skin and the memory of Number 1.

Later that day, I spent the night before Christmas Eve at work. I was a hostess at a restaurant. Due to the holidays, few customers walked through the door, so I devoted my time to coloring inside the children's menus when I suddenly felt my phone vibrate.

"Oh my God, it's him," I thought, surprised that Number 1 was calling me so soon. I ran to the bathroom to answer my phone.

"Hi, Maggie!" he exclaimed in his fake, happy voice. "I had so much fun with you last night!"

I wasn't crazy about him, but I liked the attention.

"Hey…um…yeah, I had fun too," I replied, trying to sound sincere.

"Marshall and I are having a party tonight," he continued. "Please come," he almost pled.

I was shocked. It had not once crossed my mind that Number 1 would want a continuing thing.

"Maybe it'll be a good distraction," I rationalized.

Sure, Number 1 didn't make me giddy or even happy, but he was interesting. He was different, older, and popular among my circle of friends. I figured they saw something that I overlooked and if I spent enough time with him, I would find it.

"Here I go, my first trip to a rehab," I nervously told myself, trying to bring humor to the situation. "Think of this as an adventure."

I stepped through the sliding doors into what looked like a hospital. Instantly, I heard screams in the background. They weren't shrill, agonizing cries. They sounded like the incoherent shouts of a mentally retarded patient. I always felt awkward around people with mental disabilities. Even with a child's mind, it felt rude to speak to an adult like one. I had always rushed by the mental handicap section of my school.

A plump, middle-aged nurse with a mud brown curly mom-bob greeted me. Her stern frown strongly distinguished her forehead wrinkles.

"Please sign in," she ordered flatly.

She pointed to a stack of necklaces tagged "visitor" beside the sign-in sheet. "Visiting time ends in an hour."

I glanced in my large, bedroom mirror before heading out to Number 1's party. I was dissatisfied with the bags under my eyes from malnutrition and sleep deprivation. My thick, blonde hair looked like a lion's mane framing my round, childlike face. My bulimia and drug use had gradually destroyed the healthy glow in my skin. My relatives assumed I was ill at Thanksgiving.

I considered myself fairly attractive. I had been told my entire life that I was blessed with a pretty face. My body was my ultimate vice. I was grateful that the weather was cold enough to blanket it with a baggy, baby blue hoodie.

Number 1's street was packed with rickety used cars accessorized with dents, window cracks, and bumper stickers of assorted marijuana leaves, Darwin fish, and bands ranging from classic rock, grunge, and modern metal. Number 1 and Marshalls' apartment boomed with a mush of bass and laughter.

I climbed the stairs to his apartment and opened the same screen door I slammed behind me earlier that morning.

The moment I walked in, my eyes caught the last thing I wanted to see.

"Oh FUCK!" my brain screamed as my heart jumped into the back of my throat.

Straight in front of me was my old boyfriend with his arms around his blowjob girl. Her name was Kari.

My brain immediately went into defense mode as I summarized all the ways in which I was superior to her. I scanned every inch of her to compile the most thorough degradation I could muster. Although I could not confirm her figure while she was curled up on the couch, she looked about 5'2" with a plump frame. She had a fine, black bob pulled into short pigtails. She wore an unflattering pair of worn, baggy jeans and an old, black t-shirt that hung loosely from her double D-cup breasts, making it look like maternity wear.

"Gross." I thought to myself. "She looks like a beached whale."

I fantasized about kicking her throat in.

Months after my first real breakup, I was experiencing the ego thrash that comes with watching an old boyfriend move on. I was lucky she wasn't a beauty queen. Dissecting her physical flaws was the aspirin that would not heal my wounds, but temporarily eased my pain. For the first time in my life, I managed to behave like a true southern belle. I lifted my lips into a bright smile and warmly greeted my enemy as if she were my new best friend.

With all the phony verbal sugar I could muster I said, "Hi! We haven't met before. My name's Maggie."

She obliviously smiled back. I knew it wasn't fair to hate her. The boy who had his arm around her was no longer mine. She most likely had no clue that he ever was. But my heart was too full of wrath for logic.

"Maggie!" shouted Number 1, greeting me with his bright smile and a hug. I returned his embrace before sneaking a quick glare at my ex.

"Fine," I thought, smugly. "If he wants to fuck around with some cunt, I'm not going to let it bother me."

Number 1 fed my revenge.

I wrapped my arms around his neck and forcefully kissed him in the middle of the crowded room. As soon as our lips parted, I looked around Number 1's dirty apartment. The party had an impressive turnout. There were a lot of people there, accompanied with the usual stench of weed and cigarettes.

"You want a beer?" Number 1 offered.

Nodding, I grabbed the forty he had in his hand. The heavy, jabbing pain of jealousy still weighed down my chest. I needed to make it disappear.

I sucked down the sour liquid, which tasted like carbonated urine. I intended to drown myself with it.

"Do you want some of these?" one Nightfall boy asked me, opening up his sweaty palm.

He held out several pills in his hand.

Pill popping added an extra touch to alcohol consumption. Although I was secretly afraid of all of the drugs I took, alcohol had a comforting familiarity. At fourteen years old, booze only amplified the fun of pajama parties. I would invite a few girls over and we would break into Carl's liquor stash. We made nauseating concoctions of peach schnapps, Goldschlager, tequila, and orange juice. We guzzled our magic potion, basking in the newness of its euphoria. We would wrestle, have pillow battles, and dance in the rain. We would even load water guns and squirt bourbon into our mouths. What I loved the most about inebriation was that it was a vacation from the shackles of my body.

After four mystery pills and what seemed like a gallon of beer, the rest of the night became a shattered puzzle. I would never recover all the pieces.

I remember getting into a screaming fight with my ex. I clearly recall climbing on top of Number 1, who was sitting on the chair we dozed on the night before. I groped him and slid my lips all over his throat and neck. I knew that I was faking passion in order to put on a show for everyone else. Even buried in intoxication, my pain and resentment didn't fade. My next memory is Number 1 on top of me on the floor in his bedroom. Our heads rested on a pile of dirty laundry. His hand was up by shirt, grabbing one of my under-developed breasts. I remember hating the way he kissed me, shoving his tongue deep inside my throat and moving it around rapidly. But I didn't fight it. I felt like a rag doll, conscious but unmotivated to move.

"BANG! BANG! BANG!" the sound jolted me to full consciousness.

Once again, Marshall was pounding outside the bedroom door.

I don't remember walking into the bathroom with Number 1, but I remember the floor. Lying on my back, the cold, grimy tile against my body, I felt paralyzed as Number 1 tried to shove his dick down my throat. At the time, I hated giving blowjobs. I had only made one half-hearted attempt with my boyfriend. The task terrified me. I didn't touch Number 1 nor did I stop him. I couldn't act and I couldn't think. As I gagged on his flesh with the occasionally stray pubic hair that made me want to hurl, I felt like I was dead with my soul barely hovering over my body. I don't know how I lost my clothes. With my extreme body insecurities, I had never been completely bare for any man and lacked the confidence to peel off my shirt at my own will.

The next thing I remember is Marshall's angry voice.

"BANG! BANG! BANG!"

"What the fuck are you doing in there?" he screamed at Number 1. "Maggie! Are you okay?"

I didn't answer. I don't remember why.

"She's fine!" Number 1 yelled back.

This was the first time I'd heard him sound truly angry. It scared me a bit.

"Chill the fuck out!" Number 1 roared at Marshall again after another loud banging on the door.

"Maggie!" Marshall yelled again. "Maggie! What the hell are ya'll doing in there?"

I woke up on the bathroom floor, naked and alone.

I was disoriented, but managed to find my clothes after a few moments of fumbling in my pitch-black confines. I quickly put them on, eager to cover my body. I stumbled out of the bathroom, through Number 1's room, and saw that there were few people left in the den. I heard angry voices outside. I opened the screen door. I was numb to the chilly night air. Number 1 and Marshall were screaming at each other. I clearly heard the sounds of their voices, but couldn't comprehend their words. I couldn't comprehend much of anything. I was a zombie going through the rudimentary motions of a human being.

Kari stood close behind me.

"Are they going to fight?" I slurred.

"I don't know," she answered blankly as she stared at them beside me.

"What are they so angry about?"

"I don't know," she repeated, still not taking her eyes off of them.

After witnessing Marshall and Number 1's heated conflict, I completely blacked out the rest of that night. I had no idea what time I went to sleep, or how I got back into the apartment. A splotchy memory was a normal night of partying for me.

I awoke on Number 1's filthy, brown living room carpet with his arms wrapped tightly around me. It was Christmas Eve. I coughed. My throat felt hot and dry. I had a severe case of cottonmouth. I felt a sharp pain in the back of my neck and my head was aching. But my excruciating discomfort was an unfamiliar throbbing between my legs.

When I forced by body into a sitting position, I fought back the tears welling up in my eyes from the pain and turned on my phone.

"Fuck!" I shouted.

"What's wrong baby?" Number 1 responded, groggily.

He wrapped his arms around my waist, squinting a bit.

"It's 3 o'clock!" I shrieked.

It was Christmas Eve. My parents have no idea where I am.

It was 4 pm by the time I pulled into my empty driveway. The cloudy winter sky was slowly beginning to darken from the short days. I unlocked my front door and walked into the warmth of the house. I loved the scent that welcomed me. Annie always covered the house with air fresheners and potpourri. She made the extra effort to light holiday pumpkin scented candles and replace floral potpourri with festive apple cinnamon. Our Christmas tree stood in plain view inside our large living room. The dark green pine needles looked picturesque against the burgundy carpet it stood on, with several wrapped gifts underneath.

"Mom!" I yelled aloud, to see if anyone was home. "Carl!"

The house was deserted of all human beings.

Groggy and very sore at the mere motion of walking, I crookedly shuffled to the bathroom. The drugs had diluted my emotions. I was not concerned about getting in trouble from my parents for arriving home so late and ignoring the angry voicemails they left on my phone. I didn't find it odd that nobody was home on Christmas Eve. I didn't think twice about my bloodstained panties.

I heard the sound of our garage door opening.

I strolled into the kitchen to greet them, as they walked through the garage door. I forced a smile and tried to appear oblivious.

"Hey, Mom."

"MAGGIE!" Carl boomed.

"Oh great, here comes the man of the house," I thought sarcastically.

"WHERE THE HELL WERE YOU?" he snapped again.

I began my usual bullshit story of my phone dying and staying up all night, talking with my friends and accidently sleeping in too late.

"Well, Helen died last night," Mom informed me. She was puffy-eyed and calm.

Helen was a friend of our family and a member of the Baha'i Faith, the religion my grandparents avidly followed. Helen had been sick for a long time, but the quickness of her death and funeral the following morning was shocking. I hadn't been close to her, but had known her since childhood.

"But, Mom, that was so soon to have a funeral," I explained. "I'm sorry, but how was I supposed to know?"

"Ya need ta remember to charge up that damn phone," Carl scolded. "We had Christmas dinner without ya. Leftovers'er in tha fridge."

I was too lethargic to care. I retreated to my bedroom, threw off my shoes, and buried my head underneath my blankets.

I continued to see Number 1. I didn't question our night on the bathroom floor. He never pushed the issue of sex with me again. We never went beyond kissing and cuddling. But his personality began to change dramatically. His cheerfulness and optimism festered into constant negativity.

"What the hell am I doing with my life?" he always questioned. "I hate Tennessee. I hate my life. I miss New York."

"Then why did you leave?" I asked him.

"I got fired from my smoothie shop job."

"For what?"

"Stealing money from the cash register."

As the days passed, Number 1's vices seemed to amplify. He was clingy, and called every day, though he seemed to resent me when we were together. He would complain about his endless problems in his life and would snap back at me when I tried to encourage him to make things better for himself.

"Why don't you go to school?" I suggested. "Go job hunting."

"You don't know anything about the world," he would sneer. "You're just a little girl."

I began to laugh at him.

"Yeah, a little girl with a job and a car, unlike you," I snapped back.

I had to admit that I was proud of myself when I saw his round, black eyes widen. But then, he would cry.

"I hate myself!" he'd whine. "I want to die."

I tried to be kind and comfort him. I built up his good qualities, though I secretly despised his weakness. Coddling his self-esteem was too much work for a man I couldn't even get excited over.

"Why are you so down on yourself?" I'd ask, trying to sound as sympathetic as possible. "Everyone loves you. You have so many friends."

"I guess you're right," he'd sniff.

"And he thinks *I'm* the little girl?" I thought, sarcastically, rolling my eyes when he wasn't looking.

Number 1 grew erratic and paranoid. He questioned me every time I talked to another male and would erupt in a jealous rant every time I even spoke to Marshall. The hostile dynamic was Marshall's playground. At that point, their abode was a boiling pot of water.

The more time I spent with Number 1, the more he irritated me. It was no longer his fake, happy voice that bothered me. That voice would have been refreshing to hear again. It was his whiny, petty persona that made my skin crawl.

But I had my own weakness. While Number 1's kryptonite was life, mine was men.

About a week after our clouded Christmas Eve, I awoke to the loud ringing of my cell phone. Shocked to consciousness, I looked at the clock on my nightstand. It was 2 am I looked at my phone, and realized it was Number 1.

"I spend one fucking day away from him and this tool is waking me up in the middle of the night," I thought, frustrated.

When I picked up the phone, I could tell that something was wrong.

"*Baby!*" he sobbed.

At that point, I was so exposed to his emotional outbursts that I'd developed immunity.

"What?" I groggily mumbled. "Are you ok?"

"I just drank a bottle of Jack Daniels and swallowed two bottles of Motrin IB!" he shouted. "I'm scared. I don't want to die!"

A sick part of me saw humor in a weakling overdosing on such a weak substance. But two bottles of anything mixed with that much alcohol could be lethal.

"Shit!" I shouted, shocked. He may have been annoying, but I didn't want him to die.

"You need to dial 9-1-1 now! Do you need me to come over there?"

"No, it's ok," he sniffed. "I'm going to call an ambulance."

I didn't add to the conversation, nor did I take off in the middle of the cold night to make sure he was alive. But I wasn't oblivious to the fact that, since I had first met him, his personality was almost unrecognizable. Day by day, he seemed to lose more and more of his initial charm.

Number 1 called me from the hospital early the next morning after his stomach was pumped.

"Baby, can you please come pick me up," he pleaded. "I don't want to stress my mom out about this and I really need to go home."

I'm pretty sure Number 1 wasn't even aware that he was using a man's deadliest weapon against women. He exposed his vulnerability. Over the years, I would repeat a pattern of chronically caving to that same behavior. It didn't matter whether or not I liked or respected him. Every time he dared to let his guard down and unveil some of his ugliest, grittiest faces, I whole-heartedly believed I was the only person on earth being let in on a secret. It was a mirage of a connection.

Despite his faults and my prior resistance, I felt an obligation to uphold that bond. No matter what kind of person he was or how toxic he could have been, I saw beauty in that fleeting defenselessness as if he were an infant, innocent and untainted by the evils of the world. I always fell in love with that face in every man. I clutched that memory tightly, despite the fact that its weight wore my arms and drug my pace. I was so focused on remembering their moment of weakness that I was blind to who they normally were.

From that day, I continued to stay with him from guilt instead of revenge. We had only been seeing each other a little over a week, but I felt as if I had been in this intense, exhausting relationship that bound me in obligation. His depression and mood swings intensified. But I did my best to end my sarcastic responses to his complaints.

"Baby, I'm having some friends over tonight, but I really want you to come," he told me when I returned his phone call after a shift at work. "I'm still feeling kind of down and I'd like you to just be there for me."

More than willing to prevent him from eating another bottle of pills, I quickly made up one of my nightly lies to my mother about staying at a friend's house.

When I arrived at his dirty apartment, I was surprised to see that I was singled out by gender and age. Besides Number 1, there were about eight men at the apartment. All of them were from the Nightfall crowd and over eighteen. I suddenly felt incredibly young, blonde, and female.

"Hey, Maggie, you want some yellow jackets?" Marshall's friend, who I had met a few times before, held out some pills in his hand.

They were perfectly legal in the state of Tennessee, but banned from many because they had ephedrine. Yellow Jackets were speed pills, sold at gas stations for a fairly cheap price. Although they made me feel jittery and nauseated, I enjoyed the extra boost of energy that weed didn't provide. As a boyfriend once told me, I was an "upper" girl. Before crystal meth and cocaine, there were Yellow Jackets.

"Sure. Thanks!" I replied, as if he had just offered me a cracker.

I popped three of the black pills with bright yellow stripes in my mouth.

Once the speed kicked in, I began to bounce around the apartment and stirred up conversation with several of the guys in the room. The hours passed as I drank a forty.

Meandering around the room, I noticed Number 1 sitting in a corner alone. I sat down beside him and cheerfully greeted him.

"Hey! What are you doing sitting here all by yourself?" I asked him.

"You're not paying any attention to me," he whined.

My mood instantly declined, but the speed from the yellow jackets bubbled to anger.

"*UGH.*" I thought. "Everyone's having a perfectly good time and he just *has* to be a little bitch about it."

I was so sick of babying him. I was over the constant caretaking of the biggest emotional rollercoaster I had ever met.

"What the hell are you talking about?" I replied, my volume rising. "Why are you so mad?"

"I know, but you've hardly been with me all night."

"So you want me to just stand on your arm all the time? I can't talk to anyone else? If you want to talk to me, then talk to me!"

The guys stood in little groups all over the living room, smoking cigarettes and drinking their beers.

Number 1 stood up from his pouting corner and walked to the middle of the room to start his usual rant.

"I am so over this place!" he whined. "I hate my life! I hate Tennessee! I just want to go back to New York!"

"I can't listen to this shit anymore," I thought.

I could feel the yellow jackets pump adrenaline through my veins. A surge of heat scorched through my body. I was done being sympathetic. I stood up and walked towards Number 1 in the middle of the room.

"Will you just SHUT THE FUCK UP?" I shouted.

The room immediately went silent. The guys stared at me, shocked by the little blonde girl's sudden outburst.

"You screwed up!" I continued. "You couldn't make it in New York! You had to run home to your mother because you were too much of a pussy to live in the real world! Quit bitching about it! Either do something with your life, or get the hell over it!"

The room remained dead quiet. I looked at Marshall, whose eyes were gleaming as he struggled to suppress laughter. Out of everyone in that room, he was having the most fun.

Number 1's eyes darted around the room. He looked humiliated and as usual, on the verge of tears.

"Fuck you!" he shouted back, without knowing what else to say.

I was startled by the anger in his voice that was so uncharacteristic. I was shocked, but bulletproof. I just felt free. I had a reason to leave without a guilt trip.

I shrugged my shoulders.

"Alright. We're done," I said, nonchalantly.

Just as I was about to turn around and escape that horrible apartment for the last time, Marshall seized his opportunity to throw more spice in the pot.

"Maggie," he spoke calmly.

"What?" I snapped back.

I didn't want to drag the unpleasant scene any further.

"Did you have sex with him?" he asked me, his eyes peering at Number 1.

The amusement from Marshall's eyes was gone. For the first time since meeting him, he looked very serious.

"No!" I said confidently. "No! I didn't screw this loser."

"Maggie," he repeated. "Did you have sex with him?"

"No! No fucking way! I did not have sex with him!"

I didn't understand why he was repeating the question, but it made me nervous.

Marshall's volume slightly increased. His face gained some expression back, but it wasn't amusement. It was anger.

"Maggie! Did you fuck him?" he asked again.

"No!" I yelled, becoming mad again.

"Maggie, you had sex with him?" Marshall asked *again*, but his voice calmed.

My body began to tremble and my chest tensed with uneasiness.

"What are you talking about, Marshall? No, I didn't. I'm a virgin. You know that."

"But you did, Maggie," Marshall informed me. "Maggie, he fucked you. He fucked you that night when you two were in the bathroom. You were passed out. That's why I was banging on the door."

"He's lying," I thought frantically. "How could I have had sex without knowing about it?"

My mind raced back to all the strange events that occurred that night. I ended up naked without memory of removing my clothes. Marshall and Number 1 were fighting and I had no idea why. And then, I remembered the pain and the blood stains.

I turned my head and looked at Number 1. The second we made eye contact, he dropped to his knees and burst into tears.

"I'm so sorry, Maggie!" he began to sob.

"IS IT TRUE?" I screeched.

He only cried.

"*MOTHER FUCKER!*" I screamed at the top of my lungs. "IS IT TRUE?"

He looked up at me with his wide, black, blood shot eyes.

"Yes," he whimpered.

I walked to him and looked at his face. He was blatantly petrified. Without a thought, I lifted my right arm. With all my strength, I hit him across the face.

The loud "SMACK!" pierced the silence of the room.

Still on his knees, his cries grew louder.

"You all *knew* about this?" I asked Marshall.

"Yeah, I did. We all did," he told me while looking around the room at the rest of the boys. "He told me about it the next day."

"So every single one of you knew about my virginity before I did?"

"Yeah," Marshall replied, looking down at his feet.

I looked around the room at all the men who had witnessed the entire scene. I waited for someone to comfort me, defend me, or make some remark about how fucked up it was for a twenty-one-year-old man to fuck a sixteen-year-old virgin while she was unconscious. However, the silence was a clear indication that nobody would rescue me.

I walked down the long hallways of Moccasin Bend with my visitor's sticker taped to my chest. I flinched at the echoes of the mentally ill. I had always hated hospitals, nursing homes, or any place that was crawling with sickness, but a mental institution was worse. I avoided the eyes of the patients as if contact would turn me to stone.

I entered the lounge where I agreed to meet Number 1. I saw him sitting in one of the chairs. He looked like he hadn't slept in weeks. His face lit up at the sight of me entering the room and his wide, fake smile I recognized from when we first met spread across his face. As he wrapped his arms around me for a hug, I noticed his bandaged wrists.

"Was this my fault?" I wondered. "Who's the villain in all of this?"

I couldn't understand how he could be so excited to see me after everything we'd been through.

It was past midnight when I left Number 1's apartment.

"So that was it?" I asked myself. "Was that the big virginity loss?"

Suddenly, I was unable to remain cold and stoic. Out of nowhere, I was flooded by the emotion I had been lacking for weeks. I pulled my car over.

"I didn't even like him," I thought.

As soon as I parked, I screamed. I let myself taste the warm, salty tears that dripped down my face.

Although I did drugs, drank, and had fooled around a bit, my virginity meant something to me. I saw it as the final remnant of my childhood. I knew that casual sex could have been in my future, but I wanted my first time to be meaningful. I at least wanted to choose when it happened.

Even after our nasty previous encounter, Number 1 could only stay out of my life for a few days. I received another startling phone call in the middle of the night.

"Maggie, I'm so sorry!" he sobbed.

His voice sounded even more panicked and vexed than it had during his Jack Daniels and Motrin IB binge.

"Haven't you cried enough?" I snapped.

The pace of his voice suddenly quickened.

"Maggie, I didn't rape you. I didn't do anything."

"Then why was I so sore the next day?"

"That was my hands. I didn't fuck you."

"You idiot. You act like I've never been finger banged before! Why, of all the times that you've done that, was I in so much pain that one particular night?"

"I don't know!" he yelled. "I have no idea. But you have to believe me, I didn't fuck you."

"Are you on something right now?" I asked, trying to lower the volume of my voice so I wouldn't wake my parents.

Number 1 didn't answer my question.

"What are you on?"

"I didn't fuck you, ok!" he shrieked.

He sounded like someone was holding a gun to his skull.

"Then why did you say that you did? And you didn't just tell me. You told *everyone*."

"I don't know," he whined. "I wanted to be one of the guys. I wanted them to think I was cool."

"So you told them all you fucked me unconscious?"

"Maggie, I didn't fuck you!" he screamed. "You're fucking sixteen! I don't want to go to jail!"

Then I realized exactly why he was calling me. Number 1's apology was not out of respect of me, or shame for anything he said or did. I had my gender and my youth, both qualities, which would vouch for my innocence in a Tennessee courtroom. An attempt at justice was guaranteed jail sentence.

Suddenly, all I felt was hatred.

"You piece of shit," I muttered. "I wish you were dead."

I wanted to kill him myself.

"Go into your bathroom," I ordered.

I could hear him whimpering and sniffing on the other end of the phone.

"Pick up the razor you shave with," I continued. "Put it against your wrists and cut your veins."

"I'm sorry," he mumbled again.

But before I let myself hear another one of his meaningless apologies, I turned off my phone and threw it across the room. I lied awake in bed for several hours. Without tears, I let my thoughts drift and my heart race. I eventually fell asleep before the sun rose.

I got the news of Number 1's suicide attempt the next morning. Of all people, it was Kari who called me.

"It happened last night," she informed me. "I didn't see him do it. He was alone in his room for a while. Me and a few other people were hanging out in the living room."

"Oh, *fuck*," I thought in shock. "I wonder if she has any idea that he called me last night."

But Kari's voice didn't sound accusatory or bitter.

"He was *really* fucked up," she added.

She didn't elaborate what exactly he had been on, but I hoped that it was something that blacked out his memory.

Number 1 called me later that evening from Moccasin Bend. He showed no recollection of his phone call from the night before. In fact, he treated me as if we'd been dating the entire time.

"Baby, please come visit me this weekend." he begged. "It would be so nice to see your pretty face."

The only reply I could force myself to give was "yes."

As fucked up as it was, a small part of me wanted to continue dating him. There's no way to define an inclination to be with the one who damaged you. But it was then that I understood why so many people remained shackled to abusive relationships. With or without my permission, he was still the man who took my virginity. I believed that if I could force a relationship with him, I could magically bring some beauty or meaning to what happened.

"You look beautiful," he told me as he grasped my right hand and pulled me into a hug.

We were sitting side by side in the lounge. I looked through the large glass windows at all the patients and wondered if they all were there for suicide attempts.

"How are you feeling?" I asked him, once I uncomfortably freed myself from his arms.

"I'm much better!"

He looked at my face and squinted his black eyes with a look of concern.

"What's wrong?" he asked me.

I wondered if he actually expected me to be perky and chipper in such an unpleasant scenario. I tried my best to lift the muscles on my face into a smile.

"I've never been to rehab before," I said lightly. "Here, I brought you some colored pencils to draw with."

I handed him the bag and watched Number 1's face light up as he saw his gifts. His face reminded me of the way my brother looked while opening his Christmas presents. For a moment I forgot about every horrible thing that had happened.

"Thank you so much for bringing me all this. It really means a lot to me."

"It's not a big deal," I replied, trying to sound as cheerful as possible. "I stole most of it anyway."

"So I have some exciting news to tell you," he stated, with one of his wide smiles.

His black eyes were gleaming with happiness.

"Something exciting here?" I asked. "In rehab? Wow. Ok, what is it?"

"I met someone!" he exclaimed.

Shock struck my entire body. Not knowing whether I was supposed to pretend to be happy or not, I was instantly jerked out of my newly constructed la-la land.

"In fucking rehab?" I snapped.

"Maggie, don't be mad!" he groaned. "I knew you were going to be like this. Listen, we met a few days ago and really connected. She's here for a heroin addiction, but she's getting better. She has a kid and I really think I could be a good father to him. I think I'm in love with her."

I was astonished by the utter stupidity of his words.

"In *love*?" I said, so heated that I was nearly yelling.

"Yes, and I really want us to stay friends. I care about you and I know you'll really like her."

"You think you're in love with someone you met in fucking rehab? With a child? You've only known her a few days!"

"Maggie, what would you know about love? You're just a child."

I always imagined rape as this violent scene of a woman walking alone down a dark alley and getting mugged and beaten by some masked criminal. Rape was an angry man forcing himself inside a damsel in distress. I would not carry the trauma of a cliché rape victim. I would not shriek in the midst of my slumber with night terrors. I would not tremble at the sight of every dark haired man or the mention of Number 1's name. I would not even harbor ill will towards him. My damage was like a cigarette addiction- subtle, seemingly innocent, but everlasting and inevitably detrimental.

Number 1 never opened his screen door to furious crowds waving torches and baseball bats. Nobody punched him out in my honor. The Nightfall crowd never socially ostracized him. Even the ex-boyfriend who'd second handedly fused the entire fiasco continued to mingle with him in drug circles. Everybody continued with business as usual. And when I told my parents I lost my virginity against my will, unconscious on a bathroom floor, Carl did not erupt in fury and demand I give him all I knew about his whereabouts so he could greet him with a rifle. Mom blankly shrugged and mumbled, "Oh, that's too bad," and drifted into the kitchen as if I'd received a stubbed toe rather than a shredded hymen.

Everyone in my life took my rape as lightly as a brief thunderstorm that might have been frightening when it happened, but was easy to forget about. I adopted that mentality as the foundation of my sex life. I would, time and time again, treat sex as flimsily as it started. I would give it away as if it was cheap, second hand junk, rather than a prize that deserved to be earned.

Number 2

I didn't cry when Number 2 died.

I sat in my car alone and summoned tears the way a phony medium invokes ghosts. I didn't understand my pathetic attempts to dry heave devastation. At twenty-eight years old, I'd softened with womanhood. It only took a photo of a puppy with paralyzed hind legs to moisten my eyes, yet my heart seemed immune to the image of my first boyfriend's cold, pale corpse lying stiffly in a cheap motel bed. I'd been anticipating the day a prior lover perished like the death of a first grandparent, aunt, uncle, or childhood companion. As I crept into my mid twenties, every Facebook login displayed the union of a couple, the birth of a child, or the death of a loved one. However, the passing of a peer instills a diluted dose of the dread Granddaddy felt during Korean War combat when he was the only soldier to stumble out of a foxhole alive. All I can think is, "It could have been me."

However, that wasn't the case with Number 2. Although I never found out his official cause of death, word was it was a cocktail of Methadone, Methamphetamine, Klonopin, and whiskey. To an outsider, the combination reads like suicide. But to those who knew him, it was his typical Friday night.

An eerie aspect of social media is the way the dead's account lingers in digital space as a floating memorial. Friends post emotional farewells as if the departed will read them. But we all know that those words are for the rest of the world as if to flaunt their bond with the deceased like a new car or engagement ring. Just like any material possession that ceases production, a person's value amplifies when they are dead. They have no future. They have no present. Their past becomes a limited resource that everyone is desperate to snag a piece of. I had a big one with Number 2. Even more than taking his virginity, I was the only one who truly understood what killed him. It wasn't his drug problem. It was his burning desire to *have* a drug problem. Number 2 didn't fall into addiction. He pursued it. He desperately *wanted* it.

I found out about Number 2's death from one after another Facebook wall post about the tragedy of his overdose, how adored he was, how kind he was, his love for music, his talent for the guitar, and his endless potential. They raved about their shock at his fate, their final conversations with him, and the great things he proclaimed were coming his way. They highlighted his kind heart and adventurous spirit. They said he was robbed of life. They said he was *trying* to do better, but would sadly never get that chance.

I was also a hypocrite. I prattled on with bullshit about the beauty of our adolescent courtship before the drugs and complications of life. The truth was I thought he was a complete loser. The truth was I dodged his invitations for grabbing a beer every time I visited Chattanooga. The truth was, for years I had been Google image searching his mug shots, screen capturing his statuses on arrests, drug charges, probation violations, and court dates, texting them to friends, rolling my eyes and sarcastically snickering about how he was "the one that got away."

I sent flowers to his grandparents. I searched myself for every drop of compassion I could muster and forced it to the tip of my tongue. I called them and voiced my condolences, while doing my best to suffocate my wrath for raising an ultimately pointless life. If I ever loved Number 2, that emotion has been gone for thirteen years. If I ever mourned his death, I recovered a decade prior to it. But I still sleep with the white, fluffy teddy bear he gave me. It remains as the only romantic gesture I've received. I find myself, again and again, clutching its feather-soft fur in the midst of the aftermath of a slew of one-night stands, fuck buddies, or the abandonment of a charade of intimacy as if I am a child waking up from the nightmare of my eternal status as a living sex toy. I suppose looking at that bear ironically ignites the same feeling of sifting through photographs of the dead. I know I will never be that girl again. My brief role as the woman men find worthy of pure, wholesome affection died far too young. But, just as out of gratitude for the dead's existence, I take comfort in knowing it was once there.

It was a dreary January night around 3 am. The clouds seemed to be so bloated from moisture that they collapsed to the earth and smothered Chattanooga in a blanket of frigid steam. My mud brown 1988 Nissan Altima was parked at the edge of the parking lot of Lake Winnepesaukah, an amusement park that was a white trash version of Six Flags. I grew up hearing headlines of its rickety roller coaster cars colliding, swing chains snapping, and children flying into its toxically polluted, algae crusted, man made lake. Patrons attended the park with the same attitude of purchasing lunch from street vendors. They grudgingly accepted the threat to their livelihood. But the lot was eerily desolate in the late night darkness. Number 2 and I were tangled in my back seat, awkwardly fumbling over each other's bodies. I couldn't shake our disappointing transition. What resulted with losing a Trojan between seat cushions in a rush to see if my hymen was still intact actually had a darling beginning.

Number 2 was once the teenage boyfriend who clutched my hand until our palms were hot and slippery. We spent hours burrowed in the back of movie theaters shoving tongues down each other's throats until they were paralyzed by friction and parched of saliva.

The first time I met Number 2 was in fourth grade. He had chubby cheeks and grey-brown hair that curled at the end. He was spazzy with ADHD and made funny noises in class that sometimes erupted into little temper tantrums. But despite the immature mannerisms, he was placed in all the gifted courses.

It wasn't until a couple months before my sixteenth birthday when we crossed paths again. My friend, Robin, invited me to a church lock-in. We were supposed to bring our sleeping bags and spend the night in a gym, play beach ball volleyball, and watch movies. I was uneasy around churches. They usually ended in arguments about Satan with Sunday school housewives.

"I just don't believe you have to be a Christian to get into heaven," I'd protest. "I mean, what about people in countries who haven't heard of Jesus? Why should they burn in flames forever? It's not their fault."

"Well," a forty-something with a southern drawl and puffy bob would usually reply," That's wah it's our job ta spread tha word of tha Lawd. We wanna save them from goin' ta hell."

"But what's wrong with having our own opinions?" I'd reply. "What if the stories of the Bible don't make sense to us? I mean, it was written so long ago. How do we have proof that everything in it is true? How do we know that Jesus really existed?"

They'd nod their heads, seeming to take my words seriously. Just when I began to believe that they were opening their minds a little, they would shake their head and say, "Oh hunny, you poor thang. Tha devil's talkin' to ya."

After enough condemnations, I avoided my friend's Sunday school invitations. But Robin and I rarely got to see each other anymore.

As we played badminton with several other girls, I watched Robin with her tall, lanky frame and strawberry-blonde hair, realizing how different we had become.

Though Robin and I were zoned for the same public high school, she chose to go to their rival school, while I switched to Chattanooga School for the Arts and Sciences downtown.

CSAS was known for its unconventional teaching methods. They encouraged freethinking, which was a rarity in The South. Their classes were smaller so teachers had a more one-on-one relationship with their students. Every class had a seminar, where students sat in a circle and discussed the topics they were studying. The outspoken and argumentative students were praised, while the meek received lower grades. CSAS pushed for diversity.

"We try to get as much of a mixture of races, religions, and cultures as we can so students can learn about different people in the world," explained one of the teachers during my admissions interview.

But my desire to attend had nothing to do with its uniqueness. I spent years in my suburban middle school desperate for popularity. I knew that my only shot at reaching the top of the teenage social ranks was a clean slate.

Strict social classes were clearly distinguished by the cafeteria tables at lunch. The lowest were the nerdy and the poor, redneck kids who lived in trailers, wore ragged clothes, and smelled like stale cigarettes. The highest were usually full of rich kids decked in plain, overpriced Abercrombie & Fitch ensembles. Despite their parents' annual income, cheerleaders and football players were automatically welcomed into this crowd.

I did a thorough analysis of how to sneak my way into it. For the life of me, I couldn't comprehend the formula. At first, I assumed that I had to be pretty, but I was much cuter than quite a few popular girls. Carl's yacht did nothing to elevate me. By the end of eighth grade, I realized that my allowance purchased Limited Too clothes, orange spray tan, or souped-up house could not alter some personality trait that pigeonholed me in the preteen middle class.

By freshman year, I developed into a bleach blonde bombshell. My braces had been removed and after a summer in the sun, I was a five-foot, size two, one hundred pound, fourteen-year-old Barbie doll.

But CSAS had its own definition of cool.

I might as well have attended high school on Mars. My first day was the most reality shattering culture shock I'd experienced in my short life. With the exception of an occasional Asian, the student body appeared to be half white and half black. Up until that day, I was accustomed to a dash of pepper in a sea of salt.

Fashion statements were as varied as the student body. Some kids were dressed in the mainstream jeans and t-shirts, while others did their best to defy every definition of normal. There were boys with long, greasy hair and baggy jeans. Others dressed in all black with matching black nails and dark eyeliner. A few just gave up on dressing themselves entirely and wore slippers and pajama pants. One boy even wore hospital scrubs.

"They're comfortable," he said, with a shrug.

I was baffled by their fearlessness. I came from a world where the wrong collar tag guaranteed social crucifixion.

"That shirt," a boy pointed at me in class.

His name was Dee. He had shaggy, ginger hair, faded jeans, and a black Korn t-shirt.

"Where did you get that from?" he asked me a bit aggressively.

Dee seemed to be speaking to the kids around him more than directly to me.

"Uh." I stuttered, caught off guard by such a random question. "Abercrombie & Fitch?"

"How much did you pay for it?" he interrogated.

"I don't remember."

"I bet it was a lot."

I looked down at my fitted navy blue, three-quarter inch collared shirt.

"It was like thirty bucks."

"Thirty bucks?" he said with exaggerated shock.

I glanced at the expressions of the others suddenly looking down on my fashion choice.

"That's a lot of money for a plain, blue shirt. Especially since it was made by Thai children slaves for a tenth a penny an hour, " he continued. "And I bet you only bought it because it was from *that* store."

I was dumbstruck. I remembered my rare trip to the mall with Carl. He promised to buy me one shirt from Abercrombie & Fitch, which became highly popular once Limited Too became too juvenile. Shopping trips for me beyond obligatory back-to-school stocking were rare. And I could count on my hand the number of times Carl and I spent time together outside of his Jack Daniels back porch medicating, so the shirt had been precious to me. I wore it all the time and purposely let the tag stick out of the back of my collar for both its origin and its size extra small display.

Dee continued to condemn the materialistic attitudes of America's youth.

"That's what I don't understand about *society*!" he exclaimed, throwing his hands in the air. "You buy this plain shirt for all that money for what? So that you can say that you buy your clothes at a trendy store. I can't believe that people actually buy into that shit. I could just take some ratty shirt from a thrift store and stick an Abercrombie & Fitch tag on it."

At first, I rolled my eyes as I watched Dee swiftly glide through the halls, but his rebellious friends fascinated me.

I soon realized that Dee was one of the most popular kids at school.

I once watched Dee enter a crowded hallway one morning before class. It was packed with a group of black girls chattering and braiding each other's hair.

Over the mass of brown, I observed Dee's pasty figure strut right through.

Turning his fiery locks left, and then right, he smiled and shouted in his most Caucasian tone, "WHAT'S UP, MY NIGGERS?"

I gasped. I knew that word as evil and forbidden, especially for a white person's use.

"Why the hell did he say that?" I thought, trembling just from being a white witness.

"He'll get expelled if he doesn't get lynched first."

There were a few excruciatingly long seconds of silence. Right when I expected a mob of girls to scream and claw at the pasty little bigot, a flood howling of laughter ripped right through the tension.

"Oh Dee! You're so crazy!" they laughed.

At that moment, I knew that people like Dee dominated the social totem pole.

CSAS was certainly different. Styles went from Hollister to "skinless and boneless" stickers, meant for grocery store meat packages but worn on crotches. Instead of candy sales to support cheerleading fundraisers, there were brownie sales in support of the legalization of marijuana. While the girls from my old school dabbled in low lights, CSAS girls dabbled in bisexuality.

I began analyzing the fuck out of every commercial, religion, and lyric. I questioned all rules enforced by my parents. A repressed ferociousness started leaking. By sophomore year, I had bright red streaks in my hair and the ego of a renegade.

At the lock-in, Robin and I hung around two goody-two-shoes church girls who annoyed me. One was a plain-faced brunette named Allie who attended a local Christian school.

In between badminton sessions, Allie began chattering about some boy.

"He's so cute!" she gushed. "He has the best body. I think he likes me, too, because when I asked him for his number, he gave it to me!"

"Let's call him," one of the girls suggested. "I dare you."

We all clustered around her cell like jumpy baby chicks.

She timidly dialed his number and began chatting with him about her weekend.

"Blablabla," I thought, quickly bored from the whole setting. "Let me talk to him!" I chimed in, hoping that he was more stimulating than my current company.

I had no master plan to steal Allie's crush. But I somehow ended up outside the church gymnasium with her phone cradled against my ear. By the end of the conversation, he had my number.

I was ready to date. I had been attracting the opposite sex for two years. Although I liked the attention, I didn't know what to do with it. I had spent many evenings on the docks near Carl's boat, strolling around with his friend's sons. There were a handful of all-nighter phone chatting marathons and summer camp escapes to dark, deserted playgrounds. There were even a couple real dates that had me ducking and turning cheeks, horrified at the foreign lips diving straight for mine.

But when Number 2 came around, I was almost halfway through high school with only one sloppy truth or dare kiss on record. I had friends who were already touching penises. I was rapidly feeling like a ripe fruit on the verge of decomposing into an old maid. I kept a hawk-like vigilance for any intimate opportunity.

Opportunity knocked a month after my blind phone conversation with Allie's mystery crush.

"Sorry I took so long to call," Number 2 said, sounding half asleep. "Uh... I wrote your number down on a napkin, but I lost it. I found it again with some trash on my floor."

"He's kind of a pothead," I remembered Allie telling me. "That's how he ended up at my school."

Number 2 had been attending McCallie, an all boys private school that was known to be the best in the state. It was a full-on rich kid campus with water polo, lacrosse, and boarders from all over the world. According to Allie, Number 2 had been kicked out for selling weed.

To me, this was a red flag. But not the "I don't want to date you," kind. No. Number 2's bad boy reputation drew me in.

"He's really into sports," Allie mentioned at the lock-in. "He swims and plays soccer."

I developed my own fantasy of a chiseled athlete and rebel to the elite private school system.

In actuality, we were both amateurs inebriated by second-hand bong smoke. Of course we tremendously exaggerated our experience. Our newfound intrigue of the drug world became our bond.

A few days after he called, we were set for our first date. Since neither of us had our licenses yet, his dad was driving us to the movies. Though I was ecstatic about the date, I was terrified by how blind it was. The only social media around back then was faceless AOL chat rooms. My only idea of what he looked like came from a mix of Allie's descriptions and my fourth grade yearbook. I certainly had nightmarish daydreams of a buck-toothed, acne-crusted dweeb ringing my doorbell, but I was even more concerned with what he would think of me.

I stood in front of my full-length bathroom mirror, pivoting to the side as I evaluated myself in my red, body hugging v-neck and padded bra that covered my underdeveloped boobs. I sucked in my stomach, smoothing my abdomen as I cringed at the tightness of the size four jeans I was outgrowing.

"I need to quit this bulimia thing," I thought. "I'm obviously digesting too much food. I need to just starve myself again."

I was grateful that I'd only eaten an apple that day.

When I met Number 2, I had been a bulimic for nine months. There were days that I felt thin and days that I felt fat. The days that I threw up more or ate less were not necessarily thin days. My eating disorder transformed from a weight loss mechanism to an addiction. I craved the process. When I did it, I felt filthy and ill. My head ached and my throat throbbed, but I couldn't stop. When I was depressed, my cravings were stronger.

I didn't like myself throughout most of my teens. I didn't meet the personal standards I set. I wasn't attractive or smart enough. Damaging my body was my outlet and my punishment. But sparking a boy's interest told me that I was doing something right. I hated myself less and that urge to vomit faded.

My belly flip-flopped as I saw a car pull into my driveway. I rushed to my mirror to double check my makeup. My long, blonde hair was combed straight and curled under at the ends. I wore a light coat of brown eye shadow and with my lids painted with thin, black liner. I had the girlish, round face that would have passed for a German World War II poster of an Aryan Hitler youth had I worn braided pigtails.

I rushed downstairs to answer the door before my parents could. Their awareness of the whole song and dance was embarrassing enough. I peered through the stained glass in the door as I cracked it open. When I saw Number 2 strolling up my front walkway, I was stunned.

Number 2 was tan with face-framing chocolate brown curls. He wore khaki shorts and a bright yellow t-shirt that hugged his chest enough to reveal his chiseled, athletic physique. I looked at his arms, which were practically carvings from an ancient Greek god sculpture. His calves were thick and muscular. His square jaw was prominent, which made his face look very masculine but his eyes softened it. They were round, golden, and framed with thick, sun-kissed lashes that curled they way his hair did.

"Woah. I lucked the fuck out," I thought. "He's beautiful."

Number 2's infatuation with marijuana was even more apparent that night. Once his dad dropped us off at the theater, we ditched the movie to smoke weed with one of his friends. I was grateful for any form of intoxication to conceal my nervousness around him. When we got back to the theater, we waited for his dad in the lobby. High and happy we stretched back in the cushiony chairs. I was finally relaxed enough to let myself look deep into his golden brown eyes.

We didn't kiss on our first date, but I sensed a mutual attraction. Unfortunately, our blossoming relationship was put on hold when Number 2 was kicked out his second school for, yet again, selling weed. His dad put him in rehab for a month.

"Crack, cocaine, heroin, any of those I understand," I thought. "But marijuana? Really?"

I later found out that Number 2 was genetically destined to be an addict. His "parents" were actually his grandparents. Their daughter was a junkie who snorted, smoked, or ate any substance she could salvage. Number 2 suspected that he was the love child of a crack dealer his mother prostituted herself to. His mom gave him up to her parents and lived her life like an aimless gypsy who sporadically popped in and out for holidays and cash. He referred to his biological mother as his sister. A baby was never motivation for his mom to clean up. She continued using while pregnant, giving Number 2 a mild form of Tourette syndrome that made his eye and hand twitch from time to time. After Number 2, his mom had another fatherless baby with Down syndrome and a life expectancy of thirty.

Number 2's sister-mom would die of drug-induced seizure during our senior year of high school. From what I observed, Number 2's parents were pushovers. Although they loved Number 2, they didn't implement discipline when necessary and their attempts at punishments were ineffective. Their walk-on-eggshells parenting tactics were the greatest detriment to his future.

At the age where the first kiss established commitment, Number 2 became my first boyfriend right after his rehab stint. The magic happened at Nightfall. I was somewhat familiar with the scene, but it was Number 2's first time mingling with Chattanooga's outlandish, wayward youth. Private school kids rarely graced Nightfall unless it was to blow their hefty allowances on schwag. When I saw Number 2 stare at JNCO wearing druggies with immense respect and admiration, I felt a twinge of guilt for introducing him to that world. But I was far too distracted by my lovey-dovey euphoria and drunken stupor for those thoughts to linger.

Earlier that night, Number 2 and I paid a homeless guy to purchase Southern Comfort. We guzzled it in the corner of a nearby parking garage, squatting over gravel behind a cement structure. As disgusting as it was, I welcomed the stinging flavor.

We quickly became drunk and lost our juvenile timidity around each other.

After chatting with some friends, he took his hand in mine as we walked off to be alone. We stumbled to the opposite side of a water fountain in the park and plopped down on a grassy hill as if it was our bed.

"It's coming!" My brain squealed when I knew that he was about to kiss me.

With SoCo surging through my bloodstream, I laid my head on his shoulder and felt his chin on my forehead. Before I knew it, his lips were against mine and his tongue had worked its way inside my mouth. Had I anything to compare it to, the kiss would've seemed sloppy. He thrust his tongue too deeply down my throat and couldn't seem to keep my face dry. But with this being my first actual make out session with a boy, the saliva swapping was sublime.

At the beginning of that summer, my life seemed perfectly in sync. Along with my sixteenth birthday came a driver's license, a thousand dollar 1993 Grand

Am, a chunky Nokia cell phone, a grocery store cashier job, and a boyfriend. I lavished in my newfound freedom. But even better, I finally had someone to romantically romp around town with. Number 2 and I spent our recent release from tenth grade hiding in the back of movie theaters and ducking behind bushes to dry hump on moist, dew-glazed grass.

Our relationship lacked depth. Number 2 had a brilliant mind on some levels, but I think he subconsciously masked it. Even when he wasn't high, he had a stoned surfer twang. Somewhere in his adolescence, he learned that Spicoli was cool and articulation was not. If it weren't for his previous straight A's, I would've dubbed him a complete moron.

"Uh. This one time I got a nail stuck in my foot for three months," he told my friend's mom once when I brought him over.

"What, you didn't notice?" she asked.

"No, and I played soccer on it and everything!"

She started laughing to tears.

Number 2 was dense, but attractive. People doted on him like an adorable, golden-eyed puppy that fumbled into walls when he played fetch.

But he didn't embarrass me. I didn't desire anything more. Declaring him mine was all it took to fill my voids.

I actually enjoyed being intellectually superior to my boyfriend. It made me feel like I had control over him. He was sweet. He doted on me. He never challenged me.

But, when it came to the physical stuff, I fell right through my safety net.

Our lack of mental compatibility was replaced with fooling around. And Number 2 and I fooled around a *lot*. I'd barely been kissed before him. Even *that* was horrifying enough. The initial touch of his hands on my B-cup knockers nearly set me in a panic attack. The harsher our denim rashes, the greater the pressure intensified to remove that clothing barrier.

I had no clue how to jerk a guy off.

"How hard do I hold onto his dick?" I wondered. "What kind of rhythm do I move my hand in?"

I certainly didn't know how to give a blowjob. Just thinking about it made me want to guzzle a gallon of Listerine.

"So, I'm supposed to just put my mouth right where a guy pees?" I wondered. "And then suck it? What if he pisses in my mouth?"

Oral sex sounded gruesome. Sperm couldn't have had a tasty flavor.

I knew Number 2 had a bit more experience than me, but his stories were vague.

"Uh. I can't remember if I had sex before," he told me. "I know I had a sixty-nine with this chick when I was fourteen. Maybe."

That was enough to intimidate me.

Although he didn't push it, I knew that the excitement of boob fondling would eventually expire. Though I could navigate the Bermuda Triangle better than a penis, my own lady parts were their own issue.

How the hell would I make my vagina presentable?

Sure, it was youthfully uncharted, but was it attractive? What qualities defined a visually pleasing twat? Was it the size of the clitoris or the shade of its flesh? Was it the difference between a full bush, landing strip, and baby smooth? Did different men prefer certain variations?

I never dealt with excessive body fur. But having barely made love to a tampon, my privates were truly untainted.

Inspired by a *Sex in the City* episode, I decided that the safest route was to exterminate the entire light brown bush that had been blooming since age nine.

In the privacy of my room, armed with a mirror, shaving cream, razor, and bowl of water, I sat on my floor with a towel propped under my bare ass. Leaning back against my bed with my legs wide open as if I were about to give birth, I shaved everything off. My vagina looked like a barren desert after a massive forest fire. I saw parts of myself that had long vanished beneath pubescent growth.

Suddenly, I felt sexy. There was something about going bare that made me feel sensual and touchable. But that was short lived. I was ill prepared for my skin's reaction to the change. I completely broke out. My pussy flushed as razor bumps shot across my flesh as if I'd had an allergic reaction to my underwear. It took weeks of applying antibiotic ointment to calm my skin.

After enough shaving and treating, the inflammation faded. I finally let Number 2 finger-bang me for the first time. We were in an empty park late at night in downtown Chattanooga. It had just rained and we rolled through the grass behind a thick, cropped garden. In the heat of the moment, I pushed myself on top of him. When he slipped his hand up my leg for probably the millionth time, he was pleasantly surprised when I didn't swat it away.

I felt his hand go down my shorts and through my underwear. The whole experience wasn't the hype I'd expected. I had no orgasm, nor any intense feelings of pleasure. It felt like the same thing I'd done to myself for years except that I did it better. As he aimlessly fumbled his hands inside of me, I realized that we were equally clueless. That made me brave. I unzipped his pants and pulled out his erected dick.

It wasn't as scary as I'd expected. Instead of monstrous and intimidating, it was fairly small and silly looking.

I'd only seen one grown male penis before. I was six and my mom was dating Carl. The three of us went camping. We all shared a tent, but Carl had been discreet when he changed his clothes. The morning after we all spent the night in the tent together, we were lying around. I made up my mind that if I was ever going to see a penis, that was the time. Feeling like a pioneer about to embark on an uninhibited jungle, I crawled under the covers. Carl, who is fat with a body suit of man fur, slept in only his underwear, so reaching his penis would be easy. Under the blanket, I grabbed his briefs and yanked them down.

There it was!

The only thing I remembered about his penis was that it was small, red, and ugly.

"WHAT THE HELL ARE YOU DOING?" Carl shouted.

Number 2's penis was not as red. It was erect, so I could give its size more credit than Carl's.

I gripped my hand around it, and began stroking it up a down like I'd observed in porn. Although I heard a few groans from Number 2, I still had no clue as to what I was doing. We were exploring our sexuality together. I dropped a great deal of my insecurity that night. I figured that until he rocked my world, there was no pressure to rock his.

It didn't take long for trouble to cloud my paradise.

"Let's get some hash!" Number 2 demanded when I picked him up one night.

In the month we had been together, there was never a drug free date. If Number 2 didn't have weed, he was equipped with stolen pills from his relatives. If he was completely drugless, we were hunting Walgreens for Coricidin or Robitussin. He even had us hiking through pastures to scavenge mushrooms in cow shit.

"Here he goes again," I thought, annoyed that we had to waste yet another night on a drug search.

I knew that my best bet was to snag the drugs as quickly as possible or else we would spend the entire time looking for them.

"I bet I know someone who's got something," I volunteered.

"Really, who?" he asked eagerly.

I remembered a girl who rode my school bus sophomore year. Her name was Whitney. She had two sisters. The three of them were known as the biggest whores in school, but she was really sweet. She told me once that her dad sold weed. I called Whitney and got directions. He lived in a trailer in the outskirts town.

When we arrived, Whitney wasn't around, but her dad knew we were coming. The trailer looked like a run-down crack house. Her dad was Holocaust skinny with grey facial scruff and missing teeth.

"So, yaller lookin fur sum hash?" he asked.

"Yeah, dude. I'd like to get a gram, man," Number 2 strained to sound cool as if he were meeting Mick Jagger rather than a white trash meth head.

We took our gram and drove away. We found a secluded area in the countryside to park and smoke.

"I'm not sure if I want to smoke this stuff when I have to drive," I said.

It bothered me that Number 2 didn't have a car. It was late June and he didn't turn sixteen for a few more weeks. Even then, his parents didn't get him a car and I would be faced with constantly hauling him around town.

"You'll be fine," he urged. "Relax. Smoke this with me."

I hadn't had my license a month. I was already extremely paranoid driving sober and hash was brand new to me. I didn't want to take my chances.

"Look, I really don't feel like it," I retorted.

"You're always so worried about stuff!" he exclaimed.

He was sounding annoyed and I really didn't want to fight.

"We came all the way out here. Just smoke it. You'll be fine!"

When he saw the worried look on my face, his eyes softened.

"Here, just take a couple hits and we can stay here for a few minutes," he assured me. "Your high can wear off and then you can drive."

That option sounded safer. I took the pipe he made from stolen plumbing parts from one of his dad's construction sites. I felt the high right away. It was much stronger than any marijuana I had tried before. I looked up and saw an explosion of bright flashes and neon lights zigzagging up and down the interior roof of my car.

Number 2 must have been sharing hallucinations because he let out a big, dumb stoner laugh and said, "*Cooool.* Hehehe."

I looked at him and he looked back at me affectionately, stroking my hair with his hand. It was as if my smoking the hash made me more attractive.

I felt relieved by the sudden affection. Enjoying my high, I was perfectly content with where I was.

Suddenly, Number 2's head perked up.

"Ok, let's go," he said.

Fear cut through buzz.

"Let's go?" I asked. I couldn't believe what I was hearing. "What's wrong with here? You said we could stay for a bit."

"Yeah, but I'm bored," he said, chuckling like a stupid pothead again.

"No, I don't want to drive!" I shouted. "You said we could stay for a while."

"And we just stayed for a while. Relax, Maggie," he said, sounding annoyed again.

"But I'm too high to drive!" I exclaimed.

"That's a bunch of bullshit," he said. "You can't drive drunk, but anyone can drive high. Being high won't fuck up your driving."

"Fine!" I snapped. "I'll drive. But if we wreck, I'm blaming you!"

Within five minutes, my first car was totaled.

As much as Number 2 urged me to drive, he took none of the blame. Since the passenger's side got hit, he actually acted like quite the victim.

I'd never been so terrified in my short, sixteen-year life. Driving through the fog on hash had given me some scary hallucinations. I knew I was unfit to drive and needed off the road as soon as possible. In a panic, I veered the right lane and slammed into a car.

"Are you ok?" I asked the man in the other vehicle as I stumbled out of mine.

"What the fuck, lady? Look what you did to my car!" a bald, black man in his forties screamed at me. "You better have insurance!" he threatened.

Once he found out that I was covered, he was giddy. He later sued my insurance company, claiming that the wreck had traumatized him. Luckily he had no idea I was high.

Number 2 ate the rest of the hash while we waited for the cops. He would later crack jokes about how fucked up he was that night and how the cop lights played tricks on his eyes. From our glazed, bloodshot eyes and dry lips, the police knew we were high, but didn't have solid evidence.

"I'm not gonna give you a DUI for this," said a middle-aged officer with a thick, brown mustache. "But I'm gonna tell your momma when she gets here."

There was a significant difference between Number 2's parents and mine.

His folks took pity on me. They hugged and kissed me.

"Are you ok, precious," Number 2's mother asked me in her raspy smoker's voice. "You poor thing. You must have been so scared."

My own mother had a much less subtle approach.

"*Drugs*? Maggie, really? DRUGS?" my mom shouted. "What the *hell* were you thinking driving your car high? You're in deep shit. Just wait until Carl gets to you!"

Carl had been out of town on business and I thanked God he wasn't around for my wreck.

I laid in bed that night, shocked but full of gratitude. The wreck had been by far my most traumatic event.

"I could've died tonight," I thought to myself. "All for drugs. Drugs are so stupid. What was I thinking driving on them?"

I was positive that I had learned a valuable lesson to live a stone sober life. I vowed to come clean to my mother and change for good.

The next day, I approached my mom. She was in my eight-year-old brother's room putting away some clothes.

"Can I talk to you for a second?" I asked her in tears.

I had been crying all day. I lost my car, was grounded, and lost the privilege to see my Number 2 without parental supervision.

"Sure, honey," Mom responded.

She had calmed since the night before.

"I've done a lot more drugs than you think I've done," I confessed. "And I want to come clean with you because I want to stop."

I spilled it all. I told her that I had rolled ecstasy, tripped acid, smoked weed, smoked hash that was probably laced with something, and had abused several prescription pills.

As my truthful words crept into her ears, my mother's soft, sympathetic eyes widened into a stunned expression. She had been clueless.

"I can't believe this, Maggie," she sounded afraid. "It's as if you've been living this double life. I don't even know you anymore."

In hindsight, I think my parents had been looking for a reason for me to leave CSAS for a while.

"We don't lak wat that school is turnin' ya into," Carl would bitch. "All that free thinkin' bullshit is turnin' ya into this back talkin' smart ass."

"And now it's getting you into *drugs,*" Mom said, looking like a toddler seeing her favorite stuffed animal being thrown in the yard with the dog.

They forced me to leave one of the state's best education facilities for our local public school where being intelligent was no longer considered cool. I was back to the narrow minds of the Chattanooga suburbs.

Though their intention was to teach me that drugs would not be tolerated, I learned that honesty would be prosecuted. From then until I left home, I was a compulsive liar.

My three-week devotion to sobriety was enough to ruin Number 2 and I. We broke up at the end of the summer. While he escaped the wreck unscathed, I lost my school and my place on the crew team I joined that summer. I was left with a totaled car and heart.

When Number 2 and I broke up, he didn't exit my life. He called me constantly. He wanted to chat. He wanted to hang out. He wanted to play his stupid guitar on the phone until I passed out from boredom. He was never any good at it. His singing was worse.

I answered his calls, drove him around town, and maintained a volatile friendship. I didn't like Number 2. I didn't respect him, but I gripped onto every last inch of him because I couldn't shake the rejection. My self-esteem could not mend unless I got him back.

Over the months, Number 2 fell deeper into drugs. His beautiful curls grew long, greasy, and unkempt. His chiseled, Greek god physique became thin and frail after getting into harder drugs like crystal meth. He traded his khakis for saggy JNCOs and ratty hoodies. A bloodshot glaze smothered the flicker in his lion eyes.

Number 2 became a poster boy for a "say no to drugs" campaign. What started as a beautiful, straight-A athlete spiraled into a junkie dropout. But Number 2 was something much worse than a drug addict. While typical teenage heroes are athletes, celebrities, or even politicians, Number 2's idols were strung out on street corners. He honored the drug overdoses the way Christians honor The Bible. Number 2 loved drugs for the love of drugs.

Nobody, including myself, could understand why we still associated with each other. We broke out in spats every five minutes, which were usually provoked by me. I mocked and made fun of him. I was downright cruel, yet he kept coming around. He introduced me to his friends, who I blatantly flirted with just to piss him off. I took my pain and anger out on him. I quickly learned that I could sneer scathing remarks and he would just take it. I got a twisted kick in abusing and controlling. But no matter how much my verbal lashings stung, Number 2's desperation to be loved and accepted kept him boomeranging.

I wasn't the only one who took advantage. His drug friends were even worse. He was the dumb, clueless laughing stalk of his crowd. He was viewed as weak. He was the first one to get ripped off in his apparent "drug deals," often receiving crushed baking soda posed as cocaine or Pepsi moistened sugar cubes as "acid hits." Guys would often sway him to snort crushed Benadryl. He willingly, without question, abided all orders and ranted about how much the mystery pills fucked him up.

By the time we had sex, Number 2 felt like an overplayed one hit wonder that made me want to put a gun to the speakers every time I heard it. Although I was sick of our friendship, the curiosity of my virginity status overpowered my irritation.

"Take your shirt off," I muttered, as soon as I parked my car in a desolate lot outside Lake Winnipesaukee.

We had actually gone to Lake Winnipesaukee the summer before. We were that cliché teenage couple, sucking faces in the line to rides and oblivious to the bad manners of our PDA. As he wrestled his t-shirt over his curly head of hair, I thought about that trip. The memory made me sad.

I wished we had sex in the beginning when affection was there and when sex could have meant something. We would have been kind to each other. We would have found a room somewhere with a bed and blankets to spoon in afterwards. Maybe I would have enjoyed it. Maybe I would have felt loved. Maybe I would have felt *something.* Anything. But on that rainy January night in the backseat of my car, shielded by the windows fogged by our heavy breathing, my actions were robotic.

"Life never turns out the way you plan," I thought to myself, as he went inside of me.

"Hmm. No pain," I thought. "No, I guess I wasn't a virgin after all."

Number 3

"Ya need ta be very ca-ful what ya wish for, Maggie," Grandmother warned me. "Because ya may just get it."

Adele Young was referring to my desire to be a grownup. I was seven years old. I wanted to drive a car and eat chocolate whenever I pleased. I had a right to stay awake past ten and watch bad TV shows.

"Your life'll fly bah so fast. Before ya know, you'll be as old as me. Than you'll wish you were a child again."

It's natural to want what you don't have. The "grass is greener on the other side" mentality is usually healthy. It fuels motivation. It gives the daily grind a little spark.

But every now and then, wishes come true. And that seems wonderful at first. There was a time when I wished for a boyfriend. But finding Number 3 was like winning a million dollar jackpot that funded a cocaine addiction. Some prayers are better left unanswered.

I spent two years latched onto a man who was wrong for me in every way. When I questioned life after death, he said my fate was to rot in the dirt. When I dreamed about traveling the world, he assured me that there was nothing worth seeing. While I wanted to meet new people, he said that everyone was as dull as him. While I spoke of any career aspirations, he called me narcissistic for believing I would accomplish them.

"Ugh. What did I see in this guy?" I asked myself after a phone conversation with Number 3.

I was twenty-four years old. Over five years after our breakup, we were having that uncomfortable 'catch up with the ex' chat.

Since the split, communication was sporadic. I was hesitant to keep in touch and he was difficult to keep in touch with. I saw him about a year after leaving Chattanooga. But by my next trip home, his number was disconnected. Number 3 was a bit like a groundhog most comfortable in hibernation. He tended to scurry away from the noises of civilization.

Then, Myspace erupted. Every ex, one-night stand, and grade-school enemy was suddenly on the radar. My generation was free to stalk and judge anonymously. I dug through the depths of my past. I found his profile picture, baby and baby's momma included. My jaw dropped. I've heard that ugly people can produce beautiful children. Number 3's little family was a prime example. His baby, who was about nine months old, was a stunning blonde-haired, blue-eyed girl. Her mother had a pasty complexion, a sharp, pointed nose and jaw, and a thin head of long, greasy black hair. She was posing at an unflattering angle, with the camera being slightly too high, she was lifting her chin. Her lips were chapped and cracked, spreading into a broad smile that framed a set of crooked, plaque-crusted teeth.

Number 3 didn't look much better. When we first met, he had a subtle, country boy cuteness to him. His copper brown hair was thick with bushy waves.

He had small, beady brown eyes with a few freckles around his button nose. At twenty, he still had a baby face. My least favorite feature was his overgrown chin goatee. He wasn't bone skinny, but he didn't have any excess fat. However, the years hadn't been kind to him. His matted mane was shagged to his ears. His round, freckled cheeks had plumped. I envisioned him gobbling Dollar General Hamburger Helper and Budweiser in front of the television the way he did when we lived together, letting his looks go long before thirty. He wore a baggy t-shirt. His goatee had grown into a wild puffball that looked like a thick bush of pubic hair on his face.

"Oh my God," I gasped at my computer screen. "I had sex with that guy. A *lot.* Gross!"

I pictured his sweaty body on top of mine, his cigarette ash-flavored tongue in my mouth, and his chin puff scratching my cheeks.

I heard through mutual friends that she had been a one-night stand gone wrong. Their daughter was conceived on New Year's Eve in a dive bar bathroom. Number 3 had never been a big fan of condoms.

I clicked through their photos. I paused at an image of his girlfriend standing by their bed. It lacked a frame and headboard, standing as a queen size mattress atop a box spring. I cringed when I realized the mattress was still wrapped in our old sheets. My parents bought them while I was in high school. They were white with a green, watercolor leaf pattern spackled all over them.

Every time Number 3 and I caught up, his familiar words towards the end of things ran through my memory.

"I love you," I remembered him telling me right before I left for the Navy.

We were preparing for the day I was shipping off to boot camp and getting far away from Tennessee.

"But there's no point in us being friends in the future," he continued. "We'll move on with our lives and the only thing we'll have left to talk about is the good old days."

He rolled his eyes as he said the "good old days." Number 3 loathed cliché small talk like football season or the weather.

He was right, though. We laughed about the good, the bad, and our childish stupidity. But every time we spoke, the bonds of our past fizzled into negative tension.

"Guess where I start school in the fall," I started, a bit smugly.

"Um," Number 3 said, mumbled, already bored with the topic. "That really good school you wanted to get into?"

"UC Berkeley," I said assertively.

"UC fucking Berkeley. It ranked the third highest in the country this year," I boasted.

I was full of fury. Number 3 had always been quick to rain on parades. Berkeley was a pile of shit I wanted to rub his nose in.

"The only schools above it in the United States are Harvard and MIT. This year it outranked Stanford, Princeton, Yale, Duke, Columbia...." I said, trying to sound as pretentious as possible.

"Well *congratulations*!" he said sarcastically.

I knew I was provoking him. Number 3 never genuinely celebrated achievements because he didn't have any of his own. He didn't make it through his sophomore year of high school. He never obtained his GED and had been painting houses since his teens. Realizing that I was taking my suppressed aggression too far, I switched subjects.

"So I went to a really cool party last Friday," I continued. "It was with this huge Mexican family and I was the only white girl there."

A classmate invited me. After five years of living in Latin-dominated southern California, I hadn't explored its family life. I loved the way such a huge clan could be so close. For every birthday, holiday, or graduation, hundreds of them gathered in backyards to drink beer, dance, play music, and shoot the shit all night. I loved the way everyone was natural and relaxed around each other. The bash gave me the urge to crack open a keg in the middle of my reserved southern family's staunchly passive-aggressive decorum.

"I bet you got hit on by a lot of dirty Mexicans," Number 3 said in a failed attempt to tell a joke.

Number 3 had always *tried* to be funny. When we were together, I was constantly faking laughter and orgasms.

"Actually, it wasn't like that at all. Most of the guys my age were pretty mature. They were all college students," I replied defensively.

"Yeah right," he sniffed. "I've never known a Mexican with a college degree."

In the midst of obtaining my politically correct education, I was appalled.

"Actually, most of those *dirty Mexicans* are transferring to UCLA," I snapped. "Isn't it you, the member of the 'superior race', who doesn't even have a GED?"

We continued to bicker like vengeful divorcees until the conversation ended.

After my awkward conscious virginity loss, I kept things up with Number 2 for a little while. But at the dawn of my sex life, I was already feeling like a middle-aged hooker who mechanically put out like a vaginal vending machine.

"Well, I've already been fucked," I rationalized. "I might as well go fuck some more."

I wasn't even enchanted by the rush of promiscuity. I didn't know intimacy, passion, or even of the climax I was supposed to be aiming for. I just got naked, lied down, spread my legs, and tried not to cry while Number 2 awkwardly maneuvered in and out of me.

In, out, in, out, in, out, whoops, slip, in, out, jerk, grunt from Number 2, pull out, and that was sex.

"Wow, this really *is* overrated," I thought, remembering my mother saying the same thing to me.

But after a drunken doggie style session on stained brown carpet at a trailer park party, I awoke more hung-over from Number 2 than the previous night's Sauza binge. I began actively seeking a replacement. Number 3 was the first thing I found.

Number 3 was buying weed from my friend's ten-year-old brother. The kid had been riding his bike around his neighborhood when he saw a speeding car swerve to the curb. Apparently a duffle bag was tossed out the window. The mystery car took off with cops on its tail. The curious boy found a pound of marijuana inside.

Number 3 was an acquaintance of my friend's boyfriend. So the four of us, along with our pint-sized drug dealer, met in a church parking lot to sell Number 3 a sack.

"That had to be the lowest point of my life," Number 3 said once, laughing at that memory. "When I realized I was buying weed from some little kid riding up to me on his bike."

Number 3 stood in front of his red 1995 Chevy Blazer. I took a good look at him, trying my best to not seem obvious. He stood a few inches taller than me. He wore a tie-dye shirt that read "Mary Jane" on the front. I stared at him harder as he smiled back at me. His appearance didn't have the wowing effect of the first sight of Number 2. I looked at him and thought, "He could be attractive with a good personality." I strained an attraction. I had already decided to ditch Number 2 for good and was in a panic from my state of complete singledom. Number 3 was decent enough. Plus he had a car.

"So I heard you went to my high school," I mentioned, feeling very brave for initiating conversation.

My friend mentioned our similar pasts before the meeting.

"Oh really? Small world," he replied.

He had that smiley, amused look in his eye that I was beginning to recognize as attraction.

"Yes, but I hate it," I said.

"What do you hate about it?"

"I hate the students, the teachers, and the dress code," I went on.

Since my parents forced me to transfer schools the previous summer, I felt as if my life had been tumbling into a gutter. Just before the accident, I reached the first point of contentment I'd known since Mom married Carl. I had a boyfriend and was receiving an affection that filled a void that had been aching for as long as I could remember. But even beyond the adventures of my romantic explorations was CSAS. Adjusting to the oddball school was awkward at first. But by sophomore year, I saw it as a black hole that launched me out of the shackles of the Republican Bible Belt and into a world that challenged rules I never thought to question.

I was learning Spanish and developing an intrigue with Latin America. My voice became articulately booming once I mastered talking across an auditorium. I became obsessed with literature and dominated mock court sessions in defending fictitious villains in Greek mythology. I joined a crew team in downtown Chattanooga. I was gradually discovering my first niche as an intellectual Birkenstock-wearing, Rock Creek Outfitter-shopping, outdoorsy hipster who smoked grass atop mountain parks and dissected poetry verses.

My parents blamed CSAS for my drug use, even though my classmates were my only straight edge acquaintances. They took me out of crew, despite the fact that athletic obligations were my only hope for bulimia salvation.

"That goddamn, free spirit, hippie school is makin' a disrespectful smartass oudda ya!" Carl lectured, rolling his eyes.

Although it was Mom who I poured my drug experimentation confessions to, she followed her typical tendency of spilling it all to Carl like a tattletale child. Uprooting me from a good school to a bad school seemed like a drastic move considering Carl had knowingly seen me intoxicated several times and never cared. Back then, I figured he was just mad at me for getting caught and forcing him to deal with my mother's panic. But in hindsight, I think he spotted the birth of the monster he would fear for the rest of his life.

The brain is like any other muscle. We're born with certain ones, but there are times in our development where its construction is vital. Just as a six-year-old and seventy-year-old can't build a six-pack the way a twenty-year-old can, the brain has certain points in life where its absorbency is higher. During Mom's teenage years of mental hypersensitivity, she was pampered and babied, giving her a permanent need to be cared for. Carl became an alcoholic during his adolescence, cementing an everlasting reckless, party boy mentality. During my sensitive years, I was immersed in a culture that bred educated rebellion. My school was a miniature epicenter of progression tucked in the belly of southern tradition. Our teachers opened our eyes to daily tests in our own yards, making us constantly ask "Why?"

"Because I said so," was always Carl's answer.

In just two years, CSAS ignited the flame Grandmother lit years before. Carl would never succeed in his attempts to extinguish it. But his parental authority was able to keep it dormant and unthreatening for several years. At Ooltewah High School, I was like a lion forced into captivity after a liberating romp in the jungle. Nothing challenged me. Nothing motivated me. Nothing moved me. My claustrophobia itched to the point where clawing at my own skin seemed to be my only method of relief. With no social outlets and no intellectual nourishment, I caved into self-destruction. My bulimia amplified from throwing up obligatory family dinners to driving to grocery stores and gas stations, shoving junk food into my purse in security camera blind spots, devouring the calories in the corners of desolate parking lots, and scurrying into remote public restrooms in the outskirts of town. My knees would rest on the cold, sticky tile floors as I wrapped my arms around bleach-scented toilets as if embracing an old friend.

There was a time when one finger tickling my tonsils was enough to provoke stomach jerks, but my gag reflex built a tolerance to it over time. One finger became two and then three. By the end of my junior year, my throat was nail scratched and knuckles were scarred with tooth marks. My fingers reeked of a constant sour scent of my stomach acid.

"Do ya actually think it's workin'?" Carl interrogated my eating disorder during one of our "family meetings."

The term, "family meeting" my parents occasionally summoned was always code for, "We're going to lecture Maggie on everything she is doing wrong and then punish her."

The announcement was usually typed up in a semi-official Times New Roman format used to summon gatherings in professional establishments. Mom and Carl posted it on our refrigerator with one of Mom's puppy magnets.

"Your bulimia sure as hell aint' makin' ya skinny," Carl jabbed, darting his eyes at my stomach. We were all sitting in the living room. Carl was in his large Lazyboy black leather recliner that he would have likely even forbid the president to rest in. To the left of it was a table that held a coaster for his large Jack and Coke mug and about four remote controls for his big screen television, DVD player, and stereo systems. To the left of the table was Mom's smaller peach, patterned cloth recliner that was typically hers, but was sometimes occupied by guests. But that evening, I was cornered to the couch on the other side of the room as my parents sentenced from their thrones.

"You've packed on at least ten pounds since last summer and you're always wearin' those godawful baggy sweats 'round the house. You're in denial that you're gainin' weight."

I knew that my eating disorder wasn't achieving its initial goal, just as any alcohol or drug addict knows that their substance won't fix their lives or numb their pain. I was a junkie far beyond feeling the satisfaction that initially enticed my addiction. I felt my headache and my heart pound post purging. I felt the hot, regurgitated chunks of sopping wet food burning my throat as my stomach erupted, splattering toilet water back into my face from the vomit's cannonball. I saw my complexion morph into a pale yellow that illuminated the deep, dark circles around my eyes. I knew that, sooner or later, somebody would spot me throwing up in the woods or unveil the vomit filled Tupperware I hid in my closet. I knew that I was committing gradual suicide. It's not that I disregarded logic because I couldn't see it. I disregarded it because I didn't care. I didn't stop because I *couldn't* stop.

My parents' attempts to stop my habit were through guilt and force. They grounded me several times. Carl made cracks when he felt that I was eating too much and snide comments on my weight yo-yoing. They sent me to psychiatrists who tried to quick fix me by Paxil, Zoloft, and Effexor prescriptions. All were antidepressants with weight gain for side effects, which might as well have been rat poison for a bulimic.

I would take them a few times, feel my emotions and sense of reality fuzz, and look at my mother who had been doped up on them since we moved to Chattanooga. I would see her blank, hazel eyes, and her bright, but empty, smile with chronic, artificial, exaggerated cheer, and become scared. I often wondered if she was buried under layers upon layers of southern sugar. I would make bitchy, inappropriate statements and look for her. I would say something, *anything* to shake her and look into her eyes for something real. I saw it when she was upset or afraid. I saw it when she'd spot me exiting my bathroom, hair tied back, knowing what I'd done. I saw it when she found out I was raped. I saw it when I told her about the drugs I used. I saw flickers of a real person, but she quickly disappeared within herself once she gathered composure. I decided not to be like her. Even if it meant embracing my demons, I wanted to be real. After a couple doses, I would toss the meds in the garbage.

It was Number 3's mediocrity that drew me to him. He seemed safe, simple, and effortlessly comprehendible. I looked into his beady brown eyes and saw no passion or inner fire that would send him racing across the planet on a mission to find himself. He wasn't smart enough for college or motivated to embark on any lofty dreams. From my first encounter with him, I could tell that he didn't have the temperament to hurt me. I saw Number 3 the way a toddler sees a stuffed teddy bear. He was something empty and lifeless that I could hold tightly and pretend to love. That delusion was my lifeline.

When I expressed my interest in Number 3 to my friend later that night, she played matchmaker and brought me to a party where he would be. The bash was on April 20th, 420, the birthday of Hitler and international marijuana smoking day, at a guy named Eli's house. The place was in Ringgold, Georgia, just about fifteen miles southeast of Chattanooga.

Eli was twenty and lived with his parents. He was a chunky, kind-hearted country bumpkin type. His parents allowed him and his friends to throw parties on their several acres of land, absorb hefty amounts of drugs, and couch surf for long periods of time. I later found out that Number 3 was one of a whole group of orphaned, homeless teens that squatted on every couch cushion and crevice of the modest three-bedroom.

Number 3 seemed to immediately catch on to the purpose of my attendance. He adopted me as *his* guest, introduced me to everyone, and asked me a series of first-date-like interview questions that ranged from my musical preferences to religious beliefs. By the end of the night, we were camped in the back of his Blazer.

Number 3 was one of five siblings. He was born in the Ukraine and moved to the United States when he was six. He described his parents as cold and strict.

"Ukrainian parents aren't like American parents," he explained. "They don't talk to you about sex or the things you're going through in life. They don't celebrate birthdays unless you are really young. Once I became a teenager, they quit buying me stuff for birthdays and Christmas and shit like that."

I felt sorry for him. Birthdays were one thing my parents always did well. Even Carl would participate in taking me to a theme park or my favorite restaurant with a group of my friends.

"I even paid for the furniture in my room," he added. "That's why I dropped out. I had to work full time."

Number 3 was awkward around unfamiliar crowds. He would be a boyfriend that I couldn't bring to a party or introduce to my friends. He would retreat inward and remain stoic and pouty until I agreed to leave with him.

After that first night in his Blazer, we continued to see each other. We never went to the movies or strolled in parks. He didn't even come to my home to meet my parents. Number 3 skipped all dating rituals. We hung out with his friends on the farm, got incredibly stoned off weed and painkillers, and crept into the nearest dark corner to fool around.

He seemed to like me rather quickly. We would drive to isolated areas around town from countryside cemeteries to lakes, smoke out, and have various deep, buzz-inspired conversations. He noticed my wit and sarcastic tendencies. He seemed to enjoy me poking fun at him for things like the marijuana leaf Mardi Gras beads he hung on his front mirror.

"Oh that's really smart," I said, flinging the beads with a little swat. "A cop pulls you over and asks if you've got weed and paraphernalia on you. What are you going to say? 'Oh no, officer. Marijuana is wrong and illegal. I would never touch that stuff!'"

"You're a little smartass aren't you?" He said with an amused grin, finally catching on. "You're funny. I think you're the first girl that's been able to make me laugh."

What gripped me was the way he made me feel about myself. He liked me. He wanted me around him. He told me I was beautiful. He told me I was strong. After years of starvation, he fed my self-esteem.

In southern society, it was the female's job to be the guardian of morality within a relationship. She was expected to have the willpower to control the proper time and place to have sex. If she allowed a man between her legs too soon, she was a whore unworthy of a relationship. The man was allowed and *expected* to be constantly sex driven. He was only responsible for strategizing how to get his penis inside her vagina. Whether or not it was too soon in the relationship was not his concern. I was taught that females sought affection and males sought penetration. The woman withheld from penetration in order to obtain affection. The man distributed affection in order to obtain penetration.

I implemented Carl's fatherly advice and withheld from sex with Number 3 for a month. His dick was ignored. His needs were intentionally overlooked. I allowed him to take my shirt off, feel me up, and go down on me as much as he pleased. Refusing to give physical gratification was part of my method. I had to give him a chase. That was how I was taught to establish power.

"Always surround yourself with people you wanna be like," I remembered Carl advising me.

He was sitting back in the Captain's chair of his yacht.

When I was about eight years old, Carl discovered a love for boating. He bought a small pontoon for summer family outings. But Carl was always obsessed

61

with having the best of all material things and eventually upgraded to a yacht. Nothing made him happier than to lean back on the boat paid for with his hard-earned money. On humid, summer nights, he would relax with his large mug of Jack Daniels and Coke.

"*Whaaaaaada country*," Carl would exclaim with his slow, southern slur.

"Why do you always say 'what a country'?" I asked.

Comments like these were usually the beginning of one of his drunken tangents of life instructions.

"Cause this country is tha mightiest, richest in tha world," he'd say, preparing for some good old southern "God bless America" preaching.

"In other countries, people'r dirt poor. They live their whole lives workin' the shittiest jobs you'd imagine with barely enough food ta eat at tha end of tha day. Ah mean, you gripe bout'school, but kids your age in India would kill ta go ta school. But they're stuck sellin' stuff on the streets to turists."

"But in America," he'd continue with a smug grin on his face, "You can git anything you want with the right work ethic. I mean, look at me. I have a yacht and a stereo system that could blow yer socks off, an ah didn't even finish college. An ah have tha fortune to sit here on ma boat with a drank in ma hand on a beautiful Tennessee night. It's all cause of America. That's why I say 'whadda country.'"

I looked at Carl, hearing the summer crickets chirping around the marina. He slouched back in his cushioned chair with his well-fed gut hanging over the front of his belt. Lounging on his yacht, named "What a Country," he was indeed a symbol of a southern man who had gained his American dream.

"I wanna be rich," Carl carried on. "So I surround ma'self with rich people, like tha boaters on this here marina."

He gestured to the other yachts parked on the dock, much more luxurious than ours. The boats were literally millions floating on the murky lake.

"That's why you have to be very careful with who ya hang 'round. If ya surround yerself with losers, it'll be tough to be a winner."

The first month of our relationship was fun. We spent every day together hot-boxing his Blazer with his friends, sipping Budweiser in front of a bonfire near a shed on the farm while analyzing Tool lyrics, and sucking face in random baseball field dugouts. Carl and I were in one of our buddy phases. I would drive home after drinking, smoking weed, and taking a few Vicodin's or Xanax, stumble into the house past my mom who was likely in her room drying her toenails and removing her makeup for her mud mask. Carl would be lounging on the back porch. I'd spot the bloodshot glaze of his eyes and know I was safe. Still, he'd humor himself by belting out a few sarcastic parental interrogations, just to fuck with me.

"How wuz that movie y'all wentta?" he'd ask, his face hot and balmy with his lips spreading into a toothy grin he never displayed sober.

"Good."

I tried to remain as short as possible. My tongue felt like it was made of cement.

"Wha-jall see?"

"Ummmmm. *Panic Room*?"

"Oh, reely?" he chuckled. "Whutzit about?"

"Um. Jodi Foster," I mumbled, incapable of conjuring even the most rudimentary story. "Was in this room. And she panicked."

Carl let out a long belt of laughter and offered me his one-hitter.

I liked Carl when he was inebriated because that seemed to be the only time he liked me. As the daughter of Jack Daniels, I found drugs to be my gateway to male affection.

Just like Carl warned me, putting out changed everything with Number 3. He began disappearing, sometimes for weeks at a time. I played the submissive southern belle my mother was. I didn't flood him with calls or even show concern. I suffered in silence and eventually assumed that he wasn't coming back. But every time I considered us over, he called. Instead of scolding him, I put a smile on my face and welcomed him. I didn't let out the slightest hint that I even noticed his absence. I later discovered that he'd been hiding on drug binges.

I began to see darkness in Number 3. His musical taste was depressing, usually consisting of metal with some band screaming, or the eerie tone of Tool or the Deftones. He never seemed to like much of anything beyond curling up in a corner and smoking a bowl.

"I'd like to live in a cabin in the middle of nowhere so I can be away from stupid fucking people," he would say all the time. "People are all the same, doing the exact same shit every day. They carry on fake conversations of small talk and ask each other stupid questions that neither one of them give a shit about. Like the weather," he'd ramble. "Why the fuck does everyone always have to talk about the *weather*? Who gives a shit?"

Leaving him always felt like finishing a sad movie. His bleakness was infectious. A month into our relationship, my depression spiraled. My relationship with my parents grew even more distant. When I was home, I spent all of my time in my room with the door shut. My only human interaction was through my cell phone. When my eight-year-old brother would say a word to me, I'd give him such a mean glare that he'd instantly look away.

"Why do you treat him like that?" Mom would ask. "He's terrified of you. He loves you. He just wants to talk to his sister."

Dating was my desperate game. Number 3 was the prize and it was my job to strategize how to get him. He was a simple man, so it was easy to discover a formula. The trick was to analyze him as much as possible. Once I learned what he wanted in a girl, I would simply become that.

My looks weren't a problem. Number 3 hadn't been shy about calling me pretty early on and consistently did so. But once physical attraction reached its limit of appeal, and I realized how badly our personalities clashed.

"I don't get why you like metal so much," I told him one day.

It was just the two of us blazing in his Blazer. We were parked in the countryside. The sun was beginning to set. After a few hits from the glass bowl Number 3 kept handing to me, I was feeling relaxed and silly.

"What do you mean?" he asked suspiciously.

"Well," I said, reclining the passenger seat back so I could lie down. "When I picture a metal fan, I get the image of someone with lots of tattoos and piercings - someone tougher looking."

"So are you saying that I look like some kind of pussy?" he asked, sounding angry.

"No, no, no," I slurred, stoned at that point. "But you have that baby face. And with that shaggy hair, you should be listening to the Grateful Dead or something."

He gave me a suspicious look, his eyes squinting at me as if I'd said something highly offensive.

"Hey!" I said cheerfully, too delirious to read his body language.

Reclined, I turned over on my side and looked at him.

"Has anyone ever told you that you look like that Grateful Dead teddy bear?" I asked him, laughing loosely.

Number 3 erupted.

"Is that what you think of me?" he raised voice. "I'm supposed to be some lazy hippie because of my hair? Do you think you're better than me? What the fuck are you doing with me in the first place? You should leave. You can do better."

I had to spend half an hour taking back my jokes and stroking his ego, reiterating every specific reason I liked him. I quickly learned to walk on eggshells.

By mid summer, Eli's parents had finally kicked out the lost boys. Five of them were crammed in a dumpy motel room in a sketchy part of town. Number 3 was always up for an escape. We spent most nights driving around town to do drugs with various groups of his friends.

I was used to surrounding myself with drug addicts. They were usually slightly older than me. Most of them looked like they'd been gnawed at by a household pet and tossed in the corner of the garage for a few years. But Number 3 introduced me to a whole new level of bad crowds. As a house painter, he associated with men in construction. Many of them were middle-aged, poverty-stricken rednecks with snuff leaking out of their toothless traps. Marijuana and painkillers were their crackers and juice boxes.

"Try this," Number 3 urged me.

We were visiting Cody, one of his work buddies. Cody was a tall, fair-haired and skinned guy. His shoulders and face were sunburnt from working outside and his hands were callused. Cody claimed to be twenty-eight, but his worn, sunken face looked at least thirty-five. His body looked like a flesh-toned skeleton.

"What is it?" I asked.

I was introduced to new drugs on a regular basis. I'd long tossed caution aside.

"This is how ya smoke an orgasm," Cody chimed.

I looked where his thick, southern drawl came from and noticed that he had a few teeth missing. Cody held a piece of tin foil folded down the middle. He poked a few holes at the bottom of it with a pen and dumped some white, powder on top. Lighter in hand, he set flames to the bottom of the foil. I saw a small amount of vapor rise. With a straw between his teeth, Cody greedily sucked every trace. He didn't hold the smoke in like marijuana. He quickly blew it out with a satisfied, euphoric grin like he'd just received a blowjob from Angelina Jolie.

"Yer turn babygurl," Cody said.

I had no reason to reject him. I felt like it was just as rude to turn down Cody's drugs as it was to turn down a neighbor's home-cooked meal.

Number 3 held the foil in front of my face while Cody lit the bottom. As soon as the vapor rose, I heard Cody say, "Suck it all in."

With the straw in my mouth, I took the deepest breath that my lungs could hold. It was the smoothest hit I'd ever taken, much more pleasant than heavier, scalding marijuana smoke.

"Don't hold it," Cody ordered.

As soon as I exhaled, I truly understood Cody's term, "smoking an orgasm."

There are no words to pinpoint the feeling of one's first methamphetamine hit. Those who have used understand. The world suddenly seems more beautiful than it's ever been. You have nothing but immense love and compassion for everyone. You are infected with an overwhelming sense of hope and optimism. You suddenly transform into this beautiful, immaculate soul. You love yourself with every inch of you. With no rhyme, reason, or requirement for that sort of logic, you are suddenly powerful, strong, and brilliant.

Meth gives you a rush that you can practically feel pumping in your heart and tingling in your skin. Without movement, your adrenaline seems to furiously race through your soul. That one hit makes you believe in your strength to climb a mountain or win a war.

One hit was never enough. When I smoked, I bathed in every bit of happiness my body could produce. In my body's attempt to balance itself, I had to come down. My nirvana faded. That broke my heart every time. I was willing to do anything to get it back. We bolted across town in the middle of the night and emptied our wallets. But just as with all poisons, there always came a point where we had to either stop or die. Luckily we were too poor to die.

My comedowns from meth were as devastating as the highs were pleasant. Even warmly nuzzled against my boyfriend, I felt utterly alone with the weight of sorrow heavy on my heart. My beautiful world was crumbling. I was suddenly overcome by an unexplainable urge to scratch filth out from underneath my skin. My bones ached. My body became my prison.

I clutched onto Number 3 for as long as I could. Knowing that he was experiencing this horrible feeling with me was a bit comforting. But I was seventeen and had to face my family and school. I drove home feeling uncontrollably depressed. In hopes of lifting my spirits, I turned to another addiction. I stopped by a local grocery store.

"I've already damaged my body today," I rationalized. "I might as well fuck it up some more."

I strolled in, still aching and a bit dazed from my earlier adrenaline rush. I grabbed several bags of candy, stuffed them in my purse, and walked out.

I became quite the kleptomaniac the summer before and had been hooked on shoplifting ever since. The trick was to carry a large purse, watch out for sensors, and keep an eye on security cameras. Most security systems had several blind spots. Some stores didn't even have cameras. This particular grocery store had few, if any, so it was a routine place for me to pick up food that I intended to vomit right back up.

It was my bulimia that prevented my full on meth addiction. The high I got from binging on forbidden food outweighed the meth euphoria. I was too focused on my former addiction to develop another. So I only smoked meth with Number 3.

Of all the bad habits I partook in, Number 3 was my most destructive. As I constantly struggled to curb my personality and tip toe around his ego, I lost sight of my friendships and any ambitions I may have had. When Number 3 graced me with his presence, I remained at his heels like a well-trained puppy.

Our dates were random late night house parties. My dinner was the toxic substances he graciously paid for. Those nights were a complete blur. Number 3 and I would take a pill, smoke some weed, drink some beer, and snort some random type of speed all in one night. I couldn't recall whom I'd met or what we talked about. There were times that I drove home so cracked out that I would suddenly wake up in my shower, not remembering how I got there.

"Maggie," my mom began in her serious tone one evening.

Her blonde hair was cut in short layers that framed her face. She was thirty-seven with barely any wrinkles. She looked pretty that night, having made the effort to put on makeup that brought out her hazel eyes. Everyone always said that my mother looked just like me, except with fairer skin and a sharper nose. It was always strange to see her serious side. Even during the times that we argued, her smile remained intact as if it were porcelain carved.

It was one of the nights where Carl, Mom, my brother, and I were all eating dinner together. I hated our family dinners because I knew that my parents sharply observed everything I ate. If I consumed too little, I was starving myself. Too much, their ears were on guard for gagging noises in my bathroom.

"Oh, shit, am I in trouble?" I wondered anxiously.

I was always paranoid around my parents. Although Carl didn't know that I ventured into the more dangerous territory of meth, he was well aware that I smoked pot and took pills on a regular basis. He kept his mouth shut and in return, I didn't rat on him for sharing his weed and partying too hard when my mother was out of town.

"Yer a teenager," he told me once when my mother had gone to bed. Carl's large body reclined on a cushioned lawn chair. As usual, he held a cigarette in one hand and his Jack and Coke in the other.

"Yer gonna git high. Yer gonna drink. Just don't do stupid shit 'dattal gecha caught and you won't get flak from me."

"But," he warned, "Don't think for a second that I'm as dumb as your mother. Every time yer stoned, which is a lot, ah can tell. Ah can see yer bloodshot eyes, yer di-lated pupils, and yer dry lips. Take one hit and I'm gonna know."

"Has Carl told on me about something?" I thought, panicked.

"Carl and I have been talking about it," she continued.

"Fuck! Fuck! Fuck!" my mind screamed because I was sure that I was in trouble when she mentioned Carl's name.

The second half of her sentence was the last thing I expected to hear.

"And we think you should move out," she said coolly.

I was shocked.

"That's if you can find a place to live," Carl added.

"We're not *kicking* you out," Mom said. "You're only seventeen, so you're free to stay here, but you can leave if you're ready."

After shock, came rejection.

"They want me gone," I realized.

"We're tired of dealin' with yer smart ass attitude. We hope that you livin' on yer own will change ya," Carl added more sternly. "You'll appreciate a job when you have to pay rent. You'll appreciate food when you have to pay for it. Maybe you'll stop throwin' it all up."

In less than a month, I was on my own. After working all summer as a hostess, I earned enough money to pay my Middle College tuition. Middle College was a program at the local community college that gives both high school and college credit while attending the college full time. I was miserable at Ooltewah. My parents would not allow me return to CSAS. The tuition for Middle College was around nine hundred dollars a semester. My parents earned far too much money for me to qualify for financial aid, but were unwilling to pay the fee. When I saw my checking account hit a thousand dollars, my mouth gaped open at my fortune. The bindings of high school and my parents were cut a year early. I was thrilled.

My roommate was Jolene, a classmate about my age. She had wavy, chestnut hair, large brown eyes, and a plain, round face. She looked like an average girl at an initial glance, but she had a wild side. She was bisexual and in need of someone to live with because she'd hooked up with her former female roommate who had fallen in love with her. For me, a girl who'd been around very little homosexuality, it was shocking to imagine feminine, soft-faced Jolene in bed with a large, butch lesbian with a military crew cut. As a fellow castaway teen, I looked at Jolene's independent survival for guidance. She had been on her own since sixteen. Her grandparents owned a tiny house in a Podunk town called Sale Creek, Tennessee, about a forty-five-minute drive from Chattanooga.

The house was in the middle of nowhere with at least a fifteen-minute drive to any Wal-Mart or grocery store. With rolling green hills, stray, matted Chow dogs, and dumpy trailers with Cameos parked outside, the area reeked of a white trash. Turning onto the street where I would be living, I couldn't keep my mind off of Jeff Foxworthy jokes.

"You might be a redneck if," I remembered, as I observed one beaten down house with what looked like a junk yard in front.

"You might be a redneck if you have to go outside to get something from the fridge."

And there was the antique, brown refrigerator within feet of the front porch.

"You might be a redneck if," I thought, watching a skinny man literally with a red neck, strutting across his lawn with tight jeans and a NASCAR t-shirt, "three quarters of the clothes you own have logos on them."

I looked down at his belt.

"You might be a redneck if your belt buckle weighs more than three pounds."

"I can't be picky," I told myself.

I made seven dollars an hour. With the five fifteen minimum wage in the state of Tennessee, I was doing quite well for a minor.

"But very few people my age have to deal with paying their own rent," I thought. I was pretty scared.

With a crumbled sheet of notebook paper in my hands with Jolene's scribbled address, I followed the numbers leading to the house. Looking at a cluster of three houses, I glanced at the tiniest one in the middle. It made the Jeff Foxworthy homes I'd been rolling my eyes at look like Buckingham Palace. I could have built it myself. It was a box with four walls evenly placed into a square and a cheap roof that rested at enough of an angle to allow water to run off. The box house was awkwardly elevated with a large block of cement in the front that was used as a step to the door. The home would have made a cute children's fort.

"Man, that would be horrible if that was Jolene's house," I laughed.

But I looked at the numbers placed on the mailbox in front of the box house and realized that it was the address that I was looking for.

Shit.

"The rent for the entire house is two-fifty a month," I reminded myself. "Did you honestly think it was going to be nice? This is your first place on your own. You're going to have to deal with living in shit holes for awhile."

I kept optimistic. My home would be my own, not my parents'. I would have the freedom to come and go as I pleased. I would not be tiptoeing around the signs of whether or not Carl was playing good or bad cop that day. My food consumption and every slight weight fluctuation would not be observed, critiqued, and humiliated.

Looking at the little box house in the middle of nowhere, I thought of my mother and wondered why she'd allow me to live like that. I thought about how far we had come. Long before Carl and boyfriends, it had been just the two of us. She had been the center of my universe, just as I thought I had been hers before Carl.

I faced the harsh realities of the real world quite abruptly. Right after moving, I got fired from my hostess job when I had been too strung out with Number 3 to show up for my shift.

Being only seventeen, it was extremely difficult to find a job. I began to realize that my suburban teenager work ethic wasn't cutting it when I had to pay rent. I hated The Box from my first night there. My furniture was so crammed into my miniature room that could barely walk in it. Jolene's cat loved to run into my room and shit in the hard-to-reach places under my bed. Between the old house and cat stench, there were never enough candles at the dollar store to create a pleasant aroma.

The worst part about box life was its location. I hated making the long commute to the city. Because it was such a journey to run errands, once I was home, I was stuck. The dumpy house was lonely and isolated. I had horrific daymares of being murdered and dragged into a nearby ditch, my carcass rotting for weeks before discovery.

I spent most of my nights with Number 3. He finally moved out of the motel and into an apartment with his buddy just a few minutes from my school. Meth smoking became routine.

Despite Cody's suggestion, our sex life never escalated on meth. Although it usually made men fuck like the Hulk on Viagra, it had an opposite, wilting effect on Number 3. Despite my surging sex drive, I struggled to ignore his shortcomings.

On meth, Number 3's quiet nature became chatty. We would spend entire weekends tweaking and talking about things that we would never recall, yet somehow made us feel closer. When two people use a potent drug together, their mutual distance from reality creates a bond. Number 3 and I went through the emotional rollercoaster of meth together. We shared our euphoria. We came down together. We bonded over our sorrow and clutched onto each other during our downfalls.

I never considered the danger of what we were doing. I didn't notice the bizarre behavior of my next-door neighbors who had the body clocks of vampires. I never paid attention to the decaying flesh and sunken eyes of Number 3's coworkers. I didn't question why Cody looked nearly twice his age. I just didn't *think*. I looked at it as an unhealthy habit, like eating junk food or smoking cigarettes. But it never even registered that I was consistently inhaling a mixture of ammonia, iodine, ephedrine, ether, Drano, brake fluid, lighter fluid, and whatever else the redneck in some remote shack felt like throwing in. I had no idea that it would have taken something as simple as an electrolyte imbalance from my bulimia or a night of drinking to kill me if paired with meth.

I began to lose weight. My olive skin that was already grey toned from my bulimia, turned into a pale, sickly yellow. I began constantly grinding my teeth, which became a permanent habit.

After an entire weekend of tweaking out with Number 3, I showered at his apartment and left for school on Monday morning. I had not eaten a bite of food since Friday. The only calories I ingested all weekend were from the gum that I incessantly gnawed. As I got out of my car, the sunshine beamed. Suddenly I felt like my eyes had been maced. I immediately snapped both hands over them in agony.

"What's wrong with the sun?" I wondered. "Why is it so bright?"

I ran into a friend, looking ridiculous with my palms cupped over throbbing lids.

"Does the sun seem brighter than usual?" I asked her, squinting out tears.

"Uh, no dude," she giggled, finding my absurd question funny. "The sun is the same as it always is. At least I hope so. It would be really bad if the sun was coming closer to burn up the earth."

"Then why is the sun hurting my eyes?" I asked her, knowing that she would not have an explanation.

"I don't know what's wrong with you," she laughed. "It's not even summertime. It's cold outside and you're complaining about the sun."

She was right. It was only a few days before Thanksgiving. The chill air had the familiar, crisp scent of fallen leaves.

Even after several minutes outside, my eyes never adjusted to the sun. I stood closely by my friend's side and wrapped my hand around her purse straps like a blind old woman with her seeing-eye dog.

"You look like crap," she blurted. "Did you sleep last night?"

"No and I'm so exhausted."

I felt like I'd spent the night under the wheel of a semi truck. I wanted to crawl into a dark, moist cave and hibernate.

I struggled through the only two classes I had that day. It was a miracle that I wasn't failing.

"You're the only person I know who was able to do all of those drugs and not flunk out of school," Number 3 often joked.

My school fully encompassed a miniature southern suburbia. Its juvenile society considered athletic ability in boys and beauty in girls to be their most credible attributes. Social statuses were defined by those qualities, the economic wealth of their families, and most importantly, whom everyone was friends with.

The cliché of not caring about *what* one knows, but *whom* one knows is a southern gospel. One's popularity defines party invitations, club memberships, and even career opportunities. In my hopeless desperation to wiggle my way up the social totem pole, I found that there was no formula for promotion. No amount of weight I lost, highlights I got, tan I acquired, name brand clothes I purchased, or brace-free smiles I plastered on my face would grant my entry into their circles. Even when I sat at the popular tables in the cafeteria, distributed Christmas cards, and invited them to my birthday party on Carl's yacht, they merely twirled their hair, smiled to my face, and then gossiped about me the moment I got up to dump my lunch tray.

One has to be able to walk along blurred lines and follow unspoken rules to harmoniously mingle with southerners. I was a lost cause from the get go. It wasn't because I didn't look the part. I never learned to speak their silent language. Something about my persona gave them the sense that I did not belong.

By high school, I was fed up with the struggle. I surrendered to it with ferocity and rebelled. I refused to even try to interact with my peers. I got high and napped in the back of class when I wasn't ditching. From the day Mom and Carl's courtship began, I carried that same sense of mute ostracism. It went beyond just being the baggage from an unwanted pregnancy. We didn't understand each other. Everyone had a place in my nuclear family. Carl was the breadwinner, the king, the *man*, the maker of all rules, dictator of all opinions, and distributor of all discipline. My mother was his soldier, surrendering any personal opinions and ideals she may have had and swearing her unquestioning, unconditional loyalty to him. My brother, Carl's son, would learn to repress himself inside a shell of the mainstream Tennessee teen who played sports, ran with the cool crowds, and cheered for the Vols. I was supposed to be a younger version of my mother, but an even more upstanding, devoted citizen to show my everlasting gratitude for Carl graciously taking me in. I was not supposed to demand things, question him, or challenge him. I was expected to remain as little of a burden as possible. I was supposed to be easy. I was supposed to devote my entire life to earning my privilege at their dinner table. My greatest dilemma was my lack of respect for Carl. I didn't even respect The South.

The culture I was raised in had a beauty to it. I grew up around woods, twisty gravel roads, secret trails, and cow pastures. I had plenty of places to play. I, along with my cousins, made forts in the woods or in trees planted all over the several acres of garden my grandparents owned. They had apple and pear trees, raspberries, strawberries, and rows of juicy muscadine vines, which I would often venture to with a large basket. My childhood was not contaminated with fancy, technologically advanced toys. I spent most of my younger years outside. I lived with unlocked doors and the freedom to roam as far as I pleased before dark.

There is an old fashioned politeness in southerners that is unique from the rest of the world. I was taught to say "yes ma'am," "no sir," "please," and "thank you." The men I knew opened doors and were instinctively protective over women. Strangers said hello to everyone who passed with a chummy grin and wave. But The South's density of social games and politics were stifling.

By high school, I had big dreams of breaking out. Although I planned to see the world, California captured the most of me. It was the media's image that made star-studded Hollywood look like the foundation of dreams. I pictured a paradise of white sand beaches, glamour, and excitement. Through the rose-colored lenses of a sheltered southern girl, it was a farfetched destination. I reminded myself, without truly believing it, that I would get there.

As time passed, my peers seemed to lose track of their own freshman aspirations. There were friends, family, sports, activities, drugs, and relationships to get caught up in. Many of us were terrified of straying too far from home. The fear only intensified as graduation neared. Others realized how expensive out of state college was, binding them to their homeland. I, on the other hand, surrendered my sights to Number 3.

I left school that afternoon, still stunned by the bright light. It was the last day of class before Thanksgiving break. I headed to my parents' home to attend a family pre-Thanksgiving dinner that evening. Even with sunglasses, it was a tough drive with the blinding white light jabbing my pupils.

I pulled into the driveway. Since moving into The Box, my parents' suburban home seemed to transform into a luxurious mansion. It was a nice two-story, four-bedroom, three-bathroom house that they spent nine years personalizing. The mailbox was covered in vines where pink flowers bloomed in the spring. The yard had a few trees in front of the flowing pond my parents built themselves. It was made of pastel-colored flat stone and decorated with yard décor and lily pads.

When I walked inside, I noticed the special touches I always took for granted, like the autumn wreath on the door. I admired the spotless burgundy carpet and the leather furniture in the large living room. I missed the convenience of having a computer with a printer at home and a kitchen with new appliances. I missed having an abundant supply of plush towels in the bathroom and a refrigerator of food that I didn't have to pay for. I missed the perky yips of the dogs greeting me when I walked through the door.

The house was empty. I climbed up the stairs, dehydrated enough to feel my bones creak. I knew that I needed to eat, but I wanted sleep much more than food. I peered into the first room, my old room, at the top of the stairs. My parents began ripping up the carpet in my room about an hour after I moved out. They turned my old room into my brother's room and my brother's room into the new guest bedroom. I peered into his new room with his green comforter and dark wooden bunk beds.

I trudged into the new guest bedroom and plopped down on the stiff Queen bed. The blankets were warm, plush, Downey-scented, and topped with about six fluffy pillows.

"Finally, I can get some sleep," I thought.

I lay there with my eyes closed for several minutes. My body and mind were beat, but a leftover meth rush lingered. Suddenly, I began heaving dry sobs. I was too dehydrated to produce tears.

"I'm so tired, but I can't sleep!" I thought, hopelessly. "What am I supposed to do?"

I was losing my mind. I desperately needed rest and had no idea how to get it. Had my brain been functioning properly, I would have realized that my irrational emotions were my meth comedown. My sleep deprivation, dehydration, and starvation were also major contributors. But for a few miserable moments, I breathed heavily in a panic. I rubbed my itchy, red eyes and pulled my composure together. I decided that I needed to eat. Despite the fact that my appetite had not yet returned, I knew some nutrition would revive me.

As I lifted my body out of bed, each stiff muscle felt like concrete. With a struggle, I managed to get on my feet. But as soon as I was fully standing, my legs gave out and my entire body collapsed. I stayed still, face down on the carpet with my legs twisted in an awkward position. Gradually, I crawled on my knees, pushed my arms against the bed and successfully lifted myself to my feet.

"No more meth," I told myself. "I'm done."

My relationship with Number 3 plummeted shortly after I moved into The Box. He broke up with me twice within a month.

As much as I hated my single stints, I thrived alone. I cried and bitched about him to my friends. I dyed my long, blonde hair dark brown. The change was therapeutic. If I could move on with my hair, I could move on with my life.

I began working as a waitress at a small Italian restaurant. I was paying my bills. I was already learning the ropes to surviving on a budget. Although I was sad, I was focused on school again. Without dedicating hours out of my day to being fucked up on drugs and cuddling on a couch, I had more time to accomplish things. It was my senior year and I was thinking about college or taking a year off to travel.

After some poverty to knock me to my senses, I began mending my relationship with my mom. I was healing. The more I emotionally distanced myself from boys, the more my turmoil faded. The drugs were gone and the self-induced vomiting lessened.

The call came right before Christmas. Although The Box was still my official residence, I was developing a habit of sneaking home to spend time with my mother while Carl was still at work or out of town on business. One night during winter break, I was sitting in front of the television with my mom, nine-year-old brother, and the glow of our Christmas tree. The scene was a Hallmark-worthy vision of family bonding. Life felt safe and intact for the first time since puberty.

"You know, you could always move back in," Mom offered. "We could turn the game room into an apartment for you."

I had somewhat emotionally distanced myself from Number 3, but one phone call was enough to detonate every bit of progress built. When he begged for me back, I claimed victory. And when he asked to move into The Box and pay all of my bills, I considered my struggles over. But they were just beginning.

Once Number 3 moved in, I was bound to The Box. Without my permission, he got us a dog. At seventeen, I was living the life of a country housewife. All I needed were some offspring.

"And just to let you know," I told him once he moved in," If you ever knock me up, I'm going straight to the abortion clinic."

I carefully took my birth control pill every day.

The first few months of our cohabitation actually went quite well. I knew it was a make or break move. Overall, it made us. We fought a lot, but learned to talk out our problems. When I unleashed my sarcasm, he explained why it bothered him. He often elaborated on how he grew up and why he was so sensitive to my attitude.

"I think the key to a relationship is communication," he always said.

He was right. I took it as a permanent life lesson.

Number 3 made life convenient. He paid the rent and the cable. He decided to quit drugs altogether. In following my mother's relationship chameleon characteristic, I mimicked Number 3's newfound sobriety. Number 3 seemed to flip a switch the day he decided to move in. He told me he loved me daily and seemed to do so unconditionally. Our modest home became a sanctuary.

Any chumminess Carl and I may have had soured the moment I moved out. I avoided the house when he was around, but found myself alone with him shortly after Christmas. My parents, brother, aunt, uncle, and cousins planned to meet at a Japanese restaurant for my aunt's birthday dinner. We were all taking separate vehicles and Mom took off ahead. The moment Carl and I were alone, he charged at me with a list of what I needed to do to get my shit together. I didn't remember the exact words that were exchanged, but I ended up running out of the house humiliated and in tears.

"I can't come to dinner," I sobbed to Mom. "Tell Aunt Libby that I'm sorry. I just can't be around Carl right now."

Although Mom was angry with him that night, her reaction was no different than every other time Carl drove drunk with her kids in the car or lost my toddler brother in the woods for several hours. She would glare at him, pout a bit, and maybe be bold enough to stir up an argument. But I assumed that things were back to normal the next day because Carl's behavior never changed. Even upon gaining sobriety several years later, he continued to be the type of father to dump garbage all over his son's bed when he forgot to take it out.

Before Number 3 moved in, I could barely afford my own food. Mom would meet me for secret lunches, slip me forty bucks here and forty bucks there, and sometimes gave me old jewelry to pawn. But after gaining some distance from Carl, I realized that he was the bane of my home life. The free rent, plush, detergent-scented towels, and pine-scented hallways were not worth living with Carl again.

For the first time in my dating history, I felt safe. I quit calling my friends for boy advice and trashed my "how to please your man" *Cosmopolitan* articles. I no longer lived with the paranoia that he could dump me at any second. I ended the struggle of trying to transform into his ideal woman. I got what I wanted. It was empowering. I didn't hesitate to argue with him, make fun of his music, or be as opinionated as I pleased. If he fought with me, I fought back harder.

"You completely changed once we got serious," he told me after a few months of living together. "I treated you like shit in the beginning of the relationship and you were patient and sweet. Once I began to treat you well, this whole other girl came out."

He was right. With every "I love you," I let my guard down a little bit more. Our roles were almost immediately reversed. Having once bowed to his every gesture, I suddenly dominated him. But with the sacrifice of his manhood came the benefit of our sex life.

In the beginning, I fucked like a corpse. Sex was a bizarre combination of grunts, tongues, bodily fluids, and a stick of flesh maneuvering in and out of my vagina. I was too focused on the fear of any love handles, stomach bulge, or cellulite dimples being spotted to enjoy it. Every time Number 3 began to initiate, I

74

cringed with each article of clothing he tugged at, silently praying that the room was dark enough to disappear between his flesh and blankets.

But once Number 3 moved in with me, I owned him. With a surging newfound confidence, I dismissed my fear of being seen naked. I developed rhythm. I went with my impulses. If something felt good, I released my whimpers and moans freely. We began experimenting with different positions. I got very familiar with his anatomy.

"Your dick is strange looking," I said to him once after sex, staring at his shriveled little sausage just after it puked up a pool of unborn babies on my sheets.

"That's because I'm not circumcised," he said casually, as if he'd expected me to pipe up about it sooner or later.

His penis wasn't large, though it wasn't as small as Number 2's. I assumed that it was average, if there was such a thing as an average dick size. Although I've never found penises all that pretty, his was particularly unattractive. His foreskin was rounded like a sucking mouth, which reminded me of some sort of hagfish or parasitic worm.

"That thing belongs at bottom of the ocean, not between the legs of a man," I thought.

I lightly flicked it and began laughing.

Regardless of the hagfish, I didn't shy away from oral sex. Because Number 3 wasn't circumcised, stimulation was difficult for him to obtain. Blowjobs required me to jerk his dick off hard enough to qualify as a full cardio workout.

Through a routine sex life, I learned a lot about myself. I got bored easily. I did my best to push boundaries. I endured the pain and awkwardness of anal sex, which felt like taking a shit backwards. I got him to fuck me in public restrooms and corners of the woods. I gave him road head. I even put a Listerine mint strip on my tongue after reading about the oral stimulation of mint in *Cosmopolitan*. My little experiment practically set his privates on fire.

"At least my breath smells good," I laughed.

Number 3 was not amused.

I was discovering the things I wanted. I enjoyed intimacy, but craved a roughness that Number 3 refused to aim for.

"I don't want to hurt you," he explained, after my incessant demands to fuck with some fury.

He was drenched in sweat. Although he was only twenty years old, he just didn't have the stamina I needed.

Early on, I saw our differences. I wanted my hair pulled, my ass slapped, and body slammed against the wall. My sex drive was significantly higher than his. I demanded a minimum of two sessions a day.

"Baby, we live together," he whined. "We don't have to have sex every day."

"You act like an old man," I snapped, rolling my eyes.

This was our most common fight.

Sex was just one of our obstacles.

Although I thought that living with my boyfriend would sway me to stop purging, I kept up my old habits. He worked days and I worked nights, so I vomited in the morning. There were several times that Number 3 would come home for lunch and hear me gagging in the bathroom through our paper thin walls.

"You need help," was all he would say, unable to do anything else.

Another conflict with living in close quarters was our basic bodily functions. I am a human being. I eat, drink, shit, and fart. Sometimes my crap is the size of a small toddler. I am also a woman, which means I have a vagina that bleeds a monthly flows that ranges from rosy spots on my panties to black ovary clumps. Even though every woman has that in common, we are taught to keep it a dark, filthy secret. While men have a bit more social leeway, a woman revealing her mortal grossness is just plain dangerous.

I was terrified to take a dump while Number 3 was home. It was okay that he did it, but at first, I didn't dare. For several months, we acted as if the food I consumed just magically dissolved in my stomach. The vile act of farting was even more crucial to hide.

Farting was never done in public, except by a humiliating accident or old ladies whose ancient buttholes were just too tired to clench.

"I've had five children," my grandmother would say with her nose in the air after ripping one out in a public parking lot.

But there were certain people I could let loose around. As little girls, my cousins and I had farting contests, trying to define the noises our ass flapping mimicked and competing for the foulest smell.

"Yours sounds like a motorcycle," one would say, pointing at my butt.

"Yours sounds like a pile of books falling off a shelf!" I responded in fits of laughter.

But after a year of getting naked with my boyfriend, I continued to hold in my stomach pains.

"Have you ever farted in front of Carl?" I asked my mother a few months into my cohabitation.

"Nope," she answered.

She had a smirk on her face, as if she had tricked him into believing that her body was physically unable to produce them.

"You two have been married for over ten years!" I exclaimed, in disbelief.

My mother managed to create a child with a man while keeping her unladylike stomach gas completely elusive.

Carl was a man who openly belched, farted, and lounged around the house in tight briefs with his hairy, fat stomach falling out for all to see. I didn't understand how my mother could still be that uptight in front of *him.*

It just seemed like way too much effort. I decided to let myself go. Alcohol gave me that bravery.

The day Number 3 confessed his love to me was the day he flipped a 180. He vowed to forfeit drugs for a life with me in bumble fuck Tennessee. To feed his addiction and my severe boredom, we became heavy drinkers. One night, after chugging an ungodly amount of vodka and several beers, I awoke next morning in a different change of clothes. I noticed Number 3 had changed our bed sheets.

"Do you remember what happened last night?" he said, grinning.

"No," I said, confused.

My blonde hair was in a tangled mat and I could have sworn that I'd fallen on a sledgehammer the night before."

"You pissed in the bed."

My jaw instantly dropped.

"What?" I asked, horrified.

"Calm down. It's ok," he said laughing.

I had been so hammered that I lost all control of my bodily functions. I could not believe I had wet the bed like a toddler.

Once Number 3 had cleaned my urine and changed me while I was unconscious. I completely let myself go around him.

Within months, my claustrophobia intensified. Nearly eighteen and at the birth of my independence, I grew desperate for a bit of socialization. But I felt light years away from any enjoyable companions, both geographically and culturally. I sometimes sought company with the Sale Creek locals.

Our next-door neighbors were a forty-something year-old couple named Johnny and Helen. Helen was plain woman with wavy, tangled reddish-brown hair. She never wore makeup and was rail skinny. Her skin was freckled and sunburnt with parched crow's feet around her tired eyes. She looked a bit like Julia Roberts after a prison sentence.

Johnny was a rough-necked ginger who usually wore cut-off denim and grease-stained wife beaters. He had a long, untrimmed mustache that made him look like a Confederate soldier.

Helen had an eight-year-old daughter whose father was actually Johnny's brother. He died in a car accident when she was a baby. So, the little girl's uncle was also her stepfather. In traditional stereotypical fashion, they were racist as fuck.

"Ders dis place in da hills dat'r infested with niggerz," Helen told me once, as I tried to hold back my shock of hearing that word. "All dem dirty lil niggerz hide up der. Dey got der own stores an everythang."

I imagined that Helen had once been a pretty girl before surrendering her body to meth. Her cheeks were sunken, teeth decaying, and she had horrendous mood swings. Number 3 and I often heard her screaming at Johnny at 3 am.

"Johnny's a crack head too," Number 3 commented once.

"How can you tell?" I asked.

"Well, he's in construction. Pretty much every guy out here in construction does meth or crack. Just look at the way he twitches. Notice how they're always up in the middle of the night?"

It was true. I never saw their kitchen light off. Johnny was always outside in the pitch black, completing basic daytime tasks like changing the oil in his truck. Number 3 and I often woke up at 2 am to the purr of Johnny's lawn mower.

Meth was a common Sale Creek past time. A tiny town that lacked wealth and entertainment, it was cheap and could be cooked up with household cleaning products.

I remembered the way I lost contact with reality. Time seemed insignificant because I never grew tired. My desire to function in the world like a human being diminished. I was perfectly content being locked up in a small room, busying myself with incessant cleaning, drawing, taking things apart, or any other useless task to occupy my speedy little hands.

"Maybe that's why they never leave Sale Creek," I added. "They're too cracked out to think about it."

Nearly everyone I passed by in Sale Creek looked like they'd had heavy objects dropped on their heads. Even the children seemed to be a result of fetal drug exposure. With every person I encountered, I got a little more scared. I wondered if I would become just like them if I remained in Sale Creek much longer.

Despite their detrimental meth cycles and damaged lives, I understood how they fell into it. Though I wasn't sure if other young locals felt the same way, I found Sale Creek severely depressing. I won't deny that it had its beauty. I took many walks through its scenic, grassy hills with an abundance of trees that bloomed bright colors in the spring. I lived only a mile away from a cluster of hiking trails that had yet to be tainted by tourism. I spent hours hiking and discovering swimming holes. Afternoons in those woods prevented several breakdowns.

But there was little more to do than that. I knew I was missing out on my life. I had gotten everything I thought I wanted. But over time, Number 3 wasn't enough.

Stuck in between my shackles and my fear of freedom, I medicated with alcohol.

Once Number 3 turned twenty-one, he began bringing home twenty-four-packs every night. It was always something cheap and urine flavored, like Bud or Coors Light. I'd drink that or vodka and orange juice. The higher our tolerance got, the more he brought home, and the heavier we drank.

At first, being drunk made me happy. My little box in the middle of nowhere became a charming, country cottage. The redneck, meth-head neighbors made me laugh. Number 3 and I had better sex. We were mushy, romantic drunks.

But over time my liquid courage unraveled different emotions.

"What's wrong with you?" I asked Number 3 one morning when he was acting very distant.

I had gone overboard the night before and completely blacked out.

"You hit me last night," he muttered.

"What are you talking about?"

"You slapped me right across the face."

Neither of us could remember what the confrontation was about.

Though I never got physical again, there were numerous incidents where we broke out in screaming matches. Sometimes I would drunkenly drive out to the woods. It was the only place in Sale Creek where I felt at peace. I'd stumble out of my car to literally lie on the ground by the river and sob.

There were times that we'd be having sex when I began feeling trapped. With him inside of me, I would suddenly have problems breathing.

"Get off of me!" I'd scream. "GET OFF! GET OFF!"

"What's wrong, baby?" he asked, terrified of my panic attacks.

I would push him away, curl up in a fetal position while still naked in the corner on the hardwood floor as Number 3 watched me helplessly.

After over a year together, he had yet to give me an orgasm.

"So you've really never had an orgasm?" he asked me, looking a bit hurt.

We had just had a decent round of sex, which Number 3 had just dubbed our best sex yet.

"I just don't understand what I'm doing wrong."

"Maybe it's me," I said, trying to be helpful. "Maybe there's something wrong with my body."

We tried just about everything to make things more exciting. We did it in nearly every position imaginable. He had gone down on me in my sleep, which was an amazing way to wake up. And, yes, the sex had been very enjoyable. But there was none of the explosive pleasure that led me to moan and scream uncontrollably. The Big O that I had heard of all my life just never happened with Number 3.

About a year into our relationship, I was bored. I craved variety. I wanted to feel the exciting newness of someone different. I began fantasizing about random encounters. I would look up at Number 3 while he was inside of me, and pretend he had blue eyes or black hair.

I was petrified of being alone. But the day that Number 3 didn't show up for my high school graduation was my ultimate deal breaker. I had to leave, but I was well aware of the emotional crutch he was.

I began devising a plan for what I was to do with my life. I was barely out of high school. In the midst of my Number 3 and crystal meth haze, my post-grad planning had been put on hold. Mom and Carl had long forfeited their obligations as guardians and never asked me about my plans. I decided to take a semester off to work and then apply to a university. I hadn't pinned down a particular one. I knew that I wanted to major in journalism, but that experience would be pretty limited in Tennessee. Out of state tuition was outrageous.

"I have a question for you, Maggie," my mom said when I called her about my college situation.

She sounded a bit anxious. "Do you know if your grandmother is paying for your other cousin's colleges?"

My grandparents on my mother's side were the financial heads of the family. Born during the great depression and raised during the World War II era, they were always extremely frugal. My grandfather spent decades earning a lucrative income, but living a modest lifestyle. For as long as I can remember, my grandparents were cheap. They refused to trash breadcrumbs or buy new shoes until their soles were falling out. At the end of every week, my grandmother would collect all of the leftovers in the fridge and make a soup out of them. Finding random chunks of pasta, tuna, and sandwiches, my stomach would curl. My grandmother always made me drink milk that was past the expiration date.

There was plenty of evidence of a fortune. It wasn't uncommon to rummage through my grandfather's drawers and find one thousand cash rolled up in one of his socks or buried in the floor mats in his truck. I'd seen statements for accounts in the Netherlands and Ireland with just under a million dollars in them. It was rumored that they had about ten of those accounts as well as a great deal of property ownership. And when it was needed, their pockets seemed bottomless. In fact, every family member I knew had some kind of assistance with college, business startups, bankruptcy bailouts, and even thirty-thousand-dollar rehab getaways. Although he never practiced the religion, Carl signed a Baha'i Faith membership card so he could be in my granddaddy's good graces for a loan.

"Because," Mom continued, "we haven't saved anything up for your college fund."

I was devastated. It was true that I hadn't been the most ambitious person the past year or so, but even on drugs, I still managed to graduate with a 3.0. College and a career had always been the plan.

I drove home that day, infuriated by their financial priorities. Carl was a flamboyant spender. His job as a mobile home dealer was unsteady, but allowed him to earn a load of money when business was up. Carl earned plenty, but spent even more. Being the type who craved the best of the best, he owned a nice yacht, had the highest quality stereo systems installed throughout the yacht and house, and was always the proud owner of the latest electronic gadgets. My parents seemed to have a new truck or SUV every year.

My parents also had a history of filing bankruptcy, had sketchy credit, and a large chunk of debt. What bothered me even more was the fact that Carl once told me during one of his drunken ramblings that he had made a promise to pay for my college when he first married Mom.

"Yer granddaddy and I shook onnit," he said. "Cuz he was willin' to pay for yer eye surgery so I had ta git your college."

A family friend once told me she'd sworn my grandparents had a trust fund for me, but I never heard a word about it from my parents.

I was the absolute last person that anyone expected to join the Navy. My mother always claimed that I came out of her womb kicking and screaming. I was never an obedient child. I talked back to my parents, questioned every decision and delivered scathing sarcasm until they grounded me. When Carl would thump me on my head for saying something rude, I'd barely stop myself before swinging my furious little arms back at his face.

"There's no way you could ever be in the military," Mom joked with me once when I was a kid. "If an officer told you to do fifty push-ups, you'd just tell him to kiss your ass."

Typically, there are three main motives for enlistments. The most honorable, and least common, is strictly out of patriotism. Of course, the government knows how rare this really is or else the enlistment bonuses and college money would not be so heavily advertised. Another reason is for people who simply don't know what else to do with their lives. The military is packed full of young ones who didn't excel educationally or have the patience to sit in a classroom. My reason, and what I found to be the most common, was pure escape.

The military is there to rescue wayward youth from a fate of lounging around their high school campus for eternity. It is there to rehabilitate drug addicts, criminals, and alcoholics. It straightens out the bad kids and gives direction for the aimless wanderer. The military provides the poor a steady income.

Overall, the military is a paycheck with an honorable image and immense sacrifice. You loan your soul to the government, and in return, the government shoves you on your feet. It is the job of the enlistee to stay standing.

I had no idea what I was getting into when I strolled into my recruiter's office on a hot July day. I just knew I was desperate.

I pulled up to the building divided into Marine, Army, Air Force, and Navy recruiting offices. I'd seen it several times because I used to pay my cell phone bill next-door. I would look at it, rolling my eyes at the thought of anyone wanting to enlist. It seemed like such a ridiculous establishment full of rules and mindless drills. But there I was, feeling as out of place as ever at the mere thought of what I was about to do.

President Bush had just declared the War on Terrorism a few months before. I knew that joining the Army and Marine Corps would be a one-way ticket to some Middle Eastern battleground. I may have been loaning my freedom, but I was never willing to die for my country. I felt zero drive to sacrifice my own life for oil and greed. With no desire to wind up in some nowhere town like Tinker, Oklahoma, I skipped the Air Force section and went right for the Navy. With the Navy, I had a high probability of getting stationed by a beach. It was also the traveling branch. I relished the thought of sailing around the world. Those tiny, unrehearsed details directed my fate.

I timidly entered the recruiting office, feeling the chill of the air-conditioned room against the scalding July heat outside. I saw three men sitting at nice desks in white Navy uniforms. The first man I saw was a large, African American in his late thirties. He was tall and burly. He reminded me of a grizzly bear.

"HEY, YOU!" he shouted at me.

His deep, booming voice matched his body.

"YOU READY TO JOIN THE NAVY?"

I'd never been addressed so boldly in my life. I would later learn that this tone was typical in military society. When they left sea duty, sailors often had trouble softening their demeanors.

The grizzly intimidated the fuck out of me, but I shyly walked straight to his desk and took the seat in front of him.

I glanced at the other two men in the room. The one behind him was white in early forties. He had brown hair and a thick mustache over his lip. I got the impression that he was the head honcho as he sat in the back of the office and watched over everything. He had a kind, fatherly face.

The man at the desk on the left looked like he was in mid twenties. He had a tall, lanky frame, shaggy black hair, and a wide, boyish grin. He wasn't James Dean, but his smile emulated confidence with a hint of flirtation. I felt a brief flip-flop in my belly, but quickly dismissed it when I heard the booming bear voice again.

"LET'S GO AHEAD AND SIGN YOU UP!" said the grizzly.

"Leduc," I read on his nametag. "Petty Officer," I thought. "Is that supposed to be his rank? *Petty.* It sounds so *degrading.*"

"Calm down, Leduc," said the fatherly man in the back.

"Petty Officer Randal," I read on his nametag.

"You don't want to scare the girl off," Randal laughed.

I talked to Leduc and Randal for a while, though I aimed my words at Randal since he was less scary. They told me all about Navy life and, in typical recruiter fashion, made it sound like a glorious adventure.

"The Navy is just like any other job," Randal assured me.

I could tell that he sensed my hesitation. And it was true that I was having doubts. The thought of swearing into the government for a four-year contract felt dicey. Until the age of twenty-two, I would be at the president's mercy. And I didn't even like the guy.

"You enlist," Randal began to explain. "And then you go through boot camp. Boot camp won't be fun, but it's only two months. Once you get that over with, the Navy is no problem. You're assigned to a job before boot camp. Then you work that job out in the fleet, but you get to travel. The Navy will pay for your health care, housing, and when you get out, it'll pay for your college."

"Can I be a Navy journalist?" I asked Randal.

My mom's next-door neighbor was an anchor for the local news. She had gotten her start with Navy journalism.

"Yeah, a JO," Leduc said. "That's what we call em'."

"The Navy has a whole new language," Randal informed me, reading the confusion on my face. "Don't worry. They'll teach you in boot camp."

Within days, I found myself gearing up to be a sailor. They were sending me to this place called MEPS in Knoxville, which was where potential recruits were physically and mentally tested for placements.

"You'll be taking the ASVAB test," Randal explained. "That's the test that qualifies you for certain jobs. Then whatever job they have available will be offered to you and that'll determine when you go to boot camp. Now, you have to be stubborn with them," he warned. "They will say whatever they can to convince you to join. Don't let them give you a job you don't want."

I obediently nodded, already feeling thrown into a world of trickery.

"Now, let's talk about the medical part," he said, looking more serious. "I need you to be honest."

I nodded again.

"Have you ever been to a psychiatrist?"

"Yes."

I had been to a few from the age of eleven to seventeen.

"What for?" he asked.

"Eating disorders."

"What kind of eating disorders?"

"Anorexia and Bulimia."

"Do you still have an eating disorder?"

"No," I lied.

I lied to everyone about that one, even myself.

"Have you taken any prescriptions in the past?"

"Zoloft, Paxil, and Effexor."

"Ok," he said, not sounding surprised by my answers. "Now, have you experimented with any drugs?"

"Yes."

"What kinds?"

I looked up at the ceiling for a moment, trying to remember all the drugs I'd taken over the years.

"Ecstasy, acid, weed, meth, coke, opium, maybe crack - I'm not sure. It was out of a crack pipe, but it might have been meth," I said, beginning to feel a little regretful of my honesty. "Oh, and several prescription pills."

"That you weren't prescribed to? Like what?" he said.

He kept his face completely professional.

"Hydrocodone, Xanax, Lithium, Oxycontin, Adderall, Klonopin, Vicodin, Valium, and, well, that's all I can think of. "

"Ok, thank you for telling me," he said, looking me in the eye. "I'm warning you now, you can't be honest with the doctor who is going to interview you at MEPS."

"Wait, so you want me to lie?" I asked, shocked.

"Yes. You *have* to lie."

"Won't they know? It's the *government*," I asked, eyes widening when I said "government."

"No," Randal said, his voice transforming from serious to very nonchalant. He took a swig of the Taco Bell paper cup on his desk and slurped the last bit of liquid from the ice at the bottom.

"It's illegal for your medical records to be searched. You haven't been arrested for any type of DUI or drug possession, have you?"

"No. I've never been arrested."

"So if your criminal record is clean, you're fine. Just don't talk about your depression or eating disorders. I'm sure you're just fine. They're putting kids on anti-depressants for everything these days."

"What about drug use?" I asked.

"Lie," he told me again. "It's ok to mention that you've smoked pot once or twice, but don't tell them you did it on a regular basis. And don't dare tell them about coke, meth, or any other hard drugs. They'll disqualify you in a heartbeat."

I continued nodding.

"Now, when was the last time you smoked marijuana?"

"I think about a week ago."

"We'll schedule you to go to MEPS in about three weeks. That'll give you thirty days to get it out of your system. It takes marijuana about a month. Coke, meth, or any type of speed take about three days, but I recommend that you stay far away from that stuff anyway."

"Oh, I have been for a while," I assured him.

"Good."

His smile was comforting.

My testing at MEPS was a taste of the discomfort I would consistently experience during my enlistment. I rushed through the ASVAB test, not really focusing on a thing. My score was decent, though not extremely high. I was too stressed out about the physical that followed.

Throughout middle school, I was obsessed with scales. Once I hit one hundred and ten pounds during my chubby phase in sixth grade, I weighed myself several times a day, determined to get that number as low as possible. With enough starvation and obsessive exercise, I got down to seventy pounds at the age of twelve. But it was an impossible weight to maintain. I began to feel sick, light headed, and lethargic. I stayed active, hiking trails and riding bikes, but I began to eat little by little. By the age of thirteen, I cringed when the scales reached ninety. I was terrified of hitting the hundred-pound mark. I began avoiding scales altogether. Then, at a doctor's appointment around my fourteenth birthday, I was horrified to see that I weighed one hundred and four pounds.

"That's not much at all!" the nurse assured me when she saw my horrified expression.

"Are you kidding? That's *huge*!" I exclaimed, struggling not to cry.

"Maggie, one hundred and four pounds is really nothing," my mom said, likely worried that I would have an anorexia relapse.

What they said was true. I was a petite, five-foot tall girl who wore a junior size three. By no means was I fat, but there was no way to convince me otherwise. Rather than facing the dreaded scales, I ignored them. Eventually, puberty set in. I shot up six inches, grew breasts, an ass, and hips. My size fluctuated due to the bulimia. But I lived in denial of the horrible number that would define my weight. Every time I went to the doctor's office, I instructed them not to tell me my weight. The process was a nightmare. With my heart pounding, my eyes tightly shut, I stepped on the scale like a decapitation platform.

I began starving myself the day before my weigh in. I'd been popping laxatives all week. I was determined get as light as possible, even if my intestines bled out. Me, along with a pack of other young adults, piled up in buses and headed to the medical facility.

It was five in the morning when we arrived. Nearly the entire staff was dressed in military attire. With scowls on their faces, they reminded me of embittered DMV staff.

"You think this is bad?" said a bulldog-looking man in camouflage as he scanned our tired faces. "Wait till you get to boot camp."

He let out a loud cackle, shook his head, and walked away.

Although the first part of the day was not unbearable, I felt like a vulnerable, lost calf confused in a herd of cattle. The fat, troll nurses were blunt and rude without a hint of the hospitality that had been handed to me my entire life.

"Give me your hand," demanded one nurse as she slapped a wristband on me.

It was my identification tag.

"Go get your blood work," she said without looking at my face.

The bitch loathed my existence.

We were shuffled here and there in small groups. In one room, I would get my hearing tested. Then I would wait for a while. I would then be called into another room to have blood taken, then back to more waiting.

"The pace of the Navy will always be 'hurry up and wait'," I remembered Randal warning me. "Just play their game and stomach all their bullshit."

So I waited and got tested in every way, shape, and form. It was tedious, but fairly easy for the most part until it was time for my drug screen.

"Take this cup and urinate in it," one of the trolls ordered.

"But I don't have to go yet."

I honestly couldn't. I probably could have gone without a problem if it wasn't obligatory. But my bladder had performance anxiety.

She nurse rolled her eyes.

"See that fountain," she said as she darted her pupils at the water fountain about twenty feet to my left. "Take one of those paper cups beside it. Drink until you can go. It'll help to walk around the room."

Had I not been so exhausted, I would've laughed at the spectacle of the dozens of teenagers pacing in circles, guzzling down cup after cup.

"KEEP DRINKING!" a nurse would yell when one of us would go more than thirty seconds without taking a swig.

"My stomach hurts," a tall, acne-faced teenage boy complained.

"*Drink until you can urinate!*" the troll demanded again.

I must have downed two gallons. I finally filled my cup, getting a bit of urine on my hand from the overflow.

"Gross," I thought.

But the worst part about the whole process was that a nurse had to actually watch me pull down my jeans and pee into the cup. It was embarrasing, but child's play compared to my next endeavor.

With my deep-seated physical insecurities, duck walking in my bra and underwear in front of a room full of people was more humiliating than smearing my face with my own period blood.

But the military found the charade necessary to make sure our spines had no deformities. The males and females were separated.

"Just be glad you're not a guy," Randal told me. "They have to get their prostate examined."

We were grouped into fives. Every girl in my group just so happened to be petite and rail thin. We waited for what felt like an eternity, frequently excusing ourselves to use the restroom, despite the nurse's scowls.

"Come in now," ordered one of the trolls.

We entered a plain, white room with tile flooring. I looked to my right and spotted a gigantic scale that was taller than me. It reminded me of a life size version of the scales used for fruit and vegetables at the grocery store.

"Ugh, could those numbers be any larger?" I thought to myself with an overwhelming sense of dread.

We sat on a long bench beside the scale. It was cold, hard, and uncomfortable- descriptions that would be all too familiar in boot camp.

"Strip," the nurse demanded.

I grudgingly removed my clothing, sucking in my stomach and cursing everything I had eaten in the past decade.

"Step on the scale," the nurse instructed.

"One-oh-one pounds," she announced the first girl's weight. "One-ten pounds."

"Fuck! These girls couldn't even give blood!" I thought, wondering why it was necessary for the nurse to announce our weights so loudly.

I was last to step on the scale. Although I had the freedom to shut my eyes, which I did, I could not stop the nurse from announcing the horrible words that revealed my weight.

"*One-fifty-one pounds*," she bellowed.

I wanted to shove a grenade up her ass.

The number repeatedly rang in my head.

"ONE HUNDRED AND FIFTY ONE POUNDS?" my brain screamed.

"That's only forty-nine pounds lower than two hundred pounds," I thought, as my cheeks became a hot, crimson red. "I'm officially closer to two hundred pounds than I am to one hundred pounds."

"You can step off the scale now," the nurse commanded in the uniformed rude tone everyone seemed to be using that day.

I sat on the bench, crossing my arms over my exposed stomach, wishing I had a blanket to hide my body with.

I watched the next stick figured girl step on the scale.

"One-fifteen pounds," the nurse announced.

I officially felt like Jabba the Hut. I looked down at my wide hips and lower belly fat, wishing I could shed every inch of it off the way a snake sheds its own skin.

To be fair to myself, I wasn't fat. A daily dose of the gym and a nutrition upgrade would have done me justice, but I certainly did not have a plump physique.

I wore about a size ten at the time. My body was curvy, with wide, high-set hips, a rounded, perky butt and slim legs. Since I didn't work out, my body was soft and fleshy. I had very little muscle definition and was unhealthy due to all the self-induced vomiting over the years. Plus, the fluorescent lighting and Godzilla-sized scale didn't ease my self-esteem.

One by one, the nurse made us squat to the ground and waddle like ducks across the room. Being a clumsy girl since birth, I nearly lost my balance with each step. But I finished the routine and was finally allowed the protection of my clothes.

"None of you are done yet," the nurse warned us, wiping off our relieved expressions. "The doc has to meet with every one of you."

The "doc" was a short, shriveled man who didn't look a day under ninety. He wore thick glasses with black rims. His face reminded me of an angry opossum's- white, hissing, and ready for attack.

I was ordered by the nurse to once again to remove my clothes. This time I was shielded with a blue paper gown. The doc examined my vaginal area and performed the yearly exam that I was used to. Then he ventured behind, spreading my ass cheeks with his pruned, gremlin claws.

"I wish he'd at least let me get a little drunk for this part," I thought, shivering.

"Doesn't look like she has any hemorrhoids," he said to the nurse who stood beside him as if the ass's owner was not in the room.

"You need to watch your weight," he said to me, once he was finished with his examination.

The nurse nodded in agreement. I shot her a glare.

"Ha! I weigh as much as your single leg does, you rhinoceros," I thought.

But a pang of hurt feelings still shot through my chest. There was not an adjective more brutal in the English language to me than "fat." The word infected me with rage. I wanted to push the gargantuan nurse on the doc and crush his deteriorating bones.

"You're 5'6", the doc began to explain in his crackling voice. "The weight limit for women in the Navy is one hundred and sixty three pounds. The minimal is ninety."

"No way in hell I'll ever be ninety pounds again," I thought miserably.

"You need to be in the middle of that. Aim to weigh at about a hundred and twenty-five pounds. The Navy will have physical fitness tests and weigh-ins twice a year. You better get to working on your weight quickly."

I stared at him blankly, but there is no doubt in my mind that he saw the hatred in my eyes. Realizing that the Navy was going to constantly revisit my darkest monsters, I left the doctor's office with a heavy heart.

After hours of being poked, prodded, humiliated, and insulted, I felt as if the worst part of the day was over. And indeed, the painful stuff was behind me. But in retrospect, the greatest damage was done while sitting in a cushioned chair in an air-conditioned office.

After hours of hurrying up and waiting, I headed to another waiting room for even more waiting. There were several rows of chairs with at least a hundred other people crowded inside. There were several offices with large, glass doors and transparent windows. Each office had a sign over it that read either "Navy," "Air Force," "Army," or "Marine Corps." Inside, I could see one or two people in uniform behind a large desk with a squeamish kid in front of each of them.

I took a seat, getting elbowed by a boy with large arms on each side of me and tried to tune out the buzzing of the crowd. I stared straight ahead wishing I had a book to read. For what felt like days, I sat in the chair and fought sleep. It was the sound of a booming voice reciting my last name that awoke my fog.

"YOUNG!" he roared.

Throughout my four years in the Navy, I would be referred to by my last name.

I entered the office that was labeled with the Navy sign. I sat down with a woman wearing the same white uniform as my recruiters back in Chattanooga. With her mousy brown hair pinned back into a tight bun, she was plain and a bit rugged. I guessed she was about thirty-five years old.

"Hello," she greeted me without looking up from her computer.

She typed away at her desk before looking up to make eye contact with me.

"So, are you ready to find a job?" she asked me.

She had no cheer in her expression. I could tell she went through this process over hundreds of times a day and was trying to rush through it as quickly as possible.

"I already know what I want," I said with all the confidence I could muster.

"Be firm with them," I remembered Randal warning me. "They'll try to convince you to take whatever job they want for you. To the Navy, you're nothing but a billet- a number. They'll offer you bonuses, but don't take a job that you don't want. They'll lie to you and say anything to get you to take the job they want to give you."

"What job is that?" she asked me.

"JO."

She squinted her eyes in an expression that was already said "no."

"I'm afraid that rate is all filled up," she said. "Plus you're ASVAB score is a few points below the requirement."

"I want JO," I repeated.

I did my best to sound aggressive and ignore my nervous, clammy palms.

"I already told you, we can't give you JO," she repeated.

"Well, that's the only job I'll take."

Had I possessed the slightest street smarts, I would've read the twitch in her eye. It was vital for me to understand the way the military functioned. It was a system of lies, deception, and keeping its members as in the dark as possible so that they can be shuffled around at the government's convenience. To the Navy, the individual's wants and goals do not matter. An ideal enlistee is a robot, designed to serve its programmed purpose.

But I was a baby minnow entering the murky waters of the vast ocean. I did not know how to swim in the currents or dodge the sharks. I was easy prey.

"Wait," she said, almost yelling, right as I was about to get out of my chair. "There is a way for you to become a JO. You have to go through this new program."

And there was her hook.

"It's the Seaman Apprenticeship program," she began to explain.

She opened up her desk and reached for some papers.

"Basically you enter the Navy undesignated, meaning you have no rate or job. You go to a ship and you try all of the other jobs to see what you like. Once you know what you want, you choose that job. You can work with the JOs and decide if you want to do it or not."

Sold.

I would be shipping off to boot camp in Great Lakes, Illinois in January.

Those last few months were a series of farewells. I said goodbye to drugs, smoking one last joint after MEPS before tossing the habit for several years. I said goodbye to the drunken laziness I'd acquired with Number 3. I eased off on the booze and began jogging on a daily basis. Though I wasn't marathon training, it turned out that running came easily to me. Most importantly, I said goodbye to nearly four years of chronic bulimia.

My last session of self-induced vomiting was unforgettable. About two weeks before I left for boot camp, I found myself alone in The Box. I had eased up on my habit since MEPS. I went from purging at least three times a day to once every few days. Running was simply too painful after vomiting. When I first began forcing myself to throw up, the only damage it seemed to do was leave a bad taste in my mouth. Over the years, it evolved to scars on my fingers, a sore throat, chest pains, altered taste buds, and blurry vision. By the time boot camp was approaching, vomiting brought on dizziness, fatigue, and migraines. As I fought to get in shape, I felt my bulimia crippling me. But Number 3 had just left for work and I had several hours to myself. It was the perfect opportunity to enjoy some forbidden food and gag to my heart's desire. I did just that, gripping the side of the toilet with my left palm and shoving nearly my entire right fist down my throat. When I first became bulimic, it only took one finger to gag me. Towards the end, my gag reflex was nearly gone.

With a good deal of struggle, I coughed up chunks of food that splattered all over the toilet, causing a few drops of toilet water to splash up into my face.

"Ugh, I hate when that happens," I thought.

Along with the food chunks were a few streaks of blood. I had been coughing up blood for a few months, but I convinced myself that the bleeding wasn't internal. I convinced myself that my nails were just scratching against the side of my throat.

I flushed the toilet and I hopped in the shower. I stood nude under the hot water with my arm pressed against the shower wall to keep my balance. After a few moments, everything stopped spinning and I was able to finish cleaning myself off.

After turning off the water, I stepped out a towel wrapped around my body; I reached in the medicine cabinet for a Q-tip. I dipped the cotton swab in my ear, took it out, and was horrified at what I saw. There was blood at the end of my Q-tip.

"No way," I thought. "My ear has to be scratched."

I dipped the Q-tip in my other ear and pulled it out. Once again, the swab was covered with blood. I was indeed, bleeding out of my ears.

"We do not want to be the parents who are forced to identify their own daughter at the morgue," Carl had lectured me after they first discovered my bulimia.

But I'd never really taken medical precautions seriously. I'd vomit, feel my heart pounding against my chest, and remember all the times doctors told me about bulimia triggering heart attacks. Like most teenagers do, I felt invincible. Death was never comprehensible until I found myself bleeding out of every orifice.

"I'm done," I decided.

Finally, I meant it.

Number 3 dropped me off at the recruiting station for boot camp. Although I was sad and a little bit scared, I didn't cry.

I walked into the office, greeted by Randal, Leduc, and the young, shaggy-haired recruiter.

"Well, looks like I just broke up with my boyfriend," I said with a sigh as I sat down in the couch in the front of the room.

"Oh, you'll get by. You're only eighteen. There will be plenty of boys for you in the Navy," Randal reassured me.

"You've got a few hours before the van ships you off to MEPS and we've still got to get your transcript from community college. This guy's gonna take you."

Randal walked over to the young recruiter, patting him on the shoulder.

I looked at his slightly cocky, but genuine smile and bright eyes. He wore his black Navy uniform, referred to as "working blues." The fleet changed their uniforms seasonally. The white uniforms were for the spring and summer. The blues, which looked more black than blue, were for the fall and winter. Black suited him much better. The uniform complimented his dark hair, which was grown out rebelliously past military standards. His small eyes were charcoal and his skin was fair. His nose wasn't large, but was a bit pointed at the end. He was clean-shaven with neat eyebrows. He wasn't ugly or particularly attractive. Besides his demeanor, everything about his features screamed "average." I only had to be in the same room with him to feel a pull. His smile was captivating. I could tell that he charmed women very easily, but there was no maliciousness in his way of doing so.

"Let's go, Miss Maggie," he said, darting another one of his smiles at me.

I realized for the first time how country his accent was. It almost made me laugh.

"This guy is such a dork," I thought.

He opened the passenger door of his little black car for me, let me in, and closed it behind me. Within minutes of being in his presence, my nervousness about boot camp, the Navy, and leaving my boyfriend faded.

"Boot camp really ain't a big deal," he assured me, his smile never leaving his face. "It'll jus' be cold as hell up there. You'll get negative temperatures out there," he continued. "But you'll be fine. Jus try ta keep yer mouth shut and blend into tha background. You'll realize that once ya get it all over with, it'll be the best thang you ever done. It's so important you get out of here and experience the world. That's what the Navy will do for you. You'll get to travel and see things that civilians will only read about in books."

"You grew up in Chattanooga, right?"

He nodded.

"So why did you come back?" I asked him.

"My ex-wife wanted to come out here," he said.

"Ex-wife?" I said, shocked. "How old are you?"

He seemed far too young to have an ex-wife. He looked at me, his grin still constant.

"I'm twenty-six," he said. "I was nineteen when I got married. We have a daughter."

My eyes widened again. He seemed to know exactly what I was thinking.

"You'll see that a lot," he warned me. "A lot of people in the Navy get married young and have kids young."

"Why?" I asked him.

"I thought I was in love. But the atmosphere can get very lonely in the beginning. It can push you to want someone to be with. Plus, a wife will get you out of the barracks and ships. The Navy gives extra pay to married people. They give you even more pay for kids. Plus, you get free medical benefits so havin' a baby is free."

"So what happened? With you and your wife?"

"She cheated on me."

He said this very casually. His smile shrank to a smirk, but he seemed like he had gotten over it long before.

"She was banging some guy in base housing with my daughter in the other room."

My mouth gaped open.

"That's so sad!" I exclaimed.

"It happens a lot in the Navy," he said. "Some people can't handle their spouses being gone for so long. There's a lot of cheating."

"Did you ever cheat?" I asked him, not caring whether or not I was invading his privacy.

"Nope," he said, looking me dead in the eye.

I didn't think he wasn't lying.

"I liked being married. But it didn't work out for me. Oh well. I'm happy being single. It's much more fun," he said with a playful, but innocent wink.

"You must hate her now, huh?"

"No, not at all," he said. "We have a beautiful daughter. I'm grateful for that. She's remarried and has more children."

"Now, don't get mad at me when you're in Great Lakes and wonder what the hell I got you into!" Randal told me right before I got into the van to ship me off to Knoxville.

I would be spending the night in Knoxville again, then going through MEPS for one more medical checkup and drug test. I was going to have to duck walk again, but I was dreading it less since I knew what to expect. I also was feeling healthier with my daily runs. I would be boarding a plane to Pittsburgh and then finally Chicago. From there, I would board a bus to Great Lakes.

"It's gonna be cold as hell," Randal reminded me again. "They're going to yell at you and you're gonna be scared out of your mind. Just play the game, suck it up, and it will all be worth it. It's only two months of your life."

I nodded, feeling queasy.

"You're a tough girl. I can tell," Randal assured me.

"You'll be fine, Maggie," said the young recruiter behind him.

His smile made me feel a bit better.

"Time to get this over with," I told myself.

Swearing into the military was surreal. Me, along with a few other boys going into various branches were called in to take our oaths that bound us for four years. A few gruff men in uniform escorted us. We must have looked like flimsy infants in our jeans and hoodies. I observed a soldier with his upright, stiff posture and wondered, "Is that what I'm going to turn into?"

We entered a room with wooden walls, a red carpet platform, and a large American flag hanging behind it. Some families stood behind us to watch their children swear in, taking photographs of the flag afterwards. A man in camouflage stood on the platform behind a podium. He had a buzz haircut that made him look like a life-sized GI Joe. He gave us a brief speech of the significance of the oath we were about to take, explaining that we were giving our citizenship up in service of the government.

I gulped.

"Does anyone have any questions or concerns?" he asked us in his deep, authoritative voice.

"No sir," we all answered obediently in unison.

He instructed us how to stand at attention, with our arms to our sides and our wrists against us with thumbs pointing down.

"Now, raise your right hand and repeat after me," he ordered.

We looked at him, frozen, but prepared to follow orders. I did my best to look as militaristic as possible, though I knew I was just a kid playing make-believe sailor.

"I, state your full name," he told us.

"I, Maggie Young," I repeated with the mild southern accent that would soon disappear for good.

"Do solemnly swear," he said.

"Do solemnly swear," our scattered voices tried to repeat in unison.

"That I will support and defend."

"That I will support and defend," our voices sounded timid.

"The Constitution of the United States."

"The Constitution of the United States."

"Against all enemies."

"Against all enemies."

"Foreign and domestic."

"Foreign and domestic."

I repeated the rest of the oath, trying not to let the flashing cameras distract me. There were several family members in the room, tearfully capturing every moment. The whole scene was very American propaganda, with the parents of the good 'ole boys of The South leaving to defend their country. I pictured those boys returning home for 4th of July cookouts in their uniforms and wondered how real the glamour of military service really was.

I tried to feel honor in my oath, but I couldn't muster any genuine patriotism. It wasn't that I lacked gratitude or didn't recognize the privileges of being an American citizen. But I knew, should I ever be sent into combat, that I would find a way out of it. I would fake insanity, homosexuality, or break a leg if necessary. I had gratitude for the perks of my country, but I didn't *love* it. I didn't even identify myself with it. My enlistment was a meal ticket and a stepping-stone to take me beyond the doom of becoming Number 3's wife.

In boot camp, I was told that I sold my soul to the government. I knew it was just a loan.

The caution from my recruiters that boot camp would be more mentally challenging than physically challenging turned out to be very accurate.

Of course, there were plenty of physical obstacles. The frigid, January air of Great Lakes, Illinois, seemed to ice my every breath. I grew up loving snow. The winter wonderland signified school vacations and sledding adventures. But after two months of trudging through slushy, slippery ice, it ruined me. For months after, I didn't even want ice cubes in my drink. I was forced to become accustomed to sleep deprivation and early, abrupt, wake-up calls by screaming Recruit Division Commanders.

Our workouts were a challenge in the beginning, especially when the RDCs wanted to demonstrate their authority. We had the occasional "beating" session of being ordered to do push-ups, mountain climbers, and anything else to knock out our energy. Some of the recruits handled physical exercises quite well, while others were degraded to tears. I was relieved to discover that I was not the only recruit who wasn't in top shape. Only a few recruits in my division actually were.

One of my favorite boot camp memories was after our first physical testing session, called the PT.0. In the Navy, or the "fleet" as the RDCs called it, there were two physical tests a year called the PRT, short for the Physical Readiness Test. In boot camp, we had the PT.0, the PT.1, and the PT.2. We had to pass the PT.1 and PT.2 in order to graduate boot camp, but the PT.0 was to see exactly how out of shape we were. Depending on our age and gender, we had to do a minimum amount of push-ups, sit-ups, and run a mile and a half in a specific time. For someone in decent shape, the requirements were easy. But our division's first attempt at a PT was a pitiful display. With our RDCs screaming out words of encouragement, we ran thirteen laps around the gym that felt like a million. My lungs burned, but I didn't resort to vomiting in the garbage cans along the side of the track like several others did. We all got through the run, which I proudly passed.

Recruits were the sheep, and our RDCs were the sheepdogs that herded us around base. Every move we made was organized in groups. We got from place to place by marching in step. If one person was out of step, others tripped, the formation would be ruined, and the RDCs would bark.

We were trained to line up quickly in the order of our height, with our RDCs growling in the background to make sure we did everything in a timely manner. We were petrified of standing out in any way and struggled to blend in. We nearly shit ourselves every time an RDC called our name out.

After the PT0, we lined up in ranks in the snow. We listened to a heated lecture from our RDCs about how horribly out of shape we were. We stood at attention like statues. When one of our RDCs finished speaking, there was dead silence. Suddenly, I saw a thin, tall, boy two rows ahead of me jerk his head forward. I heard the gag and saw chunks of white vomit gush down the head and neck of the recruit in front of him.

Our workouts were miniscule compared to the cultural shock of basic training.

"The purpose of boot camp is to break you down and build you back up," explained our RDC during a lecture.

Indeed, they were quick to break us down. Within minutes at arriving to base, we were stripped of our own clothes and changed into NAVY sweats. We were fitted for uniforms within the first week. The boys had their heads shaved. The girls got their locks butchered to above chin length. The barber didn't care if he cut evenly. He just took a pair of scissors and hacked it. A lot of girls cried.

"You'll look like a Britney Spears when I'm done with you," my barber said sarcastically as I watched blonde chunks fall into my lap.

Our Navy uniforms were unflattering to the female figure. We usually wore what were called "utility uniforms." Utilities were navy blue pants, a blue shirt, black boots, and a navy blue cap that was boldly labeled "recruit" in yellow lettering. The pants were high waisted, fitting uncomfortably on our belly buttons. Even on the thinnest girls, the pants created a pudge right below the belt that I'd always seen in my grade school teachers. In the Navy, we called it a FUPA (fat upper pussy area) or a BIF (butt in front). Something about those pants dissolved our butts. Besides our new FUPAs, our feminine curves were well hidden.

"They make you look like shit on purpose," Petty Officer Hunter told us.

Hunter was our female RDC. She was a husky woman with dirty blonde hair pulled into a bun and a sharp, makeup free face. Her voice was deep and aggressive. She reminded me of a cliché butch high school gym coach. She was extremely sarcastic and tough as nails.

"That way all those men won't want to fuck you."

Her demeanor was crude, which helped her function in the very male-dominated career that she chose for herself.

"But it still won't work," she added. "Men are dogs. They'll fuck anything," she gave us a crooked smirk. "I hate to say it, but within your first year half of you are going to be pregnant."

She looked out at all of the females in our division, as we glanced at each other uncomfortably.

Hunter had once been a recruit herself. To her, our thoughts were transparent. She watched us cringe in the mirrors at our exhausted faces, stripped of makeup. She laughed at the girls who cried from their haircuts.

"This isn't the fucking prom," she mocked. "You're here to become a sailor, not bang one. Nobody gives a damn what you look like."

The RDCs were bullies. They screamed us into acting quickly. They threatened us into folding towels, shirts, and our beds perfectly while being timed. If we fell behind, they did all in their power to single us out and humiliate us for letting our guards down.

Like the offspring of emotionally abusive parents, we became weak submersion in an unkind atmosphere. We were isolated from our families, friends, the media, or any source outside of base. We were theirs to be tampered with. There was no kindness or nurturing during the early stages of boot camp. There was only marching, exercising, yelling, snow, ice, cleaning, and a bunch of timid teenagers chaotically smashed together.

Privacy was not an option. Our division was filled with about a hundred recruits, half male and half female. About fifty females resided in the barracks across the hallway from the males. We slept in rickety old bunk beds, which we were drilled daily to make a specific way. I was horrible at folding sharp triangles in my sheets and smoothing every microscopic crease. The situation was much worse when our RDCs timed us, yelling, "GO! GO! GO! You have thirty seconds," in our ears. We made our beds, known as racks, as if guns were being held to our heads.

With fifty females in one room, there was no alone time. Showering was always a reminder of exactly how many of us there were. Each day, we had ten minutes to take a shower. Although that may seem like plenty of time, this involved fifty women showering under eight showerheads of cold running water. In the beginning, it was shocking to see so many naked broads. To a man, the idea of fifty unified pussies seems quite jerk-off worthy, but the sight was not sexy. There were moles, fat clumps, sagging breasts, and bushes. We were forced to trash our modesty. Everything we did was rushed. Our showers were timed. Folding our shirts, underwear, which was called "skivvies" in Navy language, and getting dressed, was urged with a "HURRY THE FUCK UP! YOU'VE GOT SIXTY SECONDS!"

Losing alone time was the best thing that ever happened to me. There was no possible way for me to be bulimic in boot camp. Every sound I made was within earshot of at least one girl. Self-induced vomiting would've been an instant trip to a psychiatric hospital. I was forced to quit, but I had no desire to throw up anyway. With the constant activity of boot camp, I needed the energy that food gave me. I began to eat very healthy. I took advantage of the fact that Navy cafeteria food, known as galley food, was not tasty. Boot camp was my rehab.

After a few weeks, I became accustomed to the uncomfortable racks. I was too exhausted for insomnia. Tears stopped welting when I saw my pale face and tired, sunken eyes in the mirror. Beauty quit mattering. I was able to strip in front of all the girls in my division without internal panic attacks. I became used to being cold and uncomfortable. Every night, we were sent to bed with our hair wet. The windows were left open to keep germs from circulating, but outside temperatures were usually in the negative. Wet hair and cold climate gave me a two-month long cold.

Disgusted by the galley meat that was rumored to be grade D, I was a vegetarian in boot camp. My complexion became white with deep, purple circles under my eyes. Me, along with most of the girls in my division began slimming down. By the end of boot camp, I was too anemic to give blood. I became comfortable in the routine of being told what to do. I grew accustomed to feeling constantly on edge. Marching became second nature, despite my earlier troubles with clumsiness. I just kept doing what I was supposed to do and looked to the future. Boot camp was just an obstacle I had to get over with. Inevitably, the end of it was coming.

Our RDCs changed as well. They went from being our bullies to our leaders. They were like the parents whom we had a slight fear for, but respected and admired. We were obedient to their orders and aimed to please them. Despite their early methods of putting us down, they took time out to have encouraging talks with us.

"You're doing something amazing with your life," Petty Officer Hunter said to the division females once. "Not many women can do this. Just enlisting shows character and courage."

She prepared us for the end.
"You're going to go home and it won't be the same," she warned. "People will be doing the same old shit, and you'll have changed. You'll feel out of place there."

I saw the change in myself. I got stronger. My skin grew thicker. Most of all, I knew that it was possible to survive outside of Chattanooga. I was determined to start experiencing the world.

My orders were to San Diego, California. I was moving to my dream state. It felt like a lottery win.

I was going to be stationed on a ship called the USS Higgins. I knew little about the ship except that it was a destroyer that carried a crew of about three hundred.

"For those of you stationed on small ships," Petty Officer Hunter warned, "I hope you don't get sea sick. You'll definitely feel that ship rocking when you're underway."

I would be boarding the ship as an "undesignated Seaman." I remembered the program the woman at MEPS convinced me to join. Already, I was learning the manipulative functioning of the Navy.

"Those of you who are undesignated," Hunter informed us, "Are screwed. Congratulations. You're in for some real bitch work. Prepare to chip paint and scrub a lot of rust."

But I shrugged off her parade rain. Regardless of what my job was, I was going to live in San Diego. I was going to be aboard a ship that deployed around the world. My great escape was set.

"It can't be that bad," I reassured myself.

After boot camp, I went home for one last goodbye to my previous life before flying off to my new life in California.

I thought about the warning Hunter had given us in boot camp about coming back home.

I had two weeks leave in Chattanooga before heading west. My return was, indeed, bizarre. Although my parents attended my boot camp graduation in Chicago, their lives seemed to comfortably continue in my absence. They worked during the day, watched their hours upon hours of TV programs at night, and had their own vacation planned with my brother for the middle of my leave. When it came to their life, I was an observer and not a participant.

On my last night with my parents, we were supposed to have dinner at my favorite restaurant. Earlier that afternoon I drove to Atlanta to have lunch with my grandmother, a few aunts, and some cousins. On the way home, I got stuck in traffic and was an hour late for our scheduled time to leave for dinner. Instead of waiting for me, my parents and little brother left. I was devastated. I sobbed for hours.

"Why do you let them do this to you?" Number 3 asked me.

I called him, although I was barely able to talk. My nose was congested and I kept taking in deep breaths in failed attempts to calm myself.

"They always make you feel like this. Why the hell are you giving them your time? Come home." He pleaded. "Get out of there. Baby, just come home."

"Quit bein' so ungrateful," Carl scolded as he tossed me a takeout bag with my dinner inside. "Ah paid good money for this food. Yer gonna git some manners and enjoy it."

By the time they returned home, I had washed my eyes to sooth the swelling and calmed myself down so they couldn't tell I had been crying. Carl must have spotted a glimpse of my emotions on my face.

Once again, I found a remedy in safe, predictable Number 3.

I anxiously drove to The Box in the middle of nowhere. I watched the rolling Tennessee hills, the trailers, the meth heads, and the matted Chow dogs. I was amazed at how untouched everything seemed. I wondered how everything could be the same when I felt so different.

I parked in the gravel driveway, nervously walked up to the doorstep and opened the screen. I wondered how I looked at that moment. My blonde hair was chopped short from boot camp. I was much slimmer, but my face still had a young, country girl look.

I opened the screen door to find Number 3 sitting on the small couch that we once shared. His curly, brownish-red hair had grown out a few inches. He had gained weight, which showed in his freckled cheeks. It was obvious that he'd just come home from work because he wore a t-shirt and basketball shorts spattered with paint. His eyes lit up when I walked in the room.

He jumped off the couch and walked right to me, wrapping his arms in an embrace. He backed away after our hug to look me down.

"You look great," he said, still smiling.

I looked back at him. Finally there was something that wasn't going to yell at me or put me down. There was the same old Number 3. I kissed him, took off my clothes, and fucked him on the couch.

To say that the sex was disappointing would be an understatement.

Up until that point, my libido had been throbbing in a way that I'd never known. I didn't fully understand my body and its reaction to sex. I had never reached a full-blown orgasm. In fact, I didn't even know how to spot or define it. The only thing I knew of orgasms were what I saw on TV, which was a woman experiencing a point of euphoria while uncontrollably screaming at the top of her lungs. Although I enjoyed sex, I'd never come close to that level. Once Number 3 and I began having sex regularly, I found myself craving it. It was as if an amount of pressure was built up inside of me. Sex usually released that pressure, so I assumed that I'd had some form of mild climax.

I realized in boot camp that sex was like a drug. After a year of cohabitating with my boyfriend, I grew accustomed to regular access. The first week without the drug didn't faze me, but I began to feel it the week after. It didn't help that I had no time or privacy to rub one out. By the first month, I was on the verge of dry humping the flagpole I saluted.

For weeks before going home, I anticipated getting the shit fucked out of me. I had two months worth of tension stuffed inside of me.

"Baby, I'm sorry," he said to me after five minutes of awkwardly maneuvering the weak, half chub hagfish in and out of me.

Instead of the pounding session that I had fantasized about in my freezing, rickety rack at boot camp, Number 3's dick went limp. I looked at the wormlike thing, deflated and drooping between his legs as he sat straight up on the couch. It wasn't that Number 3 was so turned on that he blew a fuse prematurely. His penis had just quit on me at the worst possible time. It was then that I understood the level of torture I had put boys through when I wanted to fool around, but refused to have sex or give a blowjob. It was agonizing.

"I was just so nervous," he began to pout. "I wanted the first time we were together in so long to be perfect. I think it was too much pressure."

It's ok," I assured him, making eye contact. "I don't care about sex," I lied. "I'm just so happy to see you."

Though the sex improved, I became the one losing interest. During our last time, I stopped Number 3 completely. I had my left leg over his shoulder, bending it back to my chest. It was one of my favorite positions, but for some reason, I was getting zero enjoyment.

"Stop," I said in a monotone voice.

He pulled himself out of me, backing off and giving me a few inches of space.

"What's wrong?" he asked, concerned.

"Were you into that at all?" I asked.

"Yeah, I was really into it."

"I wasn't. I just got nothing out of it. Sorry. I have to stop."

He didn't put up a fight. Number 3 kissed me on the forehead and we fell asleep. He dropped me off at the airport the next day. I cried. I knew I was doing the right thing, but the separation was still rough. I continued crying on the airplane. We kept close for a month after that. Number 3 even asked me if I wanted him to move to San Diego. I said no. I later found out that he'd been planning to propose. Then, when I least expected it, I lost all attraction. Two years of drama, struggle, intimacy, and separation anxiety were gone overnight.

"What you want in a man now will change," I remembered my mom once telling me when I was in my early stages of dating in my teens. "What you want at eighteen will be totally different from what you wanted at sixteen. What you want at twenty-five won't be the same as what you wanted at eighteen."

"Hmm," I thought to myself as I sat topside of the USS Higgins in San Diego. "I guess wishes work the same way."

Number 4

"Don't fuck any of the guys on the ship," one of the girls on the USS Higgins warned me. "You'll regret it. You think nobody will know, but everyone will find out. They'll talk shit. From then on, you'll be considered a slut. You'll probably do it anyway, but don't say that nobody warned you."

It was a bit much for my first day aboard, but there was absolute truth in every precaution I was advised to take. Every girl eventually slept with at least one of her shipmates. For me, it only took a month.

Every hint of melancholy from leaving Number 3 diminished the second my plane landed in San Diego. As the sailors from the RSO drove me to my ship, I stared out the window wide eyed at the stunning city. The air was clear and the sun was luminous. Since I was a little girl, I had always loved palm trees. Whenever I saw them, I got excited because it indicated that I was close to the beach. Nearly every single street was lined with them. I loved the green shrub hills that looked lush, but were made for the arid conditions and needed little water. I loved the prickly red and pink flowers that bloomed at their tips.

San Diego was different from Tennessee in every way. Even the Hispanic-influenced architecture clashed with my norm. I noticed that even most of the street names were of Mexican descent. Instead of small cities with names like Soddy Daisy, Jasper, and Whitwell, there was Chula Vista, Escondido, and Rancho Cucamonga.

"This place is *amazing*!" I said aloud, thrilled by my vibrant new home.

"Welcome to San Diego," the sailor said with a smile.

I could tell my awe was a common reaction.

My ship was stationed on the 32nd Street Naval Base, located a few minutes from downtown and in the middle of a low-income suburb. But I was too dazzled by southern California to notice the neon colored homes packed with poverty stricken Mexican families. We were only about ten minutes from the Tijuana border. We approached the tall fenced gate that surrounded the base and I spotted several massive grey ships in the distance. The fact that the base looked like the outskirts of a prison didn't bother me, nor did it occur to me that my life on the ship would feel like one.

My heart was fluttering as I scurried down the pier towards my ship. I wore the official Navy dress white uniform required to check into my new command. Like all of our uniforms, it flattened my ass and concealed any hint of femininity. I hated the way the uniform looked on me, but I was too used to my frumpy, military-issued, birth control getups to be embarrassed. I clutched a package in my hand that held my service and medical record. I looked at my ship. It was what the Navy called "haze grey" with white lettering that read DDG on the left and right side. "DDG" stood for "destroyer." I saw several guns and other contraptions set up around the decks. There were windows at the top from where the ship was operated, with several satellite-like instruments above. There was an American flag on the top of the ship as well as in the aft (back) section of the ship. I reached the ladder that took me from the pier to the ship.

"Now, don't forget this part," I remembered Petty Officer Hunter instructing us in boot camp. "Your arrival to your command is the first impression you'll make. I cannot stress enough how important that is. *Don't fuck it up.*"

She glared at us as if we already had.

"When you reach your command, the first area you will step onto is called the quarterdeck. There will be an Officer of the Deck on watch. But before you can come aboard the quarterdeck, you must turn to the flag at the back. You will salute the flag. Hold your salute and ask 'Permission to come aboard?' Then turn to the Officer of the Deck. The OOD will say 'Permission granted.' Then and *only then* is when you can drop your salute and walk aboard."

We practiced this procedure several times in basic training.

It was nearly dusk when I reached the Higgins. The ship appeared deserted and had a quiet and peaceful aura.

"Permission to come aboard?" I asked, turning my stiff salute towards the flag that hung on the ship's tail.

I mentally pleaded that I was showing enough military bearing. Little did I know that the boys on watch were chuckling at my efforts. The Navy newbies were easy to spot. Fresh out of basic, we reeked of posttraumatic boot camp timidity. For the first week or so, 'booters' looked like mice in a python cage.

"Permission granted," said a chubby black man in his light blue utility shirt.

The Higgins had just returned from a six-month deployment on the Persian Gulf, so my crew had just spent three months in sweltering heat with few port visits, followed by brief stops in Sydney, Fiji, and Hawaii.

My crew had just begun boarding females. During deployment, there were only five enlisted women. A handful more had boarded days before me.

I was eighteen, fresh out of Tennessee, and the thirteenth female on a ship of over three hundred males.

I looked to my right at a small shack under a flight of stairs that led to an upper level of that ship. A blonde, skinny boy with a gun around his shoulder and a bulletproof vest stood with an intercom in his hand.

"WILL THE DUTY BOATSWAINS MATE PLEASE REPORT TO THE QUARTERDECK?" he announced, his voice echoing.

A few minutes later, a door opened near the shack. Out came a white male who looked like he was in his late thirties. He had light brown hair, glasses, and several creases in his forehead. He had a beer gut protruding over his black belt. His blue utility shirt read "Wayne," his last name. Our last names were all labeled on our shirts and coveralls.

"Seaman Young," he greeted me with the name I'd get used to responding to.

My arrival was expected. Wayne did not smile, but his face was not cold or unwelcoming. Greeting new sailors was routine.

"Welcome aboard," he said.

His voice seemed to project through his nose.

"I'll show you around."

Wayne took me all over the ship, leading me through passageways that I was certain I would get lost in. Every door was a hatch that had to be pulled open with a handle and then closed behind me. The doors were heavy and I feared getting my finger smashed in one of them. I found myself constantly taking steps through the ship's hallways (or p-ways as they were called in the Navy.) Several hatches that I had to step through were open throughout the ship, but were closed during drills or security emergencies.

The ship had a stench that reminded me of a musty basement.

"You'll get used to all this," Wayne assured me when he saw me nearly trip over one of the hatch steps. "After awhile, you won't even smell the ship anymore."

The ship was cold. Every surface was rock hard. There were tons of spouts, buttons, and contraptions along the walls and ceiling. I had no idea what any of them did and hoped I wouldn't have to memorize all of their functions.

The worst part about the ship was the stairways. The ship had several levels. To get to the different levels, we had to climb a nearly vertical ladder well. I was petrified of climbing any of them straight down.

"Go down backwards and grip the railings," Wayne advised me.

After going down a few ladder wells, we entered a tiny room with a desk. I realized that everything on the ship was compact. Sea duty required a mass amount of people to function in very close proximity. The office Wayne took me to was labeled "Aft Workshop."

Wayne sat down in a chair while I stood. I noticed that he had an old Coke bottle full of tobacco and saliva on top of some scattered paperwork. He picked up some of the papers under the chew bottle.

"Young," he said in a low tone, seemingly speaking to himself.

He looked up at me.

"You're in duty section two. During your duty days, you will remain on board the ship all day and all night. We normally have six duty sections, but the ship is on stand down now since we just got back from deployment. So the way it normally goes is that you work on weekdays and then on your duty days, you stay over night, stand watch, and do whatever drills the duty station is doing."

I remembered standing watch in boot camp. Someone had to stay awake for two hours at a time and guard our barracks.

"But the way it's going now," Wayne continued, "Is that you'll have a duty day, a half day, and an off day. Today would be your duty day. Tomorrow is a half day and the next day you have off."

"What kind of work will I be doing?" I asked. "Don't I get to try out different jobs? I'm in the Seaman Apprenticeship program."

Wayne busted out with laughter.

"Oh no, they got you with that shit, did they?" Wayne asked, looking cynically amused.

"That's just some shit they pull to get you to enter the Navy undesignated. That just throws you in deck. No, no, you're a deck Seaman. You do topside preservation. You'll chip, prime, and paint - that's your new life. You've officially been fucked over by the Navy. Get used to it."

I felt a pang of betrayal and regret, but still, I did not let that get me down. I escaped from Number 3 and The Box. I had four years in the Navy. I was going to get through them without making myself miserable.

"Now, once advancement testing comes," Wayne told me. "There are some rates that you can test for. If you score high enough, that can get you out of deck. It's called striking out."

My eyes brightened. There was hope. Until then, at least I was chipping paint in San Diego.

Wayne led me back up the ladder well, down a few p-ways, and to the top of a hatch that rested on the floor, or the "deck." There was a white sheet of paper taped onto a pipe beside the hatch with bold black lettering typed "female berthing."

"Here's where you'll stay tonight," Wayne told me. "Get a female to take you to breakfast on the mess decks in the morning. I'll meet you there and we'll get you fully checked in. Good night."

The racks on the ship made the racks at boot camp look like s plush bed of clouds. They were piled vertically in three, with about a foot of space in between them. There was no possible way for one to sit up in them. The beds were called "coffin racks" because they lifted up like a coffin into a storage area. This and one small locker were the only places I had to store my possessions.

I got stuck with a top rack, which required me to climb in between two middle racks across from each other in an isle. That pissed off the middle rack occupants because my foot nearly smashed their arms. Being able to organize my things inside my rack was a struggle and climbing into bed felt like an obstacle course. The lids were heavy and were held up by a small, metal bar in the middle. If the bar was knocked back, fingers and skulls could be crushed. The worst part was trying to jump down onto the cold hard deck when I was groggy in the morning. Having to get up in the middle of the night to go to the bathroom was something I did my best to avoid.

I quickly fell into the routine of ship life. Each morning I met, or "mustered," with my division. Our chief, the head of deck division, was a large black man from Oakland who loved to scream.

"GET TO WORK, SHIT BAGS!" he'd bark.

I was constantly on edge when he was around.

Our jobs were remedial busy work that could have been tackled by any breathing primate. We would scrub rust in one area with sandpaper or prime another space. The work left my nails filthy and my coveralls smothered in paint.

I talked with a few girls on the ship, though my only solid buddy was a girl named Sally. On my off time, I had the adventures I'd been missing from college life. I flirted with boys, got shitfaced, and often woke up on random couches and beds. One night, I ended up falling down on the sidewalk and scraping my knee. The next morning I entered the ship hung over in a skirt that revealed the large gash. I was dubbed a train wreck right then and there. I'd later learn that morning watches were the best times to get an eyeful of the most entertaining walks of shame.

The crew did not fit the stereotype of the Navy sailors that I expected. The media always presented Navy men as being GI Joe's in white. But a good sum of them were in their thirties and forties. Very few sported less than two chins, let alone the six-pack of a warrior. While standing at attention, I saw a slew of potbellies jiggling atop Navy belt buckles. I saw bald spots, acne, retro porn mustaches, and wrinkles, but to my utter disappointment, no eye candy.

I was also surprised by the racial diversity in the crew. Being from The South, I thought of Americans as primarily black and white. But there were several Mexicans and even more Filipinos in the fleet. I learned that it was common for Filipinos to join the Navy. The lifestyle suited them quite well. They didn't have to be American citizens to enlist. They hailed from poverty, which instilled strong work ethics and gratitude for modest military living. They could happily serve twenty years, return to their homeland, and live off their retirement pay. Though it wasn't enough for comfort in the United States, it made them quite wealthy in a Filipino economy. They were known throughout the fleet as the Filipino mafia. They often established decent rank in the military and held a camaraderie and favoritism among their people.

I never got involved with any of the recruits from boot camp. With the strict rules, busy schedule, and little opportunity for social interaction, I didn't see how it was possible. Boot camp romances actually blossomed all the time. It wasn't uncommon for two recruits to lock eyes during church or the ten minutes they had to raise the flag together for colors. Drenched with the basic training blues, they clung to any relationship they could develop. Recruits often married at the base chapel during their first day of liberty. The marriages usually ended as quickly as they started. Once they left the sheltered world of basic training, dealing with their spouse under normal circumstances butchered the primarily fictitious love connection.

Though it never happened to me, I understood it. The combination of repressed sexual desires and intimacy deprivation was treacherous. About a month into boot camp, I found my standards dropping and eyes wandering.

Nothing about Number 4 stood out to me when I first saw him on the USS Higgins topside. I had seen him on our duty days mustering in the mornings. He was always surrounded by a couple of guys, chatting and carrying on small talk. He seemed pretty popular.

The majority of the crew was married with children. Although nearly every sailor fucked either hookers or ship women, they hardly paid attention to the new ladies on board. They were coming home to their families and their lives outside of the Navy. The shenanigans had temporarily ceased. The men did not feel compelled to befriend the new eighteen-year-old with her boot camp chopped blonde hair.

But Number 4 looked at me on occasion, with a subtle, slightly crooked grin. "He's probably just trying to be nice," I figured.

He was twenty-six, with ash blonde hair that was cut short but was too long for Navy regulations, with his bangs shaggy over his forehead. His blue utility shirt was wrinkled. To any civilian, such details go unnoticed, but by Navy standards, they were signs of rebellion.

He was tall with broad shoulders that hung heavy over his slim build. His eyes were his most intriguing physical feature. They were an intense, hazel that seemed to burn into my face like lasers. His voice had the laid back twang of an old hippie. His walk was loose and relaxed, but his eyes revealed an immense intelligence that clashed with his demeanor.

His stares quickly evolved into small talk. We were on the front section of the ship, called the forecastle. One of the many pointless tasks we had to complete on duty was called "sweepers," where we would take brooms and try to sweep particles off the ship. It was nearly impossible to sweep the rough, nonskid surface with a straw broom and was a task that the ocean breeze could complete. But, like most remedial Navy duties, there was no point in finding logic to the requirement.

"Having fun?" Number 4 asked me once while I had a broom in my hand.

His smile was crooked again. Something about his face was very sly, but not in a sadistic way.

I smiled back and laughed a little. I began to notice his presence in a crowded room. When we passed each other in the p-ways, he'd smile, say hello, and occasionally start up chatter. I'd humor him a little and then carry on throughout my day, not thinking about him until we saw each other again.

Then one day, we lingered in the p-way a little bit longer. We talked about something unmemorable.

"So," he said, with a smirk on his face after a moment of silence passed between us. "Do you want to play a card game or something?"

It was after working hours. We were on duty and confined to the ship. We had the same watch later that night and had nothing but time to kill until then.

He led me down a few ladder wells, opening a hatch even further into the back of the ship than the aft workshop. He opened a door to what looked like his little hideout away from the rest of the boat. In the middle of the small room was a thing that looked like a giant spool. To my left were a computer and a desk. Behind the spool were two small chairs with a crate in the middle. We sat in the chairs, facing each other.

As we played cards, we talked. He told me more about his life. He was from a town in Northern California called Chico. He joined the Navy for the same reason as me, for college money and a hometown escape. He loathed the Navy and constantly mocked its structure.

"The Navy likes to put complete jack asses in charge," he told me. "You'll understand once you're here a bit longer. You've got bosses double your age with fifth grade reading levels."

He was funny. Something about his presence made the world feel pleasant. Our conversation flowed smoothly and naturally. I'd never felt so verbally in sync with someone before in my life. When one of the guys that worked with him entered the room to sit down and talk with us, I wanted him gone. I wanted Number 4 to myself because his company was therapeutic. I didn't mind being stuck on board the ship doing drills or chipping paint as long as he was around.

"I don't get these Navy people," I said to him about twenty minutes into our card game.

Number 4 told me crazy deployment stories and about all the times he'd smarted off and gotten yelled at by his superiors. He was a free spirit, and had issues with the macho military atmosphere with its endless rules and large amounts of busy work.

"Isn't it so weird how everyone here is married?" I asked, as we sifted through conversation topics.

"What do you mean?" he asked.

He looked intrigued every time I spoke. He would cock his head to the side and peer into my eyes with his sly smile.

"Well, from what I've heard, most of these guys cheat on their wives on deployment."

"They usually do," he agreed.

"Then why the hell are they getting married in the first place? I think it's stupid to get married at a young age, especially when you're stationed on a ship that leaves all the time."

Since boarding the Higgins, I caught wind of the incessant gossip about who cheated on who and which homes were wrecked. I already knew a few women from my berthing who were continuing affairs with married men that began on deployment. The scandal was shocking for me. The marital conflicts of southerners were private until divorce papers were signed.

Number 4's smile brightened.

"Let me show you something," he said with a faint laugh.

He brought me to the computer in the room and opened up his email account. He clicked on a file in his inbox and showed me a picture of a slim, dark haired woman holding a baby.

"That's my wife and daughter," he said, still sounding casually pleasant.

I wondered if he sensed my heart jilting in shock. I felt rude for so carelessly bashing marriage. I had no idea. Something about him seemed so *single*. He didn't even wear a wedding ring.

"Oh my God," I thought to myself. "I actually *looked* for a wedding ring."

"It's okay," he said, laughing again. "You didn't offend me. I don't get offended easily. I don't wear a wedding ring, so there's no way you would've known."

I was caught aback at his mind reading.

"Plus I'm not like those Navy fools," he continued. "I didn't fuck with anyone on deployment. You're actually the only girl I talk to on the ship."

I was pleased with my sudden elitism.

"Why's that?" I asked him.

"Oh, I don't know," he said.

He stretched his arms out as he said this. His voice stretched with him.

"You just seemed really nice. All the girls here seem bitchy, but you were like 'Hi, I'm Maggie! I'm from Tennessee!'"

He mocked me with a shrill voice and that made me blush a bit.

In a way, I was relieved that he was married. That meant we were strictly friends. We could be a man and a woman, hanging out, without the tension of it going any further. But I couldn't ignore a slight twinge of disappointment.

"Am I attracted to him?" I wondered.

For the life of me, I could not answer that question. I loved talking to him and even got a little nervous around him. His presence made me really happy. But he was eight years older than me. He was married. He had a kid. Apart from his baggage, he was just so *different*. He was positive, upbeat, and charismatic, yet strutted around in his Navy working whites like a barefoot hippie. Sure, *different* was the epitome of everything I was craving. But the thought of stepping foot out of platonic territory was terrifying.

"So. Uh... What are you up to this weekend?" Number 4 sheepishly asked me during one of our card games.

He was sitting on a chair with his face towards his hand of cards, but his eyes peering up at me. I'd never seen him look so shy before. He looked like a sixth grader asking a girl to his first dance.

I was dumbfounded by his shyness. A spasm of excitement jumped through my veins. Up until then, all of our social interaction was confined to the ship. Even that was limited. We had to keep conversation to a minimum on watch and were constantly interrupted during our card games by our shipmates. I was actually beginning to look forward to duty days. He was different than any man I'd associated with before. I felt like I could be completely myself around him and could blurt out whatever I pleased without judgment.

"What am I doing this weekend?" I repeated his question. "I'm hanging out with you?"

"So you're just going to this guy's house?" my friend Sally later demanded.

We were in the cramped female berthing on the ship. I was sitting on a very uncomfortable red plastic chair that was attached to a small wooden table in the lounge area. Sally stood in front of me with her hands on her hips like a mother on the verge of grounding me.

Sally arrived on the Higgins the day after me. She was a fresh-faced brunette from Montana who had already been engaged three times. She had just turned nineteen. Sally was a petite five feet tall with tan skin and long eyelashes. Her figure was thick without being fat and her breasts were full D-cups. She was confident and flirtatious. She quickly captured the attention of every man on the ship, except for Number 4. She had no interest in him, but I could tell that his mutual feelings mutilated her ego.

"Does he talk about the girls on the ship?" she would interrogate me.

Number 4 had just passed us. He said hello to me, but looked right through Sally.

"No. Not really," I replied.

"Not even me," she said, trying but failing to seem discreet.

"Nope. He's never mentioned you."

She pouted and came to the conclusion that he was a pervert.

"You should stay away from him," she warned me.

"He's not a bad guy," I assured her. "And I'm hanging out with him this Saturday."

She grimaced.

"You're going to sleep with him," she said, rolling her eyes.

"No, I'm not," I began to laugh.

"I bet you are."

Number 4 picked me up from the ship the following Saturday morning. It was a normal San Diego afternoon with predictable sunshine and the slight breeze that kept temperatures from feeling too hot. San Diego climate was normally so flawless that flash flood warnings were given at one inch of rain.

It was funny seeing Number 4 outside the ship environment. He drove a small, rickety pickup truck. He wasn't much of a car person and was happy with whatever functioned. He wore khaki shorts and a light blue, untucked button-down shirt. He looked like he belonged in a hammock on the beach.

We carried on the chatter that always flowed so easily as he drove on Interstate 5 through downtown San Diego. I wondered if I'd ever adapt to a city with so many highways. Every now and then he'd take his eyes off the road to glance my wide-eyed gaze outside the window. I must have looked very childlike to him, but I think that's what he liked about me.

Number 4 lived in a sunny studio apartment with a small water fountain in the front and a red brick driveway. The inside was small, but immaculately clean and comfortable. The entire place had the sweet scent of lavender incense.

"My wife, Norah, doesn't live here with me," he explained. "She and my daughter are with her mom in Chico. They stayed there while I was on deployment, but she'll be down here in a week."

Number 4 had a month left in the Navy. The three of them would make the trip north together to start a new life. It was difficult to picture the carefree Number 4 as a family man. He lacked the exasperated look that the other husbands on the ship carried.

"So what do you want to do?" he asked me.

He sat by his window and I sat at the foot of his bed. There weren't really any other places to sit in his studio.

"I have no idea," I said.

I couldn't remember the last time I'd hung out with a guy one-on-one without sex or some kind of drug use involved.

"I'm your guest," I said smugly. "So I believe it's your job to entertain me. You'll have to think of something."

"Hmm… Okay boss girl," he said. "I'm afraid that you're going to be very disappointed. You see, I'm a very boring old man."

He was so nonchalant about everything that it was difficult to give him a hard time for more than a sentence or two.

"That's okay. I'm actually just happy to be here in an apartment and off that damn ship."

With no creative effort, we decided to drink.

The fact that the outcome of that night wasn't blatant from the beginning demonstrates my inexperience with men. I was an eighteen-year-old about to embark on a drinking binge with a twenty-six-year-old alone in his studio apartment with his wife hundreds of miles away.

To any outsider, the situation would have labeled Number 4 as a creep and me as a stupid little girl. Maybe we really were those things, but even years later, I could never consider Number 4 a predator.

As we walked down the street to the liquor store, I felt a lightheartedness I hadn't felt since playing games in my grandmother's garden with my cousins as a little girl. We passed by stop signs and he would scold me for walking on the opposite side of the sign from him.

"It's bad luck," he said.

Laughing to myself, I made sure that we walked on opposite sides of every telephone pole, sign, and shrub. What I loved about Number 4 was that there was no intensity. He blurred all stress and obstacles.

"What do you want to drink?" he asked.

I shrugged.

"Miller Light?"

My beverage of choice reflected my sheltered and penniless teenage background. I'd yet to be introduced to high quality beers. Number 4 gave me a little shit, but purchased whatever I requested.

But with one sip, I was hooked on his beverage. It was a mixture of gin, red bull, and orange juice. I couldn't taste a hint of liquor.

"Fuck beer," I announced, as Number 4 laughed at me.

Our cocktail was elusive. It was sweet, juicy, and potent. We were buzzed after one cup. We were drunk after two. We were honest after three.

"Gosh, it's too bad that you're married," I slurred a bit, staring at him intently.

Having yet to blossom into social maturity, I had no grasp on how inappropriate our scenario was, let alone the conversation.

"This is the point where I'd be taking my clothes off," I joked.

I was on his bed while he sat in a seat by the window just a few feet away. My eyes were nearly as crossed as my legs were as I tilted my head to the side to run my hand through my hair. I nearly fell off the bed. I was a drunken little girl playing seductive mistress, and failing miserably.

"Well, my marriage isn't an issue," he said with his sly, mocking tone.

"What to do mean it isn't an issue?" I snapped out of my tease. "You'd *cheat* on your wife?"

He laughed as that crooked smile spread across his face.

"Norah lets me have sex with other women."

"What do you mean?" I asked, still stunned.

"Let's just say that she's a sexual deviant. She gets turned on from sharing. I don't sleep with other women often. It's actually really rare for me. But she allows me to when I want."

I glared at him.

"I don't believe you," I said coldly.

"Look, you don't have to sleep with me. I'm not saying that. You're my friend and I like being with you," he continued, remaining completely calm. "I'm just saying that *if* you did, it would be totally fine with my wife."

He could tell by the look on my face that I wasn't swayed.

"Look, I'll call her right now just to prove I'm not some pervy asshole," he said, still laughing.

I wasn't thinking clearly. I was too young to comprehend marriage and Number 4's was one of the most bizarre relationships I'd ever encountered. But it had been nearly a month since I'd had sex. The gin only amped my libido and drowned my morals. All it took to get me to jump Number 4 was the approval from the missus.

"Have fun," her sweet voice giggled over the phone.

I could hear her smile.

"And take good care of my husband, Maggie."

I'd had a night full of firsts. Number 4 was the first sailor, husband, and father I'd been with. He was also my first run with casual sex. But because of my newfound love for gin, juice, and red bull, my memory of those firsts, along with several of my brain-cells, were dead. Reality quickly registered when I awoke with him inside of me.

Any normal girl would've felt frightened, insulted, and invaded, but the longer I strayed from The South, the more I realized that normal was the last adjective that suited me. I was caught a little off guard, but my shock transformed into an adrenaline rush. *Finally* I was doing someone *new*.

Number 4 was very intimate. He liked to fuck smoothly, taking his time as if he wanted to absorb every sensation. After a few requests to go harder and faster, I could tell that he wasn't willing to bend. He had his own his style, which wasn't particularly mine. But after a while, I let him do his thing and enjoyed it.

I saw Number 4 like a pair of shoes. The shoes belonged to his wife. They were her style, not mine. But if she didn't mind sharing, I was certainly willing to wear them for a few nights out. Despite his softness, he had a slightly sadistic look in his eye as if he fancied himself a fifty-year-old nailing a teenager.

I caught a glimpse of this filthy side of him and knew exactly what it was about me that he found so captivating. I was a stumbling, wide-eyed girl strutting into the cold, volatile world that Number 4 despised. I was outspoken and opinionated, yet untactful. I shared his free spirited nature and, like him, would be constantly at war with its bindings. But, when Number 4 first laid eyes on me, I'd not yet learned the ways of the Navy or how to articulate those qualities. I was a feisty kitten, aimlessly swatting at swinging objects, but missing every time. From day one, Number 4 aspired to violate that kitten. Conveniently, that kitten badly wanted to be violated.

His dick was average, maybe slightly bigger than Number 3's.

"Six inches," he later told me. "Yeah, I measure it."

But he seemed cleaner and much better kempt than my ex. He trimmed the hair on his balls very short. I appreciated his effort.

I, on the other hand, was a pitiful mess. My chin-length blonde hair had a rat's nest tangled on the back of my head. I was in dire need of a shower and some fresh makeup. I wasn't prepared to wind up naked; my underwear was a pair of full coverage, black Target panties. Retouching my lower region with a razor would have been a plus.

Once we were done having sex, reality set in and my embarrassment at being bare skinned with a new man overwhelmed me. Number 4 didn't seem to care though. He briefly teased me about the underwear, but I think they only added to my juvie-erotic appeal.

"I understand. You just don't want to waste the sexy lingerie on some dirty old married man," he joked.

He watched me struggle with getting my hair tangle out with his brush.

"Calm down," he said, laughing at the way I furiously yanked the brush over my scalp.

He took the brush out of my hand and sat beside me. He patiently combed my hair and managed to painlessly remove the stubborn tangle.

Once we had sex, a completely different Number 4 took form. He went from being my nonchalant ship buddy to a cuddly lover. I saw a sweet and nurturing side to that I didn't know how to confront. Instead of enjoying the closeness that actually felt really nice, I squirmed away. Once I was sober, I began to think about the moral structure The South instilled in me. He was my coworker and a married man. I had gotten myself into a situation that I was warned to stay away from. I had a sudden urge bolt to the ship and scrub off the scent of his body.

"I've got to go," I told him. "I've got a ton of stuff to do."

"No!" he pleaded.

We were on his bed. He was lying on his back as he pulled me on top of him and kissed me.

"Who is this guy?" I thought, still surprised by his new character.

Eventually, after making several excuses as to why I had to leave, he called me a cab that he refused to let me pay for. I rode back to the base in disbelief of what had happened the night before. For the next few days, I would play that night in my head repeatedly.

I returned to the Higgins to face the fact that I'd officially fucked one of my shipmates. Anyone who isn't in the Navy would assume that I had a right to my privacy. What happened between Number 4 and me was not the business of the rest of the crew and the Navy didn't have to know. But, there were only fifteen girls on the ship in a very small berthing. We always noticed when somebody did not return and absences were *always* for the same reason.

"You slept with him," Sally announced loudly "I knew it when you didn't come back to the ship last night."

It was just a week before when Sally had gone to "hang out" with one of the guys in deck. She returned the next day with hickeys on her neck and rug burn on her elbows.

In boot camp, I was warned about the double standards in the Navy. Petty Officer Hunter told us that Navy men were horny animals eager to stick their dicks in something warm and wet. That was socially acceptable. However, *females* were held at a higher standard. Females serving sea duty was a new concept, only a decade or two old when I enlisted. I was one of the first women allowed on destroyers. Therefore to show our gratitude for being granted one inch towards male equality, we had to work a hundred times harder for a worthy image.

Hunter informed us that we had to work hard to establish a decent reputation at our command. If we acted like a slut, we would be treated like a slut. One slip would permanently brand us.

Before the Navy, I knew nothing of promiscuity and was confident that I could resist it, or at least avoid it with my coworkers. But just as it became too easy to lose sight of The South, it was even easier to dismiss its moral implications.

As a virgin, I planned on saving myself for love. I had high standards for my first sexual experience. But once my virginity was taken away, I quit waiting for meaning and hopped right into a sex life. I did the same with my childhood moral code. I slept with Number 4. That fact was obvious. Word would spread before I could even open my mouth. Once my reputation was trashed, I let go of all attempts to salvage it.

I owned up to what I did. I was also honest with myself. I felt zero guilt. There was nothing deceiving or malicious about what we did. Their unconventional marriage wasn't my business to dictate. I was *very* attracted to Number 4. I planned to fuck him again. After a brief taste of promiscuity, I wanted more. Between my righteous 'wait until marriage' family and the outdated sexist military culture, attempting to abide by their blurry standards didn't feel like a battle worth fighting. While service members were supposed to surrender their freedom upon enlistment, I enlisted for my freedom. I intended to have it.

After our hookup, I blushed the first time Number 4 passed me in the p-way. From that point on, he looked at me with the same sadistic expression he had during sex.

We were scheduled to stand watch together on our next duty day. It was especially uncomfortable because the other two guys on watch with us were buddies of his. In my drunken state, I left a red mark on his neck and also elbowed him in the face.

"What's up with that mark, man?" they asked, grinning. "Does your wife know about that? Did the girl that made that red mark give you that black eye, too? What, did she punch you in the face while she rode your dick?"

Number 4 made up an obviously bullshit story about wrestling with a buddy, but couldn't keep a straight face while telling it. But he never got angry about his battle scars. The boys on watch knew that I did the damage, but calling me out directly wasn't as fun.

Our duty card games also became more interesting. We never fooled around on the ship. Getting caught could have been detrimental for us both. But there was thick sexual tension in the atmosphere. Since we couldn't touch each other, I was learning verbal seduction. It was actually very easy. All I had to do was talk about sex, the things I liked, and the things I wanted to do with him. We were up until 1 am and seconds away from pouncing on each other when I decided that it was time to call it a night. I returned to female berthing. Number 4 stayed in his workspace to jerk off and fall asleep.

"Boss girl, I have the funniest story to tell you," he told me the next day when we ran into each other on the ship.

He crouched down closer to my face, making sure that only my ears could hear what he had to say.

"So last night after our-uh- *heated* discussion I-uh- relieved my sexual tension in a fast food bag that was in the garbage can."

"Okay," I said, smiling.

I wondered where this story was going.

"So I guess you could say I came in a burger that was in the bag," he continued. "Well, apparently, the burger belonged to Byron."

Byron was one of the guys that worked with him. He was sweet and welcomed me in the space without hesitation. He often joined in on our card games.

"When I walked into the space this morning after muster, Byron was eating the burger! I didn't have the heart to tell him what else he was eating."

I was never able to look at Byron the same way again.

I assumed that our sexual escapades would be over once Number 4's wife and daughter came to San Diego. Even though Norah was not a typical spouse, I certainly did not expect for us to meet. I anticipated that Number 4 would act like a cheating husband and avoid my existence for the rest of his enlistment.

"I really want you to meet Norah," he said to me, holding his hands up as if bracing for an attack. "If you feel weird about it, I understand. But it would be really cool if you two could just hang out."

Suddenly, a memory from our flirtatious, gin-infused chatter flashed through my brain. Norah was bisexual.

I gave Number 4 a scrutinizing glare. Once again, he read my mind.

"Maggie, I want you to know that I'm not expecting you to fuck my wife or anything," he said with a laugh. "And you don't have to come over and meet her. If you don't want to, I understand. It would just be really cool. I think you're awesome and I'd just like you two to meet. Norah really wants you to come."

I decided to say yes. I figured that if I was going to do her husband, I should at least show her enough respect to accept her invitation.

I was terrified by the time Number 4 picked me up from base that weekend, though he repeatedly assured me that there was nothing to be nervous about. But I couldn't understand how she, who'd been married to him for five years, would not lunge at me with a box cutter.

But the moment I set eyes on her, a state of tranquility washed over me.

She had long, chocolate brown hair that reached her mid-back. There was a slight natural wave to it that flowed around her face. Her eyes were round and brown to match. Her body was slender, but soft. I could tell that she had been really skinny when she was younger, but having a baby provided her with natural feminine curves. She wore no jewelry or makeup. There was nothing flashy about her. Her beauty was naturally subtle.

"Hi Maggie!" she welcomed me with a bright smile.

I remembered the words "take good care of my husband" from the last time I heard her voice. She said my name as if she already knew me. He was very open with his wife, calling her several times a day and filling her in on every detail of his life. The bond and comfort between them was evident and I knew that there were no secrets between them.

She was very easy to talk to. Conversation flowed between us as easily as it did with Number 4. We had Number 4 as a common lover and were able to tease him when we put our heads together. I found out a bit more about their marriage.

They dated in high school. She was a year younger than him.

"I knew who he was years before we dated," she gushed. "I was *obsessed* with him."

But a year into their high school relationship, Norah started doing a lot of cocaine.

"I despised her for that," Number 4 told me. "I hate coke and anyone who's associated with it."

When Number 4 joined the Navy, Norah contacted his mother who gave her his boot camp address. By that time, Norah had cleaned up and cut out all drugs other than marijuana. They exchanged letters and she went with his family to his basic training graduation. The two of them quickly married and had their daughter a few years after. It took me a while to notice their little girl, who was a year and a half old. She was well behaved and kept very quiet as she toddled around the studio.

Norah tolerated Number 4's six-year enlistment. It was difficult to tell which one of them hated the Navy more.

"For the longest time it's felt like I was never going to get out," Number 4 told me. "Like I was trapped forever."

By the end of the year, I would fully comprehend his claustrophobia.

After a few hours of chatting, which flew by like minutes, we all began to drink Number 4's gin, orange juice, and red bull drink. It only took a few sips for me to realize that I was being gradually seduced.

Long after the baby was asleep, we were pleasantly buzzed. The three of us sat comfortably close on Number 4's bed. Norah was the first to kiss me, though I didn't flinch. I kissed her right back, grasping and lightly sucking on her bottom lip.

Kissing a woman was intriguing. While I was used to the more aggressive kiss of a man, her softness corresponded with mine. I felt like I was kissing myself, so instinctively, I became more aggressive.

The act of kissing her was liberating. I got a high from rebelling against what I was taught to be appropriate. We continued to kiss. My urge to feel more of her body was not instinctive. I felt like I was an actress in a movie. I was playing the role of a woman making love to another. I thought about what I should do next and then I reached for her breast. Like mine, it was warm and soft. I did to her what I would want done to me. I kissed her neck and circled her nipple with my finger before fully cupping her breast with my hand. When I heard a faint moan coming from Norah's throat, I realized that she was enjoying it. I was in disbelief that I was actually doing that to another woman. I kept kissing her, which was comfortable and easy. I could have kissed her for a long time, but I reached my hands behind her back to unhook her bra. I tugged at it with one hand. I couldn't unfasten it.

"Shit," I thought.

I tried with both.

"Wow, now I know how fifteen-year-old boys feel!" I laughed, embarrassed by my awkward fumbling.

"You're doing great," she whispered to me.

It was strange to hear her seductive tone, which went down an octave from her regular speaking voice. I didn't know how to grasp the reality that I was actually turning another woman on.

I continued to experiment with her, concentrating on her feminine features. I ran my fingers through her long hair and kissed her warm, slender neck. We removed our clothes and I ran my lips over her breasts. I touched her hips, thighs, and then put my hands inside of her. Just as it had when I kissed her, I felt like I was touching myself. I did exactly the same things I would've done for my own pleasure in the privacy of bed. She moaned and became wetter the more I touched her. I was still in disbelief. She unzipped and removed my jeans.

"Mmmm. Nice!" she said excitedly when she saw my underwear.

Even though I wasn't planning my upcoming three-way, I had not come as unprepared as the week before. I wore a black silk thong that had two fake diamonds sewn in.

"Oh I see, you save the sexy underwear for her, not me," Number 4 said, laughing.

He was relishing in the sideline view.

"Keep these on for a while," Norah ordered.

She kept the underwear on, but pulled them to the side so that she could slip her tongue inside of me.

After several minutes of being a happy audience member, Number 4 jumped in on the fun. I was officially participating in my first threesome.

That night went against every moral that I was raised with. I was not only sleeping with a married man, but his wife with their baby sound asleep ten feet away. But I was completely void of guilt. Instead of taking the word of right and wrong from the generations before me to be truth, I tossed every rule aside and made my own. I judged the situation from my own eyes. I wasn't hurting anyone. There was no deception in what we were doing. There were no lies or vicious acts that would damage anyone's feelings. We were enjoying each other's bodies and our own.

In a way, they were my introduction to California, a state wild and free compared to my birthplace. It was a world where numerous cultures, backgrounds, beliefs, and ethics were melded together like some twisted sociological experiment. I jumped right into California with the liberation of my youth. No, it absolutely did not feel wrong.

While spending two years with Number 3, we did our best to prevent the boredom that inevitably infected me. We switched positions and rotated between the giving and receiving end of oral sex. We did it in in random locations like cars and public restrooms. We included outside materials like ice cubes. But even toy-free and restricted to a bed, there can be hours of fun-filled sexual activity between two people. I discovered that between three of us, there was at least triple that.

Even if I had been sober that first night, I still would not be able to recall every detail. There was just too damn much to remember. Number 4 would fuck Norah, while Norah went down on me. Number 4 would fuck me, while I lay on top of Norah and kissed her. Norah and I would go down on Number 4 together with our tongues on each side of his dick, getting him off and kissing each other at the same time. Number 4 would watch us, jerking off on the sidelines. Norah would touch herself while watching us. Jealousy was an emotion she couldn't comprehend. I admired that.

"He really likes you," she told me with a smile on her face when the two of us were alone outside during a water break. "He talks about you all the time."

When the baby woke up, she would go take care of her and leave Number 4 and I to keep each other busy. She actually seemed to get even more turned up by watching us.

I had underestimated Number 4's stamina. The three of us went at it until sunrise. Because Number 4 and I had to be at work that day, we only got about two hours of sleep. Waking up to a married couple in bed was even stranger than waking up to my first morning of casual sex.

The two of them were cuddled closer than I was to them. I realized that I was the outsider in their marriage. With the sun shining through the window and the real world settling in my state of mind, I was relieved that there was no time for morning sex.

In the midst of my hangover and groggy, full-body ache, I remembered that it was my birthday.

Early on in the Navy, I found the noteworthy adventures that I'd wished for when I lived in Tennessee. But none of them compared to the twenty-four hours of my nineteenth birthday. The midnight I turned nineteen, I was spicing up the marriage of one of my shipmates. The midnight after I turned nineteen, I was barefoot in a Mexican jail.

San Diego was only minutes away from the border. I loved the idea of another country being so reachable. Northwestern Mexican cities like Ensenada, Tijuana, and Rosarito were popular destinations for the young and under aged. At the time, I had traveled very little in my life. I saw the borders of other countries to be a path to exciting adventures. Mexico seemed wild and uninhibited. It lacked so many of the rules of the United States. Even though the drinking age in Mexico was eighteen, vendors never carded. The hotels were cheap and the clubs were popping with fellow young debauchery seekers.

The day after my three-way, the ship was meeting on the opposite side of base. It was supposed to be a command barbecue to kick off Memorial Day weekend. Everyone was supposed to be meeting at a park on base. Unlike our routine workdays, it was an easy day to ditch out of a command morale day early, as most of us did. Number 4 dropped me off at the park before he parked his car so the previous night's shenanigans would seem a little less obvious. As I started walking to the park, Sally rushed over to meet me.

"What happened?" she asked, wide-eyed and eager for my response.

Sally knew that I had gone to meet Number 4 and Mrs. Number 4 the night before.

"Did he just drop you off?" she asked, looking towards the parking lot.

I nodded. I knew what her next question would me.

"You did it, didn't you? You had a threesome with him and his wife!"

Although I'd never prevent rumors from circulating, there would've been no solid proof of my actions had I kept my mouth shut. But, freshly enlisted and naïve, I assumed that I could safely divulge to my girlfriend. I was about to learn that the USS Higgins was less discreet than a Hollywood tabloid and I was quickly becoming the Lindsey Lohan of the Navy.

"Yeah," I said, surprised by my confidence in my answer.

I realized that I wasn't embarrassed. I was almost proud of my bold sexual excursions. It was then that I made a mental note of a phrase that I would use for the rest of my life.

"If you're ashamed of it, you shouldn't do it," I told myself.

From that point on, I was indeed shameless. I would own up to everything.

Sally continued to interview me on my lesbian experience.

"So you kissed her?" she asked, squinting her eyes.

She looked at me they way person does when they see the aftermath of horrific, deadly car accident. They feel like it's wrong to observe, but they can't turn their eyes away.

"What was it like? Did you go down on her? Did she go down on you?"

I pursed my lips.

"No, I couldn't bring myself to go down on her," I laughed. "But I let her do it to me. She's better than a guy. It was fun."

"So does this mean you're bisexual?" she asked, still seeming very intrigued.

I stared blankly off in the distance for a moment.

"I have no idea," I said. "I think it was just an experimental thing."

After our thorough talk, Sally informed me that we were going to Mexico that day. We had been talking about going with two other girls from the ship that entire week. But because of our low rank, we were supposed to get permission from our command.

A sailor in the U.S. Navy is like a child of the government. The lower in rank we were, the more restrictions we had. If we wanted to go on leave, we had to request it in advance. If we wanted to participate in a dangerous sport, we had to get permission to do that as well. For E-4 military members and below, we had to request permission from our command to leave the country, even when crossing the Mexican border a few minutes away. We had to fill out this paper called a request chit. On the request chit, we had to write the address we were staying at, why we were crossing the border, as well as whom we would be with. These chits had to be approved through a chain of command that reached all the way up to the Captain of our ship. It wasn't uncommon for someone in that chain to toss the chit aside or lose it in a pile of other paper work. For Sally and me, our request chit never made it back to us on time.

The other two girls chickened out. Our chief threatened his sailors that we would inevitably get caught for breaking the rules. He claimed that border patrol had a tendency for picking out sailors and marines. It was easy to spot them. The boys had short haircuts and an erect posture imbedded into habit since boot camp. They would say things that civilian college kids wouldn't understand like "remove your cover." Service members, of course, knew that this meant to remove their hat. Then border patrol would search their wallets, find their military ID, and notify their command of their whereabouts.

But Sally and I were prepared to fake our way. We ditched our military IDs, prepped with some fiction about being San Diego State freshmen, and joined three boys from our ship.

We were going to Mexico with Jamie, Jack, and Elvis. Jamie was one of Sally's most recent hookups. He was a tall Mexican boy with spiky black hair and a slight lisp.

Jack was a twenty-one-year-old corpsman. He was handsome with dark hair and eyes. Out of the trio, Elvis was the only one I'd ever really talked to before that day. He worked in the ship's personnel office and processed my paperwork when I first came aboard. He was also in my duty section and had stood watch with me before.

Elvis wasn't noticeably handsome, but he wasn't at all ugly. He was raised in Alabama, but like me, lacked any hint of a southern accent. He had light brown hair, a tall, lanky frame, a five o'clock shadow, and a permanent pout on his face. His personality clashed with his boy-next-door appearance. He was rude with a bitter, sarcastic sense of humor. I fed off of his unapproachable persona, being extra cheerful and annoying in his presence.

"Hi Elvis!!" I'd enthusiastically greet him when we saw each other on duty, giving him an exaggerated smile.

"What's up, annoying bitch?" he'd ask, rolling his eyes.

We'd continue exchanging our attitudes, his rudeness with my unbroken spirit. But I knew that he didn't dislike me because he continued to approach me on the ship, walking across the mess decks to punch me in my shoulder or throwing paper clips at me when I'd pass the Personnel Office.

Although they didn't pick on me, his friends were just as twisted. I heard deployment stories about running trains on hookers.

"Once, we bought two in Fiji," one of Elvis's friends had told me. "And Elvis fucked one of them up the ass so hard that her ass bled. That bitch just fell apart. It was *hilarious*!"

I believed it. I pictured Elvis as a kid who used to torture animals.

That afternoon, the five of us hopped on the train that was right outside of base. It took us straight to the border.

I'd crossed the Mexican border once a few weeks after joining the Higgins crew. Getting in the United States required a long wait in line, a security check, and an ID check. Getting into Mexico required the functioning of legs.

Everything was dirt cheap in Mexico, including the alcohol that I was able to purchase. I felt like an obscenely wealthy duchess as dozens of children flocked my way selling Chiclets and woven bracelets. The roads were insanely unstructured with few traffic lights. The drivers had no speed limits or no loyalty to the undistinguished lanes.

Tijuana was filthy. There seemed to be a thick layer of dust over everything. It felt like a gigantic sand storm had swept through the whole town and nobody ever bothered to clean it up. The area was packed full of Mexicans selling items at stands that covered the roads and plump tourists with their digital cameras around their necks.

Most Tijuana citizens lived in deep poverty. Toilet paper was sold, not automatically placed in the contaminated public restrooms. Prostitution was legal.

The law enforcement was corrupt. Crime was abundant. And disgraceful amusements, like women blowing donkeys, could be found.

But to me, it was a safari through a dusty jungle.

The five of us crunched up into a cab that had no seat belts as Jamie gave the driver orders in fluent Spanish.

"We're going about forty-five minutes south to Rosarito," Jamie informed us in English. "It's much nicer there. Hotels are still cheap and there's a beach."

With Sally on Jamie's lap in the front seat, I sat between Elvis and Jack in the back. Once we escaped the chaos of the Tijuana traffic, the drive became a stunning view of lush hills and a rocky coast.

The town of Rosarito was still very Mexican, with brightly colored buildings and several clubs. But it was much more tranquil than Tijuana. It reminded me of a typical beach town, but slightly dirtier. We got a cheap hotel room with three beds and then took off to the bars.

Eager to be rid of my gin, juice, and red bull hangover, I didn't waste time getting drunk. We headed to a bar by the beach, taking a seat on the patio. I looked around me at the crowd that seemed to be mostly college students ready to kick off their summer vacation. For my birthday, Sally bought me a shot of tequila. It was poured down my throat by a fat Mexican in a gigantic sombrero. He gripped my head, pulled it back, and blew a whistle that was around his neck as he poured the burning, sour liquid down my throat. I did my best to ignore the taste and successfully swallowed without gagging.

The rest of the group joined me in the tequila shots, chasing them with Coronas. It wasn't long before Jamie and Sally left us to bang it out in the hotel room. Jack, Elvis, and I ventured to another bar. Things began to get fuzzy.

I would never understand the sudden sexual tension that erupted between Elvis and I. In fact, I didn't know if I'd ever been attracted to him before. Maybe I liked his attitude. His rude sarcasm was a challenge and winning his affection was a way to uplift my self-esteem. Then again, maybe it was just the tequila. But as we talked about nothing, I looked at him and out of nowhere, felt an electric current through my body.

"I'm going to take a piss, guys," Jack announced.

Elvis and I watched Jack work his way between shirtless frat boys and girls in bikinis as he made his way through the bar cabana and into the rickety wooden bathroom stalls.

The second Jack was out of sight, Elvis and I looked at each other.

"Want to go on a walk?" I more ordered than asked.

"Sure," he curtly replied.

We left our beers and walked out to the beach, hand in hand.

Almost instantly, we began making out, sloppily and passionately. I loved the way alcohol enhanced pleasurable sensations, like the touch of his lips against mine. The tequila also masked negative features, like the taste of smoke on his breath. Elvis was the worst chain smoker I'd met. We fell to the sand and continued to kiss, not caring who was watching. Our clothes stayed on, but our bodies rubbed on each other. I was enjoying the physical explorations of other men. It was fun and free of complications.

I couldn't feel the sand beneath our bodies or hear the waves crashing only a few feet away. I kept my eyes closed. I didn't think. I had no concept of time. The world around me was a pleasurable blur, when the intensity of the scene was abruptly halted.

I opened my eyes. I couldn't figure out what was happening. There were men around me who didn't speak English. I didn't know how many. I couldn't understand their voices, but they seemed aggressive and demanding. Then, there was Elvis, taking my hand and pulling me off the sand. The men crowded around us. Elvis's arms were protectively around my waist. I was afraid, but I didn't know what exactly I was afraid of. One of the men shouted at Elvis in a tone that sounded like an order. There was a truck with a cover on top of it with several Mexican men inside. Elvis got in and let me in with him. We drove off and I watched the crashing waves against the coast disappear. I began to panic.

"WHAT'S GOING ON?" I shrieked.

"Calm down, calm down," Elvis told me, trying to sound as reassuring as possible. "They're taking us to jail."

"JAIL?" I shouted. "WHAT THE FUCK? WHAT THE FUCK ARE THEY TAKING US TO JAIL FOR?" I demanded.

I was going to jail in Mexico, a country without the structured legal system of the United States. There were no solid rules for going to jail in Mexico. I'd later find out that it was a tactic for the police to get money from American tourists. Whenever they saw kids stumbling or getting a bit too wild, they'd haul them to jail if they didn't have money to pay them off. Although we were fully clothed, Elvis and I were going to jail for having sex in public. The Mexican cops saw two stumbling white kids and detected us for the easy targets that we were. But, barely a month into California, I was clueless of the way things worked in towns like Rosarito. I had visions of being taken out to a desert to be beaten, raped, and executed. It turns out a twenty-dollar bill would have saved me from the entire ordeal.

I unleashed a soap opera worthy crying fit in the back of the truck as Elvis cupped my face in his hands and tried to calm me down.

"Maggie, it's going to be okay!" he repeated to me continuously "We will make it through this!"

His words of encouragement were as cheesy as my cries. His attempts to be heroic almost made me laugh in the middle of my panic.

I realized that I was barefoot when we walked into what was supposed to be our jail. I got out of the truck as my feet crunched over the very uncomfortable gravel drive. The jail was right beside a sheep farm and looked like a shed where animals were kept. Unlike any developed country, there was no administrative process in entering this jail. I had no mug shots taken and was not ID checked. There were two cells, separated by a cement block wall. One cell was for the women and the other were for men. There was only one scrawny girl in my cell who didn't speak a word of English. My only toilet was a hole in the dirt floor, which I eventually was forced to squat over. Elvis had several men in his cell who all looked very poor and dirty.

I sat down in the dirt, realizing that the tequila hadn't worn off.

"It's my birthday, you ASSHOLES!" I shouted at what I assumed were the Mexican police guarding my cell.

They watched me, looking very amused as they chatted in Spanish.

"Damn, I wish I knew Spanish," I thought.

"*I'm in a Mexican jail on my nineteenth birthdaaaaaaay!*" I almost sang aloud.

At that statement, the situation became hilarious.

"Elvis!" I began to shout, crawling to the bars outside of my cell.

I stuck out my hands.

"CAN YOU SEE MY HAAAANNDS, ELVIS?"

"Yeah, I can see your hands!" he shouted, laughing.

All of the prisoners, including me, began to laugh at that point.

Suddenly, I heard Mexican accents shouting, "MARCO! POLO!" from his cell.

I had no clue how the hell they were playing Marco Polo, but Elvis and I joined in anyway.

Barefoot and in a skirt, I eventually crawled up against a wall and fell asleep.

It didn't occur to me how lucky Elvis and I were to get out of that jail until I was thinking clearly the next day. Someone had seen Elvis and I get arrested and miraculously found Jamie and Sally. They were drunk, but coherent enough to get a cab and find the jail. They came to the jail, got my credit card, and found an ATM. For forty bucks a head, Elvis and I were free. Jack made it to the hotel room at sunrise the next morning. The zipper of his pants was ripped off and he had bloodstains all over his crotch, though he had no idea why. The five of us were a pathetic morning after vision.

My brief kissing fling with Elvis became less attractive the next morning, but we continued it all the way to the American border. He'd smoke a cigarette and then shove his smoky tongue down my throat. But once we entered the United States, we detached hands and returned right back to our love-hate friendship. We remained friends from that point on and rarely talked about Mexico.

Nineteen years and a day, I crossed the pier to my ship after the wildest weekend of my life. Barefoot, with dirt on my knees, I saluted the American flag. I crossed the quarterdeck to the USS Higgins and walked right into my new reputation.

Number 5

Any innocence I may have had when I departed southern grounds was quickly contaminated within my first few months aboard the USS Higgins. Had anyone taken the time to get a thorough look at me, they would've noticed how quickly the softness in my face had faded. The bewildered expression of my blue eyes gazing at my big, new world lost its juvenile endearment. Instead of chaste and doe-eyed, I appeared oblivious.

"HEY YOUNG! Why you always lookin' so lost, girl?" one of my female shipmates teased me in berthing.

Many factors may have solidified my brand as a generally dumb person on the Higgins. Within my first few months in California, my southern twang melted into a west coast valley girl accent. In a world of salutes, attention standing, rigid military bearing, cement-starched uniforms, boots shined enough to use as a mirror, and ladder well after ladder well to climb, the spotlight on my inherent clumsiness shined significantly brighter in the military than in the civilian world. After all, I was the teenager boarding my ship with a short skirt, gashed knees, and a nasty hangover.

It was easy to gain a specific and very permanent label on the ship. This was why I'd been warned so many times to stay on guard of how I presented myself.

Our crew consisted of about three hundred people. The Higgins was a tiny town of floating steel where everyone knew each other's name and business. With only about twenty women aboard, we were even more vulnerable for acute observation and gossip. A female's status became mostly evident on watch. I would spend five straight hours on the quarterdeck of the ship with two to three Navy guys. We had nothing to do but talk.

"See that girl?" the Officer of the Deck would point out.

A blonde with a short pixie haircut and thick thighs walked across the pier and to the ship. She held the hand of a Latino male around his early thirties in civilian clothes. I assumed he was her husband. She saluted the flag and asked permission to come aboard. She made small talk with the three of us and introduced us to her man. As soon as they boarded the ship, I was flooded with stories about whom she fucked on deployment, the estimated number of pounds she gained after boot camp, and her husband's alleged closeted homosexuality.

"I can't believe she let herself go!" said the OOD, sadly shaking his head. "She used to be a fucking fox. I mean for a Navy bitch, she was fine as shit!"

Navy women were not typically considered pretty. Females with laborious jobs passed on applying the makeup that they would sweat off during work. Their utility uniforms were terribly unflattering and their hair was pulled back into tight, plain buns. Even the most attractive woman in normal attire was dull at best in uniform.

The females, along with the males, did not carry the stereotypical, muscular physiques that would've been expected in a military member. One's first year in the Navy usually resulted in packing on a freshman fifteen. I could never pin down a definite reason for why this happened, but it probably because of the allure of junk after two months of boot camp. One by one, I observed the females in berthing sucking in their guts and devoting all their strength to zippering their pants, stuffing themselves into their uniform like a pig in a blanket.

The guys on board seemed to have laser eyes that gave every female a thorough, full body scan. Seeing women through the eyes of men was both educational and disheartening. They noticed the ugliness in the most attractive girls.

"Ugh, see the way she looks at every man," the OOD would comment on a pretty girl. "That chick's fucking raunchy. One of my Seamen fucked her about a month ago. Apparently, she sucked him off right after he fucked her up the ass. No condoms or showers in between."

And they noticed beauty in the least attractive women.

"That girl over there," the OOD pointed out a brunette walking up the pier. "I'm not gonna lie. She's got a pretty busted face. She reminds me of that weird creature from Lord of the Rings. What's his name?" he paused for a moment.

"Smeagol?" I guessed, picturing the scrawny, bug-eyed monster from the film. As cruel as it was, I saw the resemblance.

"Yeah, Smeagol!" he laughed. "Despite her face, she's got a decent body though. She's nice and petite with a round, plump ass."

"That's what I call a butter face!" the Petty Officer of the Watch chimed in.

"What's a butter face?" I asked confused.

"It means that everything *but her face* looks good! Get it?" the OOD laughed. "That's the type of pussy you hit from behind so you don't have to see those eyes bug out!"

Although there were many exceptions, a good bit of Navy men were awful. They were mean, crude, sexist, and politically incorrect on every level. This wasn't because they were bad people. The military targets young recruits. It wants them barely emerging childhood, before they've developed educated beliefs, opinions, and identities of their own.

Training personnel to suppress their emotions is not a new phenomenon. They must be able to shoot, kill, rampage, and even slaughter on command. I was often told about situations where a toddler was sent waddling to soldiers with a bomb strapped to her.

"If you don't shoot down that toddler," they said, "Then you and your entire platoon are dead."

Being a trained robotic killer is often their only means of physical *and* mental survival. Lewd behavior, ignorant humor, and objectifying all walks of women are the collateral damage of that training. It doesn't excuse it. But it's hypocritical to dehumanize them for it.

Years after their enlistment, many would grow up, go to college, have families, and rediscover their emotions. In hindsight, there were a lot of regrets.

Fleet women were not immune to the same behavior. I was like a child mimicking my cool older brothers. I inherited their outlook. I'd observe a man whose face didn't catch my attention, but I'd notice his broad shoulders and the way his back narrowed down to his waist. A man who I'd normally never give a second glance would catch me off guard with his confidence and attitude. The guys who appeared dominant and fearless lit a spark. One bold look shot images into my brain of being slammed on the floor and fucked until my insides were paralyzed.

The men on the ship were raw in a way I hadn't known outside of the military.

"Butt hole. How we gone get bitches ta' make it tha' second vagina?" asked one of the guys from my division aloud.

Everyone called him Meaty. I had no idea how he got the nickname, but it apparently had something to do with his obscenely large penis. I'd gotten a glimpse of it once when he decided to flash all of the deck girls in one of the lockers on the ship. It was frightening enough to drive any girl into a lesbian rampage. The guys in our division claimed that Meaty had to pay prostitutes who were loose enough to handle him. Meaty was a black man in his early twenties rumored to have been homeless and sleeping under bridges right before he enlisted.

"Hey," Meaty would whisper in a girl's ear, sneaking up behind her and nudging his shoulder on hers. "*Pssssssst,*" he'd whisper again. "Put my dick in ya' hand. You'll like it."

"Hey Meaty, wanna see a trick?" I said jokingly around a group of people in my division once I'd gotten more acquainted with my shipmates. "I used to be bulimic, so I have no gag reflex. Look!"

We were all in a repair locker getting out tools we would be using to chip paint on a rusted corner of the ship, away from anybody high up in rank, so I felt perfectly safe to take my hand and shove it to the back of my throat as I'd done during my bulimic days less than a year before. I got as far as my knuckles to the back of my throat.

"Gurl, marry me," was Meaty's response.

"All women are beautiful," another guy would say. "When they have my dick in their mouth!"

"Hey… *heeeyyyy gurl*," Pepper, a young black man who stood about 5'5" and weighed one hundred and twenty pounds soaking wet would nudge one of the deck girls. "Ya wanna feel tha baby-leg," he'd coax.

The "baby-leg" was a reference to his penis.

"Yeah, gurl, just rub it a 'lil. It's lonely."

"Hell yeah, boy," Meaty would respond, "Gotta love me some white bitches."

"Nigga," Pepper would respond, "If it ain't white it ain't right!"

These were popular conversation starters during our workday. We would spread out on the ship in our designated areas to paint, prime, chip, sand, or complete any other mindless task and socially fulfill ourselves with vulgar conversation.

The guys laughed about things that were forbidden in normal society, but existed in the depths of every human being's innermost thoughts. They allowed themselves to be true to their mental images and shamelessly publicize them.

Anyone would expect a nineteen-year-old girl to get horribly offended with such talk, but I found it both funny and oddly enough, brave.

If the other girls in my division were offended, they didn't display it. We were all new to that world and in the extreme minority. The males resented the recent integration. The beginning of women aboard meant the end of public display of nude female posters. Suddenly, every man was at risk of sexual harassment charges when the wrong word was uttered. The crew was forced to watch a slew of sexual harassment videos and went through an intense training program to prepare for our arrival.

At the beginning of the last deployment, there were only a couple of enlisted women. Three months into it, three more were sent out on a helicopter to the middle of the Persian Gulf. Several of the sexually malnourished sailors practically lunged at them like a hungry pack of wolves, jumpstarting a whole new range of drama they'd never experienced on the ship. They resented the leak of estrogen in their manly haven.

"Shit was so much easier on the boat before you *girls* got here," They would say, rolling their eyes when they annunciated the word, "girls." "We used to be able to keep posters of naked chicks in our workspace. We could say whatever we wanted whenever we wanted. We didn't have to deal with these bullshit affairs and mini-dramas."

"Yeah," another guy would jump in. "Females are ultimately a bad thing for the military. They're a distraction. They tempt men into fucking them and maybe even lure them into some romantic bullshit when they should stay focused on their jobs. It's better off that the only women men have to deal with on deployment are hookers. They can just hit it, quit it, pay em' off, and they're *gone!*"

I did not want to rain on their parade more than my military orders already had. I did my best to become one of them. I adapted to their humor and inherited their language. I observed my female shipmates following the same pattern.

We did our best to appear callused. Some of the women were tougher than others. There were overachievers, who never uttered a word of complaint and vigorously pounded hammers and sanded the ship raw until their knuckles bled. There were tough women who practically ate the face off of anyone who dared to talk down to or belittle them. There were women who socially survived with sweet, endearing demeanors. These were the women who kept their sexual escapades highly classified and were considered too innocent and ladylike to be treated negatively by the men. I fell into none of those categories.

I wasn't a hard worker. Life as a Deck Seaman was a rude awakening for me. I felt like I had truly been one of the poor saps who'd gotten sucked in and thrown into the shitty position that nobody wanted.

With our duty being ship preservation, there was constantly work to be done. We'd be assigned to a spot outside. We'd chip rusty areas of the ship, sand it down with sandpaper, prime it, paint it, and then move on to another area. Eventually, we'd be back in our original spot doing the same task over again because ships over saltwater rusted quickly. If we weren't doing that, we were oiling machinery, polishing, or untying old, moldy ropes.

We were spoken down to and considered a lower class than the rest of the ship - even other sailors of our own rank. I worked a job that I'd once believed I was too good for. It gave me blisters on my hands and dirt under my nails. It was a duty that I thought was reserved for immigrants or redneck meth addicts, like my former next-door neighbors. While the kids I'd gone to high school with were sitting in air-conditioned classrooms, I was on my knees on the hot, non-skid ship surface beating the shit out of steel. I bitched and moaned.

Although I had the potential to carry a defensive attitude, I was no match for some of the girls who'd been born and raised in America's finest ghettos. I cowered in the presence of some of those women who I fully believed could rip any of the men to shreds.

Once word was unleashed of my threesome, the news spread like a summer wildfire. My chances of becoming the innocent pet were as miniscule as my chances of becoming God. Somewhere in between ladylike and ghetto fierce, I found my defense mechanism in my sexuality.

"So, Young. Uh, is it true?" one of the guys would shyly ask me with a curious glimmer in his eyes.

I knew exactly what he was implying.

"Is what true? The threesome?" I asked bluntly. "Yes, it's true. I fucked a guy from this ship and his wife."

In actuality, telling people this made me feel horribly exposed. I might as well have been hung up on the ship's quarterdeck naked, with my legs dangling below the American flag. But concealing my insecurities was my strategy. I missed Number 4 terribly. He'd been a comforting presence to me on the ship because I knew that I could be myself around him.

I felt abandoned when he left me alone with his legacy, but I did not discuss such things when I spoke of him. I wanted to be like the males on the ship. I wanted to materialize sex. Viewing it as an emotional, intimate act made me appear feminine and submissive. I felt that what would get me through a man's world was to be like them and treat men the way they treated women. They spoke of tearing up the pussies of hookers overseas and "hitting and quitting it" with bitches in San Diego as if they conquered their "hoes" the second they penetrated them with their merciless cocks. They felt nothing but pure physical pleasure and shielded all emotional vulnerability. I wanted that power.

Number 5 was the first boy I had sex with without any emotional memorabilia. He was fairly attractive, with a healthy twenty-year-old, tall, fit physique and short, dirty blonde hair. I never knew his eye color. I never really looked at him that acutely. He was stationed on my ship in another department, so I hardly had to associate with him except in casual passing through the p-ways. I knew little about him beyond that.

We had sex within thirty minutes of the first time we spoke. I had gone with Devi, one of the women from the ship, to the house of a guy that she'd been casually hooking up with. His name was Brendan and he was known for being a reckless party boy.

I liked Brendan in a nonsexual sense. He was adventurous. He was the guy that led you to places in the middle of nowhere to jump off of rocks into water holes. He surfed, boated, and had a house that was always packed full of liquor and people. I watched him plow through girls as they checked onto the ship and I decided not to be one of them. He'd already probed too many of the ladies I hung out with, causing an entertaining spectacle of catfights in berthing.

Although the two girls that Number 5 had already nailed were in deck with me, I hardly knew them and was certain that they had only been one-night stands. Number 5 seemed like fair game. He was cute, but plain. He was that typical American boy that probably played some sport for his high school and was popular among his classmates. I pictured him chugging PBR and cutting up with his boys at cookouts.

There was nothing unique about his look or personality. I saw Number 5 as a blank, predictable billet that became more attractive as I drank Everclear from the red solo cup that Brendan handed me. It was a toxic, 190-proof beverage, and I was drunk within a few swings. With Number 5 by my side, I sat on Brendan's couch and carried on light and fluffy small talk. I noticed Number 5's eyes narrow at mine, giving me the look that was a mixture between an amused gleam and a predator spotting his prey. I'd mastered recognition of this look from Number 4, although Number 5's eyes did not have that same childlike excitement. Brendan and Devi disappeared into his bedroom to have sex and I was left with Number 5 and his friend, Gibson, who we barely acknowledged.

I looked at Number 5 and knew that all I had to do was keep my body positioned towards his, keep a subtle smirk on my face, and show an interest in whatever he had to say. I spotted Number 5 giving Gibson a quick, but intense look that said, "Get out." Gibson quickly picked up on his buddy's signal and stepped out to Brendan's back porch to smoke a cigarette. I'd never recall the steps in how it happened, but it seemed that our jeans were down and Number 5 was inside of me before my vagina had time to moisten. On my knees with my right arm balancing on the head of Brendan's couch, Number 5 fucked me from behind. I preferred this position because it was as impersonal as possible. The sex was unmemorable. I neither felt discomfort or pleasure.

"His penis is in my vagina," I thought to myself, amazed about how thoughtless sex could be.

The entire scene was short lived when I glanced to my left to see Gibson staring at us through the glass doors on the porch. I didn't know whether to burst out into laughter or scream as if I'd spotted a monster outside the door. I was too drunk to have any solid emotions, but I was conscious enough to feel extremely uncomfortable.

"Men can be so disgusting," I thought, wondering what his fascination would be in staring down his friend hooking up with a random girl.

"Wait, wait. Let's stop!" I commanded.

Number 5 obediently removed himself from my body. Within moments, Brendan and Devi entered the living room and we continued the rest of the night drinking and chatting as if nothing had happened.

I was sitting on Brendan's front porch taking a phone call when Number 5 had to leave. He made the effort to bend down and plant a sweet goodbye kiss on my mouth.

"What the fuck is this guy doing?" I wondered.

I was surprised that he wasn't bitter that I'd stopped him mid-stroke.

"I had a good time with you earlier," he said, smiling. "I'll see you again."

"I guess the guy likes blue balls," I thought to myself in drunken amusement.

"Have a good night, baby," he said.

I wondered if he saw my eyes roll upon hearing the word, "baby." I hated such cliché terms of endearment, especially when I hardly knew the person using them.

He kissed me again and disappeared with Gibson in his truck.

I sat alone on the porch, wondering why Number 5 had bothered to carry on a polite charade as if something mildly romantic had just occurred. I laughed to myself again at everything that had just happened, wondering if it had been a reality. Perhaps I should've felt used, cheap, or guilty for surrendering myself too easily to a guy who didn't know my first name. But I tossed aside every belief I'd been raised with and every stereotype my culture conducted for easy women.

I was easy and I didn't give a damn. I'd chosen to be easy. I felt no guilt or pain for that night. I felt absolutely nothing.

Number 6

A certain vile layer overcame my personality after having sex with a man whose life was absolutely no concern of mine. I viewed my first one-night stand as a conquest, as if I was a gang member who just made my first kill. I didn't make a grand announcement of what happened. I didn't climb atop one of the mess deck tables while the crew was having breakfast, point to Number 5, and scream, "I fucked him the other night on Brendan's couch!"

But I told a girl or two. Devi told a girl or two. Brendan and Number 5 released the night's events to a few of their buddies in their department.

Higgins gossip was a constant game of Telephone. Its rapid pace grazed the ears of nearly everyone within days. Every crewmember had their own juicy, gossip-worthy background. When a man and woman boarded the ship together, the crew instantly assumed that they were boning. Whether they were married or single did not alter the likelihood of its truth. Enlisted members told stories about officers hooking up with Seamen or each other in their Ward Room spaces on deployment and duty days. Nearly every married member aboard had cheated on their spouse or had been cheated on. The typical sob story was of the married man taking off on deployment, while his wife stayed at home, got fat, and nourished her sorrow from her absent husband by nailing his best friend who had promised to take care of her. The man deployed would also cheat, but believed that his philandering had moral justification. Deployment was considered a different dimension, where the rules on American soil didn't apply. A common understanding was "what happens on deployment stays on deployment."

"After all," one of my shipmates explained to me while we were discussing his experiences overseas, "Hookers aren't real people."

When the man got home, he dropped his underway affairs and she dropped hers. Within a few months she'd be pregnant. They'd have their baby and they would be happily divorced by the time their child reached kindergarten. This story is simply a generalization. Not every person cheated on deployment – only the majority.

The stories that bothered me the most were of the very occasional guys who actually stayed faithful to their wives, but still got cheated on mid-deployment. These were the men who spent a hefty chunk of their sea pay on phone calls to their significant other and stayed aboard the ship when it was docked in some of the most snatch-infested stops, like Thailand or Australia. They were determined to prove their commitment, even if it meant losing their first chance in months to stand on a surface that didn't roll with the ocean's waves. Until my own deployment the following year, those stories were merely rumors.

"Don't listen to 'em, Young," one of my superiors said while trying to comfort me after catching the gossip of my threesome. "There will always be rumors. You just have to brush them off your shoulders."

I'd later discover how often people lie when defending themselves, but speak the truth in the whispers that pollinate gossip. Rumors were almost always true. Mine certainly were.

"Young, you really need to start keeping your private life private!" one my female shipmates advised me in a sharp tone.

Her name was Bambi. One could not stifle a giggle at the discovery of this woman having a bubbly stripper name on her birth certificate. Bambi had a strong, sturdy figure. She wore no makeup and had ash blonde hair that was always pulled back. She seemed unnoticeable at first glance, but the second she opened her mouth, her dominant personality overwhelmed whatever area she infiltrated.

Bambi was one of deck's leading overachievers and seemed to sweat work ethic. She came from white trash beginnings in a small town in Texas and enlisted to escape a psychotic ex-boyfriend. While most of the deck girls entered the Navy as teenagers, Bambi enlisted at twenty-two. She carried herself like a lioness through the African Sub-Sahara with her claws protracted. The world was both her hunting ground and an area where she was vulnerable to attack.

Bambi wasn't eager to make friends with everyone. She had matured beyond an adolescent's dire need to be accepted and she considered most acquaintances a waste of her time. She kept a small handful of friends and warded off any negative words uttered about them. One had to be initiated into a friendship with Bambi. Respect and trust had to be earned. Bambi saw me as a nice girl with a good heart, but as a wild, short sighted teenager on a fixed path for self-destruction. She did not consider me her friend, but was kind enough to ration warnings of my behavior, like a reprimanding big sister.

Upon overhearing about boarding the quarterdeck hung-over and with gashed knees, my threesome, my Mexico extravaganza, and my Number 5 encounter, Bambi pulled me aside.

"You need to watch the fuck out," she said in a low tone.

We were sitting at the small and very uncomfortable plastic tables and spinning chairs that were our little lounge area in berthing. Bambi spoke barely above a whisper so that any other females in the room were out of earshot. Her eyes narrowed at mine in a glare that was more of concern than anger.

"Look, if you want to get laid, fine get laid. You're nineteen and single. You have every right go to get fucked whenever the hell you feel like it. But quit making it obvious. Don't enter the ship barefoot or with scraped knees still drunk from the night before. Don't brag about the guys you fuck to Sally, Devi, or any of your other so-called friends. Do you know what people think of those girls?"

She had a point. Devi was considered barely above mentally retarded and the fact that she constantly held her mouth open like a kid on the short bus did her no justice. Sally had been known as the Jenna Jameson of the USS Higgins until she'd lured Jamie into a relationship. Everyone laughed at this because Jamie notoriously fell in love with every moist orifice in reach. He'd sworn on deployment that a few Fijian hookers had been his soul mates and was now on the verge of proposing to

Sally three months into dating her. Girls like Devi, Sally, and I were predigested punch lines to anyone with a trace of wit.

"The more you hang around those bitches, the more you're placed into their category," Bambi continued. "Those girls will never be taken seriously on a professional level. They'll never get a decent evaluation and I doubt their rank will ever advance. The higher ups think they're stupid hoes and if you keep acting like them, they'll think of you in the same light."

I stared at her intently and focused on her cautionary words. Bambi knew what she was talking about and it amazed me how she obtained such a levelheaded grasp on the USS Higgins society. The Navy world felt like a complicated mess to me. Ship social life was full of so many rules that seemed like they were written in a language that I'd never been taught to speak.

"Just remember, the Navy is just one big game," Recruiter Randal warned me a year before. "Just play their little game and life in the Navy will be easy."

My entire enlistment would have been significantly less painful if I followed Bambi's lead. Instead, I caved to my natural drive to rebel against every structure that dared to cage me.

"How come we have to be so discreet about the things we do?" I asked Bambi. "I mean, how many stories have we heard about the deck guys running trains on hookers and banging the new chicks on the ship? Most of them even cheat on their wives and they don't get shit for it!"

"Because they're men," she said flatly.

She rolled her eyes at her statement. I could tell that she resented this double standard even more than I did.

"I know," she said, reading my irritation. "It's complete bullshit. It's hypocritical and unfair. I don't like it anymore than you do. But, honey, that's the way the world works. Hopefully that will change some day, but you are not going to change the world by yourself. You can't just switch everyone's mindset."

She was probably right, but I was too stubborn to care.

"Fuck that!" I thought to myself. "Fuck anyone who wants to judge me. If I want to have sex, I'm going to have sex. And when I do, I'm going to own up to it. I'm not going to be secretive like some coward. I have every right to enjoy my life as much as any man."

Number 6 was a stolen item from Devi. I first saw him a few days after the Higgins had been ported into the shipyards for construction. The ship's residents were moved to barracks on Coronado Island, across the San Diego Bay. The barracks were designed like the ones in boot camp, with rows of eight to ten bunks in one large open space. It wasn't a luxurious setting, but it was definitely an elevated status from our coffin racks and cramped lockers on the ship. We could also enter our new digs without having to climb down several ladder wells. There was even a lounge area with a TV, fridge, and a rigid couch with itchy cushions and wooden armrests.

The entire section of the base that we were on was filled with other barracks rooms, which housed the males from our ship, sailors going thorough Navy Seal initiation (Buds), and Marines preparing for the Middle East. With bulging biceps and youthful energy, the Seals and Marines made ideal visions.

While the girls and I were still fresh into our new lodging and unpacking, I answered a knock on the door. I barely kept my jaw shut when I saw a stunning young thing in a fitted tan shirt, camouflage pants, and combat boots.

"Good God. Who the hell is this?" I thought to myself.

His face was tan and his short Marine cut was a marble black that matched the long, thick lashes that outlined his round, chocolate-brown eyes. He couldn't have been purely Caucasian. I guessed that he was mixed with some Hispanic blood, considering nearly everyone in southern California was. His lips were soft and his smooth face was absent of stress lines. He had to have been about nineteen and was definitely fresh from basic training. His shoulders were very broad and strong, setting the structure for his toned biceps. He didn't have an inch of fat on him. Number 6 looked like the beautiful killing machine that The Marine Corps strived to mold from ripe high school graduates.

I smiled at him flirtatiously, giving him a sharp, piercing look into his brown eyes. I felt confident in his presence, unaffected by the intimidation I usually felt around men. Although there was no doubt that he had the body of a very strong and potentially destructive man, I could tell that he had the mind and maturity of a boy. His eyes were happy and amused. Number 6 was preparing to deploy to Iraq in the bloodiest period of the Iraq War, but the entire scenario was a game to him. He was a child fulfilling his dream as GI Joe, playing with violently exhilarating toys and popping off the bad guys. His beautiful fresh face lit up as I'd seen so many times in my little brother when he was a five-year-old doing Power Ranger karate kicks in front of TV.

"Hi!" I greeted him with a smile.

There was a skinny white boy behind him with orange hair, freckles, and a crew cut. He was barely noticeable next to Number 6.

He smiled back, seeming as intrigued with me as I was with him.

"Who do you want?" I asked, assuming that he'd knocked on the female barracks door to see one of the girls from the ship.

"Is Devi here?" he asked, still looking into my face and smiling at me intently.

I struggled to suppress the pestilent scowl that was forcing its way out of my throat.

"*Devi*? Seriously?" I thought, rolling my eyes.

I couldn't comprehend why the hot piece of ass standing two feet away from me wanted Devi. Devi was a sweet girl that did not have enough strength in her soul to utter a harsh word to anyone nor enough intellect to deceive a three-legged kitten. Unlike the other Navy girls I knew, Devi lacked severity, attitude, and the cattiness most of us acquired for Higgins survival. While the rest of us were finding our own ways to adapt to the Navy jungle, Devi was the runt who had to be fed, bathed, and cared for into adulthood.

Of all the Navy women I would meet, Devi would be the weakest member of the species. I liked her for it, though. With Devi, I felt as safe as anyone else would feel safe with a frail little girl. She couldn't have damaged me if she wanted to, so we were friends.

But I never understood how she attracted so many men. Devi was always involved with at least one or two guys at a time. Her hair was chopped short above her chin in an uneven cut. The color was bleached blonde with about two inches of brown roots. At 5'5", ninety pounds, and a flat chest, her gaunt body matched the boyishness of her hair. Her face had the same androgyny as her body. But it wasn't her facial features or body that I found unattractive. I'd always been a firm believer that any girl could be quite becoming if she went through the effort of taking care of herself. Devi was an incessant chain smoker who did not shower regularly and often neglected to wear deodorant. With some soap, a brush, and some personal hygiene lessons, her ditsy personal and hanging-lipped gaze could have been endearing. But by aesthetic standards, Number 6 was out of her league.

"Devi, there's a boy here to see you!" I yelled, turning my head over my shoulders with my body still facing Number 6.

His lips pursed into a pout.

"*Boy*?" he asked, gleaming at me with a smile curling on edge of his lips. "You mean *man*!" he proclaimed.

I began to laugh at his accidental emasculation.

"Oh, I'm *very* sorry," I smiled, friendly but sarcastic. "Devi, there's a big, tough, *manly* MAN here to see you!" I shouted.

He looked pleased with my correction, smiling brightly again.

"We're having some beers with some of the guys at our barracks. Do you want to come?"

I accepted Number 6's invitation without even asking his name. Devi came along with me, completely oblivious to the chemistry brewing between Number 6 and I.

The only girls, Devi and I sat at a picnic table outside of the Number 6's barracks drinking beers with several other young Marines. They spoke excitedly about their first deployment, bragging about all the "sand niggers" they would obliterate. This was the first of many social interactions I would have with Marines, except they would be the only ones I would associate with who hadn't yet killed another human being. The difference between the newborn booters and the killers would later be easily identifiable to me. These boys lacked the permanent expression of a kid recently awakening from a nightmare.

Moments into drinking with the guys, I realized why Marines were stereotyped with the nickname, "jarheads." Devi and I watched with amusement as the drunk boys took turns throwing each other across the grass lawn in front of their barracks and taking turns punching one another as a pain endurance test.

"Look what I can do!" Number 6 said as he walked up to the bench I was sitting on with enthusiastic delight. He gripped his hand around his nose and pulled it to the right until I heard a crack. When he removed his hand I saw that his nose was crooked and smashed into one side of his face.

"Ew!" Devi and I shrieked in unison. "Did you just break your nose?"

"Yeah," he said, deepening his voice to sound as tough and indestructibly masculine as possible. "Don't worry. I can fix it. Watch."

With another loud crack, he pulled his nose back in place.

"What a moron," I thought while laughing aloud. "A very *attractive* moron."

The boys' vigorous energy eventually calmed as we all sat down at the picnic table, continuing to drink. While Devi sat across from me, occupied by the other young Marines, Number 6 sat close.

I drank enough beer to get a buzz, but hadn't reached full-on intoxication. Still mildly sober and fresh into the world of casual sex, I wasn't in the mood to make the effort to pursue Number 6. I was also on my period, so I knew that intercourse was simply not an option that evening.

As Number 6's hand ventured to my knee and up my thigh, I realized that our plans were not in sync. The rush of sexual tension with a new guy flooded my entire body and I quickly became engrossed in the attention. I didn't stop his bold behavior, nor did I reciprocate. I wasn't dressed impressively that day since I'd been hanging around the barracks unpacking my things. I wore only a t-shirt and a thin pair of running shorts. As Number 6's hands crept further up my thighs and closer towards the spot where only thin cloth came between his fingers and my tampon, I jumped up from my seat.

"I've got to use the bathroom," I said abruptly. "I'll be right back," I said, smiling at him, with every intention to return to the picnic table.

I strolled back to my barracks and changed my tampon. When I walked out of the all female section, through the lounge area, and out the back door of the building, Number 6 was waiting for me. Without a word, he walked right up to me, grabbed my waist with the hands that felt even stronger than they looked. He forcefully pulled me towards him until my body clung to his. He kissed me right away. Though I wasn't even slightly attracted to his denseness, every inch of my body sizzled from the combination of his hard body and soft lips.

"I want to get laid," he stated bluntly after our kiss. "And I know you do, too. I can tell by your eyes how bad you want it."

"When boys wave at you, don't ya *dare* wave back," my grandmother, Adele, advised my cousin and I.

I was thirteen years old, anorexic and underdeveloped, but with an attractive face. I'd been noticing male attention for about a year. My cousin was twelve with a full set of C-cups. We'd both become curious about the male gender and were testing out our flirtation skills when we spotted boys waving at us on the roads while we were riding the back of Grandmother's car.

"All men wanna do," Grandmother cautioned us, "Is pin you down and *pork* you. That's all they eva' think about. They'll say anythang- and I mean *any*-thang-ta have yer panties 'round yer ankles!"

Grandmother always talked about men like they were aimless predators ravenous with lust. Only when shackled by matrimony were they sanctified as human beings.

A distinct memory I kept from my childhood was watching a movie with her. There was a scene where two lovers greeted each other. The man grabbed the woman by the waist and pulled her into an affectionate and slightly erotic embrace before kissing her on the lips.

"Girls," she announced in the familiar tone that meant that she was teaching us a lesson. "If a boy eva' grabs you like that, I want ya ta *smack* em' with every bit of strength in ya body."

I thought about my grandmother's warnings as Number 6 handled me with pure aggression and zero tact. I was not the proper, respectable young lady my grandmother raised me to be. Just as lust driven as any male she had warned me of, I didn't respond to Number 6's statements with defensiveness. I liked his attention. He wanted to bang a girl before he was subjected to a year of jerking off in the Iraqi desert. I was turned on by his fearlessness and even more so when he grabbed me by the wrist and pulled me into the lounge. The second we were in the door, he dropped to the floor, jerking me down with him. Lying on our sides, legs wrapped around each other's bodies, we began making out on the carpet as his hand darted up my shirt. There was no lock on either the door that led to the female barracks or the door that led outside. Anyone could've walked in on us.

"Wait!" I nearly shouted, remembering the wad of cotton in my pussy. "*Dude*," I began to almost laugh. "I'm sorry, I can't do this. I'm on my period."

His brown eyes met mine as he gave me a mischievous grin. Suddenly, his hostile, eager hands yanked down my shorts, ripped out my bloody tampon and threw it across the lounge.

He quickly and furiously thrust himself inside of me. Despite his rapid moves, I was soaking wet and ready to take him.

Number 6 wasn't concerned with my comfort. He handled me like a rag doll, fucking me on the floor with my back banging against the wooden couch. When he wanted to switch positions and fuck me from behind, he didn't bother asking. He gripped his hands around my waist and flipped me with his muscular arms. My knees banged against the carpet and I knew I'd have rug burn - a little souvenir from our encounter in the lounge. Barely keeping my balance, I pulled myself up, leaning all my weight on my right knee and lifting my left leg so he could dig his dick in even deeper. I was already in pain, but I liked it.

Wrapping his right arm around my waist, he reminded me that he had complete dominance. Taking his left hand, gripping the hair around my scalp and tugging my head back to where his lips touched my ear, he whispered, "I could break your neck right now." Instead, he softly sank his teeth into the back of my shoulder. I didn't say a word. Although he couldn't see me, I was gleaming and on the verge of breaking into wild fits of laughter. The boy was exhilarating. His strength, masculinity, youth, and stupidity gave me the same rush I got when I jumped off cliffs into the lake as a kid. He made me feel like I was on the verge of death.

Like many of my future sex partners would be, Number 6 was a quick shooter. I doubt he lasted over seven minutes, nor was he tactful and skilled in the way he moved his body with mine. He fucked me like a boy with inexhaustible energy, but with no knowledge of how to channel it.

And just like every other man I'd been with, I didn't reach an orgasm of noticeable intensity. But despite his shortcomings, Number 6 taught me how to unleash the feelings inside my body and abide by my very animalistic sexual urges.

Once again, thinking of my grandmother as I sat in the lounge with my ass on the filthy carpet, I wondered how enjoyable sex would be if I'd been more ladylike.

Number 7

I was twelve years old the first time my parents sent me to a psychiatrist. Within a year of crash dieting and excessive exercise, I managed to drop forty pounds and halt the repetition of my first period. At seventy pounds with protruding ribs and knobby knees poking out of my scrawny chicken legs, I stood at 4'10" as a pre-teen in a child's body.

"So, Maggie," Dr. Sullivan, a middle-aged psychiatrist with a silvery-brown beard and a calm voice began our conversation. "I spoke to your mother and she says that you are obsessed with losing weight. Why is this?"

His eyes darted up and down my entire body - not in a perverted, kiddy porn way - but in amazement that such a thin girl could be so desperate to lose weight.

I began to elaborate on the humiliation I felt during the chubby phase that seemed to creep up on me unexpectedly the year before. I explained the shame I had in that body and the excessive flesh that I could literally feel weighing down my confidence. Fat was ugly to me and for a young girl in dire need of approval from her peers, ugly was worse than cancer.

"Every time I eat," I explained," I can just feel the fat piling up on my body."

"And what is it that you do when you feel this way?" he asked, squinting his eyes in concentration.

I resented his obvious judgments and attempts to label me with some sort of disorder. I imagined the list of mental illnesses he had in his head, waiting for my explanation of symptoms as he placed each of them in his disease categories.

I knew that he had no answers for me. There was no cure for whatever the hell was wrong with me. In my insecure, pre-adolescent brain, the only salvation for my obsession was a magic pill that would enable me to consume all the food that dominated my fantasies and daydreams and made my stomach growl in the midst of my starvation, without gaining a pound.

The number on the scale that I habitually stepped on several times a day was at an all time low. With my body forcing itself into puberty, I knew that my days at seventy pounds were numbered.

"When you eat, you feel fat, correct?" Dr. Sullivan asked.

"Yes," I answered, looking directly into his eyes to show him that I had no fear of his judgments. If I was fearless, I was guiltless. If I was guiltless, I was perfectly sane and justified in my actions. I was simply a girl wanting to stay in shape - that was all.

"And what do you do when you feel fat?"

"Well, I have to burn the calories I eat," I answered him as if he had just asked a very stupid question.

"What do you do to burn the calories?"

My stare turned into a glare and my jaw slightly dropped to express the ridiculousness of his silly, meaningless questions.

"I exercise," I answered bluntly after a moment of silence. "I rollerblade, I ride my bike, I swim, I jump on my friend's trampoline with her. I love to be outside. There's nothing wrong with that."

Although I wasn't lying, I left out the fact that I had gone from playing outside for fun to being constantly on the move for the sake of burning every fat cell in my bony body. If it was raining outside, I sat in front of my television doing crunches or running in place. If the summer heat was too intense for children to play outside, I ignored my mother's warnings of heat stroke and was comforted in knowing that I would sweat even more than usual. My cousin nicknamed me Richard Simmons because I took every opportunity to squeeze in exercise. If she was watching TV, I was walking in place beside her, or standing because I read somewhere that standing burns more calories than sitting. Even at the movies, I imagined the fat accumulating in my body as I sat motionless. To ease my mind, I tapped my feet in order to burn at least a few extra calories during the hours I was required to sit still.

I never understood why Dr. Sullivan got paid a hundred bucks an hour to follow every sentence with "How does that make you feel?" then prescribe me antidepressants, and tell me that putting ketchup on a baked potato is lower in calories than French fries.

Dr. Sullivan never asked me about Carl. Even if he had, I would have given him the same filtered explanation that any other child would have. Children are often like hostages under the care of authority, with spankings and groundings nudging them like guns pointed at their skulls, threatening to shoot if the wrong words are uttered.

Even if I had trusted Dr. Sullivan, I didn't have a grip on the reality of Carl. My stepfather wasn't a villain. Yes, he was an alcoholic. He was chronically selfish and flamboyant with his money. He was negligent. He was a cliché trailer salesman with a silver tongue that made trash seem like treasure. He was highly inappropriate in ways that, without him even knowing, would permanently tatter my developing mind. But none of these flaws were potent enough to do the real damage.

Carl never loved me. I think he wanted to. And I think by his standards, he tried. Carl did everything for me that would pass him as a socially acceptable parent. But a child can hear silent rejection.

The phenomenon of gender equality is still in progress. When I was growing up, women had only been able to hold financially supportive careers for a few decades. The women of my generation are still awkwardly maneuvering through the remnants of centuries worth of patriarchy. In the past, a woman had no income of her own, no property ownership, and no legal rights. Her level of success solely depended on the husband she landed. So naturally, every dress she wore, book she read, and word she uttered was intricately designed to gain male approval.

Although women have gained the legal rights of men, I don't think that social evolution has fully taken place. The underlying message that men were in charge of determining my worth was all around me. It was in my music, television, *Teen* and *Cosmopolitan* magazines, and the fashion industry. Nearly every form of entertainment I indulged in was based around being appealing to the opposite sex. Carl's sharp critiques on my body were solid evidence that I was failing. I starved myself. I got thinner. Without realizing it, I chased the father I would never obtain. Deep down, my worthlessness seemed inescapable. So I caved inward. My eating disorders were the abuse I felt I deserved.

My parents didn't hesitate to inform me that Dr. Sullivan racked up their bills with slew of drugs that would never work. As Dr. Sullivan predicted, I grew exhausted from starving myself. My anorexia evolved to bulimia. Once I joined the Navy, my own personal rehab, I lost all of my privacy for two months and was forced to quit. By the end of boot camp, my bulimia was completely cured. I began using sex to fill my void.

Sex began to conquer the majority of my thoughts by my first enlisted summer. With every man that crossed my path, my eyes examined his face, expressions, body movement, and voice. I was eagerly seeking the fuckable. My only standard was that he be attractive enough to stomach his perspiring body panting on top of mine.

Once a potential was spotted, I had to assess my chances with him. I didn't bother to pursue him if he was in a committed relationship. In seeking a man, I also had to take in account that I was not the most irresistible woman alive and that no man was automatically property for my taking.

Months after boarding the Higgins, years of bulimia abruptly backfired. Society's stereotype of bulimics is that they are ultra thin. This is why most people begin to binge and purge.

Despite warnings of the decay of tooth enamel, heart attacks, strokes, and numerous other health risks in bulimia, the bulimic's ultimate goal is a thin physique. They are not focused on their health. Their only vision is weight loss and to them, this is the only thing in life that matters.

But the after-school specials and *Lifetime* movies fail to mention the one thing that could probably prevent people from falling into bulimia. A bulimic has two choices: they must either quit or die.

A life of forcing one's body to vomit daily will inevitably trigger some deadly physical reaction. Just like any starvation or crash diet, bulimia destroys the body's metabolism. After years of binges and purges, along with frequent hard drug use, my metabolism was shot. I didn't keep up the heavy workout routines and constant movement of boot camp upon entering the fleet. After two months of marching and PT beatings, nobody jumped straight into a workout mode. Although I didn't gorge on fast food daily, I ate what the other girls around me ate and I partied.

I got lazy for about three months. Instead of the slight pudge on my peers, my body inflated from a size ten to a size sixteen. The weight seemed to pack on instantly. One week my body was fine, the next I was incapable of squeezing my jeans over my knees. Instead of thinking "Damn, I can't fit into my jeans. I better hit the gym and quit drinking," I lived in denial. I didn't buy jeans that actually fit. I just wore tacky skirts with stretchy material that would hide the dreaded size of how big I'd gotten.

The weight was instantly visible on my face. My small, blue eyes sunk back into my head. Despite the insecurities I had been plagued with throughout my adolescence, I had always been confident that I had a pretty face. My issues were with my body, but never my face. But suddenly, my puffy cheeks concealed my beauty. It literally horrified me to look directly in mirrors. So, I stopped looking in them.

Most women are known to get curvier as their bodies thicken. But my womanly bone structure was masked in fat, causing my ass and hips to disappear. My hourglass figure diminished. Suddenly, the winks, whistles, and stares I'd been getting since age twelve were gone.

In the beginning of my life as a fat girl, I desperately sought men to relieve my sorrows. I needed reassurance that I was still attractive and able to be wanted. I knew that one-night stands were not a sign of love, but I would've cut my clit off for any subtle sign that I still contained enough desirability to seduce a guy.

I had no interest in Number 7. I remember waking up beside him on an air mattress in some random beer-stained room in a Huntington Beach dump full of strangers.

With black hair, tan skin, dark eyes, and thick, groomed eyebrows to overshadow them, Number 7 was actually a good-looking guy. He was twenty, a year older than me, and stood half a foot higher than me. His body was lean and muscular, but in an effortless way that came from fortunate genetics. He was Mexican and grew up in Northern California. He said words like "dude," "gnarly," and "hella" every other sentence.

He arrived on the Higgins about a month after me, causing a brief stir of gossip in female berthing about the new cute guy on board. Number 7 had just gotten kicked out of Buds, the Navy Seals Initiation program, for bad conduct. He was a natural athlete who could easily run a marathon after a night of binge drinking. But he had a serious attitude problem with military structure. I enjoyed his company for that very reason.

Number 7 and I met while we were cranking. "Cranking" was when new sailors on ships were assigned to kitchen duty with the cooks for three months. Although most sailors considered cranking to be a shitty initiation, it was a huge break for the Deck Seaman. We often had to wake up at 4 am to serve breakfast, but we got a full night's rest. Our twelve-hour cranking workday was a vacation from life underway as a Deck Seaman. We were free from endless underway ship operations and our loud, obnoxious chief. I worked in the deep sink. I scrubbed large pots and pans in the back of the kitchen.

My deep sink partner was Ramsey, a twenty-two-year-old ginger with broad shoulder, sculpted biceps, and a perky, tight ass. His body was phenomenal, but his face made me cringe. Ramsey was pale with a face full of freckles and a sharp, pointed nose. Despite the wealthy family he claimed to come from, money did not show in his rigid teeth that were begging for a pair of braces.

After several weeks of washing dishes together several hours a day, Ramsey and I became friends. The two of us were the classic case of the girl who was too shallow to be attracted to the sweet male friend because he lacked handsome good looks. I'd made the mistake of making out with him at a party when I was very drunk, with his facial features blurred and my libido explosive after about ten shots of vodka. I woke up on Ramsey's friend's couch, still drunk from the night before and thanking God that Ramsey had his cranking duty early that morning.

My negligence led him on. Ramsey clung to me like a starving stray dog that had just been given a slice of lunchmeat. He chased me around the ship and insisted that I had deep, romantic feelings for him.

"You're just scared of getting hurt, Maggie!" he pleaded. "I won't hurt you. I promise. I like you. I *know* you like me!"

"I was drunk!" I shouted back. "I mean, HAMMERED! I'm sorry. I would've made out with ANYBODY that night. You're my friend, but you're just my friend."

"I don't believe you!" he stammered, angrily. "You're full of shit. I know you like me!"

Number 7 was the unlikely listener I spilled my Ramsey issues to. He was a friend of Ramsey who both pitied him and understood my situation. We began talking in the pulper room, a room a deck below the deep sink where the ship's garbage was separated and broken down. It reeked like any other dumpster and lucky Number 7's job was to operate it.

"Dude, the problem with guys like Ramsey," he said in his nonchalant surfer voice, "Is that guys like him aren't used to girls givin' him the time of day. The second you talk to him, you lead him on. You become friends with him, and he falls in fucking love."

"But it's not like I'm the only chick he's had physical contact with. He's fucked like twenty-five girls," I stammered.

"Yeah, all *hookers*!" Number 7 laughed. "See," continued Number 7, "I refuse to pay for sex. I can get pussy for free. It's not that Ramsey lacks looks. Lots of ugly dudes can get chicks. Ramsey has no game. And don't forget that the poor guy was dumb enough to have feelings for the hookers, too."

I gasped, remembering some of Ramsey's sad stories about the poor Fijian women who had been sold at the age of twelve as a child prostitute.

"I wish I could've taken one home and married her," Ramsey had said.

He spoke of foreign prostitutes as if he'd seen far too many cute puppies at an animal shelter that he could not adopt.

My eyes rolled as Number 7 peered down at me in amusement.

I was irritated with emotions and the complications that came along with physical intimacy. My sex drive was at full force. I just wanted what I wanted, when I wanted it. Sex, sex, sex was all that clouded my mind. I felt guilty for

Ramsey's hurt feelings, but was more concerned about the fact that I was desperate enough to shove my tongue down his throat.

"Wow, I am a bitch," I said to myself. "I totally led him on."

"Yes, you did," Number 7 said with a laugh. "You made the poor guy think he had a chance."

"Ugh I don't get it!" I said, frustrated. "I mean, isn't it the guy that's supposed to not have any feelings and the chick who gets all clingy? I honestly just want to have sex right now. Just sex. Fuck all of this emotional bull shit."

Number 7 laughed out loud at this. His vocal chords just exploded into a very free sound. It was a laughter that defined him, unstructured and uncaring. He was the last person I expected to meet in the military.

"Do you have any idea how easy it is for a chick to get laid?" he asked me. "Dude, I've got so many friends who would fuck you if that's all you wanted - no strings attached."

"Great! Introduce me!" I said, only half serious.

Number 7 was somewhat of a man of his word.

We didn't become good friends, though we talked occasionally and said hello when we passed each other in the p-ways. Though this was enough interaction to send Ramsey into a few jealous fits.

Suddenly, Number 7 caught me very off guard when he burst into the female berthing, not bothering to knock. I had a horrible cold and was sitting on the hard wooden tables watching a movie with a large pile of used Kleenexes at my side. My chest jumped when he walked straight inside, because no man dared to enter female berthing without shouting "male on deck!" after a few knocks. But as his attitude was with every other rule, Number 7 didn't give a shit.

My nose was red and my eyes were watery, but Number 7 wasn't fazed by my ragged appearance.

"WHAT THE HELL ARE YOU DOING?" I shouted, though I was more humored than angry.

"Get off your ass. It's Saturday night. We're going to a party."

"*Now?* I'm sick."

"You're not *that* sick," he rolled his eyes.

Initially, I was offended by his lack of concern for my health. Then I remembered that not only was he not my boyfriend, he wasn't really my friend either.

"The party's about an hour away. I'll give you gas money. You'll get free drinks and there's tons of guys there," Number 7 assured me.

"And who knows," he said. "If you play your cards right, you might just get laid."

I was suddenly feeling perfectly healthy.

Our drive to Orange County was almost completely silent. I didn't push a chemistry that wasn't there. We arrived at about ten o'clock at a small house packed with beer pong tables and kids in their teens and twenties. After saying hello to a few strangers, I began pounding down the Jell-O shots that were being handed to me by the tray-full.

Jell-O shots are tricky. The taste of alcohol is barely detectable. Doing a regular shot, a buzz follows close. But the toxicity of Jell-O shots creep up on your confident sobriety.

I remember little of the rest of the night. My former bulimia habit made me a very interesting drunk. After years of self-induced vomiting and losing most of my gag reflex, my body would not hurl whatever toxins I ingested. Instead, I was a blackout drunk with the ability to walk around and socialize for hours without remembering a thing the next day.

I talked, mingled, and ended up on a mattress that rested directly on the carpet in an empty room. My next memory was a random guy walking in, pulling his pants down, and exposing his cock. Judging from his mumblings about me being a "down chick," I assumed that Number 7 had gotten hammered and sent him in here as some sort of favor to me. Lying flat on my stomach, I lifted my head up and peered at him.

"Does this guy seriously expect me to just suck him off?" I wondered. "Like, was I gonna say 'sure, random guy, please let me choke on your cock!'"

I was easy, but not selfless.

"No dude. No," I mumbled, letting out a slurred giggle.

A few hours later, I awoke to Number 7 lying beside me. Without a word, he shoved his hands down my jeans.

Though I had never been particularly drawn to him, he met my standards. He was cute, single, and would not develop the misled emotions. Number 7 fucked around all the time. I was a dime a dozen to him and didn't care to be anything more. And his hands felt really good inside of me.

Just for that night, Number 7 intrigued me. I'd never met anyone so reckless. He was unafraid of breaking rules or the repercussions that followed them. His sexual behavior reflected his lifestyle. He didn't care if I rejected him. He went for whatever he wanted. I remembered little about sleeping with him. Even the next morning, I couldn't recall the way he kissed or how the touched me. I wasn't even sure if I'd been completely naked or if he'd just ripped my jeans off and seized only the necessary parts of my body. All I could remember about Number 7 was that his dick was slightly above average and thick enough to be pleasurable. I knew I'd gotten some physical satisfaction from him, but nothing that gave me a giddy afterglow.

Whether it was the Jell-O shots, mediocre sex, or both, I was realizing that a passionate one-night stand was a lucky strike. Although I was dodging physical bullets with Number 7, who I foolishly screwed unprotected, I was emotionally safe.

Like Numbers 5 and 6, I escaped sex emotionless. In seeking random men, I was shielded from loneliness, rejection, and waking up the next morning full of guilt and emptiness. I was desirable enough to get used. At the time, that was all that mattered.

Hung-over and slightly sore in my thighs after fucking for the first time in a month or so, I awoke next to a man who didn't hold or kiss me. We were practically strangers with a similar interest. We swore secrecy of our night together from our shipmates. We drove back to San Diego in silence as I admired the stunning blue-green water of Laguna Beach that reeked of wealth and superficial beauty.

The sun was shining and the weather was flawless. The morning after nonchalant sex with a nonchalant guy, it was a typical day in southern California.

Number 8

By fall, I hated my life.

I had come down from the high I got from the San Diego sunshine, men, and my newfound freedom from The South. I finished cranking and returned to life as a Deck Seaman. When I first boarded the ship, our workdays were hard, but much lower key than usual since the ship had just returned from deployment. But by the time I finished cranking, the USS Higgins was in full swing in constant drills and underway operations that lasted from one to three weeks. We were out and in, back and forth with no steady schedule. The Higgins would be leaving for my first deployment the following spring.

I was welcomed back to deck with my temperamental chief screaming, "NOW GET YO' ASS TO WORK, SHIT STAIN!"

I realized how much I hated deck. Cranking had been a humbling job, spending my days elbow deep in large grease pots and rubbery meat. I worked twelve-hour shifts and had burn scars from the scalding water that sanitized the dishes. But I found peace in it. I was left alone in the back of the kitchen with the company of Ramsey, without the higher ups critiquing our salutes or nagging us if we weren't appearing mindlessly busy.

Just as the ship's chow times were steady and predictable, so were our hours. In deck, our underway schedules were chaos. Everyone was required to wake up at 6:15 am for breakfast. Every division on the ship met at 7:15 for morning "Quarters." From there, our chief assigned us to our areas that we had to work in.

We broke for lunch and then worked until sunset. Had this been our entire schedule, I would have had little to complain about. But our daily work was a small portion of our full duties. Our division was split up into four watch sections. There were five of us per section. We took turns as lookouts, rotating from aft lookout, port lookout, starboard lookout, the helm, and the messenger. The helm was steering the ship, which wasn't nearly as exciting as it seems. We basically turned a wheel slightly back and forth under the orders of the Officer of the Deck.

As the messenger, we ran whatever errands were needed around the ship. Each position was one hour long and each watch was five hours with the exception of the 10 pm to 2 am watch.

The job title "lookout" was self-explanatory. Our duty was to *stand* -not sit- on the sides of the ship's bridge and "look out" at the water and report every object we saw. This task seemed pointless and outdated to me since the ship was chock full of radar to detect objects in the water long before a lookout could spot them.

"But there's things that a lookout can see that radar can't pick up," a Boatswain's Mate, who ranked one pay grade above me explained.

"Like what?" I asked.

"Well, uh, like a stick in the water."

We were honored with the essential duty of spotting sticks in the water. I learned how to fall asleep standing up, though the consequences for getting caught were Captain's Mast, which was like a criminal trial within each command.

With the deck monkeys split into four watch sections, we were rotated back one watch per night. Sometimes our watches weren't a major inconvenience. The best watch was the morning watch, which got us out of half of our workday. The worst was at night.

My least favorite was the Rev watch. The title was short for the military term, "Reveille," which was traditionally a bugle, trumpet, or pipe call used to wake troops up at sunrise. For ships, Reveille was the whistle of a Boatswain's pipe done over the 1MC, usually by one of the deck Petty Officers. Rev watch lasted from 1:45 am to 6:45 am I would have to wake up at 1:15 to be on the bridge by 1:45. I would stand my watch all night and fight sleep at the helm. Then we would break, have breakfast, work an entire day, get a nap in after dinner, and then wake up again at 9:15 to be at our next watch at 9:45. We would finally get to sleep at 2 am, only to wake up for breakfast four hours later.

But even those crazy hours would have been bearable if it weren't for ship operations. Although every division had some sort of role in each operation, deck seemed to always get the shit jobs. For Flight Quarters, which was the preparation for helicopters landing on the flight deck in the back of the ship, we were required to "man the boat deck." This was an area where we kept a small boat manned with a crew to rescue the passengers in case the helicopter crashed into the water. Our job was to help steady the boat with rope as a Boatswain's mate operated the machine that lowered it into the water. Whenever we heard the announcement over the 1MC that echoed "man the boat deck" throughout the entire ship, we were required to drop whatever we were doing and sprint to the boat deck. This call often had us jumping out of our racks in the depths of our slumber. If we slept through it, we were in major shit.

Deck division had their own role in other operations, like refueling the ship. During the refueling process, we had to hold a line called the P&D (phone & distance) line. The P&D line was a long, wire rope with several triangular flags attached to it. Its purpose was to show the Officers in the ship's bridge the distance between the Higgins and the vessel that was refueling it. Standing on the forecastle holding a rope sounds easy, but it was one of my most grueling operations. Refueling often took hours and the rope cut into our hands. We weren't allowed to wear gloves because they could get caught on the flags and pull someone into the ocean.

We donned helmets and puffy orange life jackets that were obnoxious and uncomfortable. When the seas were rough, and they often were, waves of frigid salt water would splash on deck and soak us. By the time the ship was refueled, our legs ached and hands burned.

Every day underway was a battle. It was constant movement and relentless, mindless work. Our mornings were full of the bullshit of mustering with the division and standing in ranks while our chief bitched at us for something-

anything. Whether we messed up with priming the wrong area or one of our shipmates came late to muster, I was certain that the chief just enjoyed roaring.

After muster followed clampdown. Clampdown was when the entire crew spent an hour making the ship spotless. Each division was assigned to one specific area. If a couple sailors were tasked to a p-way that didn't take long to clean, they had to keep sweeping, dusting, and polishing it over and over again until clampdown was over. Then, either the Captain or the Executive Officer (XO) who was the second ranking commander after the Captain would walk through each section. Our XO stuck his finger in every crack in search of one dust particle. When the XO did the inspection, every crevice of the ship needed to be immaculate. About once a week, our Chief or a First Class Petty Officer (one pay grade below a chief) in our division inspected our uniforms for miniscule little errors like a wrinkle in our shirt, a scratch on our boots, or a strand of hair from a female's bun that came loose.

I understood the reasoning for having inspections in our dress uniforms. Looking sharp and professional is essential to maintain a respectable image, but the crew wore coveralls underway. The entire purpose for coveralls was to get them dirty. A Deck Seaman's coveralls were wrinkled and paint splattered. In our very cramped and limited storage space, we had to keep one pair of pressed, flawless coveralls for inspections only and an extra pair of boots that were ideally shiny enough to show your reflection.

"This shit is so stupid," I would whine. "Why the fuck are we spending hours polishing a pair of boots we'll never wear?"

Despite his temper, my chief was actually a good man. But back then he might well have been Hitler. I hated standing at attention and staring straight ahead as if I were still in boot camp, waiting for his booming voice to poke fun at me or call me out on some flaw in my uniform.

"Do you honestly think that makes you look skinnier?" Petty Officer Hunter chuckled at me in one of our first uniform inspections in boot camp. Instead of tucking my utility shirt completely in, I let part of it puff out. Already self-conscious of my figure in the hideously unflattering Navy uniform, my face was burning hot. I powerlessly stood at attention and absorbed the belittlement.

My perspective on uniform inspections was abstract from its intentional focus on the condition a sailor keeps their work attire. To me, they put the horrible bloated version of my body on display. I was finally coming to terms with how much my figure had inflated. Long before I noticed it myself, I got several comments about my fat face from Dino, my fellow Deck Seaman.

Dino was not an attractive guy. With a large round head and bug eyes, he looked like a blonde Chucky doll. Dino was very much like the one bully every kid has in grade school. He was the class clown that picked on everyone. When he blurted out an insult to someone, his eyes lit up from the reactions he provoked. He was the first person to tell me that I looked like a cabbage patch doll and crowned me with my first Navy-issued nickname, "Sponge Bob Square Ass," from my flat, shapeless butt in coveralls.

Dino's personality defined the Navy's method of social interaction. Since the majority of the crew enlisted fresh out of high school, few sailors developed maturity past that age. The entire atmosphere was full of forty-year-olds telling dick jokes, superiors screaming at those lower in rank like the bratty playground conquerors obliterating the little kids' sand castles with one, nasty kick, and enlisted members fearing the presence of officers like their stern teacher.

Just as high school had its sharply defined cliques, the same went for the Higgins crew. Each division had its own type of personalities. The Quartermasters were the laid-back fraternity brothers. The electronic technicians were the tech-savvy nerds. The Gunner's Mates (GMs) were the sadistic type of kids who stuffed dynamite in frogs. Many GMs saw themselves as ferocious killers, but for some reason, neglected to join a military branch that actually put them in face-to-face combat. The engineers were the good 'ole boys with small town personas, even if their hometown was a major city. They stuck together like a pack of wolves, both professionally and socially, guarding each other's backs. Most of them resided in the East County, which was the Texas of San Diego and four-wheeled in the desert together on the weekend.

We Deck Seaman were the Navy's rejects. Rarely did anyone enlist knowing they would become a Deck Seaman. Most of us were in deck because we were too naive to see through the tricks of the Navy system or had an assigned rate, but got kicked out of our training for bad conduct. Sailors in other divisions were sent to spend a day with us for a punishment.

It was deck and the engineers who worked like dogs with their workspaces often getting as hot as one hundred and fifty degrees during summer deployments. But the engineers got respect. They were recognized and rewarded for their duties. I was once told by one of the guys on my ship that the big difference between military and civilian employees was that civilians were babies that needed a good pat on their back every five minutes.

"You gotta remind them constantly how good of a job they're doing," he said, rolling his eyes. "In the military, they don't do that shit. You're expected to always do your job well and when you fuck up, yo' ass gets tore the hell up!"

So I suppose that deck's high school role was the poor, trailer park, and project kids with abusive parents. While some of those kids bitterly rebelled, got in trouble, or flunked out, others became stronger individuals from surviving in a tough atmosphere. The only make-or-break definer for a Deck Seaman was time.

Just like the middle and high school cafeteria, each table was divided into cliques on the mess decks where we ate our meals. It was usually a different division to each table, but most of the first class petty officers sat together - except for the cool ones who didn't throw their rank in other's faces.

There was also one table where all the black people sat. I always found the racial segregation irritating and unnecessary. By the time I was cool enough with the group, I sat down with them for a few meals just to feel courageous.

"Black power," I said as I sat down, throwing my fist up in a Jane Fonda mug shot "power to the people" salute.

We all laughed together.

The Higgins had its popular kids who everyone wanted to befriend. Number 4, who the crew talked about endlessly, had been the effortless rebel without a cause.

My male shipmates worshipped his laid-back personality and ability to smoke weed every day in the Navy without once popping on the thirty-seven "random" drug tests he had throughout his enlistment.

It had its bad boys, like Number 7, who were always in trouble and never seemed fazed by military authority. There were the overachievers who practically sucked the salt off of every chief and officer's dick to gain favor for high evaluations and rapid advancement. The ship labeled its sluts, which were a large chunk of the females aboard, including myself. And, of course, the crew had its ultimate losers. There was one in every division.

The electronic technicians had Rusty, a short, scraggly man with a creepy mustache that grew over his chapped lips. He didn't just *look* like a pedophile. He had been caught with child pornography on his laptop during a trip out to sea.

The cooks had Lank, a scrawny redneck boy from West Virginia who stood at a whopping 5'2". The poor guy was constantly getting pieces of food thrown at him and getting slapped in the face with wet fish.

Operations had Hank, a tall guy who jerked off to Anime porn and had an unusually huge watermelon head. Dino named him Omega head.

It was deck division who proudly owned the Higgins's most tortured, un-cool kid, Booger. Of course, the poor guy's real name was not Booger, but the crew rarely remembered that. He was called Booger because he looked like Booger on *Revenge of the Nerds* and was known for being a dirty, smelly guy who didn't shower regularly. His lack of hygiene had even reached the point of mandatory supervised showers on long underways. Booger was in his early twenties with a stubby, stout body, wide brown eyes, and a short head of brown hair that always had a hefty amount of dandruff that peeled in curdles. Booger always looked like he just walked inside from a roaring blizzard.

Every day at morning muster, Booger was a live demonstration of how a sailor's reputation depends on their presentation. His uniform was always dirty and wrinkled. Booger was rarely clean-shaven and always had hunks of dirt or oil wedged inside his fingernails. He was notorious for uniform malfunctions.

"BOOGER! Where the fuck is yo' belt, shit stain?" our chief would demand, sometimes at the volume where the entire Higgins topside could here.

"What the hell are you thinking, dude? Shave yo' dirty ass face! And wash yo' dirty ass, pig! How hard is it to dress yo'self?"

Though Booger was usually a slacker, his appearance made it far more noticeable when he wasn't busting his ass. Because deck was assigned so many tedious, empty tasks, most of us did what we called "skating." Skating was when we put off the image of working when we were really doing nothing. During my first few months in deck, I along with the rest of the newbie's tried to be "shit hot" sailors and busted our butts pounding into the topside of the Higgins with determined force. We would finish our job and then go to one of the Boatswain's Mates. He'd give us another job. Then we would rush to finish that. We would run back to our boss and be handed more work.

To simply be assigned a production goal for the day, finish it, and be done made far too much sense for the Navy. Navy culture was all about image. They did not care very much about real productivity, just *looking* like it cared about productivity. Whether we painted a five-foot space or the entire topside of the USS Higgins in one day made no difference to our chief. What mattered was that the Deck Seamen were seen with tools in their hands and sweat dripping down their faces. That way, the officers would gaze topside and proudly observe the Navy's little grunts laboring away and think, "Damn, their chief sure has a firm grip on those Seamen."

I quickly realized that it didn't matter whether or not I sanded the ship until my hands fell off. I was a hamster on a wheel that could sprint myself into a heatstroke or mosey along slowly and steadily. Either way, I was going nowhere. My fellow deck monkeys and I usually finished what was required and then held a paintbrush in our hands without painting. When someone important walked by, we painted. But otherwise, we skated.

I quickly found that skating was crucial. With the constant watches, workdays, and operations, I needed to preserve as much energy as possible.

"Shit! Ya'll think this is bad?" one of the guys who had been in deck for a couple years asked a bunch of us new kids when he saw our weary faces. "These little underways aren't shit! You should've been out with us in the Gulf. Those were tha *slave* days! Just wait 'til deployment. It's gonna be 'Man the boat deck! Man the boat deck!' all night long."

My military time could have been much worse. Instead of being camped out in the desert choking on the dust of the Middle East, I lived in a beautiful beach town that millions of people vacationed to. I wasn't dodging grenades. My face was splattered with paint instead of blood.

I often felt guilty for complaining when I thought of Granddaddy, who barely escaped the Korean War alive. He rarely spoke of his experience, but I occasionally caught wind of my relatives telling stories. Granddaddy was apparently the only one of his eight-man operation to escape a foxhole. The explosion lodged bits of shell shrapnel all over his body and nearly paralyzed him.

I've never denied that I did not join the Navy to serve my country. I did it for survival. Enlisting in the United States military is a catch-twenty-two. Sure, I could have gone to college. I was an eighteen-year-old, able-minded adult when I chose to enlist. Carl often said that he was responsible for feeding and clothing me until eighteen. Then, at my voting age cutoff, I was on my own.

The tricky contradiction is that my financial aid is based on my parents' income until I hit twenty-four. At the time I was graduating high school, my parents' six-figure yearly earnings detonated nearly every chance for help I had. The government seems to assume that since my parents could afford my college tuition, they would pay for it. But because they were not legally obligated to do so, my parents chose to financially prioritize liquor, booming stereo systems, and yachts. Unless I ventured throughout my family tree and begged for donations, I would have had no choice but to contribute to America's one point two trillion dollars worth of student debt.

Had I gone to college straight from high school, I would have graduated in 2007, the first year of The Great Recession. As of 2013, the average student graduates with approximately thirty thousand dollars worth of debt. Only half of them obtain jobs that require a degree. And *that* lucky half earns salaries that have dropped fifteen percent since 2000. Living on my own at seventeen instilled a deep fear of poverty that would haunt me for the rest of my life. The military lured me with promises of financial stability.

In high school, I couldn't get through a television show without seeing two or three commercials containing fit young adults repelling down mountains, jumping out of airplanes, twirling rifles, and circling in for group high fives and back pats after succeeding in a mission. Those commercials offered an adventure, a family, a gateway to a new world, and of course, a hefty enlistment bonus.

Recruiters scouted every high school and community college job fair for fresh bodies. Like most teenagers, I didn't understand war back then. I was like many of my fellow recruits. I hailed from a relatively humble culture that ate up patriotic propaganda, referred to their nation's leaders as wise, and considered it treasonous to question their intentions. I grew up in America the beautiful, the land of opportunity, and the greatest country on earth where soldiers were heroes, politicians were leaders, and our enemies were villains. But even during the days that I busied my thoughts with boys, booze, and all things superficial, something rubbed me wrong about treating countries like football teams. One is born within a border and must absolutely under all circumstances swear loyal devotion to that chunk of soil, even if that requires having their blood splattered across it. Maybe it was easy to reject the beliefs of the world I grew up in because I had always felt rejected by it.

I admire the service members surrendering themselves like Romeo driving a knife into his heart for Juliet. There is a beautiful tragedy in somebody loving something enough to die for it. Whether or not they are truly protecting their nation, they sacrifice, suffer, and often die believing they are. That certainly earns them the title of heroes.

Granddaddy's service was recognized at his funeral, with an American flag over his coffin. All active duty and veterans were asked to stand up as a recording of Taps was played. I was one of three to stand and the only female. I knew that my family had wanted me to wear my uniform, but I chose to mourn him as his granddaughter, not as a sailor. Back then, I felt guilty for that. But now I wonder if I was just oblivious of how much I really understood.

The USS Higgins was the least appropriate environment for an opinionated nineteen-year-old. The ship was only sixty-six feet wide, five hundred and five feet long, and carried a modest-sized crew of three hundred. Not only was the Higgins a workplace, it was meant to be a military establishment in which the crew was supposed to set a higher standard than the average civilian employer. We were expected to be in proper uniform at all times. Women had to wear their hair in tight buns with only two natural colored bobby pins, skin-toned nail polish (if any), and no visible jewelry besides one tiny silver stud per ear. The men were expected to be clean-shaven every day with short haircuts and shaved sideburns. Enlisted members had to salute every officer that passed by while topside of the ship. Every crewmember had to stand at attention and say "Captain's on the bridge," "Captain's in combat," "Captain on deck," or wherever else the Captain was whenever he entered a ship space. We stood at attention until he would say "carry on," allowing us to return to a relaxed stance.

It was frowned upon to bring our personal lives and baggage to the ship. The standard was "This is a place of professionalism. Don't let your shit outside of work affect your job." We were not allowed to date or fuck people from the ship. Married people could be sent to Captain's Mast for getting frisky with a shipmate. Anyone could get demoted, put on restriction, kicked off the ship, or out of the Navy for banging someone subordinate in rank.

These standards would have been reasonable except for the fact that the ship was our entire life. While underway, there was no privacy of our own home to escape to. We had no couches to relax on, beer to drink, or even a quiet, secluded spot to sit down and think. We were at work twenty-four hours a day, seven days a week.

Our shipmates became our fathers, mothers, bosses, employees, brothers, sisters, aunts, uncles, friends, and enemies. The majority of enlisted members barely had enough time to log onto a computer and send an email. Our communication with the world ashore was very limited. Trapped on the ship, if we needed to vent out our frustrations, we had to do that with a shipmate. If we were desperate for someone to tell our secrets to, we prayed that we could trust the shipmate we chose. We turned to each other for friendship, affection, and often the relief of the sexual tension that built up in all of our very human bodies.

In the year and a half I was stationed on the Higgins, the people who escaped that boat without a single affair with a shipmate were scarce. I could count them on my hands and I'm not discriminating the chiefs and officers, either. And from the first kiss, first fuck, and first spotting of two shipmates eating on the mess decks together or lingering in the p-ways, word of the new couple buzzed through every inch of the destroyer.

It's not that sailors were more promiscuous than the average civilian or were spiteful gossipers eager to trash talk out of pure malice. I always saw the Higgins as one enormously twisted science experiment. Three hundred people were thrown on a floating chunk of metal with ridiculously cramped living spaces. The ship had no cheerful colors. The outside of it was haze grey, which blended in with the endless horizon of grey water against the sky. Unless we got close to land or saw another vessel, there was no life beyond the ship. The Higgins seemed to be the only civilization left in the world.

There was nothing comforting about the inside of the ship. The racks were not fluffy and soft like a bed. Our berthing lounge chairs were hard plastic. There was no art, beauty, or music. We were forbidden to listen to our iPods or a radio during work, while chipping and sanding.

There we were in the middle of the ocean. We were told to work, and when our work was done, we had to find more work to do. If there was no work to do, we had to pretend to do work so that we looked busy.

Our bodies were exhausted, but our minds were rotting with agonizing boredom. Sometimes someone would bring DVDs of a TV series like *The OC* or *Smallville.* Even if we hated the shows, we begged the owners to borrow them. Our eyes were glued to the television screens. We would sacrifice the few hours of sleep we got for the show and talked about it amongst each other because there was simply nothing else in our lives. This was all we had, so we gossiped just to give our brain cells a little nudge.

We dusted, primed, chipped, sanded, painted, and the gossip kept our emotions alive. When our lives were a chipping hammer, haze grey, and the Navy's precious military bearing, we missed being hugged, kissed, and touched. We were humans that craved the feel of others' skin. Eventually, our bodies, minds, and emotions surrendered to our abnormal scenario. The crew inevitably found each other.

"I don't associate with people *from* work *outside* of work," Bambi proclaimed when we first met. "You get involved with your shipmates and you're asking for trouble."

But a few months later, she began dating one of our engineers.

My friend, Myleen, began fooling around with one of the married Quartermasters.

Diana, a thick, Midwestern girl with short blond hair, fair skin, and enormous boobs fell into a few flings with married men from her division.

Because we were a west coast ship, our deployments to the Persian Gulf were called Westpacs, short for West Pacific. It was common for a married man or woman to have a deployment girlfriend or boyfriend. Sailors called those temporary mates "Pac Snacks." Maybe the infidelity was dishonest, immoral, and bound to end horribly, but at the time I truly envied them. We all craved intimate companionship.

Ship socialization was madness. Once we stood topside and watched the land fade into the haze grey sea, our typical definition of right and wrong went with it.

I began to make friends. Just like every high school, the Higgins had its groups who generally stuck together. Mine were Yolanda and Myleen, the Filipino girl who was sleeping with the young married Quartermaster.

I couldn't fathom how Myleen ended up in the Navy. At five feet tall with a flat chest, Myleen always seemed like a little girl. Myleen didn't have the tough, raw attitude like Bambi. She cried easily and was embarrassed about simple things like her period. We became friends because of our similar situations. One of her best ship buddies had gotten pregnant and the other was kicked off for an affair with a married man.

Sally, my best ship friend, married her boyfriend, Jamie, and faked a sleepwalking condition to get medically discharged from the Navy. She, along with most Navy wives, packed on about sixty pounds shortly after.

Yolanda joined the crew about six months after my arrival. She was a Mexican twenty-one-year-old from Chicago. With long black hair, tanned skin, brown eyes, and a sharp nose, she initially seemed like a tomboy. But her curvy, perfectly proportioned figure and a light coat of eye shadow revealed an alluring side of her out of uniform.

Yolanda wasn't new to the Navy. She had to leave her former command because she married one of her shipmates. The two of them had a whirlwind romance that involved them going on a thirty-day unauthorized absence from the ship, followed by a Captain's Mast and demotion in rank. Despite her sketchy military record, Yolanda was made for the Navy. She boarded the Higgins with Bambi's sharp intuition and a thick skin.

It took a certain person to thrive in deck. It's easy for a new Seaman to arrive in clueless and the Boatswain's mates took advantage of that. We were instructed that busting our tails would gain us respect in the fleet, but in deck an enthusiastic work ethic was nothing but a verbal punching bag for superiors. Because they hadn't learned to navigate the bizarre social obstacle course of deck, new guys were given plenty of busy work for kicks.

"Your job today is to untangle those lines," one of the head Boatswain's mates instructed some of the new sailors.

He pointed to what was probably a hundred pounds of moldy, wet rope that had been abandoned in the cool, moist depths of the ship for several months. Of course, the amount of fungus that had eaten through its threads made it far too dangerous to use in any ship operations, but the Boatswain's mates weren't going to tell their Seamen that until they struggled over it.

Once people wised up, they skated. This was the route I took. It wasn't a respectable path. But once I realized the pointlessness of being a young deck monkey, I just waited for my time there to pass.

Until Yolanda joined our division, the only way I knew that anyone in deck could spare subtle bullying was by making rank. But Yolanda was taken seriously from her first day. She knew not to associate with people like Booger, she saw straight through any trickster assignments and she diverted her energy appropriately. Without guidance, she knew how to play the Navy game. When she knew she was being observed, she vigorously sanded the shit out of the ship. When she was out of sight, she relaxed. It wasn't just her work tactics that allowed her to fit in. Her personality was deck. I never understood why, but Yolanda befriended me instantly.

"I don't trust most of these bitches on board," she told me. "They were talking shit about everyone on my first tour around the ship."

With the Higgins being her second ship, Yolanda knew what a gossipfest ships were and had no desire to be a part of it. She carefully chose her friends and revealed very little of her personal life.

Although I enjoyed the company of my clique, I still felt very lonely and out of place on the ship. My existence felt monotonous, uneventful, and unfulfilling.

A melancholic feeling that I would be wasting my life away until the age of twenty-two hovered over me. I wondered what my life would have been like had I gone to college.

I got homesick. I missed my room in my parents' home, my dogs, and an overall sense of security of having family nearby. Since my freshman year of high school, I made every excuse I could to avoid my mother's trips to South Carolina to visit my grandparents, aunts, and cousins. Suddenly, I was unable to attend birthdays, holidays, or big family dinners. I wanted them again. I missed my mom the most and began to call her every other day. Despite my shame in being seen from the weight I had gained since boot camp leave, I looked forward to my visit home for Christmas.

For a short time, I was distracted from my rut by an unbelievably coincidental run in. It was an early November afternoon, cold anywhere else, but another seventy-degree sunny day in San Diego. I was walking from my car in a Wal-Mart parking lot when I heard a man say in a strong southern accent, "*Miss Maggie Young!*"

I was shocked to hear my full name called in an oddly familiar voice. The sound came from the window of a black car driving through the parking lot. I looked inside the window. Just before I could stutter, "Hey, do I know you?" I realized that it was the young recruiter from Chattanooga, my Number 8.

His twang made me realize how long it had been since I heard the familiar southern accents I had been submersed in since childhood. His voice alone gave me a world of comfort.

"Hey!" I greeted him enthusiastically, walking up to his car. "What the hell are you doing here?"

He looked good. I hadn't found Number 8 attractive until that day. He was out of his Navy working white uniform that made him look like a 1950s ice cream truck driver. What got to me the most were his glasses. I've always had a thing for guys with glasses.

"Ah've been in town for bout'a munth," he said, gleaming as he always did. "Don't ya remember, butt-face. Ah told you ah was comin' here."

Number 8 loved giving women childish nicknames. Instead of endearments like baby, honey, and sweetheart, it was butt-face, ass-eyes, sexy-pants, and my personalized name, "Maggie-pants."

"I'm on my way to a marina around here," he continued. "My dad's got his yacht docked there."

"*Yacht?* Wow, I didn't know you came from money!" I said, being obliviously untactful.

Number 8's smile just widened. He seemed to enjoy the way I spoke before thinking.

"Well, my dad is rich, but that's his money, not mine."

Number 8 had always been fiercely independent. His father was a prosperous businessman who had millions, but Number 8 refused financial help past high school.

"That's why ah joined the Navy," he later explained to me. "Ah wanted independence from ma parents. Ah figure, imma grown man and ma dad don't owe me a damn thing. I joined tha Navy to get on ma own two feet."

Number 8 was the only one out of his three siblings who did not experience an estranged relationship with his father.

"There're rumors that ma dad cheated on ma mom b'fore their divorce," he explained. "I don't ask because that's his business. But my brothers and sister quit speaking to him for a long time because of it."

"Why didn't you quit speaking to him too?" I asked.

"The way ah see it, him bein' a bad husband doesn't mean he loved me any less as a father."

Over the years, I would realize how similar he was to his dad. After the end of his first marriage, he showed little desire to hold a stable, healthy relationship with a woman. Number 8 was, and still is, remarkably fortunate for upholding his charming, loveable personality and an STD free dick. Number 8 was a sex addict.

Of course, at nineteen, I was oblivious to this side of him.

I didn't repeat my mistake of not leaving my phone number to Number 8. He called me a few days later.

Number 8 brought a bit of excitement back into my life and it was refreshing to have a new crush. I hadn't felt a hint of attraction for anyone since Number 4 and my new situation with Number 8 felt strangely familiar with that era. I wasn't full fledged into Number 8. Like Number 4, Number 8 was an average looking guy with a magnetic personality. Thinking about Number 8, I was still asking myself, "I never noticed him before, so why am I noticing him now?"

It's because I was desperate.

Several months after permanently letting go of my ex-boyfriend, I told myself that I was independent and strong. But truthfully, men were my validation, self-esteem, and my drug. I needed them like a crutch for a limp. I could barely walk.

"Am I going to sleep with him?" I wondered to myself as I drove to Number 8's place.

I didn't know myself well enough to realize that if I was questioning it, I was going to do it.

I looked like a mess with the wrinkled up, ink-stained paper that had the directions to Number 8's duplex. I was driving down some very confusing circular roads that went to the beach. I could see the sun leaning towards the westward ocean as the day got later.

"Hmmm. I'm going to Mission Beach, near Pacific Beach," I read to myself from the paper.

Seven months of living in San Diego and it still seemed enormous. At first, I was intimidated by any city with more than three interstates. As I got closer to Number 8's place, the electricity I felt when first arriving at the San Diego airport sparked again.

"Pacific Beach," known as PB to San Diegans was absolute paradise for any single person between the age of eighteen and twenty-five. Even as it got later into a November day, PB was still a lovely vision of coastal bars, skateboarders, surfers, Barbie's in bikinis, and shirtless white boys with board shorts and six-pack abs.

For those who only know California through movies, there is a major misconception about it. The stereotype is a visual of a Beach Boys song. But California is the most culturally and geographically diverse state in the nation. There are beaches, mountains, desert, redwood forests, and nearly every type of climate imaginable. Some parts are dryer than a hundred-year-old corpse and others are balmy as a rainforest. Those who have never been to California believe the entire state is Los Angeles, but I've driven through teeny, manure-scented towns nearly replicating the meth-saturated town of Sale Creek, Tennessee. But PB embodied the California stereotype.

All my childhood fantasies of the paradise that I imagined California to be came flooding back. I was there.

One of the most interesting things about San Diego County was how every little section fits a certain type of person. Chula Vista and Imperial Beach, which lined the Mexican Border, were filled with mostly Hispanic and military families. East San Diego areas like El Cajon, Lakeside, and Santee reminded me of Texas. The majority of people I knew who lived there literally wore cowboy hats and boots, went to rodeos, monster truck shows, and four-wheeled through the desert on the weekends. The north coast areas like La Jolla, Del Mar, and Solana Beach were the homes to San Diego's wealthiest residents. Ocean Beach, next to Mission and Pacific Beach, was for the laid-back hippies and hipsters.

Pacific Beach was the wildest section of the party town. It was an overpriced land of sketchy landlords, horny frat boys, and of course, cocaine. In PB, it was common to walk down the street smelling marijuana every other block or to see apartments with their doors wide open with gatherings of young adults drinking inside. It also wasn't rude to randomly show up to a shindig without knowing a soul. In the life I would later have in PB, I would spend many nights stumbling down the street after one party and randomly end up at another party full of inebriated, welcoming strangers.

Number 8 introduced me to PB.

"Hey Maggie!" he greeted me with a big hug as I got out of my car. It was so nice to be called "Maggie" and not "Seaman Young." I was a person again.

We went to a drug store and I watched him select liquor. His presence was still very surreal. I knew him from Tennessee, my old world. And here he was in the new one. The two significantly different parts of my life were clashing. There was something so unnatural about his highly distinguishable Tennessee twang by the beach. I enjoyed watching him flirt with the grey-haired woman at the cash register until she flushed pink and giggled as if he were tickling her feet. We left the store and drove back to his place. Reintroducing me to the southern chivalry I had long forgotten about, he opened every single door I walked through.

Number 8 emulated the typical Navy man stereotype that I'd come to know, except in the way he treated me. I noticed a significant difference between the way military men handled military women versus civilian woman. Civilians were ladies. Even if a Navy guy only saw her as a piece of ass, he was at least polite during the seduction process. But Navy women were below civilian women. They were treated like one of the guys as far as giving them shit about their looks, voice, the way their ass looked in a uniform, and the rumors of the people they fucked. But they were still expected to act like ladies and when they didn't, they were severely ridiculed and called whores in whispers.

With nothing feminine or dainty about my personality, I was an easy target. One of the things that hooked me to Number 8 was that he acknowledged my humanity. My standards had dropped to that.

The reason he treated me as like any civilian woman was because he knew nothing about Navy women. He was a submariner, which had yet to integrate enlisted females. On an all-male sub, he didn't have to worry about political correction. Sexually exploiting women was just another funny story in an overgrown, underwater fraternity.

After his divorce, Number 8 dove into party boy mode and never resurfaced. His life was an adventure. He worked with the boys, traveled the world, got drunk, and fucked lots of women. When he did date, he stuck to a "stripper only" policy.

The first thing I saw when I entered his kitchen was a huge photo on his fridge of five blonds lifting their shirts with their plump, silicone tits fully exposed.

"What the fuck?" I said, laughing.

"Yeah, those are some friends of mine from home," he said nonchalantly.

He skipped discretion.

"And at sum point, Ah've had every single wunnov those chicks naked in ma bed."

That photo was just one scrap of his collection. The refrigerator was completely plastered with an array of half nude, college-aged women in thongs, bikinis, or cut off shorts that showed off their bums as if ass cracks were the new cleavage. And of course, there were dozens of nipples in every shape, size, and color. They ranged from haggard to stunning. Each picture was taken at a party or bar. But one photo stood apart from Number 8's titty collage. The picture was of a little girl with strawberry blonde hair in a little league baseball uniform.

"Is that your daughter?" I asked him.

"Yeah, that's ma lil' girl," he responded proudly. "Her name's Amelie. She's six."

He'd mentioned his daughter a few times back in Tennessee, but it was when I saw her picture that her existence felt real. I tried to envision Number 8 as a father and husband.

"Just so you know," Number 8 told me, reaching for cups out of his cabinets, "Ah drink like a sailor. Ah git hammered every weekend."

I wanted to drink. Nothing did the trick of easing the tension of a first get together between opposite sexes like Number 8's concoction of hard liquor. Within a few sips, I was at ease.

We chit chatted about our families, his ex-girlfriends, my ex-boyfriends, and our Chattanooga connections. Like all PB residents, we left the doors wide open so we could face the beach and mingle with the intoxicated next-door neighbors. The guy was a thirty-three-year-old alcoholic who couldn't get past his beach bum twenties. The girl was nineteen just like me. She looked and sounded exactly like Courtney Love, extenuating her California valley girl accent with the mild vocal scratch of heroin.

Halfway into my Captain Morgan feast, details of the night got hazy. I don't know how late it was when I found myself alone with Number 8 on his couch again. Led Zeppelin's Houses of the Holy album was playing in the background and Number 8 was discussing his plans for placing an enormous plasma TV in his living room.

"That's ridiculous," I slurred. "A TV is a TV. Why the hell would you pay thousands of dollars for a fucking TV?"

Suddenly, the atmosphere felt very serious. The room grew silent and we made eye contact. We were going to kiss. It was an unspoken, mutual understanding.

"Ya know, ah always thought you were cute," Number 8 smiled.

"Cute," I mentally repeated the word to myself. "*Cute*. Thank God I am finally *cute* again."

For the first time in several months, I was more than the fat version of a girl who had once been cute. There was no way to tell whether Number 8 saw any beauty in me at all that night or if he was simply being his skirt-chasing self. But for the first time since my post-bulimia weight gain and submersion into ship life, I *felt* attractive. Just that soft, affectionate look Number 8 gave me made me want to preserve him for every time my heart grew heavy. Yes, subtle flattery got the best of me, but after months of its deprivation, I cherished it.
I wanted to bang him and not only because of how he made me feel. My vagina looked fucking *fantastic*.

"I need a ride somewhere," Bambi whispered to me about a month before my running into Number 8.

Bambi and I were in the berthing lounge on a Saturday afternoon. Our living space looked empty, but Bambi took no risks being overheard.

"Uh... okay," I tried to whisper back. "Where?"

With such intensity in her eyes, I thought she needed a lift to an abortion clinic.

"I want to get my clit pierced."

"Whoa!" I said a little too loud.

Bambi was always a mysterious person. She was serious, motivated, and very private. She never discussed her boyfriend with the other girls dishing out details of their romantic interests. Her true emotions were almost indistinguishable. She rarely wore makeup or did her hair. She allowed herself to be plain, so everyone would assume that she was just as prudent as she looked.

You had to *really* observe Bambi to understand her sexual side. Not only was she a motivated worker, she could easily combust over any hint of bullshit. Of all the females in deck, Bambi was the most threatening to the men. She not only was able to work and carry herself better than the rest of them, but she didn't allow herself to be objectified.

With women integrating into the ship, I knew many of them were secretly afraid of being professionally surpassed. This was a major reason men treated us with the level of respect of the prostitutes they bragged about gang banging. The majority of us, including me, fed into that ideology. The Navy didn't change the fact that we were products of a society that praised women for being pretty. So we cringed in our practical, but unflattering, uniforms. Us young ones smeared makeup on our faces and strutted our tails desperate for any acceptance we could earn. While we wanted to be alluring, Bambi saw through all that crap. At work, she got off on dominating the men, but was the polar opposite when it came to sex.

"Do not repeat what I'm about to tell you, Young," she told me on one of the rare occasions that she opened up. "I'm a freak in bed."

I laughed the word coming from her lips.

"I mean it," she continued. "I like for men to dominate me in bed. I like to get slapped, scratched, flung up against walls, and have my hair pulled. To me, getting the shit beaten out of me is hot. The more bruises, the better. I liked to get fucked like a cheap slut."

She called me out in the midst of my giggles.

"Whatever, Young. Don't think I don't know that you're the same way."

I didn't have a response to that. The fact was, I didn't really know myself sexually. I had never been courageous or comfortable enough to demand certain things. With my ex-boyfriend, any sexual criticism detonated his fragile ego. But, the fact that I still got chills thinking about the way Number 6 slammed me around the barracks lounge made me realize that Bambi might have been onto something.

I envied Bambi for knowing what she wanted. Although her body wasn't flawless, she appreciated it and knew how to pleasure it. I wanted to be more like her.

"Okay. I'll get my clit pierced with you," I said.

"We're not actually getting the clitoris itself pierced," she explained to me on the way to the piercing shop. "We're getting what's called a vertical hood piercing. Basically, the skin directly above the clit is pierced. Then you have a barbell with a metal ball constantly rubbing against your clit."

"Will I be able to walk after this?" I asked nervously.

"It'll be sore for a few weeks, but you'll be fine."

We walked into the tattoo shop to see two burly, inked lumberjacks at the front desk.

"Oh fuck, are we going to have to spread our legs for these guys?" I whispered to Bambi.

"I hope not," she whispered back.

To our relief, the piercer emerged from the back of the shop. *She* stood at about five feet tall with black bun pigtails to add to her inked schoolgirl look. She spoke with a British accent that added to her cutsie demeanor.

I can't remember whether Bambi or I went first, but neither of our experiences were the least bit horrible. It was a little awkward lying on a chair with my panties crumbled up in a corner on the floor. It felt like I was seeing my gynecologist, only there was the background sound of the drilling of people's skin.

I was on my back with my vagina exposed, listening to the powder puff piercer make small talk. Nirvana's song "Polly" was playing in the background. I was getting my clit pierced to a song about a girl being raped. I would forever think about that every time I would hear that song.

"Okay," the piercer warned me. "I'm going to pierce in one, two," and there it went.

It hurt for only an instant. After that, the pain completely diminished. It was the easiest, most low maintenance piercing I would ever have. My own urine was enough to sterilize it. I never had to change the barbell. It was mildly sore for three days. Three weeks later, getting myself off in the privacy of my rack got dramatically better. Although I never reached orgasm from climbing a flight of stairs, it certainly made bicycling and leg crossing a little more awesome.

For the final step in my vaginal makeover, Bambi took me to get my first Brazilian wax. We went to an overpriced, high-end salon that she visited regularly.

"For your first time, you want to be comfortable," she advised me. "Go to the cheap salons when you're used to getting hair ripped out of your twat. But for now, this girl is amazing and worth every penny."

Every spec of repressed male resentment ever harbored seemed to arise in lightning flashes of fury.

"This is what women go through for beauty?" I thought, in between excruciating rips of hair being yanked out of my flesh. "*Why?* Just so those fucking fuck tards don't have extra hair scratching their balls? Those shit heads need to suck their own dicks!"

Getting my hood piercing was a full body massage compared to waxing. With each new, never-ending rip, I wanted to scream, cry, and kick the esthetician's face in.

"You're doing good," she tried to sooth me as I gritted my teeth and struggled to suppress screams.

She got me involved as I held bits and pieces of my skin to tighten the areas she needed to pull from. I even had to roll over, get on my knees, and let her spread my ass cheeks ass as she ripped out the peach fuzz from my butt hole.

"We're just girls here," she said in a friendly tone.

The worst part was the end when the waxing was done. I knew that my vagina, which looked like it had taken a brutal paddling, was over abuse for the day. But the lady wanted me to get what I paid for and was determined to remove every single visible hair follicle. So she got a pair of tweezers and plucked, plucked, plucked.

"I'll be damned if I went through that torture for nothing," I thought.

I leaned in and kissed Number 8.

To my surprise, it was one of the best of my life.

I have no idea what it takes to create a good kiss. It's probably a combination of a lot of things from the way one person's tongue and lips correspond with the others to the type of feelings the people have for each other. I've had kisses that are great for their intimacy and their thrill. Something about Number 8's kiss was both.

I realized that Led Zeppelin's, *Dyer Maker* was playing in the background. We parted lips and I began singing, "*Ohh oh oh oh ohh ohh, you don't have to go-ohoh oh oh ohh.*" Number 8 jumped in with me and we began singing, "*All those tears I cry ay ay ay ayy ay,*" horribly out of tune. We kissed and sang, kissed and sang.

By the next song, we were in his bedroom. That is where our chemistry and most of my memory faded. I don't know how long the sex lasted, if it felt good, or if I felt anything at all for that matter. All I know was that at some point his penis was in my vagina.

I have a theory that Number 8 and I were so trashed that one of us, if not both, fell asleep in the middle of intercourse. That's if whatever we did was worthy of being called sex. I only remembered the cuddling, which was as amazing as the kiss. But it's rare that I can comfortably be held by anyone throughout the entire night. Number 8 was one of those exceptional men whose body gripped mine in flawless synchronicity. So, I let him cling to me and slept peacefully until my alarm went off at 6:00 am.

"Ugh, I have to go to the ship," I mumbled to myself.

Still drunk the next morning, I pried myself from Number 8's arms. It would be a year and a half before we would see each other again.

Number 9

The bleak period in my life darkened after Number 8.

My only friend from home had disappeared without a single phone call. Pushing a size sixteen, I was fatter than I had ever been and couldn't seem to shed it. I began jogging and ate ridiculously healthy. The berthing females were aghast at my self-discipline. Every time they made a comment like, "Damn, Young, you're so healthy," I fantasized about force feeding my fat to the girls that were thinner than me, yet spent the entire underway trips stuffing their faces with candy bars and Cheetos. Unfortunately, life's dilemmas were even bigger than my ass.

My cell phone was stolen the night before my ship went to sea for a week. I figured I'd just left it in my car. Nope. My thief racked up almost a thousand bucks worth of calls to the Philippines. I spent hours arguing, cursing, and finally pleading with my carrier. The bastards didn't budge. I grudgingly paid the bill to salvage my credit. Since I was flat broke, I was stuck spending my first California Christmas scrubbing the haze grey hulls of the Higgins. But even more disappointment came once the Navy advancement test results were released in early December.

Like the rest of my division, I was desperate to get out of deck. Although my recruiters and MEPS personnel assured me that once I did my time, I could choose any job I wanted, my chief's only response to his Seamen was, "YO ASS IS MINE, SHIT STAIN!"

The ship career counselor flashed me a glimmer of hope when he told me that I could test into an administrative field on the ship. For three months, I forfeited my free time to cram Bible-sized books with content that can only be described as a combination of dense instruction manuals and legal documents. Although I scored higher than eight-six percent of the other test takers, less than one percent was allowed to advance. My wasted months of mental masochism were the final blow to any investment I had in the Navy.

I met Number 9 Christmas Eve. Like Number 6, he was a Marine. And also like Number 6, he was dense.

One of my female shipmates invited me to a Christmas Eve party with some Marines in a base trailer park at Camp Pendleton. The base was about forty minutes north of San Diego. I would be waking my ass up before dawn to report to duty Christmas morning, but I was just grateful to be off the ship.

Number 9 lived next-door to the main party. I spotted him grilling steaks on their front porch. When my friend introduced us, I noticed his eyes lingering on me a bit longer than I expected.

I have a theory that men can smell a woman's promiscuity. It's as if their bodies are programmed to sense sexual availability so they fulfill their evolutionary role. Being vulnerable during my fat days, sex was my quick fix for self-assurance. So when Number 9 and I crossed paths, I'm pretty sure I reeked of it.

As we all got drunk, Number 9 and I attempted forced conversation. He didn't have a lot to say. It was awkward. He showed me his bowling ball collection.

"What is this dude thinking?" I thought. "Does he actually think I give a shit about bowling balls?"

"That one's really pretty," I half-heartedly chimed, pointing out a ball with green swirls.

"How many people have you killed?" is what I really wanted to ask.

Diana warned me about those dodgy topics.

"They've seen a lot of shit," she told me. "It really brings up a lot of bad memories and they don't like to talk about it."

Like most teenagers, I rarely thought about death. In high school, I lived like an immortal, snorting, smoking, and swallowing whatever mystery drug was handed to me, repeatedly vomiting my insides out. Sometimes I would lie in bed after purging, unable to sleep because my heart was pounding out of my eardrums.

"I'm going to have a heart attack," I'd think to myself.

I knew that something was physically wrong with me and it was only a matter of time before I'd push my body over the edge. Though I've never been religious, during those frightening nights, I would pray.

"God, please don't let me die," I'd plead. "I'll stop. I promise. I'm not ready to die."

I prayed from fear, not faith. Eventually, I'd fall asleep, wake up alive, and distract myself with more self-destruction.

Marines reminded me of death. Surrounded by them on Christmas Eve, there was an unspoken knowledge among all of us that they had killed. If there is nothing after death, they had taken everything away from someone else. I didn't look down upon them for it. In a war, there are very few bad guys on either side. The true villains are rarely the ones holding the guns or dodging the bullets.

I knew that if necessary, I could kill too, but I hadn't. They had literally deleted a human life. I wondered how they felt every time it had happened and if it changed them. Perhaps Number 9 and the other Marines I had met weren't dumb, but were simply a product of Uncle Sam's training. America *wants* the bulk of their troops to be unthinking, obedient dogs who will kill at the snap of finger.

Sometime late into the night, Diana stumbled me, drunk, into Number 9's bedroom.

"You can crash here tonight," she said, tucking me in his bed.

I was too tired to notice the piles of clothes on the floor, the lingering scent of Number 9's after shave, or the unmade bed that was so much more welcoming than my ship rack.

I immediately fell into a deep sleep.

A few hours later, Number 9 trudged into the room and crawled into bed with me.

I wondered why Diana had brought me to Number 9's bedroom in the first place. The whole scenario was so damn predictable. Of course we were going to fuck, but initially, I wasn't in the mood. As high as my sex drive could be, I was becoming concerned with the series of one-night stands that had been piling up. This Marine would be my fourth in a row, and I knew that we wouldn't date. We talked for a bit, discussed making out and I thought, "I love making out. I could just make out with him."

"Okay," I agreed, "but I'm not going to fuck you."

Making out turned into necking, heavy petting, and then intense dry humping. Number 9 stripped off his shirt and I was able to feel the hard arm and back muscles developed as a Marine.

"Let me eat your pussy," he pleaded.

I practically ripped off my jeans.

Number 9 truly appreciated female anatomy. He attacked my snatch like an all-you-can-eat buffet, aggressively digging his tongue inside and then sucking on my pierced clit while working multiple fingers in areas a cock couldn't reach.

"You taste really good," he commented in between mouthfuls.

"Huh?" I asked him, thinking that such an odd thing to say.

Having chickened out on eating a woman out when I had the chance, I had no clue what Number 9 was experiencing.

In my experience in having my carpet munched, most men were eager. Although I've kept track of the number of men I've had sex with, even more men have eaten me out.

I do not believe in women who do not like having their pussy eaten. They either haven't had a man- or woman- do it correctly, they're embarrassed of their taste, or feel uncomfortable with the entire position. It's not always easy adjusting to the sight of the top of someone's head bobbing and shaking so close to such a private spot. For me, once I let go of all of those concerns, I enjoyed it thoroughly.

With Number 9's face buried inside of me, my decision to stay abstinent that night seemed pretty pointless.

Number 9 was a much better pussy eater than lay, but he wasn't bad. He knew his way around a woman's body and was decently endowed. He didn't have Number 6's Marine aggression, but he was still dominant and fucked me on top.

Right before he climaxed, he shouted, "DO YOU LIKE THIS DICK?"

Shocked at the line that sounded like a cheap 1970s porno script, I could only whisper, "Uh… yes?"

"AAAARRRGGGHHHHH!!!!!!!!" he moaned.

His toned, sweaty body collapsed on top of me.

"She's not going to want a relationship or anything from me, is she?" Number 9 asked Diana about me the next day.

I woke up early, exhausted and hung-over to report to my Christmas Day duty.

It turned out Number 9 had girlfriend.

I laughed at his concern. I had Diana give him a picture that I had drawn with magic markers. It said, "I love you."

Number 10

"Something's got to change," I angrily muttered to myself.

It was Christmas Day. Instead of opening gifts by the fireplace in front of my parents' Christmas tree, I was painting the side of the USS Higgins.

On the bright side, my supervisor had been cool enough to let us deck monkeys sleep off our hangovers after the crew's morning muster.

Aside from a few people on watch, the crew got to spend a leisurely holiday dozing and watching movies in berthing. Except for us. Deck division was put to work. It had been Chief's order that the ship got painted on *Christmas Day*.

I could envision his fantasies as he sat down with his family to stuff his face with turkey for the holiday.

"Wow, deck is working their mindless asses off on Christmas Day!" he'd imagine them saying while observing us struggling not to fall over the side with a paintbrush in our hands.

"Their chief must really be determined to get things done on this ship. I hope he makes Senior Chief on the next advancement test cycle."

I didn't keep my irritation to myself either. I wasn't a proud, strong individual who kept my negative feelings secret. I vented.

"This is bullshit!" I huffed.

"Why the hell do we have to do this crap *today* of all days?"

Me, along with a couple fellow deck guys were in a bucket attached to some sort of crane on the pier. For Christmas, it was a warm sixty-degree day, but for San Diego, it felt like the Arctic. The sky was cloudy and the rest of the atmosphere matched the haze grey of the ship. We were wearing our traditional paint-splattered black boots and navy blue coveralls. I struggled to keep my Higgins ball cap on my head as the ocean breeze blew my blonde, messy bun out of place. One of the major uniform rules in the Navy was that all personnel had to keep a cover on when outside in uniform. If your cover fell into the water, you had to buy another from the ship's store. Everyone usually kept their rack stocked with two or three. The rule became so ritualistic that those few occasions of being outside in uniform without a cover felt uncomfortable. It was as if invisible acid rain fell from the sky and only our cover could protect our scalps from frying off.

"Young! Will you shut the fuck up?" One of the third classes in the bucket with me snapped. "It's Christmas Day and I'm on this goddamn boat, too. Do you think any of us want to be here? Your bitching and complaining isn't making it any more pleasant."

At that moment, the third guy in the bucket pushed a button on the control, which tilted us down towards the water, scaring the fuck out of us. The guy with the control began laughing hysterically, then the rest of us joined in.

Times like that made me think about Number 4. I missed him terribly. He hated being in the Navy as much as I did. He complained about it, but in a joking manner. The crew loved him because he was so laid back during even the shittiest situations. He probably would've helped me keep some positivity going. Six months after he was gone, it still made me a little sad.

I dwelled over both him and Number 8. I had been single since cutting things off with my ex-boyfriend. Once I was over him, I never went back. I can honestly say that I never spent a second of my life missing him or longing for him. The thought of fucking him still made me taste vomit. However, I was nostalgic about the companionship. At the peak of my chubbiness, having to work in unflattering Navy uniforms, my already low self-esteem plummeted. I *needed* that man to tell me I was attractive. I *needed* to be held and reassured that I was this amazing person that I didn't find myself to be. That man who was supposed to miraculously show up and fix my life never came.

I knew that for the most part, I wasn't liked on the Higgins. Although I won some respect from studying so hard for the YN test, almost all of it diminished when I didn't advance.

I didn't blame people for not liking me. The chronic bitterness I held in my heart showed in my personality. By nature, I was passionate and expressive. Emotions like sadness and loneliness were projected into relentless, loudmouthed whining. In an already less than ideal situation, who wants that around? What bothered me was my reputation for being the biggest dumb blonde on board. Until I got to the boat, I had always been considered intelligent. Sure, I was ridiculously clumsy and had a tendency to daydream myself into a fiction. But I'd been a smart kid and everyone knew it. There was something about Navy life that I couldn't catch onto. The way things worked, the manner in which everyone interacted, the endless rules, and the orders I was given confused me. It felt like I'd landed on another planet.

I reacted slowly to everything around me. I let my vivid daydreams conquer my brain because drowning out the real world was much more pleasant. I appeared dumb.

My relationship with the crew was a vicious cycle. They thought I was stupid. I sensed it so often that I began to believe I *was* stupid. This made me behave even more stupid, further instilling their beliefs. The crew resented me and I felt that resentment.

I mentally clung to Number 8 because he was an escape from the ship. The sex with him had been literally forgettable, so I didn't long for him in that way. I thought about his optimism, smile, warm, and comforting arms that wrapped around my body. More than even Number 8 himself, I thought about his apartment off the beach. It was his simple, five hundred-square-foot, one bedroom on the sand that I wanted the most. I fantasized about having a place like that to retreat to after a day of haze grey and scrubbing rust. I wanted the sanctuary of a couch, a bed, and a warm body to lie next to.

I blamed myself for Number 8 dropping out of my life. I took those good old-fashioned Tennessee double standards I was raised with. I came to the conclusion that it was my fault for allowing Number 8 to put his penis inside my vagina. After all, men can't help themselves. It's the woman's job to call the shots. It's her fault if she spreads her legs too soon and he loses interest.

I grew up hearing with famous cliché, "Why buy the cow if you're getting the milk for free?" No wonder Number 8 had disregarded my existence.

Our workday ended up being short on Christmas. I'd thrown a fit over two hours of painting.

We were served some dry turkey in the galley that I didn't touch. I was never huge fan of galley food. It always had a stench that reminded me of my elementary school cafeteria.

I went to the forecastle of the ship where we were permitted to make calls. I talked to my parents and retired to berthing to watch movies before bed. The next day, I was at a laundromat in Chula Vista, an area of San Diego just south of base, when I really began to evaluate my current situation.

I laid everything out, flat and simple.

"My life sucks right now," I thought. "I'm not happy. I need to fix it. What can I do to fix it?"

I listed my biggest issues to myself.

"I'm fat. I hate my body."

"I'm lonely."

"I didn't strike out of deck."

"I am constantly stuck at work. I live where I work. People from work surround me. There is no escaping the Navy. It's driving me insane."

I realized that it wasn't the chipping, priming, painting, muster, or duty days that were getting to me. What drove me into constant melancholia was not being able to escape it. I lived on the ship. In order to get to my own thin, hard bed, I had to salute the American flag, climb down steep ladder wells, and jump up to a bed I couldn't even sit up in. I couldn't sleep in late without hearing morning announcements to the duty section blaring through the 1MC. Ship life could be bearable if I had a sanctuary to retreat to.

Eating cereal in my pajamas on the living room carpet in front of the television on a Saturday morning was such a simple pleasure that I took for granted as a civilian, but suddenly it became a dream.

Since boarding the Higgins, the only times I'd slept in a real bed were after banging some guy. But my subconscious hopes of a permanent warm body to lie next to in his warm cozy bed stopped seeming like a logical expectation.

"I have to move off this ship," I thought.

It suddenly seemed vital for my survival.

"How the hell am I supposed to afford a place in San Diego?" I wondered.

My base pay was about twelve hundred dollars after taxes. I was making about the same amount of money as a full-time, minimum waged fast food worker, except that there was no overtime in the military and no ability to work a second job. Even rent in a shitty one-bedroom in San Diego would eat over half of that.

The only way I could afford a place off base was to receive BAH, Basic Allowance for Housing.

There were few ways to qualify. I could get single BAH if I was on shore duty. Although I would've eagerly eaten cat shit for the opportunity to have a work location that didn't float on water, the U.S. Navy wasn't an organization that allowed you to just pick up and transfer to any location you desired. As a Deck Seaman, shore duty was out of the question.

I could get BAH as an E5. Having six more months until I got the chance to advance to E4 in an over-manned rate, I knew that could take *years*. My patience couldn't handle years. I could also qualify for BAH if I had a dependent, like a spouse or child. This was the most popular route for sailors to take.

"By the time your first year in the Navy is over, at least half of you will be pregnant," I remember Petty Officer Hunter telling the women in berthing towards the end of boot camp.

Fertility seemed to magically bloom upon entering the fleet. It was like our tampons were soaked with semen.

Required to leave sea duty during pregnancy, girls were dropping like flies off the Higgins. Myleen and I were the only two on our isle of racks without a bun in our ovens. Part amused and part scared, we wondered if the isle was cursed and even took pregnancy tests together.

Berthing babies seemed to be the cool thing for sailors to do. Every shore duty station on base was crawling with pregnant chicks. It was impossible to update your Navy ID or get decals for your car without interacting with bloated, crabby wenches in baggy maternity utilities hanging over their protruding bellies. They were spotted all over base picking up garbage with sticks. There were more pregnant women than the Navy knew what to do with.

"Better have all my kids now while the government will pay for the hospital bills," I often heard them say. Although they had a point, those girls were usually young and in unstable relationships.

With free birth control, I wondered how pregnancy was so common. Then it occurred to me that those women were probably suffering the same struggles as I was. They were lonely, out of place, and tossed into an uncomfortable environment. Even I could see how the idea of a cuddly little life to unconditionally love you seemed appealing and I didn't even like kids. Children were a ticket off the ship and a doubled paycheck.

A baby was out of the question for many reasons. I was never really into babies. Whenever a shipmate would bring her bundle aboard, Myleen, Yolanda, and the rest of the girls would hover around it, oohing and ahhing like it was some magnificent creature. I didn't find babies repulsive, just kind of boring. I would just glance at it and say something awkward like, "Nice baby." I was nowhere near ready to become a mother. Plus, I wanted to *lose* weight.

"Too bad I'm not married," I thought sarcastically.

When I first met the crew of the USS Higgins, I found it shocking how many sailors *were* married. Expectedly, the older sailors had spouses and children, but the majority of the younger ones were also wedded. It was common to see whirlwind marriage spring from boot camp and the Navy A-schools that followed.

One of my fellow Deck Seaman met her husband in boot camp. They got married directly after the graduation ceremony.

"How did you manage to get to know him?" I asked her.

"We were in ship staff together," she explained.

Ship staff is a group of recruits that clean up the barracks building and take turns doing the ceremonial hanging of the American flag at sunrise and sunset. I, myself, had been a part of it and couldn't comprehend how anyone could form a deep connection there. We weren't even allowed to talk to each other beyond a few basic words of communication.

Although I found the marital statistics outrageous, it makes more sense when you evaluate Navy society. Sailors are human. Atmospheres like boot camp and deployment where we're restricted from affection tend to make us crave it more. Deployment is notorious for making and breaking relationships. They break because a couple can't handle the strain of separation or because that distance altered their connection. They make relationships because loneliness exaggerates emotions. After months of working long hours among the land of haze grey without so much as a hug from anyone, it's easy to fall in love.

To this day, the military still carries these 1950s values of idealizing young families. A single sailor lives in a small rack with disgusting galley food to eat. A married sailor gets a food allowance, base housing, or a big fat check that'll take care of all the rent.

This pushes couples to marry young and fast. Many times, I saw the situation where a couple was dating. Then, one got orders far away. They wanted to stay together and just decided, "We love each other. What the hell? Let's just get married." Or a military member would be dating a civilian who needed medical insurance. They'd just push their relationship up a notch and tie the knot. There were few relationships without marriage soon to follow.

As a result, divorce was extremely common, too. I knew a few guys in their third marriage before age thirty. That extra pay can be so tempting that it drives people to use any excuse to get hitched.

"A marriage certificate would more than double my pay," I thought.

The idea was absolutely insane. I came from a family barren of divorces. My mother and aunts had weddings where they donned the traditional white puffy dresses with flower girls to sprinkle their paths with rose petals. Marriage was supposed to be a sacred, long-term commitment and I was seriously considering booking it to the courthouse with some guy for the money. I knew many guys who did the same thing. Two of them even married each other's girlfriends for the money. One had a wife who was only in the marriage for the medical benefits. He collected one hundred percent of the cash and completely lost touch with her a few months later.

Many people split with their spouses, but stayed legally married. The lived in separate homes, had new significant others, and collected their marital benefits for years.

I considered how others would judge me. I knew exactly what many people would think of my actions, because I would've had the same opinion a year earlier. Until experiencing the ship living quarters while working many hours for little pay, I would've found matrimony for a paycheck blatantly immoral.

"I drink. I curse. I have premarital sex," I thought. "I already do things that others think are sins. But those aren't my morals. If I believed the things I did were wrong, I wouldn't do them."

I had to ask myself, "Would marrying someone for the BAH be *wrong*?"

According to the Navy regulations, I had to be legally married and financially support my spouse. There were no rules about having to feel a certain emotion for your husband or wife because it was an intangible restriction. There were no guidebooks instructing military members how to go about in their marriage, forcing them to snuggle or fuck a certain number of times per week. Technically, I'd be following the rules.

I didn't understand why the military would put a price on marriage. In most cases, one works a certain job and gets a salary for that job regardless of whether they are single or married with ten kids.

Why the hell does having a spouse automatically entitle someone to so much more money? My marriage was a moral grey area, but so was the way the Navy treated people on a daily basis. I thought about the manipulative recruiters and their "undesignated Seamen" programs, the debauched advancement process, and my command's lack of concern for the living conditions of *all* its personnel. I understood that I signed a contract and vowed to serve my country regardless of any bullshit that may have arisen. I *was* following their rules and if I married for the BAH, I would still be following the rules.

I made up my mind.

One year into my enlistment, I was officially betrothed. My new husband was Elvis, my former make-out fling and Mexican jail cellmate. He was the only person I wanted to get into this temporary marriage with for several reasons.

First and foremost, I knew him. I did not trust him fully and completely with every part of myself, but Elvis was no criminal. I'd never seen him do a malicious thing to anyone and he'd always given me the vibe of being a genuinely good guy. Elvis was also in the position where he needed this marriage more than I did. He had just gotten discharged from the Navy and was flat broke. I was his girl.

I called him a day or two after my deep thinking session in the laundromat. I had researched the cost of marriage and divorce, along with the BAH we'd be receiving. Marriage was easy in California. The quickie courthouse ceremony and the marriage license would total up to about a hundred bucks. Since we weren't going to have children or buy any property together, divorce would only be about three hundred bucks and would take about six months after filing to be final. Those were small prices to pay for living in San Diego for free.

"Let's get married, Elvis!" I exclaimed, thrilled with my brilliant plan. "We'll get an apartment and be roommates! Sure, we'll technically be husband and wife, but that's just according to the government on some sheet of paper."

It didn't take much convincing to get Elvis in.

"Okay, I'll do it," he said casually, as if I was asking him to buy me a beer.

Luckily Elvis's new girlfriend, Zahara, had no issues with the marriage. She actually thought it was funny. We were good to go.

We arrived at the courthouse on a Wednesday afternoon after I'd gotten off work. It was a beautiful, light pink Spanish-style building with a dark pink stucco roof surrounded by palm trees.

When I got through security and walked up the stairs with Elvis to fill out our marriage paperwork, I was ashamed of what I was about to go through with. I wasn't feeling guilty for deceiving the Navy with my motives for getting married. I was just embarrassed that I was becoming another one of the military's young wives. Of course, I wasn't falling head-over-heels in love under some misconception that we would be together forever, but the courthouse staff didn't know that. For every person that interacted with us, I wanted to shout out, "This isn't a real marriage! We're just doing it so the Navy will pay us more money! We don't even love each other! Hell, we aren't even going to fuck! I swear I am not some idiot entering a real marriage at nineteen!"

We filled out all of our paperwork that would go on our marriage certificate. For my occupation, I put "deck hand" because I didn't know what else to write.

"Ugh, how tacky is that?" I thought. "Getting married as a 'deck hand.'"

Most of the girls I'd gone to high school with were probably shopping for orange dresses for the weekend University of Tennessee game and there I was chipping paint of a Navy ship and marrying a friend for money.

With San Diego being such a Navy dominated city, I wondered how many young, lonely sailors came to the courthouse together for a cheap, immediate marriage. As Elvis and I waited in line for our ceremony as if updating our driver's license in the DMV, I knew that we were a true statistic.

We didn't bring a witness with us on our quick, matrimonial errand. The court volunteered a staff member to escort us to their "chapel."

I struggled not to bust out laughing as we recited our vows.

"Calm down, Fuckstick," Elvis whispered to me.

I struggled so hard not to combust into laughter that tears rolled down my cheeks.

"I'm getting *married*!" I thought, more and more amused as the seconds passed by in that chapel. "WHAT THE FUCK?"

As the woman, who I'm assuming was some ordained minister, recited the vows we had to repeat, I knew that our marital bliss looked as fake as our marriage would be. We held each other's hands limply. There was a camera propped in the room that recorded each ceremony. Couples could buy a DVD of it and I wish we had because it would have been so damn funny to watch years later.

"Do you two have any rings to exchange?" Our minister asked.

"Uh…. No," we both replied uncomfortably. "

"Have you written any personal vows for yourselves?"

"No, let's just do the basic marriage stuff," I replied, a bit snappy.

She proceeded to recite the "Do you take him, do you take her forever through sickness, 'til death and blah blah blah," stuff.

Both of us repeated her vows off cue as if was the most mentally challenging obstacle we'd ever encountered.

After I stuttered an uncomfortable, "I d-d-do," Elvis leaned down to kiss my lips in a stiff peck.

I wished the kiss was more realistic because of how cold and fake the rest of our ceremony was. It wasn't like we'd never made out before. But I'm assuming he kissed me like I was his grandmother out of respect for his girlfriend.

Upon getting hitched, I learned an important lesson about the military. When it comes to paying personnel, they are slow as hell. Even after my enlistment, I would have to deal with the Veterans Administration (VA) taking months to get my GI Bill payments in for school. I realized that it was essential to anticipate the government's tardiness and always store plenty of cash in savings. Unfortunately, I hadn't grasped the way things functioned at the time of my marriage. I was broke and ill prepared for carrying on the charade as a married young Seaman.

"You shouldn't sleep on the ship anymore," Elvis suggested. "It would look pretty suspicious if you got married and were still sleeping on board."

It would be at least a month until I had the BAH to get an apartment and my bank account was frighteningly low. There was absolutely no way I could put a deposit down on an apartment before my marriage money came through.

Being a courteous husband, Elvis invited me to crash at the place he had been staying. It was an apartment that belonged to one of my Higgins shipmates, my Number 10.

I had known Number 10 since boarding the Higgins. In many ways, he was the typical Navy guy stereotype. At twenty-three, he had already been married and divorced once. He would have two more marriages in his twenties.

He was a fire controlman (FC) who belonged to a clique of guys who were mostly other FCs and Gunners Mates. Elvis was the only paper pusher in the group. Generally, all of these boys had one primary thing in common: they all wanted to be hard core killers like Marines, yet ended up floating on metal.

Some of them were there because they wanted to be Navy Seals, but failed Buds training. One guy flunked out three times, but was still desperate to return. A few in the group satisfied their craving to be badasses by joining the ship's Visit Board Search and Seizure (VBSS) team where they boarded suspicious vessels to check for drugs and any other security threats. VBSS let them play GI Joe, don bulletproof vests, and hoist guns around their shoulders. Although Number 10 had been among the VBSS crew, he failed their swimming test and was eventually kicked off.

"Dude, why can't you pass the swim test?" I once heard a guy ask him.

"Genetics!" he proclaimed.

Number 10 was half black and half white, but referred to himself as "halfrican."

Hailing from a small town in Texas, I wondered if he'd been the lone interracial kid at the butt of constant categorizations. He emulated and referred to himself in many black and white stereotypes. According to Number 10, his inability to be a strong swimmer, his dick size, and love for thick white women were from his black genes. His passion for metal music and dialect were his inner Caucasian.

He lacked any kind of accent. His voice was expressive and slightly erratic. He'd watch a movie that frustrated him and instead of saying something like, "Wow, that really makes me angry," he'd shout, "That movie pisses me the fuck off! I want to go kill a motherfucker right now! I want to take those guys in that movie and cut of their cocks and force feed their own dicks to them until they choke on their own genitals!"

Despite the aggression and dire need to be a violent warrior, Number 10 was a really nice guy. He was an E5 and qualified for single BAH, therefore was able to afford his own apartment. It was a modest three-bedroom in Point Loma, an area just north of downtown and a short drive from the beach.

Number 10 had two other roommates, plus several people floating in and out, crashing on couches when in need of a spot to sleep. Elvis was one of the regulars as well as my eternally immature, but sweet, friend Devi.

At nineteen, Devi was pregnant by one of the guys on board. She was still smoking, partying into the wee hours of the night, and couch surfing in chaotic, bustling places like Number 10's apartment. Still a frail ninety pounds, there was something incredibly disturbing about seeing her protruding belly with a cigarette in her hands and no comfortable home of her own. The Navy did provide a barracks room for her, but she had no car or driver's license and relied on friends' rides. I'm sure she preferred the soft couch cushions and abundance of hookups.

Devi was a pitiful mess, going days without bathing or brushing her teeth and always asking for money. She had a horrible inability to take care of herself. She should have had her tubes tied from the first drop of period blood. Yet, even throughout her pregnancy, Devi *always* had a boyfriend. By age twenty-five, she would be through two marriages and on her fourth engagement.

But it's the women like Devi who are never single. These women are not beautiful, intelligent, or strong. They're frail, irresponsible and immature; they're legally fuckable adult children. Maybe it has something to do with a male fantasy of being the masculine hero to save the little woman from her hardships. Devi needed a lot of rescuing.

Although Number 10 and I weren't close friends on the Higgins, he welcomed me right in.

"Dude, I understand what its like going without BAH," he assured me. "I've been there and it sucks."

The living room was packed with squatters. Devi and her current boyfriend were occupying one couch, Elvis and Zahara another. There was another free couch for me to sleep on, but Number 10 offered me his bed.

Physical intimacy was nonchalant for me. I could have still been adjusting to my post-Number 3 singledom, or maybe the loneliness I felt onboard the ship was impacting me greater than I realized. I hardly knew Number 10, but didn't think twice about jumping in his soft, king-sized bed with his tattooed arms wrapped around my body.

For a week, we spent each night curled up in his bed and talking until we fell asleep. I realized that both of us had a few unexpected things in common. He, too, had done meth before the Navy. Both of us smoked it out of tin foil and had a permanent habit of grinding our teeth. Number 10's was so bad that his teeth shredded through a retainer the first night wearing it.

"A buddy of mine actually mailed me some in boot camp," he confessed. "I snorted it in the bathroom. I was a machine at PT that day."

He told me about the marriage he'd gotten into at nineteen during his Fire Controlman A-School. He was one of the many sailors who had their romantic withdrawals in boot camp and relentlessly charged into matrimony.

"So, now, I don't date. I just don't do it," he said flatly. "I have sex with women, but I don't date them."

Fortunately, I had no desire to date Number 10, but a slight physical attraction was developing. Number 10 and I had always been cordial on board. We would say hello when we passed each other in the p-way, but that was as far as it went.

But suddenly, he started smiling at me more. He got that gleam in his eye that I had learned to recognize in men. With each night we spent together, tension inevitably cultivated. It wasn't something we spoke of, but was simply a silent understanding as our spoons gradually got tighter. I began to feel chills when our skin fleetingly brushed.

Predictably, talk about sex arose.

Though Number 10 wasn't gorgeous, he certainly wasn't bad looking. He was average height, and had light brown eyes that matched the reddish tint of the very short, wool-textured hair on his head. His skin was a fair brown with a few freckles across his nose. My friend, Hannah, slept with him a month before and had flattering things to say about both the size of his dick and his bedroom skills.

"Just let me go down on you," Number 10 finally persisted one night. "You don't have to touch me. Just let me eat you out. I like doing it."

"Okay, that's innocent enough," I thought. I was never particular on who I let go down on me. "I'll just drop my pants and let him put his tongue in my vagina. No harm in that."

It had been a crazy year. I'd had a threesome with a married couple, been to Mexican jail, married a man for a chunk of money from the government, and had a slew of one-night stands. I was latching onto my southern teachings by the tips of my fingernails

I let Number 10 go down on me. He was great at it, even better than his predecessor. Hours later with his fingers and tongue still digging into me, my clit was completely numb.

The following morning, I hobbled around the topside of the Higgins, my cunt sore from its beating. The pain made me grin. Promiscuity was the only inkling of empowerment I'd felt in my life. I held my head high, assuring myself that I could do whatever the hell I damn well pleased and was morally justified in doing so.

"I'm a young, single woman," I told myself. "He's not married. He doesn't have a girlfriend. Really, what's the harm in sleeping with him? I doubt he'll tell anyone on the boat. What's so damn wrong with a woman getting sexual pleasure from a man?"

Number 10 fucked the shit out of me that evening.

As a child of the millennial generation, I was raised in a society in which we were under the misconception that women and men had reached equality. With the exception of very few matriarchal societies, women were more liberated than they had ever been in history. In America's middle class, basic education was practically handed to us. We have the ability to obtain a higher education and career without men. So it took me nearly a decade after becoming sexually active to realize that, as a woman, I was socially oppressed. I grew up in a world where a woman's abstinence until marriage was highly praised and if she must participate in premarital sex, to limit that activity to as few partners as possible. It was considered tacky to openly discuss my sexual encounters. I was also taught that, as a woman, I was hormonally programmed to be more emotional than men. If I had sex with a man, I was supposed to feel some sort of intimate attachment. If I didn't, I was a cruel-hearted slut.

"When it comes to sex, women have the control," I so often heard men claim when we were having discussions about the differences between the sexes. "Men have no willpower. They always want sex no matter what. A woman can just walk into a bar, offer her body to a man, and get laid whenever she wants to. Women always get to decide when to have sex."

This put far too much pressure on me. Males were expected to be ready to fuck any hole they could slip their dicks into. Boys weren't considered men unless they were influenced by their carnal instincts to spread their seed.

While men had the right to obey their biological urges, women had to suppress theirs until the perfect moment. From television, movies, books, magazines, my peers, and even some of my relatives, I was taught that if a woman allowed a man to penetrate her too soon, she was too easy of a conquest for him. He would move on to pursue greater challenges after he was finished using her body to relieve his sexual urges. If the woman waited too long to let the man enter her body, she was a prude and the man would eventually give up on her. Women needed to time this process perfectly so that she could "keep" a man in her life at all times.

It was the man's goal to *catch* the woman and the woman's goal to *keep* the man.

I'm pretty sure this mentality came from centuries of women's financial dependency on whatever husband they could catch. As recently as my own grandmother's generation, a woman almost always had to manipulate a man into a marriage for the sake of economic survival.

Somewhere along the line, that dependency evolved from financial to emotional.

Every book written about a woman or movie starring a woman needs to end happily with finding her Mr. Right.

Was capturing the heart of my dream man the only way to achieve true happiness and fulfillment? For many years, I believed so. I had not found the right guy. That scared the shit out of me.

There was huge variety in Numbers 1 through 9. I'd fucked a possible suicidal rapist, a drug addict, an underachieving house painter, a married man, some of Uncle Sam's finest womanizers, and a couple of his oblivious executioners. For half a second, I had secret hopes that each of these men would suddenly transform into a Prince Charming who would completely fulfill me. For one night, Number 10 set me free. For some reason, when I was with him, I felt comfortable with myself.

What the hell?

Me. Naked.

Completely naked.

With a man.

Naked and chunky, with a man who could see my rolls, cellulite, and flabby bulge at the bottom of my belly.

Before Number 10, I thought I was comfortable with sex. I would groan and moan, sometimes screaming things like "Oh, God!' "Oh, Fuck!" "Fuck me harder!" "Faster!" "Harder!" "Harder!!!"

Thanks to a two-year relationship with Number 3, I was excellent at faking orgasms. I had screwed in all sorts of positions, locations, and orifices. I was not that prude, stiffly lying on my back, terrified of the one-eyed snake. But, without realizing it, I was *incredibly* self-conscious. I couldn't have sex without paranoia for how I looked, moved, sounded. I was so focused on self-consciousness that I forgot the whole purpose of sex was to *enjoy* it.

Number 10 made me not care about how I looked to him or even whether or not he was having a good time. I didn't want a relationship with him.

I could have just bought into Number 10's racial stereotype humor and assumed that any man with a drop of African blood in him was going to be attracted to a woman with 'meat on her bones'. I rarely thought about his racial heritage, but the feel of his hair texture when his head was between my legs always startled me a bit.

Number 10 was simply a cool person. I didn't feel like he was judging me by what I did with him. It was an "I don't want to be with you forever, but let's just get it on and have a good time" situation.

He welcomed me in his home, let me sleep in his bed, and gave me the choice of whether or not to have sex with him. Since I didn't have feelings for him,

I refused to give oral. Back then, the blowjob cat and mouse chase was my method of ethical compromise. I still carried the southern mentality that only whores give head. He didn't give me hell about it and in fact, claimed that it just made him want to go down on me more.

I was on birth control and Number 10, a huge supporter of safe sex, was a condom Nazi. I felt both physically and emotionally safe. I surrendered my body to my instinctual desires. I let Number 10 forcefully strip my clothes off.

"Thank God he can channel all that aggression to the bedroom," I thought, as he roughly maneuvered his body into mine and hammered his cock inside of me.

"Wow," I thought to myself the second he went inside me. "Hannah wasn't kidding."

"Holy fuck, you're huge!" I exclaimed.

"Genetics," he huffed.

When he flipped me over and screwed me from behind, my forehead began hitting the headboard.

"Maggie, your head," he mumbled, not pausing the rhythm of thrusting himself inside of me, over and over again.

"I-DON'T-CARE!" I shouted, out of breath and far too into the sex to give a damn.

"I DON'T CARE!"

"BANG!" went the headboard, as he shoved his dick inside of me again.

"I DON"T CARE!"

"BANG!"

"I DON"T CARE!"

"BANG!"

"I DON'T CARE!"

"BANG!"

From there, I completely let myself go and did whatever the hell I wanted. In the midst of pleasurable body spasms, I began to yank the fuck out of my own hair.

"Oh my God, you're just trying to make me cum too soon aren't you?" he responded, apparently enjoying the vision.

"Put your finger up my ass!" I ordered, out of breath.

Number 10 continued banging me until my bones felt like Jell-O.

"Let me change the sheets really quick." Number 10 said, just as I noticed a rather large wet spot in the middle of the bed that definitely wasn't urine.

"Was that you?" I asked, puzzled, because he came in the condom.

"No, that was you," he beamed.

Number 11

It only took weeks into my marriage to realize that I did it purely out of impatience. It was February and the Higgins would be leaving for a six-month deployment in early May. This meant a ship training cycle with a series of underways that sometimes lasted as long as three weeks. I would have little time to enjoy that precious civilian apartment I jumped into matrimony for.

Refusing to admit that perhaps I'd done something careless, I ignored those thoughts. I ignored many things during that time. I ignored my shady landlord and the dirty condition of the apartment I put a deposit down on all too eagerly. I ignored Elvis's cigarette smoking inside our place, not even considering my lungs or the stench it left in even the bath towels. I ignored how much it bothered me that Zahara got to live with us without contributing a dime.

But they were good people and my apartment was Buckingham fucking Palace compared to the ship and a tranquil getaway next to the hustle and bustle of Number 10's chaotic digs.

We meant to have sex again, but it just never happened and he quickly moved on to another girl onboard. Soon afterwards, he was engaged to a woman in Texas. Nobody had known about the relationship. Once I moved on to fooling around with one of his other squatters, I knew I was overstaying my welcome. As soon as my BAH came in, I rented out the cheapest two-bedroom in Pacific Beach I could find. Although I was living in the same area of Number 8's incredible apartment, I was a mile from the coast and would not discover PB's glory until later. From then until after deployment, I would be grudgingly occupied with all things Navy.

In the midst of preparing myself for the endless drills, paint chipping, and watch standing, I started an affair with a guy on board. Matty was eleven years my senior and married. I initially noticed him during my early days on the Higgins. I was in the ship's Medical turning in my records. Matty was there shooting the shit with our senior corpsman, who the crew called Doc. He gave me an intense enough look to make me remember him. We never worked together in port, so I hardly spoke to him until we consistently started going out to sea.

Matty was a Quartermaster, which is one of the oldest jobs in the Navy. From the Navy's infancy, Quartermasters navigated the ship. When the ship was out to sea, there was always at least one of them on the bridge where we Deck Seaman stood watch. Because Matty didn't have to stand in one spot for his entire watch, he would sometimes step outside to port and starboard lookout to keep me company.

I knew Matty during what I assumed was a rut in his life. He had just turned thirty-one and was regretting enlisting in the Navy. Being a Navy Seal was his childhood dream, but he was dropped from Buds within the first week. He found himself aboard our haze grey, taking orders from those much younger and less educated.

Matty was in a sexless marriage. Apparently, her pussy was the Sahara.

"She has a lot of problems," he'd complain to me while we were on watch. "She was abused when she was younger and literally can't enjoy sex. I can't do anything for her."

Matty tried to have these exploitative, overly personal conversations with other Deck Seaman girls as well. But they realized how inappropriate it was for Matty to vent such personal information to them. I, on the other hand, thought nothing of it. I loved talking to Matty. He was funny and kept my watches interesting. In comparison to staring out at the ocean in silence, I was thrilled to hear about his wife's desiccated muff.

"Try therapy," I offered. "Or just use a ton of lube on her."

My suggestions were useless. More was at stake than just Matty's marriage and sex life. The guy, in all his failures, was *severely* emasculated.

My own self-esteem was at a low point. I cowered in fear of Dino's fat jokes, avoiding him when he was on one of his smart-ass rampages. Just as I had during my bulimic years, I refused to have my photo taken and struggled to conceal raging annoyance every time Myleen or Yolanda whipped out their cameras. Every time I'd watch them pose at flattering side angles, pushing out their tits and sucking in their stomachs, I wanted to yank their scalps out of their heads in a jealous fit. I used to be a pretty girl, and I fucking missed it. I wanted vanity.

Since the weight gain, I never looked at my own naked body. Even while showering, I was repulsed when I had to look down at my stomach while scrubbing myself off. But Matty was drawn to my depressing damsel demeanor.

I never met Matty's wife, but head about her from him and many of his friends on the ship. She was pretty, intelligent, and sugar sweet.

"She's put up with so much of his shit. He doesn't deserve her," I once heard a friend of Matty's remark.

His wife was educated and held a job that designated her as the breadwinner between them. I on the other had, was his ego booster. I was the ditzy blonde chunk with a plain face and no college degree. With no self-love, his attention was a gift to me. And he knew it.

One night, Matty finger banged me on every single watch station I was on - including the helm. His fingers were up my cunt while I was steering the USS Higgins. Even though no penile penetration was involved, it was definitely my riskiest sexual escapade. The bridge was packed with a full staff of officers, a Boatswain's Mate, some Deck Seaman, and an operation's specialist. It was a late night watch and the bridge was nearly pitch black except for the illumination of the buttons, numbers, and gadgets for operating the ship. With both of us legally married, we would have been fried for our escapades. One may wonder how this was possible without having to yank my pants down in the center of the bridge. Coveralls. They were our official underway attire and zipped from the top and bottom, quite convenient for male urination and foreplay.

Magically, Matty's wounded masculinity was reinstated.

"Oh my God, Maggie, you were sopping wet!" he would carry on whenever we could talk privately. "You'll never know what you've done for my ego. I thought there had been something seriously wrong with me."

I hate cheaters. When you marry out of love, you're making a huge commitment. It's difficult enough to trust anyone in general. In a marriage or any life long commitment, you are giving someone else emotionally everything. That's a scary move to make. So when your spouse (who swore love and devotion to you) betrays that trust, it must feel like death.

There was a *lot* of cheating in the Navy. It only took a few years in the Navy to leave me permanently embittered towards that world. I've never understood why I didn't feel guilty about Matty. I heard nothing but great things about how kind and wonderful his wife was; I should've hated myself. But I was absorbed in an orgy on the water. My behavior was the norm.

The Higgins left for deployment that spring. I felt a pang of loneliness as I watched the crew's families say goodbye on the pier. I wanted my family there or at least someone to say goodbye to. The pier was packed with teary children and Navy wives. Myleen, my fellow teenage Deck Seaman and married sailor's deployment mistress, cracked jokes.

"You know she's gonna have some man in her bed in a few weeks," she said, glancing at one of the wives.

We laughed about our urges to yell, "*He's gonna fuck hookers!*" to all the wives.

Myleen had been on the previous deployment and was well versed on how things went down when America was far, far away.

In the midst of our people watching and judgments, we both gasped in shock when we saw Sally. We had once been good friends. Just a year before, she was rescuing me from a Mexican jail cell on my nineteenth birthday. But my friendship with Sally fizzled shortly after she got married and faked a sleepwalking condition that got her medically discharged from the Navy.

Sally was one of the prettiest girls on the ship and shoved it in our faces. She once told me, "Maggie, I have bigger tits *and* I weigh less than you."

Which is why I couldn't help but getting a little pleasure out of seeing her. Sally, who was once a stunning brunette with a flawless complexion, now looked like the girl from the movie *Willy Wonka and the Chocolate Factory* who turned into a blueberry. Her petite five-foot frame was swollen to the point of being barely recognizable. We said some cold, awkward hellos, but I was so distracted by her appearance. It was difficult to look at her. She must have gained seventy pounds. When she talked, I heard her voice and could see her face, but it was underneath what seemed like a fat suit. It was a shock to see her squeezed into her husband's L.A. Dodgers jersey with stretchy sweat pants.

"Damn," one of the Boatswain's Mates in our division exclaimed as the ship was pulling out of port.

He had been the first guy onboard to fuck Sally and was horrified by how much she let herself go.

"It's pretty bad when you're stretching out your husband's jerseys," he continued, shaking his head in disappointment. "She used to be hot. I loved those small hands. They made my dick look big."

Most women gain some weight when they join the Navy. From what I've seen, it's even worse with Navy wives. Once they had their man legally shackled, they just let themselves go. The stereotype is that they sit at home and enjoy their rent-free base housing. They pop out kids because medical bills are paid for and they just keep that baby weight forever. Some of them look like they've never seen a toothbrush or soap.

I, along with most of the Navy girls I've known, didn't like Navy wives. They were usually rude. They ignored us when they brought their husbands dinner on duty. They gave us smug, fake smiles if they were forced to interact with us. The Navy women and the Navy wives could sense each other's resentment. They hated us because they knew their husbands would probably end up fucking us.

After enough time at sea, *all* of us would become quite provocative. We spent the time with the husbands that they lost. We hated them because they were the ones the men would go home to. Affairs would happen and in the lonely, haze grey waters. We would get attached. For most of us, these men were rentals.

I knew that Sally only came to the pier to see off her husband. Her humiliation from her weight gain was obvious. She knew the way sailors gossiped and recognized the scrutiny of women's looks because she used to be one of its cruelest scrutinizers. With such mindless jobs, our source of entertainment was to observe, criticize, and gossip about those around us. It was especially satisfying with Sally.

"She thought she was such hot shit. Look at her now!" was everyone's reaction.

It was a relief to see someone once so high and mighty ridiculed when I was so insecure. Although her weight gain gave me some satisfaction, it also scared the hell out of me. I wasn't as big as Sally, but I had also ballooned since I first boarded the ship. I knew that people had talked about me the way they did Sally. I laughed along with them, but had to stop myself. I looked at her and knew that the same thing could happen to me.

I made a real decision to lose weight. No starvation or vomiting up my food. This time I was going to do it right.

Deployment life became a mindlessly busy routine. Stand watch, eat, chip paint, drills, prime, stand watch, eat, drills, sleep for four hours, stand watch, run, eat, stand watch, sleep for three hours, run, watch, drills. That was life.

During deployment, I completely destroyed my metabolism. Galley food was disgusting, but it got worse the longer we were out to sea. Eating healthy was easy because there was little to indulge in. My normal diet consisted of oatmeal, fruit, dry tuna, lettuce, and rice. I dodged the ship store that opened at certain times during the week. That's where my shipmates got their junk food stash.

My job itself was physically active. Heading towards Asia during the summertime, deck worked outside in the blistering heat. We were issued camel backs so that we could have access to water at all times. We'd sweat so much some days that we would have to constantly change t-shirts. I sweat through eight in one day.

After spending five hours of watch on our feet, the gym was the last place I wanted to go at the end of the day, but distance running came easy to me. Even in my worst shape, I never came close to failing a Navy running test. But I had never really *dedicated* myself to running. With the ship rocking, gripping the handles because I was damn near falling off the treadmill, one mile became two, and I was soon running four miles a day.

During deployment I got an average of four hours of sleep every twenty-four hours. There were many nights where I would eat a small dry tuna dinner after a full workday of chipping paint in one hundred plus degree weather, nap for a few hours, and get up at 11 pm so I could get a four-mile run in before my 1:45 am watch. After standing that watch, without sleep, I would work another full day in the heat.

I was definitely consuming less than a thousand calories a day and burning at least twice that. But my body was stubborn. I lived like a thin person who still got treated like the fat girl. Dino, deck division's bully, would ask girls that shared my berthing if I was stuffing candy bars in my rack. He was stunned when the girls vouched for how healthy I was.

Everyone who was around me enough to get a good look at my lifestyle was at awe of my size. It frustrated me to tears.

"What the fuck is wrong with me?" I'd ask myself, cursing my body.

Then I realized that hating my body was how I got into that position in the first place. There was so much irony in my situation. I was so desperate to be thin that I abused my body throughout my most crucial developmental years. The weight would eventually melt, but the process would take years.

I've never felt sorry for fat people who bitch about their figures. I had to work twice as hard as someone who didn't spend high school coughing vomit and blood. By the end of deployment, my weight loss would be noticeable, but not dramatic. I would become an athletic, calorie-counting health nut.

During deployment, I was still the chubby girl avoiding mirrors and cameras.

Despite its slew of vices, deployment did it did have its perks. About every month, the Higgins docked at an exotic port. During my six-month deployment, I went to Hawaii and Dubai twice, Hong Kong, Bahrain, Malaysia, Thailand and my personal favorite, India.

India wasn't just some beach resort. My surroundings looked like they had been ripped out of a *National Geographic* magazine.

What I saw of India followed every stereotype I related it to. Monkeys were jumping through the trees, goats running through the streets, and women walking barefoot with large water jugs balanced on their heads.

We were in Goa, on the west coast of India, about an eight-hour drive south of Mumbai. There were a few luxurious hotels and restaurants, but I saw more poverty than riches. Clustered shacks surrounded the mountainous, windy dirt roads where crowded families lived. Their three-walled homes exposed quaint, flimsy-roofed living quarters with dirt floors. The hot summer air was fogged with suffocating humidity. These people probably couldn't fathom owning indoor plumbing, much less air-conditioning. Children in rags ran amuck, sometimes sitting with stray dogs on the side of the road. The poverty didn't sadden me though. How could you miss things like plasma TV or an in-ground pool in the backyard if you were never exposed to it?

My favorite aspect of India was the way the women dressed. Despite their poverty, they wore beautiful, brightly colored shawls and saris with the traditional dots on their foreheads.

Transportation in India was terrifying, but exhilarating. There were no seatbelts in the rickety taxis and there were no limits on traffic violations. The land was full of hills and bumpy roads. I did not see a single traffic sign or red light as the cab driver swerved and honked at the other vehicles that were so close to plowing into us. Open-bed trucks drove by us stuffed with dozens of people crammed into it, limbs hanging out the side.

There were no "click it or ticket" laws in India. I was amazed how entire families would fit onto a small moped with young children hanging onto their sibling's backs the way monkeys carried their young. The people seemed to have no fear of death, which makes sense because Goa's dominant religion is Hinduism. The reckless drivers were probably strong believers in reincarnation.

A lot of sailors were tired of traveling after the Navy. It had the opposite affect on me. Navy traveling was a tease. It showed me beautiful places without allowing me to truly experience them.

When I was in Hong Kong, my friends and I took a double-decker bus tour to the Buddha statue and markets outside of town. I liked Hong Kong because people drove on the left side of the road and it was packed with people of another race besides mine. It was different, but it was really just another big, crowded city. It was when I ventured slightly into the countryside that I fell in love with the lush, stunning green hills and the traditional Chinese architecture. I had this urge to venture further inland. I wanted to run away from the Higgins and frolic through China. Even in Dubai when I saw signs on the highways to Saudi Arabia, I was tempted to explore.

Navy travel wasn't satisfying. There were too many rules and restrictions. We got little time in many of the ports. Hawaii was a meager two days and Malaysia was two or three. Even if we did get more time in a port, like Thailand where we had five days, we still had to stand a full twenty-four hours of ship duty every three days.

I was low in rank, and wasn't allowed to stay overnight in most ports. I finally got that right in Thailand after begging and petitioning after getting a ton of Navy qualifications. There were dress codes that didn't make sense. In countries with stifling hot weather, tourists were dressed in tank tops and shorts, so when a group of white people with collared shirts and pants romped through town, the locals *knew* we were military. I understand why our command would want us to dress more conservatively in cities where women wore veils, but the point was to make us look discreet. It didn't work.

A couple days before every port visit, the command would have a "port call."

The entire crew was called to muster on the mess decks. Officers and higher enlisted members would give us a brief on information about whatever port we were about to visit.

"Now, in Malaysia," one of the chief's warned us, "Do not point. Pointing is considered offensive. It's their version of flipping somebody off. Instead of using your index finger, point with your thumb."

"If you enter the quarter deck and it is obvious that you are intoxicated," they warned, "Your liberty will be restricted in the next port. The same rules apply if your liberty buddy is intoxicated."

Our "liberty buddy" was another aspect that killed the experience of traveling. Nobody was allowed to leave the boat in an overseas port without a liberty buddy. A liberty buddy was someone you signed out with and were expected to stay with until you checked back onto the boat. You were responsible for each other's safety. If your liberty buddy broke the rules, you were in trouble, too. You had to compromise with someone else on where you went and what you did.

I understand why we had so many rules. They were there for a reason. I'm sure they're a result of sailors getting buck wild, destructive, and arrested in the past. Rules originate from people's fuck ups. This is why bottles of bleach have "do not drink" warnings. Any normal human being laughs at them, but the warning is there because one time, some dumb shit drank the bleach. And plenty of sailors would indeed drink the bleach.

The Higgins was a high school on steroids, and along with the teenage mentality were the cliques that I never fully fit into. I found myself in that same situation on deployment. Although I had a wide range of acquaintances, I was and still am a loner at heart. By deployment, the girls aboard had either coupled up with men or formed tight cliques of two or three. The closest group I came to fitting into was my trio with Myleen and Yolanda, but I could already feel a strain on that friendship.

I occasionally got stuck with a liberty buddy I didn't have chemistry with. In India, I got stuck with one liberty buddy who couldn't hold her liquor, got trashed the second I took my eyes off her, and fell flat-faced on the quarterdeck, taking away a chunk of my privileges.

It only took a few weeks into deployment for marital issues to spread. I remember how much more attractive my shipmates became. The longer we were out to sea, the better looking they got. I had to reevaluate my sanity when I found myself checking out Jarhead.

Jarhead was a Gunner's Mate who had been in the posse with Elvis and all those boys who desperately wanted to be pinned as demented fucks. He was good friends with Number 10 and like Number 10, fantasized about being a bad ass. Like Matty, who was also a good friend of his, Jarhead wanted to be a Navy Seal. He failed Buds three times and was determined to go back again. He loved guns and all things masculine.

Jarhead certainly was not a good-looking guy. Barely twenty-three, he was already balding so he wore baseball caps every day. His brown eyes were narrow and he had a permanently pursed expression on his face. However, he was in good shape. One day on the mess decks, I watched him standing and chatting with someone, faced away from me. For the first time, I noticed the broadness of his muscular shoulders and the way his waist narrowed in an upside down triangle. He wasn't a big guy. He was slender and about 5'10", but he had a lean, chiseled body that I had overlooked. I immediately caught myself and pretended that my moment of admiring his physique had not happened.

"Stop it, Maggie," I told myself. "HE. DID. NOT. GET. HOT."

You know the way people are warned about seeing mirages while wandering through the desert? Sailors are warned about people miraculously becoming more attractive after spending enough time at sea. It's true. They really do.

My sex drive was also a major judgment contributor. Some people claim that one's dependence on sex is completely mental. I disagree. Sex is a drug that one becomes physically addicted to.

After consistently having sex with Number 3 for two years, then being completely sex deprived in boot camp, I got my first taste of sex withdrawals. From February to November, I would be completely sex free. The nine-month dry spell was the longest I had ever gone without it since losing my virginity and it was absolute torture. The last time I had sex before deployment was with Number 4. We'd gotten in touch and he flew me up to Sacramento for another rendezvous with him and his wife. Expecting another wild weekend of sex till dawn, I went, only to find out how much had changed in a year. Number 4 had quit drinking and began smoking even more weed than before. His stamina was gone. After about three pumps inside of me, he blew his load. The man who had once been able to fuck two women all night had tragically lost his mojo.

I fooled around with a guy I met on the plane when I was on my way to visit my family right before deployment, but was too paranoid to join the mile high club. At the beginning of deployment, Matty began playing grab ass and even made arrangements for areas for us to get it on while underway, but his moods were bipolar. Sometimes he was very assertive, but other days he was cold. I think he was struggling with his morality and his marriage. But he and Myleen's married lover, Chicklet, kept busy enough with hookers in Hong Kong.

The first month without sex was bearable. It began to get difficult around the second month. By month three, I was in absolute agony. What made it worse was that there was so little time to get myself off. I had to sleep every second that I got. I often *made* time when I was in dire need, but it didn't suffice.

I felt like a dog in heat. My body was telling me to do something that wasn't socially acceptable to do.

After Hawaii and Hong Kong, our third port visit was a city called Kota Kinabalu, the capital of Sabah state in Malaysia. It was an urban area with a few hotels and cheap shopping malls. Even though it wasn't one of our most impressive ports, I had a lot of fun there with Myleen and Yolanda. We romped around the town, went to malls, American movies, and bars with cheap drinks, but it was our first night there that was by far the most interesting.

The Higgins pulled into port on a hot June afternoon. There was no dock and we were transported to and from shore by a small speedboat. Just like we would see in nearly every port we went to, the small base we were leaving to go to town was packed with cab drivers shouting out in broken English to ride with them. To them, we were rich.

After anchoring in, changing out of work clothes, and standing in long lines to sign out with our liberty buddy procedures, we were on solid ground early that evening. The girls and I had just enough time to wander around for a bit and then go hang out at the nearest club.

Booze was a massive part of deployment. Since the drinking age was usually eighteen overseas, the entire crew was able to consume plenty of toxins for dirt-cheap. I never intended to get as fucked up as I did.

Since Kota Kinabalu was a fairly small port, there were few places for us to go drink so the entire crew was at the same club. This was a bizarre experience. I knew the Navy as being so segregated with rank. Lower enlisted hung out with lower enlisted. Chiefs hung out with chiefs. Officers hung out with officers. We couldn't casually cut up with everyone. Navy socialization was structured like the historical days of peasants and royalty. But we found ourselves away from our ship and our country. The walls came down. I was getting hammered with my Command Master Chief and Captain.

I was double fisting Long Island Iced Teas when the lights dimmed and a Malaysian band started playing American songs like Journey's "Don't Stop Believing" and Vanilla Ice. The dancing began.

For the record, I absolutely *loathe* dancing. I have no rhythm and look like I'm having a seizure. Today's dancing is ass shaking and dry humping to some hideous pop/rap electronic contemplation. It's loud, obnoxious, and gives random creeps an excuse to grind their dicks into my ass. This is why I can only do what my generation calls dancing when I am *smashed*.

"Look, Maggie's dancing!" Myleen squealed. "Yaaay!"

Myleen was a clubber. It was impossible to drag me out onto a dance floor, so she was pleased.

Except for the sailors on duty, my entire command was probably at that club. The floor was packed with horny, drunken sailors having a grand time grinding each other's genitals together. Suddenly, Jarhead was behind me and after about five or six stiff drinks, he was practically edible.

We began "dancing" with our friends around us doing the same thing. Everyone was all over each other having the best time.

"MY WIFE'S CHEATING ON ME!" Jarhead yelled into my ear through the loud music.

She and Jarhead used to live with Number 10, so I met her a few times. They were high school sweethearts. Jane had a stunning face with a punk rock style. Her hair was in trendy, black choppy layers and she had a few facial piercings.

"WE'RE GETTING A DIVORCE!" Jarhead continued to shout in my ear over the blaring music. "SHE CHEATED ON ME DURING THE LAST DEPLOYMENT, TOO, SO I'M DONE! GOD, YOU ARE SO HOT!"

"Hot?" I thought to myself. "He thinks I'm *hot*?"

I could not remember the last time someone called me hot. It was an adjective I was once used to. But since my post-bulimia weight gain, I wasn't even considered attractive, let alone hot. It felt so good to get that attention again. It hooked me. We started making out in front of the entire command and if the crew had been granted overnight liberty, it would have gone a lot further.

Jarhead didn't let go of my hand until our curfew drew near and we had to part ways with our liberty buddies. Our spontaneous heat was ignited by lust, but an intimacy lingered in the atmosphere. It seemed that loneliness ailed the Higgins crew just as much as sex deprivation.

Riding back to the ship on the speedboat, Jarhead and I occasionally make eye contact. I think we were both in shock from what had happened. Matty was his liberty buddy. There I was on the small speedboat with both of them, wondering what conversation they'd exchange the next day.

There was somewhat of a ruckus after my Malaysian excursion. Someone got in touch with Jane, leading her to contact the ship. Because we were both legally married, Jarhead and I both got bitched out by our chiefs and the Command Master Chief. Since there was no sexual intercourse, they couldn't reprimand us. I had never been a huge fan of my chief. I didn't like the way he ruled with his temper. But I found myself ashamed of letting him down. I realized that he didn't give a damn what I did in my personal life as long as it didn't affect his image. He knew how fake my marriage was, but never said a word to me about it until I made a public spectacle of myself. I began to understand what my recruiters meant about the Navy being one big game. From then on, I decided to be more careful. I got back into the workaholic mode.

After Malaysia, we didn't see land for forty-five days. Our haze grey planet was ladder wells, p-ways, painting, priming, watch, and sleeping whenever we could. My twenty-hour workdays transformed the rough, nonskid deck into a cloud of feather pillows. The roar of helicopters simmered to soothing purrs. The Indian Ocean raped our comprehension of gravity with a month's worth of turbulent seas that flip-flopped our bodies and bellies. I found myself dangling off ladder wells and watching weights fly across the gym like a modern day Titanic sinking. The mess decks were always stocked with saltine crackers.

Our Captain tried to make things fun. He held barbeques, ice cream socials, and karaoke nights. He allowed men to grow beards and women to wear their hair down. But deployment still seemed to age us.

I remember the spooked expressions of Marines whenever the word "Iraq" was uttered. But there were no tanks, grenades, convoys, dynamite, blood, and catapulting corpses in my enlistment.

"At least we're not dodging bullets," I said on watch once.

A couple guys and I were bull shitting in the heap of thick, a balmy fog that seemed to smother the open sea.

"Word," one guy replied. "I take some ship dust over bombs any day."

"Not me. I'd love to kill some mother fuckin' Jihads!" another cut in.

"Well, that's the thing," the other responded. "The Navy is more mentally than physically challenging. The dudes in combat might die, but they feel like they have a purpose. We're just running around in circles. It drives us insane."

The Navy's use for deck was no different than an aging socialite getting weekly Botox injections, plastering wrinkles with foundation, and ducking into the ladies room to powder her nose and retouch her lipstick every ten minutes. We incessantly slaved away to make our ship pretty. We fluffed the feathers of America's peacock. Ironically, that was why we deployed.

"We're showing our presence," my superiors often proudly proclaimed.

And sadly, every year my country spends billions to do so.

My shipmates and I only grasped our roles on the very superficial level we were taught. We were fighting the bad guys. They were the bad guys because we were told that they were the bad guys. We had to control, infiltrate, and shove our authority around the world because we were its greatest nation. We had the shiniest ships, the biggest guns, the deadliest weapons, and the cockiest egos. And if we thought otherwise, we were vicious traitors. The military condemns rebels, thinkers, and doubt. The military loves obedience, loyalty, and oblivion. Its core values are, after all, "Honor, Courage, and Commitment."

My little fling with Jarhead was just a mark on the list of the crew's sexual escapades. A couple officers were caught fooling around in one of the ship's spaces. One of my bosses was spotted squeezed in a rack with a Deck Seaman in female berthing. They were flown off the ship that day. But the crew's thirty women were a meager supply for its three hundred men. Luckily, we were sailing to Thailand.

By the time we pulled into Phuket, we were exhausted from months of labor in the sweltering Persian Gulf heat. We were so close to coming home that the adrenaline rush we had from pulling into exotic lands had long disintegrated. We were overworked and homesick.

After months of the mindless elbow grease, incessant ship dusting, alarming drills, and rigid military bearing we were expected to uphold at all times, we were fully charged by each other's friction and on the brink of eruption.

Thai prostitution was a haven for the men and a nuisance for the women. The streets of Phuket were outlined with bars ready to nourish thirsty sailors with euphoric intoxication to smother their pinched nerves from their personal lives deteriorating in their six-month absence.

Thailand truly lived up to its port reputation. Hundreds of bikini-clad prostitutes littered the strip. Slim and petite, their narrow hips and flat chests appeared to be the appropriate age for the pink plaid schoolgirl skirts, dress shirts, ties, and pigtails intended to entice pedophilic eroticism. They wore heavy coats of pastel liquid shadow that clashed against their yellow tinted tans. They awkwardly wiggled to a nauseating blend of techno and Reggaeton as cotton-haired granddaddies lustfully gawked at them. Any Caucasian male cannot trek a block without the treatment of a pop culture heartthrob with a trail of Thai teens at his heels.

"*Wan hunnet baaht!*" they taunt in a nasal screech. "*Wan hunnet baht and I suck yo cock!*"

The oriental beauties cup their fists and hold them to their mouths as they wiggle their tongues against their cheeks to provide a clear visual for their performance skills.

It's easy to dismiss the humanity in Thai prostitutes. Their splotchy, heavily accented English allows the language barrier to muffle signs of intellect. They're overtly sexual in their crotch bearing ensembles, loud and vulgar invitations, and provocative dancing that makes even corner butcher shops feel like Vegas strip clubs. Swarms of them linger in front of bars holding cardboard signs scribbled with magic marker that offer a blow job with the first beer purchased. Their eyes burn into passing tourists, with acute radar for creamy, sun-flushed complexions and potbellies - signals of the deep pockets of white male privilege.

It is difficult to see the souls within the women who stand along the streets to claw for their customers like zombies in a haunted house. We overlook the fact that they *are* zombies. Their key to maintain a physical life was likely an emotional death.

Western tourists transform Thailand into its own little planet of indulgence. Time has no relevance and debauchery, no consequence.

Thailand has been dubbed a lustful playground where it is overlooked when a straight male foggily awakes with new tattoos, missing limbs, and a torn anus from a belligerent romp with a transsexual ladyboy. As my shipmates perpetually claimed in defending their infidelities, "Hookers don't count. They're not real people."

But beyond the cultural and geographical distance from home, *wealth* is the true fuel to Thailand's wild nights and ethical negligence. One American dollar is worth about thirty-five Thai Baht. A lap dance, threesome, gangbang, golden shower, pedophilia, or any other sexual deviances shunned by conventional lovers are roughly twenty bucks - a modest ATM withdrawal.

"It's so sad that they sell themselves like that," I once said on deployment.

"But you've gotta think," more seasoned sailors would explain, "They are actually really smart women. Thailand's a developing country. We're kings there. A woman can support herself for a month with one night's work."

So, we chock Thailand's flourishing sex trade up to a rigid tradeoff in an unfair world. We use them, do our best to forget them, and thank our lucky stars that we're not one of them.

By the time we reached Thailand, electric chills spread throughout my entire body every time someone's arm grazed mine. It didn't matter who it was. Just the slightest touch of another human being was on the brink of igniting a bomb of sexual tension. I was one of the few women aboard who never had sex on deployment. This had nothing to do with my moral high ground. I found that men rarely considered chubby girls to be accessories to flaunt.

Total discretion on deployment was impossible. We had to sign out with liberty buddies. It was a complete giveaway if the person we wanted to hook up with *was* our liberty buddy. Ship gossip flourished like a senior citizen's knitting circle. Any woman could get laid, especially in the Navy.

It wasn't that no man was willing to have sex with me, but I can only go so ugly. Sure, I gained weight and lost self-esteem. My standards dropped a bit. Most of the men from my past aren't exactly prizes, but none of them were hideous. Jarhead was one of my worst and I was one shot away from alcohol poisoning when we kissed. If I can't score a fairly decent-looking man, I'll remain celibate. But by no means does that mean I wasn't desperate.

On our last night in Thailand, Myleen, Yolanda, and I were granted overnight liberty. We got nice hotel rooms, shopped, laid out on the beach, and hit the bars. We had been drinking poolside prior to pub-crawling and were already pretty tipsy. Within the first few hours out, we ran into two of our Boatswain's Mates, along with their third liberty buddy, Matty.

Matty had grown fickle since our fling at the ship's helm. He'd go from our traditional chatty banter to dodging eye contact when we crossed paths in the p-way. Once in a while, he'd spontaneously grab my ass when nobody could see us and scurry away like he was initiating a game of R-Rated Duck, Duck, Goose. I didn't know the rules, but I must have been losing.

Even beyond my craving for sex was my longing for intimacy. Matty advertised intimacy. He dangled it in front of my face and jerked it away the second my arm shifted to reach for it. The moment my interest weaned, he'd dangle it again. The scraps of attention Matty tossed me was merely a flickering candle on the other end of a cold dungeon. I couldn't escape incarceration, but I was certain that its flames would thaw my frostbite.

Every joke he told me, glance in my direction, or light punch on my shoulder became factors in my Matty behavior formula. The air seemed to buzz whenever we were in the same room. I struggled to carry on casual conversation with shipmates, laugh at their jokes, smile and frown at expected social cues, as I kept alert.

I wrapped my eardrums around his every word, mixing tones and moods into a mental tumbleweed. I struggled to steal every glimpse of him I could to compile an understanding of what was going on with us. He was married. I should have ignored him entirely for that very reason. But she just didn't seem real from the other side of the world. Nothing did.

Matty, our liberty buddies, and I sat at the bar of a seedy dive small enough for only a dozen patrons to fill. I already had a few stiff drinks in my bloodstream when a Thai woman in a tight tube top poured our Long Islands. Matty and I sat at the end, with the wall at our back. With nothing but a flickering neon pink fluorescent light to illuminate the room, Matty and I were in our own psychedelic world. Matty felt safe there, warm and loose from vodka, invisible in the dark, and bold out of his familiar domestic and professional environments. He scooted his stool my way and inched close enough for our legs to touch.

"I have my own hotel room," he whispered. "A suite."

He voice was lower than usual. His lips brushed my ear when he spoke. He sounded mischievous and determined. I realized that he clueing me in on a Top Secret mission. He put his hand on my knee, looked at me with a smirk as if we were sharing an inside joke, and ran his hand up my thigh.

"I am gonna fuck your brains out tonight," he murmured. "Make your pussy *gush*."

I gasped as his hand went higher. As he began massaging the crotch of my jeans, I was struggling to prevent myself from attacking him.

Restraint was painful. In that moment, I wanted him to pound me beyond orgasmic relief. I wanted paralysis. I wanted to lose all comprehension, all loneliness, all insecurities, and all Navy. I craved the kind of sex I'd never had - the kind that shook my soul out of my body. Matty's allure wasn't about a climax, a crush, or an ego boost. I created him. I transformed him from a cliché philandering sailor to the escort to my fantasyland. As he touched me, I envisioned the two of us beneath his floral hotel comforter like a protective shell. Matty felt like my only sanctuary.

Once Matty was bold enough to put his palm against my scalp, grip a fist full of hair, and yank it back, Myleen and Yolanda cut into my trance.

"*Don't do it!*" Myleen, who was sitting on my other side from Matty, hissed in my ear. "He's a married piece of shit," Yolanda chipped in, rolling her eyes. "He's not worth it."

Even in my intoxicated state, I saw reality in 20/20. It was as if I were outside my body, watching our entire exchange like a horror movie.

I knew that his moodiness was a reaction from his guilt.

I knew he loved his wife, but loved himself more. I knew that my only appeal was my vulnerability. I made him feel strong and desirable. I gave him power.

I knew that nothing good would come from him. I was going to get hurt. I watched myself, knowing that I should run away, clutching the scraps of dignity I had left. But walking directly into the trap seemed inevitable.

I was willing to trade months of pain for one night of pleasure.

But my friends' cautionary tones were short lived. Yolanda and Myleen traded me for one of the boys. I went with the boys, faking an enthusiasm for the Thai boxing match they were headed to. Libidos were everyone's underlying priority.

From there, the night got hazy. The boys and I made it to the boxing match and at some point picked up a Thai prostitute.

"*What the fuck, Matty?*" I whispered.

I was dumbstruck. He had been so forward with me only half an hour earlier.

"Maggie, I'm not interested in her," he scoffed, rolling his eyes. "She knows the area. She's going to be our guide."

I tried my best to drown the nervous pang in my stomach with even more vodka. The next thing I remember is being led into what looked like a small strip club. It was an auditorium setting with a stage and dancing poles around our seats. There were poles on every corner of Phuket. People crowded in and some sort of music started blaring. The "Ping Pong" show began.

A Thai Ping Pong show is a performance where strippers, either lady or ladyboy, do tricks with their snatch. It was absolutely one of the most fascinating, bizarre things I've seen in my life. From dart throwing, Ping Pong shooting, egg cracking, and cigarette smoking, these pussies were incredible. One performer even pushed a live goldfish out of her lady parts. I'd heard of the Ping Pong shows before. On one of his previous deployments, Number 10 had been hit in the head with one of the darts.

"*How do you do that?*" I slurred to one of the showgirls.

"Yu jus prak-teese," she advised me in broken English.

I couldn't imagine how many Kegels it took to reach such an astonishing dart shooting level.

The dim club sparkled with the multicolored lights that outlined the stage. Blood red bulbs blared behind the boyish, flat-chested bodies of Thai adolescents scantily wrapped in lingerie. A strobe light flashed and white disco dots swam around the ceiling, walls, and floor. The strip club was strategically designed to be our funhouse of guilty pleasure. We, the wealthy westerners, were dukes and duchesses, while they were our jesters and whores. We gulped tequila shots as we sat atop our thrones. We cackled at the spectacle of people becoming objects.

I was supposed to be having the time of my life.

I felt nauseous.

But the real show was offstage. Dozens of men lounged along the tables that circled the main attraction. They ranged from eighteen to eighty, skinny to fat, stout to lanky. I saw home in them. I saw fathers, grandfathers, brothers, boyfriends, professors, bosses, and preachers. I imagined their houses, their families, their jobs, the coffee shops where they bought breakfast pastries, the hospitals their children were born in, and their neighborhood route for their dog's morning walk. I saw the gleam in their eyes as the girls swiveled around poles, sashayed in their direction, and sat atop their laps like children visiting Santa Claus. They seemed to love their oriental dolls with a toddler's English fluency. They had their happy endings. They would soon be boarding planes, flying far away from the poverty, the mental and emotional collateral damage, and the possible babies they conceived. Thailand was theirs. It was their escape, their medicine, and their sanctuary of sin.

I had no control of Matty. I watched him slip away as he cuddled up to our bikini-clad tour guide.

I envied the men. I envied the irresponsibility their surroundings and genitals allowed. I envied the artificial affection they bought. But most of all, I envied that flicker of euphoria they got to feel, like a quick sip of whiskey that warmed their chest and eased their pain. I wanted to be them.

"I *could* be them," I thought. "And I will."

I kept drinking. I pretended not to cry inside. I laughed. And when our guide took her attention off Matty and held her hand out to me, I eagerly obliged. She led me to the pole that was near our table, raised her arms, wiggled her hips back and forth, and playfully chanted, "*Dance. Dance. Dance!*" So I danced.

When she got closer, I mirrored her until I could feel her breath on my cheeks. And then I kissed her. She wasn't pretty. I wasn't aroused by her dancing, by her straight narrow hips, or petite frame. I wasn't reacting to the remnants of the fire that ignited between Matty and I just hours before. I did it to shake Matty. My actions said, "No, bitch. You can't have it all." He must have understood.

"It's time to go," Matty ordered.
His voice was sharp and stern, like a reprimanding father. He grabbed my arm and yanked me out of the bar.

"*Wheeeerrree?*" I slurred.

"Back to the hotel," he barked.

I was initially triumphant. I'd gotten his attention. We were going to hide within the shield of his suite. The streets of downtown Phuket were a blur of music, drunken hollering, motorcycles and screeching prostitutes. Matty dragged me through the sea of tourists on the sidewalks the way a child pulls a wagon through a muddy road. Suddenly, a new, familiar face popped up in my dreamlike consciousness. Matty had bumped into one of our shipmates on the way back.

"Take her," he ordered him, eager to surrender custody of me. "She's too drunk. She needs to sleep it off."

The night's alcohol binge destroyed my inhibitions. Along with those went my adult façade. I didn't force my lips into a phony grin. I did not reserve my despair for the privacy of my own room. Just as I was a child unable to get myself back to my hotel room, I reacted like one once I was abandoned. I cried unrestrained and uncontrollably.

Although I was submerged in a crowd thick enough to smell their stench of stale beach sweat, nobody was truly *with* me. My tears were merely the same spectacle as belligerent ramblings of a homeless man, screams of an infant, or the ring of a car alarm. I was a brief interruption. I was a spectacle that people glanced at, quickly looked away and tried to ignore.

My shipmate awkwardly tugged me along as swiftly as possible. I wanted to be held and consoled. I wanted my cheeks pressed against a chest. I wanted to fall into a warm cave of somebody's arms wrapped around mine. I wanted assurance that I was loved, that I was not alone, that I was worthy of real affection.

Once my shipmate released me at the hotel, I stumbled into the lobby to use their phone. It was daytime back home, but everybody I knew seemed to be caught up in their daily routine. I tried Mom first. No answer. Grandmother. Nope. Granddaddy. Nothing. And there was Carl. In my drunken haze, I never remembered the dialogue in that fifty-dollar conversation. I only remember his tone: annoyed, stoic, disconnected, and unfazed. And when we hung up, I continued to cry until I fell asleep. He kept that call a secret. We never mentioned it again.

I've always heard that after hitting rock bottom, things begin to get better. Thailand must have been my low. A few days before deployment ended, I got orders to my A-school in Meridian, Mississippi. I was done with the ship. When my supervisor told me the good news, I jumped up and down and impulsively lunged in to give him a python hug.

"Oh my God, Maggie," Myleen exclaimed when we were on watch ten day.

I was on port lookout and she was the messenger, free to roam around the bridge. She came outside to keep me company. Although it was November, it was a warm sunny day. The ship had just left Hawaii and we were on our way to San Diego.

"You lost a *lot* of weight on deployment," she said, scoping my figure up and down.

I went to berthing and looked at myself in the mirror. She was right. Finally, my work was paying off.

From the day we returned to San Diego, I had about a month left on the Higgins. Since I had no idea where I'd be based after my A-school, I decided to take my car. I would drive from San Diego to Chattanooga, spend the holidays with my family, and then head to Meridian.

I spent that month retaliating from the Navy. I never took a bite of galley food. I didn't dare wear my uniform outside of base. I still hung out with Myleen and Yolanda, but was much more drawn a new group of people.

Devi, the skinny pregnant woman who had lived on Number 10's couch, ended up being my gateway to civilian life. We had a very strange friendship. Though she was the sweetest girl, a part of me couldn't stand her. Devi wandered through life aimlessly. But by the time I returned stateside, she was a mother. She was staying with Morrison, the father of her child. That combination was toxic.

Morrison was a former shipmate of ours. He was one of those guys who joined the Navy because it was either a military enlistment or jail. He looked a bit like a leprechaun with his bushy brown eyebrows, big ears, and short stature. Morrison was just as much of a disaster as Devi.

Since getting out of the Navy, he fathered a child and worked at the front desk of a hotel. He was a compulsive spender. He would invest in cocaine before Pampers. Like everyone else, I turned a blind eye. I knew that Morrison and Devi were shitty parents, but I turned a blind eye. It was just too much of a hassle to fight with an open invitation to Morrison's nightly parties packed with tons of the PB civilians I was dying to mingle with.

He lived in a cluster of shabby, overpriced apartments that were nicknamed "Frat Row." The Frat Row crew had a routine of hitting the bars, snorting a few lines, and playing beer pong in their front yard after last call. The strong ones were able to stay tweaked out all night and feast on a pitcher of beer by 6 am.

The Silver Fox, a bar conveniently a few blocks away, opened that early. These boys would kick the day off there, have mimosas at a nearby restaurant, and pub crawl down Pacific Beach's main strip until they reached the beach. Frat row was primarily occupied with boys, but waves of bronze skinned, coked out girls would come in and out. They'd randomly fuck one or sometimes a few of those guys before eventually moving on to somebody new to mount.

I used Devi to get myself in with the frat row crew. To even things out, she mooched off me financially. I was always paying for food and diapers for her son. Morrison didn't live a life suitable for a baby. Every night, he partied with drunken strangers, snorting blow off the coffee tables while we passed the baby around. Instead of spring the infant's lungs and smoking outside, the apartment was constantly hot boxed.

Besides the booze, parties, and an opportunity to meet young, obliterated civilians, I had another motive to hang around frat row. He was Morrison's best friend, roommate, and my Number 11.

A common Navy cliché is that deployment will either make or break a relationship. Deployment broke relationships because the separation was rough. The distance provokes cheating. But even beyond infidelity, people change. Six months apart is a long time. There's a huge difference between communicating with someone over email and the phone versus being physically *with* them. As loved ones began to feel like complete strangers, the desperation for affection created a lot of relationships. Deployment is lonely. After being deprived of affection and intimacy for so long, it's easy to rush into a relationship out of eagerness just to be close to someone. After deployment, I saw a slew of quickie marriages and divorces. When I met Number 11, I was under that spell of emotional deprivation.

There was nothing special about Number 11. He was short and stocky. The collar of his white V-neck looked like a triangular garden bed of black fur. His black buzz cut was paired with a matching patch of fur on his chin.

Hailing from the laid back, red woodsy town of Santa Cruz, Number 11 never partook in the metrosexual rituals of weight lifting, tanning, and body hair shaving of typical San Diego beach urbanites. His lackadaisical grooming, paired with his warm, inviting smile, was earthy and approachable. That was an exotic virtue in PB. The moment I met him, I wanted to embrace him like an old friend.

Number 11 was the first civilian I socialized with since boarding the Higgins. He didn't know the Navy's unspoken rules and mannerisms, so he was kind to me. He asked me about my past, my hobbies, and what I wanted to do with my life. He offered me a beer. He smiled when he spoke to me.

"Hey, it was really nice to meet you, Maggie," he said, grinning at me as I left.

That's all it took. Starving for kindness, I latched onto the first person that projected it. I decided right then that I would do whatever it took to sleep with him.

I strategized my way past Number 11's fly. Since Devi and the baby were practically living there, I hung around her more. She was my spy. She got as much information from Number 11 as possible. He was single and had been single for four years. Before leaving Santa Cruz, he lived with his ex girlfriend and they had a nasty breakup. He was into camping with bonfire, beer, and lots of cocaine.

I had no problem with Number 11 being a cokehead. Cocaine seemed more dignified than the meth I did with Number 3. I was pretty sure I snorted some coke back in Tennessee, but that was southern coke cut with baking powder and baby laxatives. Being a pebble toss away from Mexico, coke in California is reputably better.

My first knowledge of cocaine was from the movie *Cruel Intentions*. I was thirteen and hadn't experimented with drugs. I was into acting and I idolized Sarah Michelle Gellar's character. The movie was about wealthy teenagers living in New York City. A spoiled rich girl, Sarah Michelle Gellar, makes a bet with her stepbrother. If the brother takes the virginity of a Catholic schoolgirl who has sworn celibacy until marriage, he gets to sleep with his stepsister. Sarah Michelle Gellar was the image of social perfection on the outside. She was a beautiful, wealthy, straight-A student with a dark, sadistic alter ego. But what defined her was the cross she kept around her neck. It was hollow, silver, and filled with cocaine. This accessory stood for the bad concealed by the good.

While crack was considered a poor drug for the lowest of low, cocaine was glamorous. It was a drug for celebrities and the rich, privileged children who lounged around havens like Pacific Beach. Cocaine snorting was a bonding ritual for beautiful, push-up bra wearing, twenty-somethings who scurried into club bathrooms together to do it. It suppressed their appetites, contributing to their lean, giraffe-like physiques.

Despite the Navy's zero tolerance drug policy, I didn't worry about popping on a urinalysis. There were certain drugs that I could get away with. For our tests, we pissed in a cup and qualified personnel watched us. Those with friends in high places were able to pull off doing whatever drug they wanted. Sometimes people would piss for them.

I didn't have those connections, so I had to strategize. Drugs like acid and mushrooms didn't show up in urine. Marijuana could stay in the system up to thirty days, depending on body fat and metabolism. I didn't think that risk was worth taking. During my entire enlistment, I smoked only once on my first night of thirty days of leave. Sometimes I'd go nine months without getting drug tested, but that was completely random. Commands loved to surprise the crew.

Uppers, like cocaine, meth, ecstasy, and crack stayed in the system for about two to three days. Once I got involved with coke, I was shocked to realize how many sailors used on Friday and at the beginning of long weekends.

I knew that sometime shortly after deployment a random urinalysis was coming. Predictably, it did. That night I blew a hundred bucks on a gram of coke.

I was definitely interested in trying it, but just as it had been with every other substance, my main motivation was to seduce Number 11. He already knew I was interested. One night while Morrison was watching the baby, Devi and I had a vodka binge. We got fall-on-the-floor drunk and decided to stroll down to Morrison and Number 11's frat row apartment. Morrison and Devi had a huge fight while I chatted with Number 11. Devi and I left and I sent Morrison an apology text message. I was hammered, but not as badly as Morrison thought I was. I knew exactly what I was doing.

"*Bi the waaaa… uree freens hot,*" I texted Morrison, intentionally misspelling the message.

I knew that Morrison would tell Number 11. Right after, Devi relayed Number 11's response. He thought I was cute.

"Cute," I mentally repeated to myself.

I was still bigger than I wanted to be, but apparently slender enough to catch some desired male attention.

When I showed up at Morrison's place to get my gram, Number 11 was being even nicer to me than usual.

I probably would have saved myself a lot of time, trouble, and money if I'd just walked up to Number 11 and said, "Hi. I haven't gotten laid in nine months. I don't have STDs. My vagina hates me because it has been so neglected. Will you fuck me, please?" But my confidence was still too fragile for such boldness.

Plus, it wasn't honesty that was the way to his heart. It was cocaine. Number 11 was the "lick it off the table when you can't snort it all, even if your snot is crusted all over it" type of coke lover. Since coke is so addictive and expensive, it's a drug that people have to be greedy with. Number 11 was a coke mooch. He could always tell when someone was high. If he caught them not sharing their stash, he called them out.

"Maggie, you're high," he pointed out a few months after our fling.

We were at a party full of people. I snuck off to the bathroom with a friend who was generous enough to share a few lines.

"Why aren't you sharing, Maggie?" Number 11 badgered me.

"It wasn't mine," I responded curtly, trying to get him off my ass.

Then, looking like a chipmunk on red bull, his eyes erratically darted back and forth across the room.

"Well.. uh," he said in his tweaker voice that shook and changed pitches all the time. "Who's got it? Who's got it?" he asked, his tempo getting more rapid.

It's no wonder I got access to his dick for coke. Number 11 probably would've ass fucked an electric socket for a line.

Morrison, Number 11, and I sat in their living room as I pulled my stash from the knitted bag I was hiding it in. I poured some of the powder onto a magazine. Morrison handed me a razor and I chopped the clumps until it was fine. I divided it into three lines. Morrison got out a straw. He had several stashed in his kitchen since he was a regular user.

He cut the straw in half and I put it in my nostril. I bent down to towards the magazine and snorted. A sense of greed overcame me before I even finished inhaling. My nostril sucked in with all the force my lungs could handle, trying to get every microscopic speck in my body. I was happy and everything felt better. I enjoyed the way the couch felt against my skin. Conversation between the three of us was more stimulating.

We hid my precious stash when more people began to crowd into the apartment. I certainly didn't want to face that awkward situation of having to either be rude or share my coke with five new guys, so Number 11 ushered me into his bedroom.

The absolute *best* aspect of using uppers is that it can do wonders for sex. The catch is that speed can be a hit or miss with male performance. Number 3's dick was putty when he was on meth. But I had high hopes for Number 11, as we snorted more lines in his bedroom. When we were done, we sat in his bed and talked. I'm a talkative person and it gets a hundred times worse when I'm on coke. I can't remember the slew of topics we chattered about or at what point we kissed. But in the midst of my high, I clearly recall how great that first kiss was. I'm not sure if it was the drugs or the fact that I'd had the longest dry spell since my virginity, but I fully appreciated every touch of his body against mine.

We continued making out and rubbing our bodies together. He was slightly aggressive, biting the edge of my lips as we kissed. However, he needed to be schooled on a few rudimentary foreplay tactics.

"Pull my hair," I whispered to him.

"Huh?" he asked, shocked.

He was on top of me. I opened my eyes and looked up at him. The dramatic, in the mood whisper stopped.

"Just pull my hair. Haven't you done that with girls before?"

"Uh… no," he looked at me puzzled. "But, okay, I'll do it."

He took a few strands of it and yanked at them clumsily. I started laughing. He laughed too. I was glad his ego wasn't bruised. I tried to show him how to take a handful from the back of my head and yank.

"You have to do it at the right time," I ordered.

I was proud of myself. I was becoming more confident director.

He was hopeless with the hair pulling, but I forgot all about it once I saw his dick. I was shocked. At that time, Number 11 had the biggest cock I'd ever seen. It was long and thick. I didn't see it coming from him, but I was pleasantly surprised enough to completely overlook his thick coat of gorilla chest hair.

High on coke after nine months of celibacy, the feeling of that first penetration was probably the most pleasurable, bottled up, seconds of my life. I almost expected to hear a church choir to burst out in song with "HALLELUJAH!" Unfortunately, all good things must come to an end.

To my despair, Number 11's ended after about seven-and-a-half pumps.

"*Urrrrgggggghhhhhhhh…*" his voice shifted to a despairing groan.

"Sorry. It's the coke."

Number 12

It was an early morning in December when I found myself driving through the rocky, desert hills of El Centro, California. I was fleeing San Diego. My Higgins days were over.

There had been a little ceremony on the boat the day before. Every time someone leaves the crew, their division lines up in two ranks with the Captain standing at the end. The departing sailor walks through the ranks to meet the Captain with a handshake and an autographed photo of the beloved ship that the sailor so proudly served.

As much as I hated sea duty, leaving was bittersweet. The ship's Command Master Chief, a very serious woman who had probably been hot before a career at sea made her face rough and stern, gave me a *hug*.

Military rank dictates strict rules for socialization. People of significantly higher rank are not supposed to befriend their inferiors. They are expected to interact with the utmost formality. My Master Chief was a thriving carnivore in the military food chain and the highest ranked enlisted member on the ship. I was a Seaman. Master Chief was a lion. I was the Bacteria that fed off the lion's shit. This was the same woman who, along with my chief, chewed a new hole in my ass for kissing Jarhead on deployment. I like to think that she secretly saw more in me than everybody else did.

Master Chief entered the Navy back in the early eighties. When she first enlisted, she wasn't even allowed to serve on a combatant ship like the one she would end up commanding. Any sexism, discrimination, or harassment my female peers and I endured was severely amplified in her early career. Through all the ass grabbing and cat calling, she climbed to the top. She had to be ten times tougher than every man around her.

I don't get why glimpses of her fondness of me were suddenly seeping out the cracks of her rigid military bearing. By no means did I present myself as an example of a model Navy female. My uniform was always ill fitted with an iron burn or misplaced crease. I struggled to keep a straight face when speaking to officers during formal inspections.

I was incessantly rebellious. My defiance wasn't loud or blatant. I didn't smoke marijuana and dodge drug tests with a quickie cleanse. I didn't stumble into morning Quarters drunk or canoodle with officers. My demeanor was what seemed to rattle so many platforms of authority. I loosely saluted the American flag when boarding the ship. I prepped my uniforms for inspection, but without furiously starching and shining with the determination to see my reflection in my black boots. I addressed officers with their proper titles as "Sir," "Ma'am," and "Captain," but my tone was that of greeting a casual acquaintance. My eyes met theirs with a confident nonchalance. I bowed down to no one.

I had debated with Master Chief a few times. When she asked me to take off my headphones while I was painting the p-way, I went on an elaborate tangent about how depressing the ship's environment was and how important music was to prevent us from slipping into depression. She kept silent as I spoke, and a smirk I'd never seen before illuminated her eyes. A week later, the Captain announced that we could listen to music with one headphone in our ear. When she and my chief chewed me out for my Jarhead kiss in Malaysia, I stood my ground in saying that kissing did not count as adultery. From then on, she engaged me like a professor engaged one of their favorite students. I was certain she would hate me after sending a farewell email to the entire crew, ending it with "Peace out, Higgins!" But no, she *hugged* me and assured me I would do great things in life.

Before leaving, I attended Captain's Call, the meeting where departing crewmembers sat in a circle of chairs with our glorious leader to talk about our likes, dislikes, and suggestions about how the Higgins life could improve.

"Sir," I jumped in with my very bold and too-loud-for-the-room voice. "When I entered the Navy, I was promised that as an undesignated Deck Seaman, I was allowed to work in other divisions and figure out what I want."

The Captain, with his elegant stature, smiled and nodded.

"I wasn't *ever* allowed to do that in deck. Deck division is currently over-manned and there are Seamen who have been aboard longer than I have. Don't you think they've done their time? Don't they deserve to at least get *some* experience in other divisions?"

The week after I left, several Deck Seamen left the division to work in other departments. With the combination of a good Captain and a chubby, twenty-year-old dumb blonde who wasn't intimidated by the big bad officers, a teensy bit of the Navy's corruption was defeated.

"Seaman Young, it was a pleasure having you aboard. You always kept us on our toes!" wrote my Captain on my autographed USS Higgins photo.

After hearing my deck chief's booming, "WHERE'S JARHEAD?" remark, I walked through the ranks, shook Master Chief's and the Captain's hands, got my Higgins photo, and climbed off that ladder well for the last time. I heard the bell go, "Ding!" over the 1MC and the Petty Officer of the Watch announce, "Seaman Young, departing!" At that moment, like a giddy little girl, I skipped my way off the pier.

Number 11 and I had sex a couple more times, but he never delivered the passion and satisfaction that my body craved. He didn't perform well when he was coked out and he was *always* coked out. Still, I craved his body.

Number 11 moved onto another girl.

My last night in San Diego, Elvis and I moved out of our apartment. I was off my ship, but Devi begged me to stay with her one more night before I left for Tennessee. I would be driving across the country to take my leave in Chattanooga, then reporting to my A-school in Meridian, Mississippi. I appeased Devi's request. That night, she got wasted and passed out around 7 pm beside her baby crib. I was stuck

As soon as I awoke, I gave Devi a quick goodbye hug and escaped.

Though in reality I was driving through the deserts of California, Arizona, New Mexico, and Texas, in my heart, I was running. I needed an escape from the Higgins and from the cokehead I'd gotten overly attached to. But as happy as I was to see my family, dogs, and the clean, potpourri-scented suburban home I grew up in, I didn't belong there.

For the first time in over six months, I was consistently around civilians. My language was full of "fucks," "cunts," "damns," and "shits," leaving a path of traumatized children and furious mothers whenever I went to a store or restaurant.

"Oh my gawd!" Grandmother whispered to my aunt in horror. "Maggie walks like a slut, talks like a slut, dresses like a slut, and acts like a *slut!*"

I was oblivious to the fact that I'd been molded by a surrounding where I *had* to be tough, bitter, and with my guard always up to avoid getting stepped on. On the Higgins, extreme defensiveness was a survival mechanism. We are all rough around the edges. From adapting to my environment, I became a very rude, aggressive person. It took me several weeks to harmoniously coexist with civilians.

Once I learned how to act like a normal human being, I was faced with another dilemma. Boredom.

Visiting home was always uncomfortable. I was never summoned with pleas for a visit or an offer to buy my tickets home. Although it was the norm in The South to make a big fuss over military members, I was never thrown welcome home parties or dinners. My parents never coordinated my leave with family vacations. Although Mom and Carl were both business owners who made their own schedules, they never took off work when I came home.

They kept their normal routines while I seemingly interrupted their lives. My family was working, cooking their meals, and completing their daily tasks while I found myself just hopping around town to visit them whenever they were free. I went from working twenty-hour days to doing practically nothing. In the process of occupying myself, I embarked on something that would permanently change my social interactions- social media.

Back in San Diego, I spent many nights in Yolanda's living room irritated with her and Myleen's constant sprints to their laptops to check their "Myspace" account.

"What the hell is Myspace?" I asked them.

"It's a website that pretty much represents you," they replied.

"What do you mean by that?"

"Well, you post pictures of yourself, describe yourself, and you get to decorate your page."

"Decorate it?"

"Yeah, like put different colors and photos in the background. And you also get to have friends on there."

"Friends?"

"Yeah. You have a friends list and add other people's profiles to it."

"That sounds pretty dumb."

Myspace failed to initially intrigue me because I didn't have any good photos of myself. When I was at my heaviest, I had a mini panic attack every time I saw my image. I avoided cameras. But after deployment, I was pleasantly surprised when I saw a photo that Myleen had taken of me at the command Christmas party.

I didn't look fat.

Since my weight gain, it was the first photo of myself where I didn't have that bloated cabbage patch face with the teeny blue eyes. I began enthusiastically jumping in front of camera flashes with Myleen and Yolanda.

"Maggie, it's time to get you a Myspace account," they decided right before I left for Tennessee. "That way we can keep in touch while you're gone."

There's no denying that then, Myspace, and now, Facebook, Twitter, and a slew of other social media sites have flourished and healthily thrived throughout the entire planet, especially among my generation. The quick and accessible online social networking it enables has a lot to do with its success, but I think people truly love it because it gives them, including myself, a completely justifiable reason to be vain.

In Myspace's adolescence, there was no such thing as "tagging" or "status updates." Users had a limit of about eight photos they could have for their profile. Myspace was pretty simple. It was a web page with the owner's photo in the top left. Below that on the left side were categories for the owner's favorite movies, television, hobbies, heroes, and also a category where they could put their relationship status (single, married, engaged, in a relationship, divorced, and so on), their height, body type, job, and other random facts about themselves. To the right side of the page were spaces for a blog, a friend's list, and their "wall." The wall was a place for other friends to leave comments. The friend's list displayed the owner's "top 8 friends," meaning their favorites of all of their Myspace friends. After a month or two of Myspacing, I would discover the significance of one's top 8 friends.

"Why am I not in your top friends, bitch?" Myleen once remarked when I'd replaced my top 8 with some new people.

"Why is Yolanda your number one, but I'm your number four?" I retaliated.

Myspace started a lot of childish spats. Myspace was known as a relationship killer.

"Baby, my Myspace says that I'm in a relationship, but yours says you're still single?" couples would argue.

"Why does it matter, honey? You know we're together. Why do I have to put my business out on Myspace?"

"Oh, I see. So you want a bunch of sluts out there to think you're single!"

"No, babe, that's not what I meant."

"Why the fuck is that skank on your top friends?"

"Why is your dumb ass ex-boyfriend still on yours?"

Myspace was a way for everyone to create their own digital representation. And as ridiculous as it may seem, you could really tell a lot about a person from their page. If someone posted photos of them doing a keg stand or always with a drink in their hand, it was safe to assume that they liked to party. If a girl's perky, glossed-up cleavage was the only thing you noticed in her photo, she was usually looking for male attention. If a guy had a hat on in every photo, he was probably balding. I could also tell how dedicated people were to their romantic relationships. If they were dating someone, but their profile still said that they were "single," they usually either screwed around or didn't take their relationship very seriously. If their profile background was a photo of them sucking the face off their partner, they were probably pretty devoted. In dating or fucking, whoever posted the most comments on the other person's wall had the most emotional investment.

Myspace opened up an entirely new world for me. It allowed me to reconnect with old high school friends and keep in touch with people I met. And also, to my pleasant surprise, it drastically expanded my man hunting ground.

My favorite aspect of Myspace was the way you could discreetly dig people's lives. Over the years since I began using Myspace, and then Facebook, I've seen the birth and death of countless marriages. I've watched men who I screwed around with when they were in their twenties, fatten and bald into their thirties. Online, I've seen cheaters get caught, plastic surgeries, drug addictions, DUIs, child custody battles, military enlistments, and military discharges. The best thing about the Internet's instant unification capabilities is that one hardly ever has to ponder thoughts like, "I wonder whatever happened to that dude in high school." I got to see who ended up at Harvard and who ended up in the trailer park. These progressions, of course, took time. In my Myspace-using infancy, I snooped around in the digital lives of guys.

I found my first one in Chattanooga to occupy my time at home. I stalked the University of Tennessee, Chattanooga profiles. I was able to search profiles by narrowing down personal information, like sex, age range, race, sexual preference, and whether they were single, in a relationship, or married. I love how this tactic disguised itself as a method for making new "friends" when everyone knew it was for potential hookup purposes. Why would I have been looking specifically for a single, straight male between the ages of twenty and twenty-nine? Of course I wanted companionship, conversation, a drinking buddy, or just someone to spend time with in a city that I found extremely dull compared to San Diego. But I also wanted to fool around with my new Myspace friend.

I stumbled across the profile of a twenty-six-year-old Jayden.

He was tall and fit with Aryan features: creamy complexion, ash blonde hair, and ice blue eyes. Those eyes were beautifully frightening. I labeled them "serial killer eyes." My stomach got jumpy with excitement when he responded to my message. He was interested in meeting me. After a few exchanged phone conversations, we decided to meet. My stomach did a series of somersaults as I drove alone to the apartment of an Internet stranger.

I was incredibly nervous. I'm sure that's partially because what I was doing wasn't very safe, especially alone.

Upon seeing Jayden in person, I immediately discovered a common trend in meeting guys online. Their photos aren't accurate. People post their most flattering images. A man with a perfectly chiseled body, but a less attractive face usually had photos of him shirtless with sunglasses on. Those with flawed bodies focused on their faces or, in Jayden's case, posted younger, fitter photos. I was certainly guilty of doing the same thing. I learned to pose at angles that slimmed my round face and back then, rarely posted full body photos. Since losing weight, I've tried to post a variety of face and full body pictures, but I definitely still put my hand on my hip and angle my figure.

Although Jayden was slightly chubbier than his Myspace photos, he still had his serial killer eyes and turned out to be an intelligent guy. We had a fun evening that ended with his fingers inside of me.

I fooled around quite a bit those few weeks in Chattanooga, even giving a young man his first set of red wings (he ate me out while I was on my period). But sex didn't happen. As promiscuous as I was back then, I don't understand why I refused intercourse on particular occasions. Sometimes I think it was a subconscious power tactic; I was receiving without giving. The fact that I could get a man to swallow my ovaries without even grazing my fingers against his cock established that I was using *him*, not the other way around.

Being away from home the Christmas before was torture. I resented San Diego and missed all the familiar comforts of home and The South. But that year, I was surrounded by the holidays from my childhood. I spent time with my family, sipped hot chocolate by the Christmas tree in front of our fireplace, and inhaled the scents of the holiday pumpkin spice potpourri that soaked into everything from my sheets to my luggage.

Chattanooga is a lot more Christmassy than San Diego. Southern California tries its best to do Christmas. The ritzy outdoor shopping malls blast carols while wealthy consumers are bundled up in their thin, fleece jackets and scarves from the abnormally chilly sixty-five-degree weather. The palm trees that were kidnapped from Mexico and artificially planted along the streets strung with Christmas light necklaces. Just like those poor palm trees longing for their home in the humid tropics, Christmas in so-cal has always seemed out of place. Chattanooga, on the other hand, has snowy mountains and pine trees. Every yard in its hilly subdivision is decked out with a flashy lights display. It's quite entertaining to drive around and see who's got the tackiest plastic baby Jesus manger scene, Santa sleigh, or where teenagers have propped two Christmas light reindeer in fornication mode. Hot chocolate and warm, fuzzy mittens are actually necessary, and though any other time of the year it annoys me, a church on every corner actually contributes to that commercialized Christmas feel.

As much as I enjoyed our classic family traditions, like going to the movies with the whole family after opening Christmas gifts, the longer I stayed in Chattanooga, the more I realized that I made the right decision to leave it.

Everywhere I went, I ran into someone from high school and their adult lives never impressed me. At age twenty, a good chunk of them were either parents or still living with theirs. Some of them were actually living a normality I would eventually envy, like attending college, spending their Sundays in orange face paint at a Tennessee Volunteers games, and pledging to sororities and fraternities. But nearly all of them were married in the same type of Tennessee suburbs they were raised in by age twenty-five.

It's not that married suburban life is a bad thing, but I pitied them because they entered it so prematurely. I never understood the rush to grow up so fast when we live in a time where it is possible for anyone, man or woman, to explore the world and pursue any career they wanted. With technology advancing and people generally living longer, there is no need to spend one's youth worrying about getting the kids to soccer practice on time or not getting the PTA meetings and the pediatrician appointments mixed up. I saw my peers as geographical prisoners.

"You're so lucky you live in California," my old high school buddies would swoon. "I wish I could live there, too."

"Well, why can't you?" I asked them.

The answers were always the same. They had work obligations, school, and money issues. They had a boyfriend or girlfriend they couldn't leave. California was too expensive. It was excuse after excuse.

"But some day, maybe," they'd reply dreamily while looking off into the distance.

Over the years, a few of them really did get out. A small minority moved to San Francisco, Texas, Colorado, Chicago, Korea, and Japan. But for most of them, 'some day' never came. They got married because that's what they thought they were supposed to do. They had kids because, "That's what's next, right?" Then they were really stuck and all that began with a deep-seated fear of *change*.

Halfway through the Navy enlistment I resented so much, I began to see its benefits. In the past year, I had been to five different countries and worked more than those kids would ever work in their whole lives. I was earning my own salary and paying my own rent three thousand miles away from my roots.

Because of the Navy, I didn't just creep into the real world. I was shoved. Once life had delivered me a few punches to the face, I was no longer afraid of it. I knew that I could pick my ass up, move anywhere I wanted, and do the work to *make* a life for myself. For the life of me, I could not comprehend how my peers could settle for dreaming about the things they had no intention of doing.

"The one thing I can't stand about you is how you carry yourself," an old friend of mine told me during a visit. "You always seem like you are so above everything and everyone around you."

Truthfully, I *did* feel a bit above everyone. I had a hard time realizing that people were different than me. Not everyone was enchanted with the southern California coast. Some people genuinely loved Tennessee culture, the mega churches, the face value politeness, the lower cost of living and the humble wages to suit it. They did not all see young parenthood as a life sacrifice of dirty diapers and stretch marks because of a broken condom. I saw what I wanted as the ideal and the fact that I was closer to it made me feel superior.

I had that same mentality with the Navy. My A-school in Meridian, Mississippi, was a culture shock. The majority of the students were fresh out of boot camp. After boot camp graduation, one's personality is a bit off. After two months of being secluded from the world inside the gates of a base of a two-mile radius as well as taking orders from someone as if they are their own Navy blue dressed God, new boot camp grads just don't socialize the way regular human beings do. I remember nonchalantly swaggering into their little building that was supposed to be their "quarterdeck" with an American flag for me to salute, checking out the cockeyed looks on their faces as I entered dressed in my civilian clothes.

In A-school, we even had to march.

"This is fucking ridiculous," I thought to myself, rolling my eyes each time.

In the six weeks I was there, I spent nearly all of my free time reading or at the gym. I refused to eat galley food and bought all my groceries at the local commissary. For the most part, I was antisocial.

When I got orders back to San Diego, I was ecstatic. There'd be no more rednecks dressed in camouflage ready to go huntin' at every gas station I pulled into. I was tired of southern accents, tired of seasons, and ready for my beach party town. Still very wild and reckless, I wanted a life of beer bongs in the sand and blow in the bathroom. With my new shore duty command, my Navy life would be a nine to five job. I only had to be a sailor a third of my day. For my second time around, I was dead set on living the civilian side of southern California.

I remember the first time I felt the west on the drive back. After two months of muggy, cold winter weather, I realized that the warm sun was burning against my left arm that was leaning on the windowsill. I was in Arizona. The warmth of the rays automatically lifted my mood as I sifted through the local radio stations. Instead of every other station containing some preacher sending the words of Jesus through the airwaves, there was Mexican polka. I was home.

Within a few weeks back, I got an apartment with Bianca, a former Higgins shipmate who also married her friend for the money. Naturally, it was in PB. Our new home was across the street from Number 8's old apartment that I had idealized. We were back in touch again, though we had barely missed each other before he took off to his new duty station in Bremerton, Washington.

Our apartment complex was shaped as a square with a hollow outdoor area in the middle that was like a courtyard. It was the perfect setting to leave your door wide open and hang off the balcony to talk to your neighbors. The back of the courtyard, the part where the square cut off, opened up to the sand and Mission Bay. The bay had a walkway with grassy areas. It was a place where everyone picnicked, barbecued, and guzzled beer in the constant sunshine. The beach was across the street. Bianca and I were smack dab in the middle of two bodies of water. It was the perfect place to party, which was exactly why I picked it.

I was instantly one with PB. I began hanging around Morrison and Number 11 again. Through them I met dozens of people. I quickly realized how great of a networking tool Myspace really was. I'd briefly meet someone. We'd friend each other, and *voila*! I instantly had another person to party with. And·unlike the

Higgins, my new place of employment seemed to hardly interfere with my social life.

My new command was called PSD Afloat West. I was at the same base as the Higgins. We were basically in charge of updating the service records of the personnel on the ships out there. The whole idea of taking care of personnel records ashore was a new concept, so my command was small but would be rapidly growing.

We were in the process of moving to a new, larger building. At the time, we were in a small, stuffy office. The higher ups had no clue what to do with us new guys, so they tossed us in the room with all the service records.

Every military member has a service record. It's a big, fat folder summarizing their enlisted time. It lists contact information, every command they've been to, every award they've won, and every time they've been reprimanded. It has the date each service member enlisted so that their command will know when to advance them or when they qualify for certain privileges, like being up for advancement or BAH rates. Their service not only has their marriage records and certificates, but it also has who their life insurance money goes to if they die while in service. A service record is an extremely important document. This is why well into the millennium, when the Internet owned the world, it made absolutely no sense why the military members' most important documents were still being kept on paper in a file cabinet.

About a year after I joined the command, someone snuck onto base and tried to burn our building down. The arson was successful enough to set off the sprinklers and soak all the records. Our entire command spent months flipping the wet records over as if we were trying to even out their suntan. Black mold sprouted all over the records, infiltrating the air and getting everyone sick.

My first few months at my new command were spent lounging around in the record room hung over. We would listen to music and nonchalantly flip through the records pretending to update them. We were called "Personnel Specialists." PS was our Navy acronym. Since I was a Seaman, I was called a PSSN, though most people just called me "Young." My "boss" was a Third Class Petty Officer Third Class named Mare. Mare was a jolly, pudgy guy of Hispanic and Filipino descent who would let me scan Myspace all day if I either flirted with him or bought him food.

Although it was limited to the kitchen of the Higgins, the Filipino mafia was in full power at PSD Afloat. Nearly every first class, chief, or officer was Filipino and they seemed to stick together and primarily assist each other up the secretarial ladder. This was especially noticeable among us newcomers fresh out of A-school.

There was a group of us who came to the command all at once. While a fraction of them were handpicked, trained, and given specific jobs, the rest of us were thrown in the corner. The Filipino kids were provided with special attention, getting the best jobs and the most flattering evaluative comments. By no means did this bother me. I had been done putting any ambitions towards the Navy for a while.

I was just completing my time while sucking as much money as possible out of the government.

I went to work for the minimum amount of time doing the least amount I could get away with. Cramming endless dry Navy bullshit into my brain for a one percent advancement rate was not worth it to me, so I didn't care how many fantastic evaluations my coworkers got.

I also had no issues with having a Filipino command. Most of them came from impoverished backgrounds, did their twenty-year careers, and retired at thirty-eight years old. After retiring, they would receive half their military paycheck for the rest of their lives, an allowance that made them wealthy back in their home country. They were smart as hell. I just found it funny that instead of a macho GI Joe or Mr. Clean type covered in tattoos, we had five-foot-tall Filipinos standing in front of ranks of chubby sailors saying, "Don't dis-reeespect my Nay-be!" in their distinguished accents.

The Higgins and PSD were alike and different in many ways. They were organizations that reflected both rapid change in the world and desperation to cling onto the past. PSD still carried on its military charade in the way their higher ranking enlisted ruled with childish malice, yelling at us during our morning Quarters if we were late or if we had colored bobby pins on our hair. They attempted to conserve our fighter physiques by conducting mandatory physical training a couple days a week. The military's obesity rate was expanding right along with the rest of America's jiggling bellies.

One of the biggest issues in recruiting military during World War II was the malnourished state of its candidates. Most young men were skeletal from the Great Depression and were underweight by military body fat standards. Thanks to technology and the economically beneficial McDonald's dollar menu, our Battle of The Bulge took place on our waistlines instead of at war. A few gung ho types would call an upbeat cadence with rows of pot-bellied sailors in Navy sweats waddling behind them. Still, every six months some fatty first class would squash his seven chins together while someone wrapped measuring tape around it, counting the flab as muscle so the poor guy could barely pass his required body fat test.

Just like the Higgins, there was avid gossip among the PSD Afloat crew. I assumed that since our job allowed us to have a life outside of work, there would be less cheating and dramatic affairs. I was wrong. People still fucked their superiors and subordinates. There were no limits. The middle-aged with three kids still got freaky with the young sailors barely older than their offspring. The married banged the married. The ugly nailed the ugly. The men fucked the men.

Dexter, my openly and quite obviously homosexual coworker was known to have plenty of straight, "don't-ask-don't-tell" pencils dipped in his company ink.

I liked Dexter because he was honest. While most sailors denied their philandering, he owned up to everything and everyone he did, unashamed of his sexuality. He also made command gossip interesting because he liked to kiss and tell.

Strangely enough, these men usually were the ones to make the moves on Dexter.

"I flirted with everyone," he explained to me. "I was a slut back then. I made it known that I was available, but I never pursued them. They were the ones who initiated it."

Although some of these men emulated that feminine, twink stereotype often pinned on gay guys, many of them were people I least expected to indulge in some sultry, sweaty man love.

"It's usually the most macho, homophobic guys who really harbor gay tendencies," Dexter explained. "The real anus munchers are the ones you'd least expect."

Though these naughty little tidbits about my workplace amused me while I was there, I rarely paid attention to PSD. I only socialized with a few of them for Friday night coke-snorting sessions. Drug usage may have been more common at the Higgins than I realized, but I wasn't aware of that world until I began using myself. Although I vowed to keep my guilty pleasure a secret upon arriving at PSD, I eventually divulged the truth to one of my fellow Navy girls. When she let it out that she indulged in blow every now and then, I realized that there was a whole underground group of sailors who practiced that same weekend ritual.

"Drugs like coke, meth, and E (ecstasy) only stay in your system seventy-two hours max," she rationalized. "But if you drink enough water and sweat enough, it can be out of your system sooner. If you snort some coke Friday night and then drink beer all weekend so you'll piss a lot, you'll be good for a Monday morning drug test."

So it became a habit for me to do coke every time I took leave or a long holiday weekend approached. I had no idea how many of my coworkers did it, but there was intense fear in the atmosphere whenever a random drug test was given. There were a lot more drug tests at PSD than the Higgins.

This could have been my guilty paranoia, but it seemed like our higher ups truly wanted to bust people. At sea, people were only reprimanded when their misbehavior couldn't be hidden. One had to blatantly be caught with something out in the open to get in trouble. I knew people who should have popped on the drug tests, but had their asses saved. My chief knew about a lot of the shit his Seamen were into, but as long as what they did off duty didn't make him look bad, he didn't give a shit.

At PSD, there wasn't a brotherly bond or loyalty among each other. The chiefs and officers seemed to fish for misbehavior. Boredom could've been a big part of that. Sea duty was much more strenuous and time consuming than the paper filing we did ashore. Also, busting the lower enlisted 'bad children' reflected a stricter, sharper parent.

Looking back on those days, I'm aware of how stupid we were to sacrifice our records and military benefits for some speedy powder to soak in our boogers. It wasn't addiction that fueled my habit. When I was at a PB party doing coke, both they and I forgot that I was in the military. During those nights, I was one of those free-spirited southern California kids indulging in shenanigans like booze, coke, and sex. Anything that resembled the civilian world was instantly attractive and Number 12 was anything but a United States Navy sailor.

Number 12 was the second man I met from Myspace. The longer I had my account, the more I saw what a great tool it was for picking up the opposite sex. Since it allowed me to browse profiles by zip code, I found myself little by little receiving messages from random PB guys who wanted to be my "friend." If they were good looking, I eagerly responded. If they weren't, I'd roll my eyes while mumbling, "douche bag" under my breath, delete their messages, and deny their friend requests.

I was automatically interested in meeting Number 12 at the first glimpse of his profile picture. With brown hair with naturally sun-kissed highlights, round chocolate eyes, and the soft teenage face, Number 12's boyish handsomeness was balanced with a white wife beater and quarter sleeve tattoos covering his arms. He seemed to intentionally emulate the message that pretty boys could be bad boys too.

He was the best looking man to give me the time of day, but that wasn't what really hooked me. In his photo he was on a stage of a dive bar. He had a guitar in his hands as he leaned towards a microphone, squinting his eyes in what looked like a mix of being intensely one with his music and painful constipation.

Just like any normal American kid, I grew up enjoying music. My interest began with the Baha'i children's cassette tapes my grandmother would put me to bed with. As a teen, I got into the punk reggae mixes of Sublime that still bring back high school nostalgia. But it was my time on the Higgins that gave me a true appreciation for music. Cold and exhausted while standing watch on the back of the ship all alone with nothing to look at but the black ocean water, the mellow, beachy tunes of Jack Johnson had a way of transforming such a bleak, depressing atmosphere into something beautiful. Even though we weren't allowed to listen to music on watch, we hid our headphones under our navy-issued beanies. Music made life as a Deck Seaman bearable.

After enough time in PB, I would realize that around every corner was a dive bar with a band that was determined to make it in the music industry. From my experience, they were a generic breed with a flask of whiskey in their pockets, a bag of coke in their wallets, and a dream of fame manufactured from some garage where it all began. Just like silicone in Hollywood, musicians in PB were a dime a dozen.

But musicians were a novelty to a Tennessee girl. The fact that they were in their mid twenties to early thirties living on the couches and futons of friends with a few community college courses under their belts never struck me as a vice. They were artists, gutsy enough to defy the mainstream norm of corporate sheep in their business suites and cubicles. In my dreamy, star-struck eyes, that was something worth fucking.

If Number 12 had a personality, he never revealed it to me.

He greeted me outside of the dig he shared with some of his buddies. It was a nice, clean three-bedroom house with hardwood floors occupied by five guys. This overcrowding was a common trend with PB's steep rent. I'd later find out that Number 12 slept in a pullout couch in the living room.

He seemed like a nice enough guy when he greeted me with a hug. He was shorter than I expected, but just as attractive in person. But other than his basic friendly mannerisms, there wasn't much to him. He was quiet. His answers were short. Conversation with him took forceful effort on my part. He sat back on his couch looking up at me as if he was waiting for all my words to crawl into his ears.

He told me a few facts about himself. He was born and raised in San Diego with three older brothers. All of them worked government jobs like the CIA and the Navy Seals.

"You know, I came from a musical family, but I'm the only one who actually pursued it as an adult," he beamed.

His voice was deep, smooth, and self-assured. Of all the men of my past, I would always remember Number 12 as having the most seductive vocals. He was twenty-four, exactly four years older than me. Strangely enough, we shared a birthday. He was the lead singer and guitarist of a band called Chubbyfunk.

"I'm the soul of that band," he bragged. "Ninety percent of our songs were written by me."

"Finally, I've got the guy talking about something," I thought with a sigh of relief.

I kept the conversation focused on him and his music, letting him ramble on about his grand destiny in the land of rock stardom.

We decided to take a short drive to Mission Bay nearby. I quickly realized that Number 12 had no car, along with his lack of a job and bedroom. As we walked together on the dewy grass, we gazed at the bright city lights of San Diego reflecting off the bay. In the midst of what should have been a romantic scenario, Number 12 gazed into my eyes and said, "You want some of this?"

I felt no butterflies in my stomach or nervousness from the anticipation of our first kiss. I just leaned into him and slipped my tongue in his mouth. After a few minutes of making out, he took my hand as we walked back to my car.

"What the hell just happened?" I wondered.

Although he failed to spark a giddy afterglow, I was very attracted to his musical talent. The night of our first rendezvous, I checked out his website and was absolutely dumbfounded at how a short white boy could belt out so much soul. He absolutely nailed tunes from music legends like Stevie Wonder and The Temptations. I would later witness him singing "Let's Get it On" by Marvin Gaye flawlessly and nearly cum in my panties on the spot. His voice truly dominated his performance.

"I'm going to be incredibly famous one day," he slurred to me one night, wasted off Captain Morgan.

"Oh really?" I asked, amused at his self-assurance. "Why do you say that?"

"Because I am *well* aware of the magnitude of my talent."

Unfortunately, my vagina never experienced the magnitude of his talent.

The night I officially became his 2 am booty call was an absolute disaster. Walking into his living room and crawling into his futon bed-couch, I quickly realized that he was intoxicated to mental retardation.

"I was on so much shit that night, I'm surprised I managed to get my dick up and inside you," he confessed later on, laughing.

That sentence sums up our first sexual encounter. He barely got hard, went inside of me, went limp, and passed out.

The following day he left for a cross-country tour with Chubbyfunk. I didn't care if he ever called me again. I had my new life to keep me occupied.

PSD began running on a twenty-four-hour schedule and I was assigned to the second shift. This meant I worked from 1 pm to 9 pm, ideal hours for partying seven days a week. Some guys from the Higgins got an apartment right next to Morrison.

My nights became filled with beer pong and Tuesday night keggers, while discreetly sneaking off to the bathroom to do a line or two of coke if I got lucky. James, Burger, Stiffler, Morrison, Number 7, and Number 11 were just a few of the people in our frat row clique. I befriended the girls they fucked. From there, I developed a web of acquaintances to have my good times with.

Sexually, the atmosphere was extremely casual. I saw previous Numbers bring around one girl after the other and it didn't faze me. There was even a situation when two other girls and I had done both Number 7 and Number 11. At one party, somebody locked all five of us in the bathroom together.

Being the first to nail both of them, I proudly stated, "Wow! If I had herpes, you *all* would have herpes!"

My social circle quickly grew beyond frat row. PB was an easy place to make temporary friends. On any given night all one had to do was walk down the road to find almost every door wide open with a group of young adults chatting and drinking. It was easy to just walk into a party full of strangers.

There were many nights when I'd black out and wake up at my apartment with several random numbers in my cell phone wondering, "Who the hell are these people?" But during that time, I loved my life. I loved living footsteps away from sand. I loved the palm trees that ran parallel to the roads. I loved the Garnet Avenue strip packed with bars and trashy, trendy, and very affordable clothing boutiques. I loved how all I had to do was hang off my doorstep to have a conversation with one of my neighbors, barefoot in board shorts with a beer in their hands. I loved the hot boys next-door who didn't seem to own shirts. I loved that my days were always jammed with barbecues and parties. I loved the sexualized atmosphere of PB, packed with promiscuous boys that only needed a brief stare to arouse them. I loved the fact that I couldn't walk down the street without some obnoxious twenty-three-year-old rolling down his car window to yell something like "OOOOOOWWWWW!" I loved that my guy friends showed up to my apartment with kegs on holidays and wore shirts that said things like "It's not rape. It's surprise sex." I loved that my girlfriends were thin, pretty in bug-eyed sunglasses, and shared my love for shopping, blow, tequila, and belligerent fraternity boys. The more of this world I got, the less I felt like a part of the Navy.

My state of mind wasn't unique. About a quarter of my friends were still enlisted, but resented it as much as I did. They used the Navy as a half-ass day job while dodging drug tests and drinking themselves into amnesia.

My Higgins buddy, James, wallowed in the PB lifestyle like a pig in mud. He was thin, in his early twenties with wavy, short brown hair and fluffy eyelashes. Everyone thought he was stunningly beautiful because of his delicate facial features and his lean, Calvin Klein model build. Although I snorted a line or two at a party or splurged on a gram at the beginning of leave or a long weekend, my coke usage never reached the capacity of his. James constantly twitched in jerky, erratic movements that intensified his already severe case of A.D.D. He was also bipolar, so in the midst of his mania he was the force behind our chaotic lives.

When he didn't have to report to the ship, his typical morning would begin with snorting a line of coke in the bathroom. His apartment would be a wreck with beer bottles, cigarette butts, and half naked twenty-somethings sprawled across the couches and floor. Exiting the bathroom feeling high and refreshed, he'd excitedly announce, "*Let's rage, brotherdudes! Let's rage like we've never raged before!*"

James was a motivational coach for alcoholism. With euphoric enthusiasm for the adventure the day had in store, he'd lead his pack of hung over guys from one bar to the next. After last call, they'd bring back whatever tan, cleavage-baring sorority girls they could scavenge and retreat home for a night of beer pong until dawn. Enough cocaine allowed James to divide and conquer Garnet like a PB god.

There were no genuine bonds between me and the people I surrounded myself with. It didn't occur to me that once I outgrew my lifestyle, they would disappear. I lived in the now.

I focused on all things shallow. If someone was fun, they were one of my best friends. I was never lonely. Every Friday night I had a plan with eight other backups because people were so flakey. There was no such thing as saying, "Let's get dinner tomorrow," and actually getting dinner tomorrow. Whatever worked within five minutes was what happened. My PB party buddies filled in the voids of the solid relationships I was lacking.

I also had a generic substitute for intimacy. I rarely slept alone. Some of my bedmates were just platonic friends who were drunk and needed a place to lay their heads. A few were practically strangers I'd met at a party. I didn't touch some and fooled around with others. I had one British traveler about my age come over for weeks only to sleep and cuddle with me throughout the night. I didn't kiss him because I never felt like it. When I wanted something physical, I had my way with them. Until I left PB, this would be my lifestyle. Real intimacy didn't exist.

I was in complete shock when Number 12 called me late one Sunday night. It had been a month since he'd given me "some of that."

"Hey, Maggie! How've you been?" he greeted me, sounding strangely excited to talk to me.

"Um, hi!" I responded, still a bit dazed from being awoken. "I wasn't expecting to hear from you."

"I've been on tour, remember? I told you I'd call you when I got back."

"What a crazy fucking weekend," I thought as I drove over for round two with Number 12.

Friday was spent crossing the Mexican border with some San Diego State University students. We were all underage and Tijuana was a haven for us young whippersnappers thirsty for debauchery. I'd gotten intoxicated enough to dance at a club, which in my case is pretty severe. Apparently, in the midst of my crotch grinding to the beat of music, I kissed three or four different guys.

"Don't worry, they were all cute," my friends assured me.

The next night I managed to have a drunken, but passionate, sexual encounter without even having sex. I've found that with many guys, refraining from actual intercourse can be more stimulating than sex itself. I think this has something to do with two people working their bodies up to so much frustration. It seems like with sex, once a guy is done, he's done. He got off and all there's left to do is sleep. When sex is abstained, he gets more creative and the whole thing is one fun extravaganza. It happened with a friend of a friend who I'd had a crush on for a while. He was one of those guys who didn't like to have sex the first time he fooled with a girl so we went dry humping and oral sex crazy. I was fine with this setup because his penis was tiny. I didn't have to be disappointed by his baby dick and blowing him was like deep throating a Q-tip.

When we woke up the next morning, my apartment was in shambles. My sheets were on the other side of my room. Items from my shelves and dresser had been knocked onto the carpet. His boxers were nowhere to be found. There was a trail of water and wet towels from my bedroom to the bathroom only to find bottles of shampoo, conditioner, and shaving cream knocked into the middle of the tub. It had been a fun night.

I was quite proud of myself for topping the weekend off with sex, even if it was mediocre.

I never understood why Number 12 kept calling for nearly six months. After that first time, the sex was never horrible, but it certainly wasn't good. He was actually pretty well endowed but he fucked the way he carried conversation - effortlessly. It was as if his only duty was to stay hard while the woman did everything else. He was lifeless and dull. He didn't pull my hair, scratch, bite, or slap my ass. He just maneuvered himself in and out. One night, I took desperate measures to get some variation.

"Just fuck me up the ass," I commanded.

Number 12 wasn't completely to blame though. Although my ego was stronger than it was during my Deck Seaman days, I was still not totally comfortable with my sexuality. I didn't demand or even hint the things I wanted. I didn't once say, "Look, if we're going to do it, you need to put some more life into it," or "Can we please try some different positions so I don't fall asleep with your shaft inside of me?"

When it came to being on top, I was a late bloomer. Back then I avoided that position. Because Number 12 was lazy, this caused a dilemma that usually ended up with me on my hands and knees waiting for him to be done. And frankly he just didn't excite me. Sure, he was cute, was in a band, and had a voice that sounded like sex on a stick, but for some reason no matter how much I'd wanted it earlier, he always sent my twat into a coma.

I could tell that Number 12 got plenty of action by his indolent I-don't-have-to-please-you mating style. Women threw snatch at him regularly. There was no value to such a frequent occurrence.

No matter how drunk or coked out he was, he remained a condom Nazi. This is a great quality, but I've found that the more promiscuous men are the most STD cautious. Plus it's common sense that with his looks and talent, women practically shoved their boobs down his mouth. I was definitely not the prettiest girl he could get his hands on. My strongest theory is that lying stoic and stiff, like his dick was a monument I was expected to worship, required less physical rigor than stroking his own.

Even though I slept with Number 12 during a phase where I juggled a few men at a time, I made myself available every time he called. I left men in my bed in the middle of the night for a quickie with Number 12 in my car. I always came to him. He never came to me. The only time he contacted me before midnight was for my coke connections. I never demanded a date, cuddling, or even a friendship. I didn't ask him if he knew my last name or the color of my eyes. I fucked him wherever he wanted to fuck, even on a car in his driveway or on top of his bathroom sink. I made myself a warm hole for his dick with free delivery.

It is appalling how much self-respect I surrendered for a man who didn't give me a single orgasm. But from my very twisted perspective, I was climbing a ladder. I was a product of a society where women are validated by the men they attract. There is an all too common theme in romantic comedies where a pitiful, ugly girl loses weight or gets an extreme makeover, eventually winning the affection of her dream guy when she has reached her beauty potential. I grew up rooting for that girl.

In the months I was fucking Number 12, I was still fresh from seeing myself as a fat Deck Seaman. The year before, I did not attract men like him. Even though he called me for a quick and easy lay in the middle of the night, I saw him as choosing me above all the other girls drooling over him while he was onstage. I didn't see myself as being objectified and used. I thought I was making progress. I had not yet earned the right to bore him with talk about my hopes, dreams, and childhood. I didn't even deserve a lunch date. I took what I could get.

Luckily, the submissive, self-loathing persona I displayed wore off. One night, Number 12 wanted coke. It took me an hour to reach my friend's dealer during which my phone exploded every two minutes with rude, impatient nagging.

The second I had his precious powder, he disappeared. I told him to go fuck himself. I grew a spine. He quit calling.

Number 13

Carl always warned me to never peak in high school.

"When yer an adult, you'll find things lak high school pop-you-larity really don't matter," he'd say. "Once ya graduate, nobody cares if you were sum homecomin' queen that ruled your school. Mosta tha popular kids ah knew from high school turned out-ta be average Joes, doin' some working class job, poppin' out kids with their high school sweetheart, gettin' divorced by thirty."

"The sad thing bout' it is," he continued, "they grew up an' weren't leaders of their world anymore. At eighteen, they got their best years behind em'. They spend the rest of their lives in their hometowns with their same high school buddies, talkin' bout the good 'ole days."

Carl's predictions were pretty accurate. Generally, while the high school nerds were pursuing successful, lucrative careers, the popular kids were still peddling around their high school football games a decade after graduation.

Many sailors experienced the same situation with the Navy. The USS Higgins had been the highlight of their lives. They were liked and respected by their superiors and advanced rapidly. Then they got out, many of their skills useless in the civilian world, longing for the rigid structure of a haze grey world.

By my mid twenties, I knew that eras in life would come and go. I began to realize I was lucky that I'd never experienced a time or place that I felt completely in sync with. I have no delusions - there will come a day that I'll be elderly and overwhelmed with the chaos of technology that I'll never adapt to. I'll find myself disgusted with the alterations of time and spend my days buzzed off cocktails because I'll have nothing else to lose besides my nostalgia for older and better times. But before my tits got saggy enough to swing around my neck, I was ready when change came.

I knew many people who adapted to the passing years quite well. Diana, my busty Navy friend who introduced me to Number 9, was an example. Although she loved the Higgins, she also loved life after it. She eagerly gave up booze-soaked, hooker-infested deployment parties for a civilian life of motherhood, a country house in the Midwest and Martha Stewart inspired baking.

Then there were people like Dino, the Higgins high school bully who constantly made fun of my weight. After his enlistment, he never accomplished much beyond mundane warehouse jobs and sprouting a couple of kids. His weight even ballooned to the size I was when he verbally tortured me and I couldn't help but poke fun at his karma. He often contemplated enlisting again and reminisced on the Navy with the fondness for his glory days.

Dino was perfectly molded for that specific place and time. It seemed like just as the Navy was Dino's custom fit world, PB was exactly that for aspiring musicians like Number 13.

Number 13 should have had low self-esteem. He was a loser.

Like Number 12, he had no job, car, or college degree. Also like Number 12, he was the lead singer of a band. Go figure.

But Number 13 wasn't savvy enough to acquire a permanent couch to sleep on. Number 13 was homeless.

Luckily he had naïve, dimwitted girls like me to house him, feed him, drive him, and give him a twenty-dollar bill here and there for the sake of his survival.

But more than not having a dime after his twenty-eight years on earth, he was kind of ugly. With a chunky, protruding belly and the oddest over plucked, jagged black eyebrows that sharply curved into his face, he resembled an evil Disney cartoon villain. Think Jafar from *Aladdin* eyebrows.

But Number 13 did not have confidence issues. In fact, to this day I've yet to meet anyone nearly as arrogant. According to him, he was on the road to immense fame. It was his destiny. He was already plastering his inspirational biography all over his Myspace page. It was about how he had grown up in New York and boldly stomped out of that world to seize the greater world of rock stardom that awaited him in California.

"The key is to follow your dreams," he wrote.

The whole thing was chock full of generic, "just go for it so you can be a star like me," advice. His words constructed this heroic, massively accomplished superstar who had risked his life for a world of glitz and glamour. He often spent his days copying and pasting his biography onto bulletins so it could repeatedly pop up on his Myspace friends' feeds.

I "met" Number 13 in the same way I met Number 12- through Myspace.

Number 13's Myspace usage was slightly more developed. Number 12 had been fumbling around with something new. He wasn't using his page to promote his band or accumulate as many friends as possible, like Number 13 did. I believe that literally every day Number 13 woke up, sprung off some buddy's couch, and frolicked to the local internet café in PB where he'd search through the land of Myspace to submit a friend request to every female in the San Diego region.

When he contacted me, I did not for a second fathom ever sleeping with him. Even though I was promiscuous, I did not fuck every male I befriended. I had guys like Morrison and the majority of frat row strictly for partying, coke connections, and access to other potential hook ups.

Number 13 just seemed like somebody worth knowing. This was because his Myspace page served another purpose that I hadn't discovered: the ability to make one appear more important than they really are. His photos were professionally taken and edited, nearly all of them featuring him with his pierced ears, shaved head, and black t-shirts screaming into some microphone as veins popped out of his neck. There was often hazy, dusk lighting in his photos with fog in the background as if he was performing some concert in a large venue. When I clicked onto his profile, the background was black with his insanely long biography in blood red font. Below this featured what seemed to be hundreds of trashed out women - mostly cougars in their mid thirties to late forties- with crispy dyed hair, equally crispy tanned skin, and stiff silicone breasts leaving a cleavage up to their necks, posting comments of how great his music was and how fun this and that show had been. This made him seem cool, like he knew where the best parties were.

Mere seconds after entering his page, boisterous metal music blared into the background. This was his band, Beating Bertha.

Beating Bertha was a San Diego metal band comprised of five men. With the exception of Number 13, all of them were middle-aged and the sight of them was the prime visual definition of a midlife crisis. Faded tattoos covered their drooping, sun-spotted skin as their black, sleeveless t-shirts hung loosely to reveal their flapping man tits and pot bellies underneath.

Their bassist fully rocked the bad ass metal guy look with painted black nails, silver rings, chains hanging down from his faded denim, a skull bandana holding back his long, greasy, black hair and smudged eyeliner, further amplifying his worn cheeks and crows feet. Beating Bertha seemed to be their last hurrah in living their childhood rock star dreams before being bound down by nursing homes.

Once I met the entire band, I realized that, other than Number 13, Beating Bertha was more of a hobby than a career aspiration. The rest of the guys had day jobs, homes, and feet on the ground.

The old guys had known each other for decades, occasionally uniting for jam sessions far before my mother lost her virginity. They discovered Number 13 a couple years back, drunk off his ass, singing in one of those sketchy hole-in-the-wall bars that smelled of smoke and stale peanuts. *Bam!* The artistic collaboration of Beating Bertha was born! If Disturbed and Metallica had sex and smoked some crystal meth during the pregnancy, Beating Bertha would have been their baby.

I've always hated metal. It's just a cluster fuck of incessant screaming and much too amplified screechy instruments. And head banging is about as good of an idea as sticking your genitals in a bowl of Sriracha.

"*Mm mm mmmm,*" my chiropractor grandmother would always hum aloud in disapproval whenever musicians head banging would appear on television. "All they're doin' is getting' their necks outta' alignment."

Beating Bertha's music sounded like an obvious regurgitation of every other metal band. Even Number 13's voice was James Hetfield karaoke. Number 13 could definitely carry a tune, but it was a watered down version of what had been done twenty-five years before his time.

But before seeing Beating Bertha live and getting to know the real Number 13, I believed him to be the image he constructed on Myspace. This was a man who was talented, driven, and willing to sacrifice things like material possessions for a shot at fame. He seemed gutsy, which was probably what landed him in my bed hours after our first in-person rendezvous.

I was not even slightly attracted to Number 13 when I met him in the dark, desolate parking lot of a post office. Actually, the only time the thought of fucking him didn't make me queasy was smack dab, mid-coitus in the heat of the oddest, animal lust I'd ever experienced. He was tackily dark, with his tan skin, broad, hairless skull, and those angular, freshly waxed eyebrows that looked like they belonged to an amateur transvestite. Number 13's presence screamed what southerners call "Yankee."

Everything about him was loud, from his obstreperous, booming voice that echoed across the parking lot to his thick, nasal New York accent that lacked charm. All of his gestures, from his arm movements to the way his eyes excitedly darted while he talked about himself were fierce and unruly as if he didn't give a shit whether he knocked someone in the face, because he was really all that mattered.

He was short and stocky, which has always been my least favorite male body type. What made his build even less appealing was his typical stocky guy walk, puffing out his chest and swaying his arms back and forth in what I'm assuming was supposed to be some kind of manly waddle. I would later find that the gaudiest aspect of his appearance was the Beating Bertha t-shirt he wore every single time I saw him.

"MAGGIE!" he loudly exclaimed, almost abrupt enough to make me piss myself.

When he walked up to me, he wrapped his arms around my body without hesitation, yanking me into his chest like a spineless rag doll. There was not a drop of gentility within him.

I was not comfortable around Number 13 and never would be unless I was severely intoxicated. I'm not sure if it was his drag queen, pirate eyebrows, or just who he was in general, but there was something very unnatural about his demeanor. Watching his animated facial expressions and exaggerated, loud vocals as he rambled on about his band and music career, I thought of the way he wrote in our earliest communication. In his Myspace messages, he ended nearly every sentence with three or four exclamation points. He was the same way in person.

He was incredibly polite, contributing multiple pleases and thank yous when he asked for things - and he asked for a lot of things. His first request was given within thirty seconds of walking through my door. He wanted a sandwich. As I slapped together whole wheat bread, turkey, cheese, with some mayo and honey mustard, I thought nothing of it. It was just a sandwich.

I sat on my red, circular futon in the tiny living room I shared with Bianca. Number 13 leaned back in our cheap, grey loveseat that we'd gotten for free from a friend.

"GOD, YOU KEEP THIS PLACE SO NEAT!" he exclaimed. "I LOVE IT!"

The men I brought over were always fond of my apartment. There was nothing impressive about it. It was a tiny two-bedroom squeezed in only five hundred square feet, an ideal example of California's ability to smash as many people as possible into a small building to collect maximum rent.

The place had the look of a college pad with flimsy, hand-me-down furniture and a few Beatles and Led Zeppelin posters held on the walls with thumbtacks. It was so small that my open bedroom door could be touched with a broomstick from my seat. Inside my room was a wooden dresser I'd bought for fifty bucks from a woman off Craigslist and a queen size mattress resting on top of its box without the frame. Royal blue silk sheets I'd purchased in Hong Kong covered it with a comforter on top. My apartment reeked of juvenile poverty, but it had a youthful charm.

On the nights that it wasn't packed with belligerent twenty-somethings and bottles of booze piled on our kitchen countertops, the place was spotless. Since living with my chain-smoking husband and his sweet, but disgustingly sloppy girlfriend, I had become obsessed with keeping my living environment in crisp, clean order. Even in the deepest waves of my drunkenness, I'd scrub the crud off dishes and drain the beer bottles at our parties. With the scented candles, potpourri, and the salty ocean air seeping through the screens of my slightly ajar windows, my apartment carried an odor that signified a suburban housewife on the premises. The place was probably the closest thing to motherly comfort these men could find in PB, which was what likely drew so many strangers into my silky soft, Downy-scented sheets.

I watched in slight disgust as Number 13 devoured his sandwich. He ate the way a drunk man would motorboat a stripper at his buddy's bachelor party. He dug his whole face into the sandwich, nearly rubbing his nose in it and gobbling slices of meat in between sentences. I'm almost certain that a pig snort or two escaped his nostrils. However, ravenous starvation did not keep Number 13 from further elaborating on his legendary life story. Myspace didn't cover everything, you know.

Number 13 was born in 1978 and raised in New York by Italian parents, whom he remained very close to. Every time he returned home for a visit, his mother spent the entire time cooking and stuffing her son's greedy face.

"I've never seen anyone beef up that fast," the girlfriend of one of Number 13's band mates commented shortly after he'd returned from a family visit.

Even though I already knew the story, he once again went into the details of how he had sprinted out of New York completely broke and was later discovered by his band mates singing in a bar. He spoke of his life the way a parent reads their child a bedtime story, like it was supposed to inspire my hopes and dreams. Then he began name-dropping, something he did during every single conversation with everyone in earshot.

"Beating Bertha has already been *really* successful."

When he said "really," his eyes widened. This reminded me of when my brother was an infant. Whenever my mom would drive under a bridge or through a tunnel, his eyes looked like they were going to jump out of their sockets.

"We've already performed with *so* many great bands."

Without having to ask what bands, he quickly satisfied my desperate curiosity.

"Disturbed, Sevendust, Stone Sour," he began, his heart palpitating like a hummingbird. "Buckcherry, Our Lady Peace, Staind, Flyleaf, Shinedown, uh, did I say Disturbed already?"

Somewhere in the midst of Number 13 breaking down his experience with every band member, what they were like, how much they adored him and the rest of Beating Bertha, and how much promise Beating Bertha had to being truly big in metal's history, I realized that I was absolutely dying to talk. I could feel the words roughly nudging the back of my throat, desperate to escape. My brain was constructing too many thoughts and my vocal chords were in pain from being restrained from the exercise they were so used to.

God dammit, I just wanted say something! But with Number 13's brassy New York accent and massive obsession with himself, I was owned. He dominated all conversation in that room. It had finally happened. I had met someone even more talkative than myself.

"Is this how it feels to have a conversation with me?" I wondered.

After he finished the detailed breakdown of every band he'd ever opened for, Number 13 did something completely shocking. He asked a question about me. *Me*

"Where are you from, Maggie?"

"Chattanooga, Tennessee."

"Oh shit! You're from The South! Are you near Atlanta?"

"Yeah. Atlanta's actually about an hour and a half from Chattanooga."

"Ugh!" he seemed appalled by this answer. "I *hate* Atlanta! I had to go there for a show once. *Way* too many niggers! I wanted to wrap a noose around the necks of all those nasty, ratchet black people!"

At first, I thought he was just trying to display an angry, metal singer image, but as the time I knew Number 13 unfolded, I realized that he had a lot of hate.

"What's your racial ethnicity?" I asked him, responding to his bigotry.

I could tell from his mocha skin tone that he wasn't Caucasian.

"My parents adopted me from Chile," he admitted.

This was the only time he ever looked humble. He seemed ashamed of his heritage and I wondered what kind of Jim Crow atmosphere he'd been raised in.

"I really like your toe nails," he remarked all of a sudden.

He nodded to my coral painted toes that were resting on the dark red cushions of my futon.

"I have kind of a foot fetish and you have really nice feet."

The fact that I hadn't kicked him out yet demonstrates how low my standards were for the people I associated with. I didn't like Number 13. He wasn't attractive or interesting to talk to.

In spite of his politeness, he didn't seem like a decent human being. Although I had been out of Tennessee and in the big, bad real world for two years, I was still that insecure teenager eager to be loved and accepted by those that she did not even love and accept. I didn't once stop to think about how odd it was that the man in my living room was twenty-eight with no car, home, or paying job. I never considered his racist remarks a bad omen in having him even further involved in my life. I didn't dub his foot fetish comment creepy, even though it was a highly inappropriate thing to say to someone an hour after meeting. And when he got up to make *another* sandwich, this time without permission, I didn't find it invasive that he was already asking for a place to sleep that night. I just answered with a prompt "yes."

I could elaborate more. I'm sure my brain could create two point six billion ways to describe how much Number 13 sucked, but words still would not escalate me to any level above him.

I had sex with him. I was not raped. Number 13 did not hold a gun to my head and give me the option of either spreading my legs for his miniature penis or having my brains splattered across my silk sheets. I *chose* to have sex with him. Not only was I one hundred percent sober, I made the first move. There aren't enough excuses in the world or insults to fling at one another to alter the fact that we are really only as good as the people we fuck. Sure, Number 13 was a delusional, self-absorbed mooch, but I willingly got it on with that delusional, self-absorbed mooch. What did that make me? A doormat? Pathetic? A slut? All I know is that whatever the hell Number 13 was, I gave him further incentive to keep on being that.

He acted like a shit head. I rewarded him with sex.

"I don't understand why I even talk to this guy," I said as I rolled my eyes with an exasperated expression.

I was at work and as usual, doing absolutely nothing. I was talking to Antoine. Antoine was one of my coworkers, a twenty-one-year-old from Chicago. We often got through our tedious workdays by talking about relationships. These topics usually bounced back between his horrendous young marriage and my fling of the week. I gave my female perspective while he gave his male. We were scanning the Beating Bertha website so I could give him a visual of Number 13. I was still at awe that I would've ever touched someone like him. Ugh.

"I know exactly what it is," he nodded with a sly smirk on his face. "He brings out your dark side - a part of you that you never knew about."

As we stiffly lay in bed side by side, Number 13 didn't touch me. His creepy remark about my feet was the only hint of any attraction he may be harboring. I lied flat on my back and remained still wondering what to do.

"He's in my bed," I thought. "But he's not touching me. Do I want him to touch me? I'm not attracted to him. No, I'm not attracted to him at all. I've fucked much hotter guys than him. Hell, I fucked a much hotter guy just a few days ago. I don't need him. Am I attracted to him? No, absolutely not. His head is bald and he's got weird eyebrows. My mom's pug has better table manners. I hate his obnoxious New York accent. But why hasn't he tried anything? What's wrong with me? Why the hell hasn't *he* touched *me*? Ugh, I totally ditched another guy tonight just to sleep next to this tool taking up my entire bed. I bet he snores. I bet he farts, too. Asshole. I should just kiss him, not because I'm attracted to him, but just so the night isn't an entire waste. What a boring night. I can't sleep. I'm really bored. Oh, fuck it."

I rolled over and kissed him. He immediately pounced on top of me with an angry passion that I'd never seen in a man before. I'd lit some kind of fuse, like he was unleashing a lifetime's worth of sexual suppression. Sex with him was one of the most inhumane, savage experiences of my life. There were no tender kisses on my neck or flirtatious coddling. Number 13 just got straight to the point, practically shredding my t-shirt and shorts on their way off.

He took my legs and yanked them over his shoulders. He ate me the way he ate the sandwich, greedily digging his face as deep into me as it would go. As repulsive as his table manners looked, they *felt* invigorating. Hot flashes sped in currents through my body as if my vagina was being electrocuted.

Like I was one of those blow up dolls sold as a gag gift at a porn shop, he tossed my legs back onto the bed and flipped me on my side.

At some point, his pants and boxers came off, but I was delirious to all reality beyond him and I.

He positioned himself behind me, yanking my top leg up and shoving his dick inside.

Number 13 had a tiny penis. Of all the men I've had sex with, he may in fact be the small penis champion. But he was also one of the best fucks I've had. For what that man lacked in size, he made up for in vigor, energy, and some very ballsy mating behavior. All the hate I'd seen in Number 13 was taken out on my naked body. The man threw me onto walls, slapped me, yanked my hair, scratched my back, bit my ass and thighs, and shoved me face down on top of my bed, twisting my arms behind my back while he fucked me from behind.

He drilled that small penis into me while prying my legs wide enough apart so that I could thoroughly feel him. He was a significantly better lay than some of my much more horse-dicked lovers. Does this disprove that size matters? A man with a needle dick and a good work ethic is much better than a lazy tripod. But if Number 13 was a great lay with an anorexic midget penis, just imagine how much better he would've been if he'd actually been packing something.

My society, one that is fighting for full equality between men and women, would dub the sex Number 13 and I had as abusive, disrespectful, and degrading to women. I look back on my Number 13 involvement with shame because of the guy he was. But I've never felt a bit of humiliation or regret for the *way* we had sex. Although I do enjoy intimate lovemaking with the right person, that violent, animalistic heat that Number 13 and I had was something I'd been craving since my earliest days of puberty. In the two years of consistent sex I had with Number 3, I never had satisfaction. Every time I made requests like "harder," "rougher," "slap this," "pull that," he either got the face of a child who had found monsters under his bed or was so emasculated that his uncircumcised sea creature penis recoiled in shame. Number 4 simply refused to intensify anything beyond soft, sweetness and looked at me like I was a schizophrenic with daddy issues when I tried to request some aggression.

Since then, I'd encountered a few men who liked to get a little rough, but I always held back in fear of judgment. Was there something wrong with me because I wanted to get slapped around in the bedroom every now and then?

All grown up and in complete control of my life, I no longer associate with men like Number 13. I demand respect from everyone, especially men who attempt to date me. But as I've gotten more and more comfortable with my sexuality, I've found that lust transforms me. Suddenly, in the arms of a man, I want to be dominated by a very masculine force and if I really trust him, I want him to do degrading things to me. There are also instances where I want to be the one committing violence. I've had several fantasies of being on top of a man in the middle of a heated lovemaking session. As I tenderly gaze into his eyes, I stretch up my arm and fiercely nail him with a SMACK to the jaw.

There are probably plenty of psychologists and women's studies majors who would love to take pieces of my childhood, virginity loss, and broken male relationships to compose dozens of disorders I may be harboring. But truthfully, I think I'm quite normal - just more honest than average.

Sure, I want a man's respect and an equal, loving partnership, but there's no sickness in wanting to go crazy in an act that's committed *because* of our animal instincts.

Even though Number 13 had scratched an itch that no other man had even reached for, he did not fulfill me. He couldn't because there was no affection between us.

"You have to have three things with somebody," he explained to me one evening. "Friendship, intimacy, and passion. If you don't have all of those things, it won't work out."

Oddly enough, this was some of the best advice I've ever gotten. I kept his words in mind with every man that followed him. Number 13 and I did not have any intimacy. We never snuggled.

"I just don't think we cuddle well together."

I agreed. In fact, I couldn't stand him unless we were having sex. We were a horrible combination for a friendship. He possessed a much more magnified, in-your-face version of all of my flaws. We were two people competing for the center of attention, which ended up being a nasty combination. His physical appearance never grew on me. I remember looking at him the morning after our first night together. He was still sleeping on his side facing away from me. I glanced at the back of his neck at the small rolls that rested where his thick, bald skull and neck met. My stomach churned as if I'd swallowed a tub of rotten butter.

But all his qualities that I found so revolting just made our sex more interesting. There was something very erotic about fucking the opposite of what I wanted. The filth of Number 13 just made our sex dirtier.

"AAAAARRRRGGGGGGG!!!!!" Number 13 shouted as his manhood vomited warm, salty goo all over my comforter.

His left arm wrapped around my neck like a hungry python as his right hand gripped a chunk of my hair. In spite of my love for rough housing, I hate being choked, but it wasn't the best time to argue. His sweaty, famished body collapsed onto my mangled silk sheets and he curled into a fetal position.

"God damn, you are fun to fuck," he flatly breathed out, still in a post-coital trance.

After a few minutes of composing himself, he rolled over on his back and put his hands behind his head to relax.

"By the way," he said nonchalantly. "I have a girlfriend."

In all the incessant rambling about himself, he forgot to mention that tiny detail. How convenient.

For the second time that night I should have kicked him out. Keep in mind that I was the same girl driving to Number 12's house at 3 am for mediocre, orgasm-free quickies. I had a very loose grasp on my morality. Because I did not have any emotional investment in Number 13, I thought nothing of his relationship with Tammy.

Tammy was the elusive girlfriend that lived eight hours north in Sacramento. Whatever shitty judgment of character I possessed, her case was significantly worse. This woman was the last person I expected to slum it with a guy like Number 13. Although I never met her, I've seen plenty of photos. She wasn't beautiful, but she was adorably feminine with a gentle face. She had fair skin, wide doe eyes, and strawberry blonde hair. Something about her seemed very clean, like she always smelled good and greeted you at her wreath-hung door with a glass of iced tea.

Tammy seemed like a very put together woman. She was in her mid twenties and in medical school. She had brains, looks, and a promising career, yet she was in a *relationship* with some shady, broke, metal head that cheated on her. She was also his only stable source of income.

"Is she faithful to you?" I asked, while we were still in bed together.

"Yeah," he replied, still sounding casual and unstirred. "That's why I try not to cheat on her very often, but it sometimes just happens. Like tonight, you made the move on me. You started it."

From what I've both seen and experienced, I've found that cheating men tend to hold bottled up anger towards their lovers. After the Thailand incident, Matty never treated me with any warmth or friendliness again.

Even though we only had sex once and it was long before anyone knew of Number 10's engagement, he still coiled up in discomfort whenever I was any social gathering where his wife was present.

The woman, and I'm sure man in other situations, becomes that evil harlot that tempted a good intentioned guy into adultery. I suppose it's easier to blame someone else. It's a cowardly mind frame, but then again, cheaters *are* cowards.

At twenty, I did not hold commitment at the level I do now. I knew cheating was wrong, but I saw Number 13's infidelity as his business. I assured him many times that I had no desire to wreck his relationship. I even befriended Tammy on Myspace just to introduce myself. She already knew he was staying with a girl named Maggie, so I let her know me to make her more comfortable with it.

"I was a little scared when you first contacted her," he admitted. "But she says you're really nice and I know you won't tell her anything about what happened with us."

It was easy to butt out. I wasn't jealous of Tammy. I pitied her. I may have been housing and occasionally fucking her parasite boyfriend, but at least I didn't love him. I didn't even like him.

Like a stray dog, Number 13 kept coming back to my apartment. Served me right for feeding him.

Sometimes he did stay true to Tammy. I believe he loved her, but more than that, he *needed* her. She was supposed to be moving to San Diego once the semester was up and her finances were the only way Number 13 could pretend to be a functional adult.

I never pressured him to have sex. When he wasn't touching me, I didn't want him. It was only when he acted like a lion diving for juicy chunk of raw meat that he stirred anything inside of me.

Most of the time, I was just his hotel manager. On our sexless nights, we pretended to be friends. Sometimes I even got to talk about myself. Then I began to realize how small PB was. Number 13 knew Number 12. I was fucking them both. There were afternoons that I went straight from dropping Number 12 off to picking up Number 13. I felt like a player.

Looking back, I was probably a pitiful sight. Both of those men were unemployed children with fantasies of rock stardom that they'd never achieve. And both were using me.

My sex life with Number 13 came in waves. Out of the blue, he'd tackle me in the middle of my kitchen or pick me up and toss me onto my bed. There were no warnings. He never asked permission. Then, after one chaotic day that blurred into the hours past dusk, I was done.

It was a Sunday in May, shortly before my twenty-first birthday. Although it was only spring, PB was filled with the dry, blistering heat of summer. Scents of salt, sunscreen, and beer filled the air. It was one of those days where all the neighbors kept their doors wide open, occasionally greeting the scantily-clothed beach goers strolling down the bay boardwalk. Number 13 popped by for a visit and we proceeded to gulp down a bottle of cheap gin my neighbor had given me.

High off the liquor, he shoved me into my bedroom and ravaged me in the aggressive way that he always did. I lost track of how many hours we were in bed. We just continued to claw at each other like wild jackrabbits.

We were too deep into our drunken sex spell to have any discretion. Bianca came home, along with some of our friends. We were supposed to have a cookout that day. Number 13 and I continued fucking in my bedroom, concealed by paper-thin walls.

We went at it in our usual violent style of screaming, scratching, slapping, shoving against walls, knocking each other onto the floor, and then continuing to screw all over the carpet, regardless of our scorching rug burns. I hate thinking about the sounds my guests had to blare out with music.

Through the evening, we'd occasionally step out of the room to socialize. Once or twice I came out in nothing but my sheet, sitting down to chat with everyone over a beer like everything was normal. But things were not normal.

Beyond my sex noises and silk sheet ensemble, it was Number 13 that was truly humiliating. It was the first and only time I brought him around my friends and he was being… *himself*. This meant cornering every person to brag about his precious band, name drop every notable musician he's worked with, and give the same speech about how he was destined to be God's gift to metal. Then, just in the way that caused Beating Bertha to "discover" him, he began to sing. This was not for anybody in particular. Nobody was asking him to sing. He just started singing at the top of his lungs, disrupting every conversation in that room.

"Maggie, who the fuck is this jack ass with the weird eyebrows?" my friends asked me.

Naturally, they hated him. We all did. Ashamed of my poor contribution to the evening, I drank. Number 13 and I retreated to my room to bang it out some more. Then it got ugly.

It's understood that alcohol is a depressant. You drink it and it initially heightens your mood and entices your senses. This is a pleasant feeling, so you drink more. But the human body always balances itself out. What goes up must come down, so after a drunken high, the body's mood lowers into depression. These ups and downs tend to be more extreme after the consumption of hobo-quality gin.

That night, I saw a new side of Number 13. Did he become tender, caring, and intimate? No. Did we cuddle? Nope. Not exactly. However, he did show me his sensitive side. He cried. Mr. Tough, I-Scream-Metal-I-Hate-Niggers-I-Am-Man-Enough-To-Fuck-You-Like-The-Whore-That-You-Are rolled off of me, sat on the side of my bed, put his head in his hands, and sobbed. And these were not guilty tears for his lovely, dearest Tammy who he was being so unfaithful to. No, these tears were shed in the name of something *much* more important - his teeny, tiny pint-sized cock.

"I-I-I….." he sniffled, "I have a small penis!" he whimpered and wined repeatedly. "I hate it! I hate myself! I hate my small penis! Waaaaaaaa! Sniff. Sniff."

I never touched him again. There wasn't enough gin in California to sway me. Number 12's method of playing possum during intercourse was just so much more appealing. However, I did get to witness the greatness that was Beating Bertha.

Number 13 and I never spoke of his baby penis tantrum. Maybe it was purely mental, but I could feel so much filth in my vagina the next day that I rushed to the clinic and got every STD test they were equipped for. I'd only found three condoms in my garbage can, which I knew wasn't a sufficient number. On top of my birth control, I took two 'morning after' pills. My tests came back negative, but something about my memory from that night disturbed me. I made myself unavailable when Number 13 wanted to crash at my place. I attended one Beating Bertha show once I was finally twenty-one. It was hilariously disappointing.

"THIS SONG IS FOR ALL YOU ADRENALINE JUNKIES!" Number 13 screamed into the microphone.

Just like his Myspace photos, there were stage lights and a foggy haze in the background. A close up of Number 13 with his open mouth screaming into the mike and veins popping out of his neck did make him appear to be performing in a large venue, but zoom out to a wide shot and only about fifteen people stood in the audience. The Beating Bertha groupies were a pack of cougars with black tank tops and orange spray tans. The only fan dancing and head banging to the music was one young and very enthusiastic man. He was mentally retarded. Really.

Yes, Beating Bertha is definitely on a direct path to iconic status.

Shortly after the epic Beating Bertha performance, Number 13 and I parted ways for good. I was on my period and my cramps were particularly vicious that day, so I was irritable. I logged onto Myspace and saw that Number 13 was once again posting his inspirational biography on his bulletins every ten fucking minutes. I dared to poke fun at him for it. He told me that he hated me for my negativity and assured me of the fool I would feel like when he finally made it big. His paranoia also surfaced when he brought up Tammy.

"If you tell her *anything*," he warned me. "I will put you in the hospital."

Beating Bertha parted ways in 2010. Number 13 is not famous yet.

Number 14

I hate birthdays.

Of course, that wasn't always the case.

I had one of those mothers who never forgot to do something special for it every year. On my first birthday, she baked a cake in the shape of a giant egg, topped with fluffy, white frosting and a face made from food coloring. It was a Humpty Dumpty cake. On my third birthday, she baked a giant chocolate kitty cake. My childhood birthdays were filled with skating rinks, sleepovers, theme park parties, and once I got older, birthday dinners with a candle in a slice of Tiramisu. When I moved to California, I got cards and "Happy Birthday" phone calls every year.

As I approached adulthood, holidays began to feel like a dressing room mirror where under the fluorescent, yellowish lights, I was forced to look at any bulges, jiggle, or cellulite on my naked body between outfit changes. Holidays turned a harsh, bright light on the reality of my relationships. My Valentine's Days were unacknowledged by boyfriends and lovers.

My social life was measured by New Year's Eve and Halloween party options.

My Christmas's left me comparing the more expensive and higher abundance of gifts my little brother, Carl's son, got to mine. When I faced a massive phone bill from a theft and couldn't afford to come home for my first holiday in the Navy, I hopefully waited in vain for my parents to offer a ticket home for Christmas. As I painted the side of the Higgins on Christmas day, I thought about the three of them opening gifts by their icy blue bulb artificial pine, wondering if they'd gotten the presents I sent the month before. They never acknowledged them and out of pure embarrassment that they didn't like them, I never mentioned or sent another package home again. That was just a spark in the fire that would that would later incinerate my illusion of family.

But birthdays are the worst because it's my holiday. My birthday isn't another party I can crash, pretending I'm welcome. My birthday isn't a family dinner I can drop in and convince myself that I am the guest of honor because everyone is too polite to tell me to stay on the west coast. My birthday revolves around me, so the loved ones who don't remember or acknowledge it are a direct rejection. I feared my birthdays in high school when the popular girls wouldn't come to my party. I feared birthdays through my late teens and early twenties when my biological father would never remember it. I feared my birthdays from twenty-nine on when my mother would stop calling. And though I wouldn't have admitted it to even myself, I was *terrified* of my twenty-first birthday.

I knew my birthday would be the final revelation of the relationships that just weren't real. And there isn't place on the planet more desolate of real relationships than Pacific Beach.

My twenty-first birthday was a big deal to me. This was the age that dramatically affected the lives of young, bar hungry San Diegans. At eighteen, I moved to a very twenty-one-and-over city. San Diego is very active in its nightlife, packed with concerts, clubs, bars, and stage venues that all required one to be of drinking age just to pass through their bouncer-guarded gateways. And when it came to fake IDs, the bars were ruthless. As a twenty-year-old Pacific Beach resident, my age regularly inflicted a harsh blow to my social life. Sure, I could go to house parties, but it seemed like every one of them was rudely interrupted by some twenty-four-year-old douchebag shouting, "PUB CRAWL!" My coked out friends would eagerly stumble to the bar. A group of friends would go to a concert and I'd be excluded because of my age. I remember one particularly pitiful scene where some of my friends decided to drink at an outdoor patio bar. I, along with another twenty-year-old, just waited for them outside on the sand. We could literally reach out our hands to high five our friends, but were not allowed to climb on the porch. I was beginning to wonder why I bothered to bang local musicians when I couldn't even go to their shows.

From the time I moved to PB, the date of my big two-one was anxiously carved into my brain.

"Two months!" I'd squeal to myself. "One month! Twenty-nine days and twelve hours! Two weeks, three days, and ten hours!"

I was convinced that my life would be forever changed once that beloved date rolled around. When the frat row boys wanted to embark on their famous PB pub-crawls, I could respond with, "Great! I'm going too!" I could finally join the gallant young men in their glorious quest to drink the entire Garnet Avenue strip dry, starting at The Silver Fox that opened at six am for only the dedicated alcoholics. Then the warriors and I would depart for our journey west to a mimosa breakfast ending with tequila and Coronas at Cabo Cantina, a gringo bar imitating a Mexican tourist trap decked out with fake palm trees, mini umbrellas, and salty tortilla chips. This became one of my favorite bars because of its outdoor patio section. Instead of that boringly cliché ocean view, Cabo's had white boys in wife beaters shouting obscenities and glitter-coated skanks tripping on their stripper heels. Finally, at twenty-one, I would be able to freely frolic through the strip and enter *any* building that I chose.

My excitement for joining the realm of the legally drunk went beyond the bars and the booze. Even after puberty, drugs, bulimia, a live-in boyfriend, sex, a fake marriage, weight gained, weight lost, and half of a military enlistment, I really hadn't changed since my fourteenth birthday party. Deep down, my only true aspiration was to be cool. This time, I was in a whole new league of popular kids.

All those people back in Tennessee were nothing to me. The popular girls in Chattanooga desperately tried to be Californian, bleaching their hair and baking in tanning beds until their skin fried orange. They could have their country music, premature marriages, and hometown drama. I lived in a heavenly beach town. I had palm trees. I had beer bongs on the sand. I had the wildness of my youth.

My friends were thin, pretty, naturally bronzed and accessorized with bug-eyed sunglasses. They slurped vodka straight from the bottle while they drove. They roamed the streets in bikinis by day and by night, skimpy dresses short enough to bare their ass cheeks when they bent over. They pushed up their breasts and snorted coke in the bathrooms of clubs before grinding their crotches into strangers until last call. And when the night came to an end, they romped through the filthy, gum-stained streets barefoot because they were too hammered to feel the glass shards beneath their soles. The PB girls were wild, edgy, and dangerously carefree. I wanted to be just like them.

It seemed like I was well on my way. My Myspace was constantly blowing up with comments from new friends, refreshing my memories of the outrageous things we said and did the night before. We joked about the Absinthe shots we took and the weird guy who fell through the glass table after trying to dance on top of it. We hysterically giggled as we filled in each other's gaps from our memories forever lost in intoxication.

I saw those people again at more parties. The girls eagerly welcomed me in their social circles, hugged me, swearing that we were all great friends. We all vowed to spend our summer parading through PB together. Loads of people all made promises of the glory of my big two-one.

"Girl, you're not twenty-one yet?" they'd all chip in. "Okay, well we *have* to all go out on your birthday. Oh my God, it's on Memorial Day weekend? That's *perfect!* We'll all have to get you shit-faced!"

"Your birthday is gonna be so rad!" James, the leader of the frat row pack assured me. "We're gonna rage like we've never raged before!"

I was certain that I would not be facing that horrible dilemma of not having people to go out with on my twenty-first birthday. PB residents were determined partiers. I'd once seen a guy with an oxygen tank taking shots.

My birthday landed on the beginning of Memorial Day weekend. Who was going to stand me up on such an ideal day for drinking?

Spontaneity is the PB mentality. There is no such a thing as making plans. If you throw a party, the people who say that they'll make it won't show and the people who say they won't show, make it. If I wanted to be a PB girl, I had to inhabit an ultra laid back, I-don't-give-a-fuck attitude or else I'd be considered uptight and dramatic. Nobody would like me. But I never could become that nonchalant. I just pretended.

When a friend and I planned on doing something later that weekend, I knew it would never happen. I could repeatedly call that night, but my attempts were in vain. I never spoke a word in opposition. I never called my precious PB friends rude, self-centered, or unreliable. And when my birthday came along, I never revealed how hurt I was when the dozens of friends who vowed to make it unforgettable seemed to scatter into the depths of the universe.

Hours before the midnight I would turn twenty-one, I fought the urge to bury myself in my sheets and cry until my birthday passed. I called my Navy friends who I much too often took for granted. After enough borderline begging, I convinced Yolanda and our friend Annabelle to go out with me. Myleen was still underage.

Annabelle was a twenty-four-year-old Georgia native. She was book smart, but naive from her small town roots. Everyone knew that Annabelle had an addictive personality, but we overlooked how dangerous it really was. She could not have a few beers. When she drank, she did it continuously until she was either purging out her intestines or naked with whoever took advantage. Under the influence of alcohol, she was a date rape waiting to happen.

Men were drawn to Annabelle. There was nothing remarkable about her appearance. She had a cute but quaint, round face and a short, chestnut bob with the tips touching her chin. Her body was a petite, pear shape. Annabelle was always a little chubby with stubby arms and legs. She looked just like Meg, the daughter from the cartoon, *Family Guy.*

It wasn't her beauty that attracted men, but her vulnerability. When it came to standards, she had none. Even at my drunkest, I was still one hundred times more selective than she was. She fucked *anyone* who gave her the time of day, but there was innocence to the way she did it. Men were attracted to her because of the immense power they had over her. Annabelle's men were the worst kind.

Annabelle, Yolanda, her husband and I legally entered the doorways of a bar around 12:30 pm. The bouncer looked at my ID, smiled, and said "happy birthday." I wanted to kiss him.

It only took one Long Island iced tea to make me forget about all the people who had stood me up, including James, who I'd seen with his frat row crew at another PB bar that very night. By the second Long Island, I was posing for goofy pictures and throwing darts with Dwight, happy with the three friends who had come out. Yolanda had not been in the barhopping mood, but sucked it up because she sensed my desperation. By my third or fourth drink, we had company.

Annabelle had invited a boy she'd met off Myspace. His name was Tony. He was about my height with a five o'clock shadow and large ears. He looked like he'd stepped right out of the Jersey Shore. A friend accompanied him. I paid little attention to either of them because I was much more focused on getting shit hammered, assuming that I would not have an appropriate twenty-first birthday if I didn't. After my fourth or fifth stiff beverage, my memory became blotchy.

I recall walking down the street with everyone to Dwight's car and falling flat faced on the sidewalk. Wearing three-inch heels on my twenty-first birthday was genius.

Suddenly, Yolanda and Dwight were gone and it was just Annabelle, Tony, his friend, and me crammed into my tiny living room. I sat on the cheap loveseat, the friend sat in the circle futon, and Annabelle curled up with Tony on the carpet with his tongue down her throat. A happy couple for the night, they stumbled into Bianca's bedroom.

When Bianca and I lived together, I was not always the greatest roommate. My rent was always on time. I did the majority of cleaning in the house and even threw her a birthday party. But I occasionally stole her tampons and allowed people to fuck in her bed while she was on duty. And when I was really mad at her, I drank her vodka.

Once Annabelle and Tony disappeared, the friend and I were left alone. We had not exchanged a single word. As he fumbled through his cell phone for cab numbers, I took a good look at him for the first time that night.

Hot damn.

He was attractive.

Very attractive.

He had brown hair that wasn't sticky with gel, but I could tell that he had styled it by the way it swished to the front and flipped into a little wave. His face was long and rectangular with a strong, masculine jawline. He had olive-tan skin, the shade of a white boy who spent his days lounging at the beach, and chocolate brown eyes below a set of neatly groomed eyebrows. His long legs hung off the side of my round little futon and I remembered how tall he had been. He was athletically lean and towered over me. He wore a crisp, white button-down shirt that hung over a pair of blue jeans. He looked clean and well kempt, unlike all the scraggly surfers that hung around PB.

I've mentioned my theory before. When I was at the height of my promiscuity, it was as if men could sense my availability, like it all fell into our evolutionary process of the male knowing which females were ready to mate. If that's the case, Number 14's reproductive instincts must have been in full swing because he somehow became aware of my sudden attraction. If any words were exchanged between us, they were very few. I don't remember them. He just put his phone in his pocket and followed me into my bedroom.

Lying on my back with Number 14 on top of me, I quickly realized how drunk we both were. Our liquor consumption had absolutely crippled us and we were about as graceful as two quadriplegics trying to fuck on a waterbed.

Clean, handsome, and cologne-scented, Number 14 was the type of guy I would have gladly ravaged under sober circumstances. But, alas, our passion channeled out to slobbery kisses and the awkward fumbling of a thirteen-year-old boy snapping off a girl's bra for the first time. After about five pumps inside of me, a severe case of whiskey dick took hostage of Number 14. Defeated, Number 14 rolled off of me, toppling off my bed and onto the floor with a loud *thud*.

"Are you okay?" I slurred.

He seemed unfazed by both the fall and my incessant giggles. Without a word, he crawled back on the bed and plopped beside me.

"Hey, can you do me a big favor?" I asked him, the way a little girl asks for a cookie.

"Yeah. Of course!" he sounded really enthusiastic and polite.

"Will you go down on me?" I slurred, sheepishly. "It's my birthday. I'm twenty-one."

"Sure!" he sounded *very* excited about giving me this birthday gift. Through the darkness in my room I saw a wild smile spread across his face. It was cute. He seemed like such a nice guy. Too bad he ate pussy about as well as he fucked, though considering the condition we were in, I didn't judge him. I appreciated the effort, but when he slid his tongue inside of me and slithered it around like a snake, I gave up on getting any action that night.

The next morning I woke up to the sunlight shining through my window.

"Fuck!" I gasped, immediately jerking upright in my bed and knocking Number 14's arm off of my waist.

"What time is it?" I said aloud, not expecting to get an answer from the unconscious man in my bed.

I jumped up and ran into living room in search of a clock. It was 9 am and Bianca would be home any minute.

"Annabelle, you guys have to get the hell up!" I exclaimed, slapping open Bianca's door to find Annabelle and Tony completely naked in her bed.

"Get up! Get up! Get up!" I ordered like a boot camp drill instructor.

We shoved the guys out of the door minutes before Bianca arrived. I hardly looked at Number 14 and sent him into the heat of the San Diego spring morning without a goodbye. I'd managed to fuck a man without catching a glimmer of his personality. In fact, if it weren't for my post-fuck Myspace stalking, I wouldn't have even remembered what he looked like. To my pleasant surprise once I'd sobered up, Number 14 had indeed been quite easy on the eyes.

According to Annabelle, he was a graphics designer who occasionally traveled to places like Japan and Hong Kong for work. He sounded like a great package, aside from the flaws of *his* package. If only we'd met outside the dysfunctional world of PB.

For the rest of my time in San Diego, I'd randomly run into Number 14. He'd be crossing the street when I was stopped at a red light or entering the club I was drinking in with girlfriends, causing me to duck behind crowds to avoid an awkward confrontation with a one-night stand. We never approached each other like rational, sober human beings that looked one another in the eye with a smile and hello.

Every time I saw him, it was still hard to believe that he existed. Our night together had been so blurry and brief. He's such an elusive splotch on my list of previous lovers that it's difficult to acknowledge that his penis had once been in my vagina.

Annabelle never saw Tony after that night, so I wondered if she felt the same way about him that I felt about Number 14. Did she walk away from that sexual encounter asking, "Did that really happen?"

Luckily for us, Tony and Number 14 did leave us one memento of our swift six-hour love affairs.

"Uh, Maggie?" Bianca emerged from her room around 11 am that same morning.

Annabelle and I were in the living room nursing our hangovers like true PB residents, with a burrito from the corner taco shop and a fifth of vodka.

"What's up?" I asked my roommate.   ·

Bianca was an attractive girl with dirty blonde hair and a very deep voice, which was uncharacteristic of her young, girlish face. Although she was a nice person, she was socially awkward. She easily befriended guys. Despite my efforts for us to become the best of friends, she could never bond with girls unless she was drunk. Her attitude was polite and passive. If we ever had a conflict living together, she never brought it to my attention.

"Uh…did a guy sleep in here last night?" she asked.

Diverting my attention away from my burrito, I looked up at her to find a man's white wife beater in her hands.

"Dammit!" I panicked to myself, trying to think of a good lie.

"Um, no, but Yolanda's husband used your room to change. Why?"

Not making eye contact with me, Bianca looked directly at the floor and mumbled, "Um, I think he has my white tank top," and retreated into her room, filled with the scent of someone else's sex.

Number 15

As James would have put it, I "raged" into legal drinking age with full force.

Despite the friends who disappeared, my birthday weekend was everything I'd dreamed it would be. Annabelle, my loyal friend with a highly addictive personality, and I spent the rest of the holiday weekend binge drinking. We began with our Saturday night/Sunday morning with one-night stands. Instead of embracing our hangovers and shame the next morning, we treated our aching, dehydrated bodies with an alternative remedy. Any alcoholic will tell you that the ideal hangover cure is booze.

"Why the hell shouldn't I be drunk by noon today?" I figured. "It's my birthday."

When I opened my door, I realized that the rest of PB agreed with me.

PB was always a bit hectic, but on holiday weekends, it transformed into what looked like MTV Spring Break. It was a shocking sight to see for the first time. What was once sand was replaced by a mass of flesh and the aroma of sea salt was overpowered by the stench of stale beer baking in the sun. The early birds that arrived before sunrise had already set up tents and coolers packed with their alcohol. Some were equipped with food and beer funnels, which would later be shoved down the throats of young ladies in bikinis being ordered to suck down the tube like a hardcore porn blowjob. Every guy wore his own unique pair of board shorts patterned with Hawaiian flowers or Rip Curl lettering while every girl wore a bikini, sometimes topped with a short, denim cutoff skirt or a little tube dress.

That night, my buddy Grizzly escorted Annabelle and me to the bars on the Garnet strip. Grizzly was my age, but looked much older because of his fuzzy, reddish blond beard and husky, 6'5" build. He was a big bear of a man, hence the nickname. He treated his female friends like cubs, protecting us from aggressive assholes and never making a move on us even when we were half conscious. A native of upstate New York, he was a small town guy and a genuine gentleman.

"Fuck all those bitches that didn't come out tonight," he assured me. "It's your twenty-first birthday. I've got your back girl. Let's gecha a Red-Headed Slut."

Grizzly bought me one Red-Headed Slut shot after the next. By the end of the night, we reached the Silver Fox.

"Have you ever had an Adios Motherfucker?" Grizzly asked me while we stood at the edge of the musty, dark bar packed with drunk guys in baggy t-shirts and backwards caps.

The Silver Fox had a much more casual atmosphere than the other PB bars, though very few places in PB were even close to upscale. By that time, Grizzly's brother along with some other frat row boys had come up to join me in my celebration.

"Nope," I responded. "What's in it?"

Grizzly laughed at me.

"A lot of shit, darlin'. But once you drink it," he continued, "You black the fuck out. Then it's 'adios, mother fucker!'"

I stood beside Grizzly against the bar, smashed between clusters of people yelling at the top of their lungs while trying to carry conversation. I never understood why bars blared their music when people just ended up trying to talk over it. Randomly, I heard a guy beside me mention Chubbyfunk. They were playing at a bar a few blocks away.

Even though we had the same birthday, Number 12 had not responded to my "Happy Birthday" text message and had not invited me to his show even though I was finally able to get through the doors. I was beginning to realize that the man I'd been sleeping with for the past three months wasn't even my friend. A few days later, Number 12 would call me drunk at 2 am, as usual, to wish me a happy belated birthday. Then I would get myself out of bed and drive to his house for fifteen minutes of his signature just-lay-there-like-a-corpse sex.

"Chubbyfunk?" I cut in.

"Yeah, they're playing just down the street," the guys smiled at me, welcoming me into their conversation.

"Oh, I know," I slurred. "I fuck their singer."

The guys looked at me shocked and burst out into laughter from my blunt statement.

"Oh really?" they chipped in. "How is he?"

"Psshh," I rolled my eyes. "That dude should really stick to singing. Once I even let him fuck me up the ass because I was so bored."

"Woooo!" the guys hollered. "Let's get this girl a drink!" one chimed in. "Get her a drink for taking it in the butt!"

After a long day of alcohol consumption and my recent Red-Headed Slut binge, I was already pretty far gone by the time I got an Adios Mother Fucker in my hands. It was a tall glass filled with what looked like Windex with a cherry on top, but it tasted sweet and I quickly slurped it down.

Two Adios Mother Fuckers later, I was a living advertisement for its title. I remember nothing after that. Apparently I lost my ability to walk. Thank God for Grizzly's strong, burly arms.

I almost immediately began drinking when I woke up the next morning. I was still in awe of my new ability to walk into the liquor store and buy whatever I wanted.

It was Memorial Day and I entered the mass of greasy, half-nude bodies to meet some girlfriends for one more day of belligerence. As I weaseled my way through the crowds, I couldn't help but notice the madness around me. Young adults, many who were underage I'm sure, were funneling beer and doing body shots off of each other. Hyped sexuality was abundant, with men openly playing grab ass with the skin-baring girls who batted their bloodshot eyes at them. Couples groped each other on beach towels, bare sand, and on the steps connecting the boardwalk to the beach. I saw every bikini pattern imaginable from bright yellows, to ruffles, to zebra print in every cut and shape. I, myself, was in a tankini because I was too insecure with baring my belly. It was cream colored with a green peacock design that flattered my long, blonde hair. Somehow through the miracle of good cell phone signal, I spotted my friends, Tiger and Ceci.

I knew the girls through some of the frat row boys. Both girls were attractive, but Tiger was the stunner who outshined nearly every girl around her.

Ceci was petite with a round face, dimples, bleach blonde hair, and angelic blue eyes. Ceci was from Idaho and had been the belle of her small town before coming to California to pursue her dream of acting. Aspiring actresses flocking to California were always a sad sight. Most had hailed from small towns, having been the stars of their local theater, certain that they had that special quality to "make it" in the entertainment industry. With their egos inflated from being the big fish in the small pond, they came to Hollywood to realize that they were one of millions, and that for every special quality they possessed, someone out there had a better version of it. There was always someone prettier, thinner, blonder, more talented, or smarter, and even *they* often spent their days waiting tables. If they were lucky, they got an audition that would almost always reject them. Ceci's attempt at stardom ended the way they usually do, so she spent her time in San Diego working an office job and partying with Tiger.

Tiger was the epitome of a PB girl. She is what white middle-aged men call a firecracker and they all probably fantasized about taming her when they jerked off in their showers.

Tiger was that type of girl who every other female hated because of the flawless body that she never had to work for. Tiger had a fat-free figure, shapely, firm ass, and a naturally full set of tits. I've always secretly loathed skinny girls with big boobs.

Tiger's body was almost always fully visible. She didn't hesitate to romp around the streets in a string bikini with boots or heels. When she did wear clothes, they were skimpy shorts, skirts, and tight fitting dresses with her cleavage distinctly visible. Sometimes she wore more outrageous outfits, like black lingerie underneath a fishnet suit or would don a hot pink wig.

When she dressed up for Halloween, it was always in a bikini. She was a zombie girl in a black bikini or Gangsta Bitch Barbie in a bikini. I envied the freedom she felt to run around everywhere practically nude without fear of degradation. She obtained her killer bod with a strict diet of alcohol, cocaine, and Cheez-Its.

Tiger claimed to drive her best when she was drunk. She was not the typical blonde California girl. She dyed her naturally ash brown hair fire engine red and decked herself out with tattoos and a belly button piercing.

She was a beach babe with rebellion and was always the soul energy of the night. Tiger was the spirit of the pregame ritual before pub-crawls, blaring up her music and dancing around her apartment while draining a bottle of rum into her mouth. Jumping on her couches and pulling us up atop the vodka-stained cushions, her voice was the highest "WOOOOOOOO!" in the room.

She'd fill her purse with dozens of mini liquor bottles that so we could get wasted on a budget. The night usually ended with bringing some guys home to snort up their blow or with about five of us girls stumbling down an alley, rolling each other around with the grocery store shopping cart we found.

Tiger was loud and bold, unafraid to shout out a loud, "FUCK YOU!" to anyone who rudely bumped into her or mumbled a sarcastic comment under their breath.

On Memorial Day, the three of us relieved our hangovers by guzzling more alcohol beneath the sun. We filled diet coke bottles with Bacardi and I drug the case of beer I'd purchased at a beachside 7-Eleven to our spot. With the crowds of guys perched around us, it was easy to score free booze off of them.

Ceci taught me to do a beer bong, which I'd never been successful at before.

A beer bong is a funnel attached to a hose. Someone pours a beer (or a stronger beverage if the drinker has a death wish) and the drinker puts their mouth on the hose and sucks down the booze. This has always been a difficult task for me, that is, until Ceci's training.

She held the bong with her right hand as some shirtless guy prepared to pour the beer in the funnel.

"Now Maggie," she instructed aggressively, already drunk. "Open your mouth. Wider. Open your mouth, bitch!"

A group of boys begin to crowd around us, obviously aroused by her erotic tone.

"Open up. Put it in your mouth and SUCK, SUCK, SUCK!" she screamed. "Open your throat and SUCK IT! SUCK IT, BITCH! SUCK IT! SWALLOW ALL THAT SHIT!"

I obediently did as I was told and with all the will I could summon, I slurped down the beer, fighting the urge to vomit it back up. As the bubbly liquid filled my belly and dribbled down the corners of my mouth, a mass of rowdy guys cheered.

"WOOOOOO! THAT'S HOW YOU SUCK IT!" They all shouted, clapping and giving Ceci and I pats on the back.

Before long, we had a group of cute boys following us down the PB strip. Ceci claimed one muscular blonde guy as her boyfriend, holding his hand and dragging him with her everywhere she went. Later that night while the two of them were cuddling in her bed, she suddenly sobered up and completely forgot.

"WHO THE HELL ARE YOU?" she shouted. "GET THE FUCK OUT OF MY HOUSE! GET OUT! GET OUT!"

The guys were Marines. Although I tried to avoid military men, I had my eye on one named Jay with dark brown hair, chestnut eyes, and olive skin. I remember little about him, except that he was sweet and at some point the two of us drunkenly danced to Journey's *Don't Stop Believing* in a bar.

All of the guys seemed polite and down to earth. And despite my history with Marines and their tendency to be a bit on the mentally slow side, I recalled one great quality about them. Few of them were from southern California and they had that small town quality of treating women like ladies, opening doors, and paying for their drinks. These guys brought me right back to the aspects of The South that I missed.

By the end of the evening, Ceci and her boyfriend for the night took off to her place. The other three headed back to my apartment. All of us were slowly sobering up and exhausted from consuming so much alcohol in the heat. We sipped water and hung out in my living room.

"So you're in the Navy?" one of them asked.

"Yeah, over on 32nd street."

The boys were stationed at Camp Pendleton.

"How long have you been in?"

"Almost two and a half years."

"Oh, us too," Jay, the one I had a crush on replied, smiling.

The second guy seemed just as friendly. Picking up on my attraction to Jay, he offered to set us up. The third guy sat in the corner just watching us talk. He was skinny with a rectangular head. He was the most quiet and awkward of the group.

"What's your pay grade?" One of them asked.

"E3."

"Us too. How do you afford to live here?"

"Oh, I'm married, but it's not a real marriage. My friend and I just got married for the money."

My parents hardly lock their doors. My cousins will carry on pleasant conversations with mentally ill homeless men for as long as they'll follow them.

Enough time in big cities taught me not to trust the human race. Once my wallet was stolen out of my apartment in broad daylight while I was in my shower, I walked down the sidewalk clutching my purse tightly. When joggers ran up behind me, I squared my shoulders and prepared to elbow them in the face if they touched me. While I was still quite young and new to California, I instinctively trusted strangers. I shared my bed with random men and waved my personal information publicly, never wondering if others would react to it negatively, or worse, attempt to punish me for my actions. It never occurred to me to take a smarter, more cautious route and keep my private life private. I was not ashamed of my marriage or afraid of being punished for it.

"My marriage is completely legal," I assumed. "Nobody can get me in trouble for it."

At the news of my marriage, the quiet boy in the corner was no longer the quiet boy in the corner.

"ARE YOU KIDDING ME?" he demanded, darting up from his chair, he angrily walked towards me.

"YOU'RE *MARRIED FOR THE MONEY?* YOU *WHORE!*"

My entire body froze.

"Marriage is *sacred*!" he continued. "I've been engaged three times and each of those cunts just threw my commitment away!"

As he moved closer to me, the other two boys stood back. Their eyes widened. Both looked embarrassed.

"I'm really sorry, he's been hurt a lot," Jay whispered.

"LOOK AT YOU, YOU PIECE OF SHIT SLUT!" the boy continued. "What man will want you? You've been drinking all weekend! Your apartment's a wreck!"

Although I usually kept my apartment spotless, I'd been drunk all weekend for my birthday. I let the house cleaning go to Bianca, who'd just let it go.

"You are so unladylike!" he shouted. "This is *not* how a woman should act!"

With that, his friends drug him out of my apartment, repeatedly apologizing. I was alone with my mess and my alcohol comedown.

I partied hard that weekend. I partied at a level that I would consider myself too old to handle by my twenty-second birthday. I had fun.

It was everything I expected my twenty-first birthday to be, but something about the crazy Marine had left a sour note in my mind. My hangover depression didn't help with this. I'd been happily drunk for three days straight and what goes up must always come down, but something about him had frightened me. It was the way he unexpectedly turned on me. His heartbreak and mental disturbance was obvious, so I pitied him, but also feared him. He gave me a glimpse of how the most unexpected of people could become fierce, angry, and vengeful.

In silence, I cleaned my apartment, showered, and retired to my bed. I would be going to work the next day and that was okay. I wanted it. I wanted some sense of routine and normality. I wanted to be among sober people and to be controlled by authority so I could feel like a child again. I wanted some sort of parent to protect me from the world's monsters. That night, Memorial Day, the end to my birthday extravaganza, instead of the companionship of another male stranger, I slept alone. And I truly *felt* alone - frightened and alone.

"Screw those stupid Marines!" Tiger laughed. "They were so dumb."

Tiger made light of the awkward episode, so I forgot all about it. I loved how she could just let conflicts roll off her back as if to say, "Fuck the world!" and continue having fun.

I decided not to let one bizarre experience be a setback in my first summer as a legal drinker. Once I was allowed into bars, my circle of friends quadrupled. I began dating a guy I'd met at a bar. We ended our first night together coked out and running through the beach at sunrise. Our connection seemed magical. He introduced me to the soulful, classic voices of Otis Redding and the Temptations. He called me nearly every day, that is, until two weeks later he dumped me for a half-Indian, half-Irish calendar model. I didn't stand a chance. I continued to carry on brief romances that rarely lasted a week.

Fourth of July in PB was even crazier than Memorial Day. Although she was out of town, a group of Bianca's guy friends showed up at my door at 9 am with a keg. I sent a mass text message out to my friends that said "Kegger at my place," left for the beach without my phone, and came back to Number 11 and another guy I knew from the Higgins snorting lines of coke off my dresser.

Everyone I knew had been at my apartment that day. I'd been drinking that entire weekend and was fed up with partying by the time the fireworks set off.

"Everyone out!" I announced to the crowd of people in my apartment. "Take your girl with you," I ordered Number 7.

He'd brought some poor, half conscious teenager who was hanging outside the front door about to vomit off my balcony. I was becoming irritated with the idiots alcohol turned people into. My neighbor grabbed both my and my friend's ass. She punched him in the face. Bianca's friend who was too drunk to drive home persistently tried to get in my pants. I later found out the next morning that Number 7 left his girl passed out on the cement in my courtyard the entire night.

I had been in bed by 11 pm and awoke the next morning to a beach full of broken glass, plastic debris, abandoned coolers, vomit, used condoms, and drunk people sprawled over the sand like they'd been puked out by a homeless shelter.

Getting ready for work, I got a call that reminded me of something I often forgot about on weekends.

"Young, you've got to come in early," it was one of my supervisors from PSD. "The command is having a mandatory urinalysis."

"Oh, yeah, I'm still in the Navy," I thought.

Nervous adrenaline rushed through my body. I had stayed clean that weekend, but barely. All weekend, I had coke and ecstasy offered to me. Luckily, I resisted.

"Do *not* do any drugs this weekend," Raquel had warned me. "PSD likes to do a command-wide drug test after holiday weekends."

Sitting outside the bathroom where a first class would watch me piss into a cup, I saw a lot of sailors pace nervously. I thought about their sweaty palms and calculations of water consumption to dilute drug consumption. I thought about how much the Navy interfered with my social life.

The more coke that was offered to me, the more I began turning it down. I'd seen many sailors pop on their tests and was getting paranoid.

"Maggie, you owe me a coke night!" Tiger reminded me.

One night after the bars, she'd brought back some Hawaiian guys with an eight-ball. It was a Saturday, too close to when I had to be back at work, so I was a dead weight at the party. I passed out on her couch while everyone else giggled and jumped around to loud music.

Tiger and I had become good buddies into the summer. It all began on a Thursday night. I didn't have to be at work until 1 pm the next day and felt like going out. Tiger and I were on the same page.

"Nobody wants to go out tonight and I want to party!" she told me as soon as she called.

I was glad to satisfy her urgent request.

As one of the oldest, my younger brother and cousins looked up to me when I was a kid. When did I something dangerous, like climbed a very tall tree or jumped off a ledge over a creek, they tried to mimic me, often getting hurt because of their miniature stature.

"You hafta be on your best behayvia' when you're around children younga than you," my grandmother warned me. "They look up to ya. They wannabe just like you so they'll copy whatever ya do."

Tiger had the same affect on me. I looked up to her. I wanted to be just like her. Without realizing it, I began mimicking her. I began dying my hair, constantly experimenting with the color the way she did. I began with having bright red streaks professionally colored in my blonde hair. When that faded, I dyed it such a bright red color that it almost looked hot pink. My command was furious with my sudden identity crisis, demanding that I change it to a more subtle color. I would spend the next two years dying it every shade of red, brown, black, and blonde.

Tiger was like a drug, hyping me up for every night out and getting high off the freedom of our early twenties. Together, we stormed PB in high heels, our tits to our necks, and damn strong determination to be rambunctious. She made me feel free. With her, I could get myself in a drunken stupor while screaming obscenities and grabbing the balls of any man I desired. Tiger was even more promiscuous than me.

"How many men have you fucked?" I asked her one night.

We were sipping liquor straight out of the bottle and putting on the finishing touches of our makeup.

"Thirty-five," she said nonchalantly.

"Oh," I replied, feeling inferior. "I'm only at fourteen, but you're two years older than me, so that makes sense."

"I'm just a slut," she laughed.

Although I didn't say it aloud, I thought about how her numbers had piled up. It wasn't that she was so much more promiscuous than I was, but she was more desirable.

I wanted to be like Tiger and I could try. I could dye my hair wild colors, jump atop couch cushions, hide a hundred mini liquor bottles in my purse, and force myself to be that ferocious, confident life of the party, but I could not be as beautiful as Tiger. She carried the personality that only the thinnest, prettiest girls could get away with. When she had it, she was a sexy firecracker. When I had it, I was trailer trash.

I couldn't wear a black lingerie, fishnet ensemble and be dubbed as hot, or grip the balls of any man, assuming he'd be turned on.

As much as I loved Tiger's presence, it also haunted me. Watching her strut through the clubs in her thigh-high leather boots, or summer festivals in her string bikini, I was constantly reminded of my shortcomings. While she was the hot chick that everyone gawked at, I was the semi-cute, semi-chubby, second string blonde the boys went for when they struck out with Tiger. This had everything to do with my weight, the insecurity that plagued me since my preteens. Even though I'd lost a significant amount of weight since my Higgins days, I was not halfway done with the progress.

I began boxing at the beginning of the summer and despite my drinking habits, I was working out harder than ever before. After an intense two-hour workout, I'd shower, and meet up with Tiger to find her in one of her bikinis with a burrito in one hand and a cocktail in the other.

"Damn, I wish I was as motivated as you. I need to get my ass in shape," she'd say as I bitterly stared at her firm, pierced belly.

What was even more discouraging is that I knew when we emerged into the sunlight at PB, that the men were staring at us, comparing us, and that with her, I would always be the ugly, pudgy friend.

The drunkest, most obnoxious boys reminded me of my insecurities.

"I want *her* not *you*," one spat out as I tried to talk to him after Tiger turned him down.

"I'm a trainer," one told me. "You're a pretty girl, but you need to work on this area here," he said as he rubbed his lower belly.

"Fuck those guys. They're assholes!" Tiger assured me. "Enough about weight. Don't you *dare* be insecure."

That was easy for her to say. In PB, the hotter you were, the easier it was to not care.

I could work out every day, but I saw no hope in reaching Tiger's level. So, I did what I'd been doing since my teens. I tried to fill my lack of confidence with male attention.

Tiger didn't care who judged her. She did whatever she wanted and fucked whomever she wanted. She was free and empowered. She motivated me to increase my number. Why the hell not? When would I get another chance in my life to walk into a club and screw whoever I wanted? I decided that was exactly what I would do.

Typhoon Saloon.

It was a casual bar by day and a dressed down club by night. The front area had a saloon, peanut-shells-on-the-floor look while the back tried to be more elegant with strobe lights and stripper poles. Every time I walked into that place, I got into trouble. This pattern began the night I met Number 15.

I don't remember his name or what he looked like. I had full intentions of hooking up with someone from that bar. Number 15 just happened to be at a certain place and time. I was conducting an experiment that night.

"How long will it take me to bang someone from this place?" I asked myself, already drunk from pre-gaming with Tiger at her apartment.

It took less than an hour.

Upon entering Typhoon Saloon, Tiger and I immediately slurped down the doubles we ordered and headed to the club area.

The club had several levels that were all circular areas of people grinding against each other to the hip hop music blaring. We veered to our left and climbed up some stairs that led to the highest level with a minibar. We began dancing with some random guys and there he was, Number 15.

We talked briefly. He was as drunk as I was. The only things I remember about him were that I found him attractive and that he was a Navy Seal. He looked young, tall, and thin, though I can't recall the details of his face.

I suppose I released my unspoken slut signals strongly because he almost immediately began kissing my lips, ears, and neck. He backed me into the corner of the bar. Although we were among a mass of people, we were also in a private place. The club was loud, dark, and hectic. I looked at him with a smile and whispered something like, "Do it. Fuck me here," into his ear.

I don't know how it happened, or what I was wearing, but I do *know* that penetration somehow happened while we were right there on that dance floor. He also managed to wrap on a condom. After a couple of minutes, we decided to take it outside. I took his hand and we stumbled out of the club and walked a block into somebody's home garage. He laid down on the cold cement floor. He looked like he was about to pass out, but somehow managed to keep his erection.

As I straddled him, something about the situation gave me the creeps. I imagined our roles switched. If I were the woman drunk and passed out on the garage floor and the man continued fucking me, there would have been something very morally wrong about the situation.

I thought about my virginity and looked down at Number 15. Despite his supposed Navy Seal profession, he appeared so vulnerable, crippled by his intoxication. I shrugged off my eerie feeling. He'd been willing enough to put his condom on and as I maneuvered myself on top of him, I watched him slip in and out of consciousness. I continued anyway.

Suddenly my phone rang. It was Tiger. Still on top of Number 15 with his barely open eyes looking up at me, I answered it.

"Where the hell are you?" she asked me, sounding concerned.

"Hey, I'll be right there," I answered. "I'll meet you outside of the bar."

"Maggie," Number 15 mumbled as I got off of him. "Maggie, wait."

He seemed paralyzed.

"I've gotta go," I blankly responded. "Bye."

I left the garage to hear Number 15 continuously mumble, "Maggie...Maggie."

I should have helped the poor guy up or tried to get a hold of his friends. At first I felt terrible, but I instantly let those emotions go as I skipped to meet Tiger. I even let out a giggle.

"This must be what it feels like to be a man," I thought. "To fully take advantage of someone and have control over them when they're so feeble - to not feel any emotions when you're done with them."

I didn't realize it at the time, but I was angry with men and the way I needed them. It wasn't so much for sexual satisfaction because in retrospect, most of them had given me very little of it. It was the way I used them to validate myself - to make me feel like I was a woman of worth. This need was what fueled my motivation in pursuing them and what made me put myself into so many awkward situations.

I wouldn't learn this until many more encounters with men who, despite our intimate relations, were strangers. But I was a prisoner of that need. Because of it, I surrendered my self-control. I thought I was taking it back with Number 15, but I was wrong.

Number 16

I don't think I'll ever be completely over my eating disorders.

I haven't binged and purged since joining the Navy. I like to think that I have a healthy relationship with food. I no longer fantasize about it like a long lost lover. I can eat the occasional piece of cheesecake without feeling the urge to shove the entire cake down my throat, licking the sugary graham cracker crumbs off the plate, and then despising myself for weeks afterwards as if I'd committed adultery on my own body.

I do rigorous workouts every day that I genuinely enjoy, like CrossFit or rock climbing. I can run seven miles in my sleep.

I almost always eat healthy, but not like a rabbit. I refuse to spend my days like an anorexic supermodel, fatigued and feeble from a diet of lettuce and vinegar.

But still, an obsession with my body lingers. With the obliteration of my metabolism after eight years of anorexia and bulimia, weight loss is difficult. I have been slowly slimming down since the peak of my post-bulimia inflation. I find that the thinner I get, the more I scrutinize myself.

In the beginning, my only desire was to look like my old self before my weight gain, beneath all the fat. Then I wanted to look directly into my reflection at the salon. I wanted to have my hair lifted from my face without feeling an urge to grab the scissors out of my stylist's hands and snip off my plump cheeks. Eventually, the cheeks faded. My face became oval with my prominent cheekbones quite visible and defined.

Later, my only major issue with my body was my lower stomach, a stubborn area that viciously held onto the fat of my heavier days despite the hours I spent sweating out my bodily fluids and exhausting my muscles at the gym.

After one too many nights of standing in front of the mirror, gripping my lower belly, crying, screaming, and pleading for it to go away, I made a drastic decision. Shortly after my twenty-fourth birthday, I underwent plastic surgery.

Two liters of fat were sucked out of my stomach. Once that flaw was gone, I found more. I began standing in front of the mirror completely nude, mentally cutting my body apart. I still do it to this day. My lower belly fat may be gone, but a slight pudge that can only be seen sans clothing is still there. Naked in my shower, I look down at it and shudder.

My hips are too wide, shoulders too broad, and my thighs still touch. I have a small chunk of fat under my left arm that's been there since childhood. I'm seriously considering getting that sucked out too.

My arms, though toned and muscular, are too meaty. I am petrified of scales. I have not weighed myself in years. I dread going to the doctor, not because I hate being surrounded by illness or fear the metal tools that I will be poked and prodded with, but because of the possibility that I will be weighed at the beginning of my appointment. When the nurse does order me to step on my enemy, I close my eyes like terrified child shielding their vision from the scary parts of a horror movie.

"Don't tell me the number," I order. "I don't want to know."

I won't bungee jump, not because I'm afraid of dangling off a tall bridge by my ankles, but because I have to be weighed before they can drop me. To me, the scariest part of having a child is not the overwhelming idea of creating a new life, but the mere thought of my weight being observed and recorded by a doctor for nine months of pregnancy.

Although I no longer vomit up my food, swallow shots of vinegar, or eat packs of laxatives in hopes of shitting out my intestines so that I can feel two pounds lighter, I know I'm still a little sick.

I should take complete responsibility for my issues. The bulimia, starvation, and the self-loathing are things I did to myself.

I want to blame the men who tell me I'm pretty, but that I would be hot if I dropped ten pounds.

I want to blame the first kid who called me fat when I was an anorexic seventh grader who feasted on saltine crackers at lunch.

I want to blame my grandmother for baking me a dozen chocolate chip cookies every day that I came home from first grade.

I want to blame Carl for praising my success with my first diet at age eleven.

I want to blame my high school boyfriend who told me I'd be beautiful if I were "super model skinny."

I want to blame the last man I was intimate with who said things like, "I'm used to dating girls I can lift with one arm." I could sense his mental comparisons. His ex-girlfriend, a 4'11", eighty pound, and ironically, *bulimic* dancer in and out of rehab who, according to him, still managed to have a "perfect set of tits and ass." He spoke of her as if she'd been a flawless goddess - the "most beautiful girl he'd ever dated." Despite his efforts to help her with her disease, she probably believed that if she lost her skeletal figure, he might have loved her less. I know exactly how those girls think and there is truth in their fears.

I want to blame him for giving me impossible standards that I will never live up to. I want to blame him for putting shame to my womanhood, strength, and health. He watched me slowly shrinking over the months and I saw the approval in his eyes. Everyone approves. "You look great," they tell me.

Whenever I go a month or two without seeing a friend, I return to them visibly slimmer. This is good. Slimmer is better. Men love small women.

"I want a girl I can put in my pocket," my male friends tell me. They want something feeble, weak, and girlish that they can easily overpower. They want a mate they can feel strong and manly beside. I want to blame them, too. Though I hate to admit it, I often envy those small, thin women. Maybe I do want to look like a malnourished teenager with "a perfect set of tits and ass."

This book is about my triumph over the need I once had for men. From the disastrous relationships I held onto for much too long to the physical gratification that made me feel like less of a woman when I was without it.

As time progressed, I found myself needing the Numbers less and less. There are days when I feel like I've done the impossible. Sometimes I truly believe that I don't need the love and affection of a man to love myself. But my body is my kryptonite. I feel satisfaction when my jeans become loose or a friend comments on how much weight I have lost. It is when I feel that pride over my "accomplishment" that I am positive I have not accomplished much at all.

I got serious about shedding my post-bulimia weight gain at the beginning of my USS Higgins deployment.

After six months of sweating in the Persian Gulf, sacrificing my four hours of sleep a day for four-mile treadmill runs, and surviving on a diet of dry tuna, oatmeal, and lettuce, I returned to the United States with a sleeker figure. I was still much chubbier than what I wanted to be, but what I *had* accomplished further motivated me to continue a fitness routine.

In A-school in Meridian, Mississippi, I refused to socialize with my fresh-out-of-boot camp classmates. Instead, I spent my liberty at the gym. I began jogging from my barracks to the fitness center and then did a full workout before jogging back to my barracks.

"Good God, you've lost a ton of weight!" my friends exclaimed when I returned to San Diego.

Naturally, I loved the positive attention. I wanted more. But my body was stubborn and my metabolism was slow. I was not like a normal twenty-year-old who could just drop the excess fat with a diet and healthy exercise routine.

"There will be no shortcuts this time around," I told myself.

I could not return to eating disorders, starvation, or crash diets. I had no choice but to whip my body into shape the old-fashioned way.

I made a decision to permanently change my lifestyle. Still quite young and wild, I was not ready to cut out booze and cocaine from my life. However, I ate healthy food and jogged twenty-five miles a week on the beach boardwalk, even under the heat of the sun during my most intense hangovers.

I ate food like grilled chicken, turkey sandwiches with wheat bread and low fat mayonnaise, and whole grain pasta. When I drank, I avoided sugary, calorie-packed chick drinks like Malibu with pineapple juice, margaritas, and daiquiris. For the most part, I stuck to Bacardi with Diet Coke and straight shots of liquor. That May, my friend, Gia, inspired me to take my workouts up a notch.

"I fucked my boxing instructor last night," she proudly announced amidst giggles.

Gia worked in the tanning salon that I regularly visited in a desperate attempt to look like a tan California girl. Originally from Boston, she moved out to San Diego with her boyfriend. Upon their relationship's destruction, she rented her own studio in PB. With a steady salary from the tanning salon and daddy's trust fund, she was able to pose as a young, independent women truly "making it" in southern California.

She reminded me of Tiger in many ways. Both girls were thin, beautiful, and very well aware of it. Their skimpy bikinis were their signature ensembles.

They were promiscuous and shockingly bold with a sweet tooth for late night coke binges.

Although I had many pretty friends, Gia and Tiger were definitely the most stunning, but in their own unique ways. While Tiger's look was rebellious, Gia's beauty was more conventional. She had the body of a swimsuit model with bronze skin and full C-cups. Her hair was straight, long, and chocolate colored with naturally sun-kissed highlights to match her sun-kissed, freckled nose. Her sex appeal had a fierceness that reminded me of Angelina Jolie in her wilder Billy Bob Thornton days.

And when she was angry, I halfway expected her to let out a loud hiss and unleash sharp, jagged claws from her hands like Wolverine. She was bat shit crazy. I would not know this until later. Gia was the I'll-fuck-your-boyfriend-then-break-into-your-home-and-stab-you type of girl. This quality was what differentiated Tiger and Gia. Both girls were the life of the party, envied, vivacious, attention hungry, and a toxic combination.

"Don't ever bring that girl around again," Tiger ordered me after I had invited frat row to one of Tiger's parties.

Gia had tagged along and the two bombshells exploded upon collision.

"It's okay," she soothed me mid apology. "She is just a horrible person. You should stay away from her."

Perhaps Tiger's comments were inspired by her spite from being subjected to someone as pretty as her, but I think that Tiger had the judgment of character that I lacked. Like any other PB resident, Tiger could be a flakey party girl, but she never did me wrong. She was never the type to use her sex appeal for evil acts, like stealing her girlfriends' men. She never verbally attacked me or pointed out my flaws. She defended her friends when necessary and kept a strong circle of them over the years, while Gia's all ran away once she unleashed her evil inner character.

But on that warm May evening after my tan, she was another role model. Though nineteen, a year younger than me, I still had that mimicking admiration for her. Gia was open with the sexuality that she frequently practiced. Our friendship was conceived during a conversation about band guys and how our standards dramatically dropped when a man carried a guitar. We logged onto the salon's computer and I showed her clips of Number 12 performing.

"Damn, you're good," she gasped, praising my conquest.

"*She* envies *me*," I thought with disbelief and immense pride.

From then on, every time I finished tanning, Gia and I discussed our recent sexual conquests.

"Girl, wait till I tell you about the man I just landed," Gia announced when I walked into the salon one evening.

"His name is Loco. He's my boxing instructor," she gushed, looking dreamily up at the ceiling while fluttering her thick, brown eyelashes. "And he is *so hot*. And man, he was packing," she said, rubbing her crotch and giving me a quick wink.

"Wait, you box?" I asked, sort of surprised.

Boxing. It seemed so badass. Gia *was* a bad ass, but I had no idea that she boxed to tone her flawless, tan body.

"Loco is really, really sexy," she continued, ignoring my question. "He's super ripped. He's all muscle from head to toe. He's twenty-five, Mexican, and has a Mohawk. He teaches Muay Thai fighting and goes to Thailand every other year to train with the crazy, intense fighters. He wears these short shorts at the gym," she began to giggle. "They look funny, but they show off his muscular legs. Mmm.. he *really* showed his fighter technique in the bedroom. He just threw me onto his bed - no- he *shoved* me. It was *so hot!* And his cock is huge and thick!"

As exciting as her night of passion sounded, I was much more interested in a different topic. I kept interrupting her sexploitations with questions like, "Where do you train? How much is your membership? Do you like it? Have you fought someone before?"

While Gia was rambling about all the things she wanted to do with Loco's shaft, I was having fantasies of my own. I envisioned myself sleek and toned, like Gia, but muscular and in the middle of a boxing ring beating the shit out of another fighter. I had an image of myself that I wanted to obtain. I wanted to be like Gia, a beautiful PB girl who lounged in a bikini by day and a tough, ferocious boxer by night.

"I'm going to join," I told Gia.

Gia trained at The PB Boxing Club, a little gym that was in the same complex as the tanning salon. It was also conveniently located steps away from the PB beach boardwalk, which I would eventually use for five-mile runs before boxing sessions.

Although fitness was my greatest inspiration to become a PB Boxing Club member, Gia's descriptions of the hot, muscular trainers were a plus. But I truly would not have predicted that one of my trainers would become my Number 16.

The PB Boxing Club was a mecca of physical perfection that can only be found in southern California. Everyone there looked like Barbie and Ken with a mild dose of steroids.

I was greeted at the front desk by a brunette Barbie named Britney. Unlike the stereotype of cute, petite PB girls, she was very down to earth. Over the months of my membership, we became good friends and I made a point to stop by the front desk for a chat with her before my workouts. Without a trial workout or personal training session, I handed her my credit card and immediately joined. I was positive that I wanted to box. I bought my first cheap pair of gloves and hand wraps along with a complimentary boxing glove key chain.

The gym was a small, simple square with a treadmill, Stairmaster, rowing machine, an elliptical trainer to the left, and a red boxing ring to the right.

Boxing was exactly the extra push I needed in my workouts. The first week of my training, I could barely sit down without excruciating muscle aches. I felt muscles I didn't even know I had burning inside my skin.

Each workout was about an hour long. The trainer began with jump roping in front of the mirrored wall as a warm up, then stretches. Next we'd start boxing exercises. Sometimes we'd do a series of jabs, uppercuts, and hooks on the bags, a series of lunges across the room, or pairing up with a partner and taking turns holding up a big pad, repeatedly beating it while running across the room.

Unlike running, which came easy to me, boxing required constantly pushing my body to exhaustion. I never left that gym without looking like I'd just jumped into a lake fully clothed. According to my trainers, each session probably burned somewhere between eight hundred to a thousand calories. Slowly, more fat began to melt off my body and I developed a muscular physique. Within three months of beginning my new activity, the men's medium wife beaters I'd bought to work out in were hanging off me like hospital gowns.

I was not attracted to Number 16 the first, second, or third time I took his boxing session. He was the cliché embodiment of a boxer. He reminded me of a young Sylvester Stallone in the original *Rocky Balboa*. Because of his Polish and Mexican descent, he had Stallone's olive-tan skin, deep-set dark eyes, full lips, and black hair. Number 16's hair was naturally thick and wavy, but cut short enough to pass Navy regulations.

In the beginning, I knew little about him. He seemed very quiet and reserved. Although he was friendly, there wasn't much to say to him beyond basic small talk; he came off as a meathead who had suffered a few too many concussions. Though his body was what most women would have considered perfection, I was never tempted to let my eyes linger too long over his chiseled shoulders while he demonstrated uppercuts and jabs. He was too bulky for my taste. When I saw his sturdy, sculpted frame strut around the ring, I imagined him in one of those body building competitions wearing an American flag speedo lathered with fake tanner and bacon grease.

I quickly learned that the gym was an eye-candy store for mommies. Since I didn't have work until 1 pm, I took the morning boxing classes. Those were the times crowded with wealthy, middle-aged housewives who lived in the upper class surrounding areas like La Jolla or Mount Soledad. Their children were young adults or college students, already fulfilling their lives in Ivy Leagues. Their rich husbands kept occupied by cruising around San Diego in their Jaguars and philandering with much younger women or in some cases, much younger men.

These women filled their free time at the boxing club. Most of them were thin and extremely muscular. They were exercise addicts and according to gossip among the trainers, severe coke addicts, snorting lines before and after their hours at the gym to suppress their appetites. They were usually blonde, with leathery faces from decades of tanning, booze, prescription pills, and cocaine. They strutted around the gym in skimpy workout ensembles made of tight spandex, fully displaying their six-pack abs with their hair and makeup fully done.

"Dolores wants my cock," Number 16 whispered to me during training one morning. "All these cougars do."

I could've slapped him for saying such things about Dolores. Although I was fond of them all, Dolores was my favorite gym cougar. She was a small woman in her early fifties. She perfectly fit my description of the gym cougars, hailing from one of the wealthier residential areas in coastal San Diego with a husband who romantically neglected her.

"We're the best of friends," she said, opening up to me one night over a few cocktails. "We love each other and I consider him my soul mate. He just has no passion for me." Looking down from her vodka cranberry as if she were fighting back tears, she said, "He only makes love to me once a year - on our anniversary."

Because the boxing club was as gossipy as the Higgins had been, I later found out that Dolores had found a hefty collection of gay male pornography in her husband's work briefcase.

"Why doesn't she just leave him?" I asked Britney.

"Well, if she did, what else would she do with her life?" Britney responded. "She's never worked. She'd have no means of supporting herself. Plus she's been married for thirty years. She probably wouldn't know what to do with herself if she got divorced."

Trapped inside her own life, Dolores spent a huge chunk of it at the boxing club. She'd show up at 8 am, do an hour of boxing and then do thirty minutes of abs before taking another hour of boxing. Sometimes she'd stay longer to do more abs or jog on the beach. Like me, she had once been overweight, so I related to her in that way. I occasionally spent my mornings at the gym with her, taking double boxing classes and joining her for an abs session in the middle. An impressive before and after picture hung in the front of the club.

"You're next honey," she'd tell me with a smile and a wink.

Whether she was a horny cokehead fantasizing about the buff trainers half her age or not, I liked Dolores. She filled that maternal void in my life. We talked about my weight issues or conflicts with my fling of the week. She occasionally took me to lunch, always refusing me every time I pulled out my wallet. I loved her old-fashioned perspective on my life. She reminded me how ill mannered the men I dated were.

"Oh, honey, if only my son were single," she said, smiling and shaking her head. "I taught him how to treat a woman. He opens doors and always pays for dinner. You should've seen the roses he just bought his girlfriend. You need to set your standards higher."

Dolores would have highly disapproved of my secret affair with Number 16, especially if she knew his real character.

Dolores and the gym cougars were nurturing and motherly towards the young trainers. They bought them manicures, pedicures, food, and in some cases, housed and clothed them. I do not know if any love affairs with younger men were involved in these exchanges, but judging from Britney and Number 16's snide, sarcastic comments, there were certainly plenty of rumors. And if there's one thing I learned from the Navy, it's that rumors are almost always true.

I completely understood why older women often developed a desire to nurture and care for Number 16. He seemed to need it so badly.

As the months passed, I saw Number 16 nearly every morning. He began initiating conversation and making jokes in the middle of training. Those jokes evolved into odd, random remarks with sexual undertones, like cracks about slipping roofies, the date rape drug, into my bottled water. When he said such things, they were under his breath, only meant for my ears. He should have given me the creeps, but he was too socially awkward to take seriously. There was something off about him that gave him a childlike innocence. He seemed afraid of something or maybe even everything.

"I spent six years in prison," he informed me, out of the blue.

Suddenly, he made sense.

Number 16 and I were alone in my car. That day, he'd been so bold as to ask me for a ride home. He had no car, which was becoming a steady pattern in the PB men I interacted with.

It was an August morning. I'd been a member of the boxing club for over three months, and recently a tension between Number 16 and I had been blossoming. This was all his doing. At some point, his eyes began lingering over me as I did crunches, stretched, and punched the bags. This made me nervous, but it also gave my workouts an exciting edge. I loved the attention and the anticipation I felt when I paired up with him, punching the pads he effortlessly held in place with his thick, solid arms.

"What did you go to prison for?" I asked him, a bit caught off guard at his confession.

"I shot a guy in the shoulder," he said blankly, staring straight ahead at the road as I drove. "I was trying to rob him."

Number 16 was a bad boy. He rarely smiled and had an intense, disturbed stare in his marble eyes, as if all the evils of the world flooded his thought process. With his broad, built shoulders, he was an intimidating sight. His body seemed to be his only method of productivity. By day, he was a buff boxing instructor winning the adoration of rich, gym cougars with the combination of his manly appearance and his charming, boyish denseness. By night, he unleashed his cold stares and gruff gorilla posture to intimidate PB drunks as a bouncer at a local nightclub. His body was his life support, not just physically, but financially.

I did not know it until after his seduction was successful, but he used his body to attract a series of sugar mammas. In a way, he was a prostitute. Although he was thirty years old, he'd never paid rent on his own. He relied on the women he slept with to house, clothe, and feed him. The year after our brief fling ended, one of them bought him a car.

During the last months of his imprisonment, his mother, who he'd been extremely close to, died suddenly of a brain aneurysm. With prison guards by his side, he said goodbye to her in her hospital bed long after she'd become a vegetable with her pulse pumped by life support. Ever since then, he seemed like he was desperately in search of love.

But instead of the love of a girlfriend, wife, and partner, he craved a mother. While his women paid his bills and most likely tenderly stroked his hair as he laid his head in their laps, he fulfilled their sex drives and desires for a sweaty, beefcake of a man to lie on top of them.

As I dropped him off at what I thought was his house, but actually belonged to one of his mommy-girlfriends, I only saw a shy charm when he nervously asked, "Do you have a boyfriend?"

It had been a month since I'd left Number 15 lying in that garage. After three months of the beautiful freedom to walk into any bar of my choosing, drink myself into a stupor, and end the night with a new, fleshy object inside my vagina, the novelty had worn off. Number 12 had quit calling the month before and I was growing lonely. I began to realize that PB, the town I'd once believed fulfilled me, was a world of strangers and intimacies as false as the silicone breasts bouncing under hot pink sports bras on its boardwalk.

"He's been through so much," Dolores said, shaking her head sadly when we were at lunch one afternoon.

We were gossiping about the trainers at the gym when she'd gone into Number 16's tragic history of prison and his mother's death.

"If he found a woman to care for him, he'd love her forever."

When I began my involvement with Number 16, my frame of mind was the same as an insecure teenager has when she gets knocked up on purpose. There's no logic in her brain. She doesn't think about the stretch marks, soiled diapers, the 2 am cries, the financial sacrifice and the lifetime commitment of raising a human being. She only envisions an adorable, pudgy-cheeked baby loving her unconditionally.

I made the same mistake with Number 16 that I made with every man that had walked into my life. I did not rationally evaluate him. I did not consider it a red flag that the man was thirty with no education, ambitions, or plans for his future. I did not take the six years of hard time in prison that he'd done as a warning sign of his mental and emotional disturbances. It didn't even occur to me that his obvious depression and addiction to artificial mothers would weigh down my youth. My heart was that lonely pregnant teenager, embarking on an opportunity to nurture.

That weekend, Number 16 called me at 4 am. I'd just returned from a night on the PB strip with friends. My phone rang just after I'd showered and crawled into bed.

"What are you doing?" he asked casually, as if he were calling during daylight hours.

"I was about to go to sleep."

"Are you at home?"

"Yeah."

"Is there a guy with you?"

"No," I laughed. "Not tonight."

"Can I come over?" he asked it like an eight-year-old wanting to play with my Legos.

"Sure. Where are you?"

"I just got off work. I'm on the boardwalk near the gym."

"I'll come meet you."

I felt like a rebellious preteen sneaking out of the house as I walked down the boardwalk. It was completely desolate with the exception of a few stumbling homeless people and the waves crashing in the distance concealed by the black horizon. I couldn't get over how odd it was to finally be associating with one of my trainers outside of the gym, especially in a manner as personal as entering my apartment at 4 am. But in usual PB style, the social limitations that conducted the rest of the world evaporated within its borders. Within minutes of crossing my apartment's threshold, his shirtless flesh rubbed against my silk sheets with his tongue down my throat.

Of all the men I've been sexually involved with, my experiences with Number 16 were the most uncomfortable and degrading, including the loss of my virginity. He did nothing to explicitly violate me. He was never overtly violent. He did not call me names. In comparison to the rest of my lovers, his intimacy was mediocre, less than the men who cared about me like Number 3 and 4, more than those who didn't, like seven and twelve. Whenever I was with him, panties down, pussy exposed, I felt like a five-year-old girl in the lap of a pedophile, being swayed to touch myself in my naughty places.

That first night, I clearly stated that I did not want to have sex. I used my period as an excuse, but truthfully, the beaver was not prepared for exposure. I needed a wax and although surprise sex was not below my moral high ground, a furry cunt was just plain unladylike. This put a great limitation on our erotic options because I was, and still am, extremely picky about my blowjob distribution. If I'm not comfortable with the guy, I just don't do it.

"No head," I stated bluntly. "Sorry, but not tonight."

"Why not?" he protested.

"Because I don't know you well enough."

"Yes, you do."

"No I don't, and I don't feel like sucking your dick."

Like a bratty five-year-old begging for a cookie, Number 16 continued with his incessant nagging.

"Please. Please. Please suck my dick. Nobody's done it for a long time. Let me just slip it in really quick. Please. Please."

I was not having fun. Then he finally suggested an alternative.

"Let me titty fuck you."

Ugh.

Who the hell invented titty fucking? What a stupid idea, right up there with ear, nose, and belly button fucking. I had only been "titty fucked" once on my life. It was during my passionate, drunken, everything-but-sex night with a friend. I suppose to him, it was a pleasurable vagina substitute because after enough pumps into my cleavage, my collarbone was soaked with millions of microscopic unborn babies. Since I did not have a clitoris growing from my chest, other than a salty, sperm bath, I got *nothing* out of it.

His begging continued.

"Please. Please. Let me do it. Let me titty fuck you. Just for a few minutes. Please."

"Well, it may not feel good," I thought. "But it won't feel bad. At least it won't hurt my throat. It requires little to no work. All I have to go is hold my boobs together. Ugh, but it's so dumb. But it will get him to shut up."

"Okay, fine," I agreed.

I reluctantly squeezed my breasts together, creating a little boob cave in between. I even faked some moans and heavy breathing and pretended to have a good time. As Number 16 rubbed his junk up and down my chest, in and out of the cave. After a few minutes of grunting, moaning, groaning, and knocking his pelvis against my ribcage, he did something that I truly should have castrated him for.

Without warning or permission, he shoved his cock down my throat. Not only did he do it after I'd specifically asked him not to, but he did it forcefully and painfully, as if my mouth did not belong to a human. Although I was not being raped, it felt a lot more like rape than when it had actually happened to me.

I wanted to scream, cry, or bite his stupid dick off. But for some reason, all the self-empowerment I'd ever had dissolved into vulnerability. I felt paralyzed and shocked. So, I took it. I did not suck or swivel my tongue around in attempt to make the experience good for him. I simply continued behaving like an object, holding my mouth open and fighting my urge to vomit. For the first time, I was grateful for my bulimia because it damaged my gag reflex.

Number 16 was decently endowed with a thick shaft and it burned the back of my throat, choking me at times. As he gripped my head with both hands, thrusting his cock into my throat, literally skull fucking me, I felt like I'd choked on a large piece of meat and was dying from suffocation. After what seemed like much too long, I felt warm liquid dribble down my throat and I obediently swallowed.

We finally had sex days later. Although he was fairly intimate, kissing my mouth, neck, and snuggling up against me in bed afterwards, the sex was almost as disturbing as my mouth rape.

Number 16 was the absolute *worst* quick shooter that I would ever know. I'd heard of "minute men," but Number 16 was a "thirty-second man." During those brief instances we were having sex, I did get a thrill out of his muscular body against mine. His dick was an acceptable size and we managed to reach good, thorough penetration. But after probably about eight or nine thrusts inside of me, his condom would be flooded with his man juice. The glorious boxer would tap out.

Number 16 was still continuously nice to me. He gave me sincere, sweet compliments like, "You suck good dick, Maggie." He thanked me for all the rides I gave him and for the forty bucks I loaned him for coke, which of course, he never paid back.

As far as I know, he remained discreet at the gym and my workout sessions never got too awkward, but he was a negative contribution to my life. He reminded me of too many of the demons from my teenage years. In many ways, he reminded me of Number 1 even beyond his disregard for my requests for abstinence.

Number 16 was a walking, talking tragedy. He suffered from chronic self-esteem issues that he did nothing about.

"I'm going to die at a gym," he'd mope and complain about his fate as an eternal boxing instructor. "I'm stupid. I can't do anything else with my life."

In response to my suggestions to begin community college courses or at least attempt to get his driver's license, he'd just look down at the ground and say, "No. I can't do it. I can't do anything."

On top of being a drug user, he was a self-destructive alcoholic. He claimed that his hazardous, self-loathing path was his fate.

"Not a single male in my family has lived past forty," he'd tell me. "I'm going to die in less than ten years. I was born to die young."

The last night we spent together, he reminded me of another depressing aspect of my adolescence - Xanax.

The drug is meant to relax people. It's a treatment for severe anxiety, but in the years I abused it in high school, it had another effect on me. Xanax gave me memory loss and severe depression. It was what I took when I'd first began dating Number 3 and accidently began to sleep with Number 2. It was what I was still fucked up on later that night during my tearful confession to Number 3 that I did not remember the next day.

I ditched Tiger and Ceci at the bars and almost immediately dragged a girlfriend over to the apartment of one of Number 16's friends. When we got there, the boys were snorting Xanax. I snorted one myself without hesitation. I don't remember the rest of that night. When Number 16 told me about a new woman in his life the next morning, the depression kicked in. In an impulsive attempt to make it go away, I snorted another line off the glass coffee table next to the couch I'd fallen asleep on, rushed my friend out the door, and sobbed all the way back to PB.

My cries came from much more than the Xanax side effects or yet another horrendous outcome with another man. I was exhausted. For a while, I pegged *that* day the day I began to feel emotions for the opposite sex for the first time since my post-deployment cling on with Number 11, but now I know they always existed.

A friend of mine once told me about a program where volunteers go to Africa to hold orphan infants. According to him, babies will die without physical affection. I think human behavior proves that physical intimacy is a natural craving that lies within everyone. But when things went to shit with Number 16, I realized that I was not an infant. I was a twenty-one-year-adult in the military with a future to seize. Even deep into my Xanax tantrum, I quickly came to my senses.

I took a day off from PB. I fled fifteen minutes east to my friend May's condo in the suburbs. May, having once been a member of frat row that matured and reformed from that world, understood my sorrows. Although she was only a year older than me, she gave me the same comfort that my mother would have. We did normal things. We went grocery shopping. We shopped at Target. She cooked for me. We watched movies. These activities were so fantastically average, belonging to the world outside of PB that I'd forgotten about.

After a night on May's couch, I drove back to PB physically and emotionally revived. Though I was not happy, I was content and in control.

It was then that I realized what I wanted, and it was not another musician, buff boxer, or shirtless PB guy on a skateboard. I wanted *stability*. For the first time in my life, I knew I was ready to be an adult. Little did I know how fate could stab me in the back. Under unexpected circumstances, I would grow up very soon.

Number 17

As my wild PB summer wound down, I began to realize that I was a closet fuck. Never the girlfriend who gets taken to dinner or invited to publicly hang out with the friends. I was that 2 am emergency lay, followed by a walk of shame unworthy of daylight.

At first, I'd felt accomplished by these scenarios. Sure, to those men I was a pocket pussy with legs. They came to me because I required less arm movement and lotion. There was no doubt that I was being used, but these men wouldn't have even bothered to use me during my Higgins days. Progress was progress. But eventually, I wanted respect, friendship, or at least a few minutes of pillow talk. After three months of excessive boxing workouts and a new, edgy layered haircut with bright red streaks to clash with my blonde hair, I felt well worthy of it.

So, when Number 12's bass player, my Number 17, invited me to a Chubbyfunk show, I gladly accepted the invitation.

Just like my other musicians, we met through Myspace. When Number 12 added me, I was just discovering that world and without hesitation, added anyone I found remotely attractive. I found him on Number 12's "top 8 friends."

He didn't have the handsome, pretty boy look that Number 12 possessed. He had short, black hair with olive skin, dark eyes and a slight five o'clock shadow. His photo was a headshot of him looking straight at the camera with a slight smirk on his face. The picture's antique coloring brought out the darkness in his facial features. It looked professionally done, like he was a co-star on some TV show and the photo was his promo shot.

Instead of the mainstream hunk that would have been the center of attention, he looked like the average-looking best friend, full of the personality that the leading man lacked. This metaphor was actually very close to reality.

Number 12 was a typical lead singer - hunky, a favorite of all the ladies, but so spoiled by the attention that he made very little effort to woo and charm. According to him, the "magnitude of his talent" was enough. He didn't need a personality or any uniqueness in his character.

Number 17 was sort of cute, but not at Number 12's level. He could not sing and his instrument was meant to enhance the lead guitar, rarely being the center of the stage. So Number 17 danced.

I've never seen anyone else hold a big bass, playing it quite well, while jumping around stage, grooving and shaking to the music. Unlike Number 12 who convulsed on stage as if he was having a mild seizure, Number 17 could actually dance. The first time I watched a Chubbyfunk video after my awkward first kiss with Number 12, I found my eye much more drawn to the bass player dominating the stage with his carefree moves. Number 17 looked so alive and *fun*.

According to Number 17, Number 12 knew very little about our communication, but their timing was impeccable. When Number 12 disappeared for the month that Chubbyfunk was on tour, Number 17 began sending me Myspace messages from the road. He was funny, clever, and a pleasure to talk to. I always felt slightly giddy when I received his messages, each entertaining in their own way.

Once Chubbyfunk returned to San Diego, Number 12 and I began humping on a regular basis. Number 17 disappeared. He deleted me from his Myspace friend's list without a word of explanation. I was disappointed, but shrugged it off, secretly hoping that Number 12 would invite me to a show so that I could finally meet his bass player. But Number 12 never invited me to a thing besides his bed, couch, bathroom sink, or the hood of his roommate's car. Conveniently, just a week after the Chubbyfunk singer quit calling, the bass player was back in my life.

Our conversations were confined to Myspace. They were never deep or personal. They were unmemorable. I cannot think of a single thing we talked about in all those weeks of constant messages, sometimes twenty each day. Both of us were clever with words, able to thoroughly express our humor and sarcasm. They were lighthearted, fun conversations that added a little panache to my day.

After enough messaging, Number 17 did what Number 12 never had. He invited me to a Chubbyfunk show, giving me a level of humanity that very few men did. I would be attending a legitimate public event. I would meet the entire band as *his* guest. Number 12 would see me there, invited by his bass player and *know* or at least suspect that something was going on. The tension I knew my presence would cause was delightful.

As I got ready to head to the dive bar that evening, I made a special effort to look good. I held my camera in front of my face and took several photos of myself so I could upload one or two of them to Myspace.

Since the birth of Internet social networking, digital cameras, and now smart phones, I'm pretty sure this is a ritual in all young adults, especially women. We get dolled up and want to capture that image to display to the world. We take one photo after the next, blinking in some, having awkward facial expressions in others. Some photos make our cheeks look too chubby or emphasize that pimple on our nose. Certain angles just aren't flattering until finally, we find the perfect one and upload it in hopes of our "friends" commenting on how much weight we've lost, how pretty we are, or how flattering our new haircut is. That day I received several compliments on my profile picture worthy photo. It was my coming out photo, introducing myself to the world as a redhead with sharp, jagged layers framing my face. I smeared on black eyeliner and brushed my eyelids with charcoal shadow, giving me a devilish look to compliment my new fiery mane.

In the photo, my head was tilted slightly down as my eyeballs glanced up at the lens. I had a slight smirk on my face, but it wasn't a smile. I looked dangerously seductive, an expression that I would find quite silly years later. But I was different back then. I wanted to seem semi-naughty and promiscuous.

I wasn't certain what my intentions were that night. I was trying to make Number 12 jealous, get some sort of revenge for disappearing without an explanation and what better way to do it than to show up with his band mate and rival?

Was I trying to hook up with Number 17? Did I even like him? Sure, I was mildly attracted to the Myspace side of him, but those were just typed words. I did know that I wanted him as my territory that night, just in case. So I brought a few girlfriends that I knew could not possibly be competition.

Dolores and another PB cougar met me at the dive bar that was in walking distance of my coastal apartment. Brooke met me at my apartment so we could walk together.

Brooke was a girl I'd met on the Higgins. She had a petite, feminine body with proportional curves. She had a very confident, seductive walk that the sailors fawned over on the ship. She was ghostly pale with large, dollish brown eyes, a pointed chin, and had recently cut off her pretty, long hazelnut mane into a jagged, pixie cut that didn't compliment her circular face.

Once I turned twenty-one, Brooke and I pretended to be friends. We never disliked each other, but we had no chemistry. We began hanging out to have someone to go to the bars with. This arrangement was ideal because she wasn't a heavy drinker, so I always had a guaranteed designated driver and, unlike my pretty PB friends, her looks never made me feel insecure. Like most of my California friendships, ours was purely for the surface. As our encounters with Number 17 proved, Brooke and I had no loyalty to one another.

Walking down the sidewalk, I told Brooke about the complicated mess between Number 12 and 17. It was an August evening about an hour before sunset. We were across the street from the beach and the Pacific breeze cooled our skin, making the summer San Diego temperature perfect.

When we neared the bar, my stomach began to crawl nervously. I'd only heard Number 12 sing through the Internet and iTunes, but there it was, powerfully full of soul. The bar was small, dimly lit, but beginning to crowd.

As I walked in, I saw Chubbyfunk on the other side of the bar. Number 17 and I instantly made eye contact as he smiled and nodded his head to say hello. We met up with Dolores and her PB Boxing cougar friend, who'd already grabbed us a table. Brooke and I ordered our drinks, a Bacardi and Diet Coke for me and a Malibu and pineapple juice for her. Sipping my booze, I anxiously awaited Chubbyfunk's break.

"Here he comes!" Brooke said excitedly as if she was anticipating the encounter as much as I was.

"Maggie!" Number 17 greeted me with a hug. "We finally meet!"

Once he spoke, my spirits dropped. His Myspace photos weren't misleading. He looked exactly the same in person. Like Number 12, he was short, but from seeing the two of them together in the band promo shots, I totally expected that. But I could not *stand* his voice. It was mousy and nasal, as if he'd been huffing helium onstage.

Way beyond details like height, weight, hygiene, endowment, teeth, to me, the biggest turnoff when first meeting a man is an obnoxious or annoying voice. A grown man with a squeaky little girl voice might as well dip my clit in liquid nitrogen. I didn't want him, so I hardly noticed him or the flirtation that bloomed between him and Brooke once she mentioned that she'd be getting out of the Navy and leaving San Diego for good a month from then.

That night, I only had eyes for Number 12 because watching him on-stage belting out Stevie Wonder covers was the most attractive he'd ever been to me. Completely forgetting about what a boring lay he was, watching him perform stirred a number of fantasies of me jumping on-stage, tying him up with the microphone cord, and violently raping him. He was attractively unreachable, not just because of his stage presence, but also the new girlfriend he strung along by his hand during their breaks.

"So *that's* why he quit calling," I thought. "Or had he been cheating on her with me?"

Infidelity certainly would have made sense. Number 12 seemed guilty and somewhat frightened of me, making a conscious effort to be extra friendly, hugging me, wrapping his arms around me as if we were old chums. He'd acted like less of a friend when we were fucking.

"You're so much prettier than her," Dolores encouraged me, being the sweetly biased mother figure that she was.

And perhaps Dolores was right to a point. Number 12's new girlfriend was cute, blonde, and unlike me, very *thin.*

Over four years after Chubbyfunk and PB were out of my life, I watched a movie for a Chicano film class called, *Raising Victor Vargas.* It's a coming of age film about a Latino teen named Victor who lives in lower east side of New York. In the beginning of the film, he is shown messing around with a hefty young lady who the neighborhood calls, "Fat Donna." When Victor realizes that she has a photo of them together, he gives her the same speech I heard from numerous Navy and PB men.

"I'm a private person. What we do is between me and you."

Once their affair is discovered, he snatches the photo of them, ignores Fat Donna, and denies their relationship. Since sleeping with Fat Donna has ruined his reputation, he spends the rest of the film pursuing the affection of one of the prettiest and of course, thinnest girls in the neighborhood.

Fat Donna was not a major character. The hurt feelings she most likely had after Victor fled her apartment with their photo clutched between his fingers, knowing that he was ashamed of her was never touched on in the film's plot. Like most fat people in the media, she was only a joke.

Though I wasn't an anorexic supermodel, I'd lost enough weight to occasionally fit in a size six dress or to be able to look at my backside from a double mirror without pure horror. When someone wanted to insult me, I was a *bitch*, no longer a *fat bitch.*

But I could not help but relate to Fat Donna. I was extremely active and in fantastic shape. But by southern California standards, I was still slightly chubby. I probably *was* their equivalent of Fat Donna. In the eyes of those men, I was desirable, but only in private. The fact that, as most men would put it, I acted like a whore and therefore was treated like a whore, is a good explanation for my closet fuck status, but I can't help but wonder if my thicker physique contributed to the equation.

At first, I didn't notice the witty Myspace banter between Number 17 and I come to a halt. I was too occupied with the aftershock of meeting Number 12's girlfriend. Sure, I'd been hopeful for a mutually revengeful hookup, but my in-person encounter with the petite, squeaky-voiced bass player was underwhelming. It apparently was for him too because Number 17 quietly took a hiatus from my life. Strangely enough, so did Brooke.

Knowing that Brooke was on the brink of getting out of the Navy and moving back to her hometown in upstate New York, I called her one afternoon.

"We've been dating since we met at the show!" she gushed a couple weeks after their introduction.

My jaw dropped at the news of their courtship. Sure, I noticed him being nice to her. I spotted him escorting her to the pizza shop next-door while Number 12 and I awkwardly chatted outside the bar. But I'd briefed Brooke on the Chubbyfunk triangle before the show. I had dibs on Number 17.

"He cooks me dinner. We go to the park. We're just enjoying each other's company until I leave."

"Those mother fuckers," I thought, angrily.

Sure, I hadn't really wanted Number 17, but it felt shady that Brooke hadn't even run her interest by me, at least to spare my feelings. It wasn't so much that she was seeing him that bothered me, but the fact that she waited so long to mention it. It was a vicious jab to my ego.

"*Brooke?*" I thought to myself. "He didn't want me, but he wanted Brooke? Pale-faced, bug-eyed Brooke?"

Publicly, I had been his guest at the Chubbyfunk show, but also publicly, he was seeing Brooke. And privately, he pursued me a couple weeks after Brooke left San Diego.

"Come out!" he pleaded over the phone as if we'd been best friends all long. "I'm at a bar *literally* a mile from your place."

By then, I was well aware of Number 17's pattern of jumping in and out of my life, skipping between conflicting mutual associations. My company was only appealing in Brooke's absence. But I was so damn curious how Number 17 would behave. If he made a move, what explanation would he concoct for dismissing me and seducing my friend?

I went in hopes for some amusement and a free vodka soda.

Number 17 gave me my regular public treatment at the bar. While we carried on small talk with a friend of his, he was warm, chummy, and personable. He did not wrap his arm around me or brush my cheek with the back of his palm. We did not graze limbs. He kept a platonic six-inch space gap between us. So, I assumed his request for a ride home was merely just that.

In the privacy of my car, it took Number 17 about ten blocks to run his hand up my thigh. I should have been insulted by his display of entitlement to my body.

A confident woman would have called bullshit, pulled over, and kicked his ass to the curb. However, I played along, eager to scrape any remnants of validation he was willing to toss me. But I still faked a bit of perplexity.

"WHAT THE HELL?" I stammered, trying to muffle my arising giggles.

"Oh, come on," he coaxed. "You know we've both been dying to do it since we started talking."

"Really?" I said with exaggerated expression. "Is that what you told *Brooke*?"

He rolled his eyes.

"*Pa-leeze*," he scoffed. "I only went for her because she was leaving. Ugh, she was a fucking *awful* lay."

Number 17 and I spent our drive home swapping bitch fests of Brooke and Number 12. I went on about what a lazy lover Number 12 was while Number 17 rattled on about my ex lover's ego. I growled about Brooke's unjustifiable vanity, while Number 17 grumbled about her sexual lack-luster.

"Is his dick big at all?" Number 17 asked about his band front man.

"No, not really," I laughed. "Average at best."

"HA! I KNEW IT!" Number 17 cackled. "He's always bragging about how big his dick is and how every chick wants it."

"Well, he certainly fucked like his dick was immaculate - just lying there with his penis erect like a monument I'm supposed to worship."

"Brooke wasn't any better," Number 17 remarked. "She fucked like a corpse - ignored my dick altogether. Ugh. Such a pillow princess."

"Then why'd you give her so much attention?" I interrogated.

"I dunno," he shrugged. "Her face wasn't the best, but she's got a cute, petite body. Plus, she was about to take off across the country. I could have all the fun I wanted - no strings attached."

"And," he cockily winked, "I knew you'd be around once she left."

Number 17 was an unapologetic asshole. But caving into his passes seemed to bring a mutually beneficial, double-whammy payback. I loved the idea of nailing Number 12's bass player while proving that ⸺ was nothing special.

Number 17 practically screamed his ⸺ looks, charm, and diverse musical talent. And he ⸺

We both had one objective that was ⸺ to be better at sex than our mutual enemies ⸺

Number 17 lived in an up and com⸺ gradually renovated from ghetto to hipster ⸺ apartment was budget friendly, he admitt⸺ official. Every musician I'd known was a ⸺

The humble abode was clean, sm⸺ was decorated with tribal artifacts from ⸺ showed me some of his most prized pos⸺ behind the adventures in acquiring his ⸺ towered well over his head.

I contemplated lunging forward, grabbing his crotch, shoving my tongue down his throat, or just flat out asking if he wanted to just cut the crap and get the affair over and done with. But I was cemented in place. Regardless of how obvious Number 17 made our fate, his rejection just weeks before still rang loudly in my memory.

I waited for Number 17 to keep pushing forward. He seemed to enjoy the process of dancing around my hesitation. He played an excruciatingly gradual seduction game of putting on a movie neither of us would watch, positioning himself close to me on the couch, and throwing a blanket over our laps. My feet were propped up on the coffee table in front of us, giving him conveniently reachable access to my legs. I sat stiffly as I let him begin with rubbing my knee and then working up my leg and into my inner thigh.

"Here we go," he said, practically reading my mind. "This is happening."

He knew that the combination of our awkward social ties left me a bit baffled. He loved it. Our whole charade clearly amused him.

And then, his hand was on my crotch, massaging my pussy outside of my black bikini underwear. We hadn't even kissed.

"Whoops!" he exclaimed sarcastically when one of my lips slipped out of my underwear. "I guess this is it."

His fingers dove right inside my vagina, which was already slick from our tediously tense buildup. Although he didn't have the pipes of Marvin Gaye, Number 17 was significantly more sexually impressive than his band mate. He actually displayed some work ethic, rubbing his fingers on my clit, kissing my neck, gently tugging my hair while playfully biting my earlobe, unhooking my bra with one hand, and massaging my nipples with his tongue.

I was still sitting upright when he scooted me up to yank my jeans. Number 17 may have not respected my feelings, but he respected my sexual needs.

By that time, he had maneuvered off the couch and was on his knees directly in front of me. After tossing my panties to the side, he spread my legs and buried his tongue inside of me. After he'd had enough generosity, Number 17 stood up to where my head was at level with his dick. When he pulled his boxers down, I was dumbstruck.

Right in front of me was a green four-leaf clover tattooed on the tip of his penis. Number 17 must have noticed my puzzled expression.

"I see you noticed The Sham-cock," he gleamed.

"Oh my God," was the only response I could muster before combusting into ʰing fit.

ˢ's in honor of my Irish ancestors. You should pay your respects."

ith Number 17 was fun and fair and square in generosity. He was ˢe passionate Chubbyfunk member, straddling himself behind me, ⁿ behind on his couch, gripping my long hair like reins that ʰoria.

ᴼVE ME!" he demanded.

ˡed.

Number 17 certainly out-fucked his rival and claimed I out-fucked mine. But hindsight made me wonder who really won. While Brooke got dinner and legitimate dates, I got a boot out the door before his roommate got home.

Number 18

There are no seasons in San Diego, only occasional spurts of rain and clouds to interrupt the usually warm and sunny skies. San Diego showed no evidence of summer rolling into fall. Instead of a crisp, cool breeze with the scent of changing leaves to remind me that my wild, carefree PB summer was over, I got a much ruder awakening.

Entranced in San Diego's intoxicating temptations, my peers and I once felt invincible. We did as we wished. Then, September came, and it seemed as if the party town was annoyed with us. It sought to teach us humility, to prove that our actions came with consequences.

After one of our usual evenings of pub-crawling the Garnet strip, Annabelle crashed her brand new sports car and earned her first DUI. If a sailor gets him or herself in trouble, they are almost always punished twice: once by the civilian world and again by the Navy. A criminal charge results in two trials. A jail sentence is usually followed with prison *and* the brig. The Navy has a way of reminding its personnel that it owns them.

Halfway into my enlistment, I lived in denial of it. As soon as I was released from work each day, I darted into the bathroom, stripped off my uniform and tossed it in the trunk of my car for the next morning. I wouldn't be caught dead by any civilian in the unflattering, ass-dissolving ensemble that made me feel so uncomfortably bound to my contract.

When I wasn't at work, I lived like a civilian. I socialized with civilians. I partied with them. I hooked up with them. I snorted coke with them. I worked for the Navy just enough to keep the paycheck that supported my beachside apartment. I loved my life in PB because it was truly a refuge from all things military. When I wasn't on base, I forgot that I was even in the military. I even forgot about my military marriage.

"Do you know why you're here?" a woman named Danita Brown asked me.

I had been summoned to the Naval Criminal Investigative Service office. With my indestructible twenty-one-year-old attitude, it hadn't occurred to me that I was in trouble for anything. Sure, NCIS was some serious shit. It was like the FBI of the Navy. There was even a prime time TV show on it that my grandmother still watches religiously. But I had done nothing wrong. Technically, I had not broken a single rule with my marriage. I was clean. Safe. They must have been questioning me about someone else. I was absolutely innocent.

I shook my head no at Brown's question.

I still wasn't threatened. Danita Brown wasn't scary at all. She was a cute, young woman with chocolate brown skin and a protruding baby belly. How could such a sweet mother-to-be intimidate me?

Suddenly, she became my enemy.

"You're being accused of committing fraud," she said.

"*Fuck*," was the first word sprung from my aloof brain. "What the *fuck? Shit. Dammit. Fuck! Fuck! Fuck!*"

That was it. I was caught.

I swear I felt my insides hemorrhaging. I wanted to run, cry, scream, and puke all at once.

I was interrogated for several hours. According to the documents Brown gave me, I had the basic criminal rights. I could remain silent and end the interview, which was exactly what I should have done. But several investigators urged me to talk. They told me silence would look horrible on my record - that a judge would be more likely to Court-martial me if I plead the fifth. So, I tried to fake my way through it. I told Brown that I had a normal marriage, that I'd been in love and that we separated like most young Navy couples do.

Unfortunately, I am a shitty liar and a failure under pressure.

"Okay!" I blurted out. "I was never in a relationship with my husband. We did it so we'd have the money to get an apartment! I can't lie anymore! I can't play this game!"

"You're not a good liar," Brown said, with a sympathetic smile.

From that moment on, I was her bitch. I gave her *everything* she wanted. I broke down in tears, feeling pathetic and weak. I spilled my guts about myself, my marriage, and my white trash, tinfoil meth smoking Sale Creek, Tennessee past. I answered every single one of her questions, even overtly personal ones, such as "Do you still believe that your marriage was legal when you never had sex with your husband?" Whatever she wanted was hers. I just wanted to escape, go home, cry, and possibly slam my face into a doorknob for a few hours.

As my interrogation unfolded, I realized that NCIS had been following me for about six months. They knew about my husband and his girlfriend, parties I'd had, and the friends I associated with. This knowledge sent me in a deep state of paranoia that would haunt me for months.

Suddenly, I was a criminal. I was accused of embezzling money from the government. NCIS wanted everything back, from eighteen months worth of San Diego rent to my spouse's hospital bill from a trip to the emergency room. It added up to $31,025.10.

I didn't pocket a dime of it. It had all gone to rent. They took my fingerprints and mug shot. I must have looked like the Navy's rebellious teenage daughter with my bright red and very out of regulations hair.

Shaken and defeated from hours of hysterical sobbing, Danita Brown smiled at me with a mixture of sympathy and assurance.

"Girl, I'm not worried about you," she said. "Yeah, you're in trouble. You're in big trouble. But look at how far you've come. You're twenty-one. You've got your whole life ahead of you. From the path that you were going, you should've been lying in a gutter somewhere. You're in the Navy, on track, and doing things with your life. You're going to get through this."

My urge to claw her eyeballs out quickly subsided. Unable to hate her, I smiled back. I knew she was right. I would become more than a petty Navy criminal. I was determined to become more than the Navy itself.

My life changed immediately. The changes went far beyond the dark cloud that loomed over me in my own mind. My supervisor, PS1 Queen, met me at the PSD entrance.

I had always hated Queen. He was tall and reasonably handsome for a thirty-four-year-old who looked forty. His hair was jet black and his arms were covered in the tattoos of his youth.

Queen was one of those men who needed the Navy. He had never pursued a college degree and had accumulated a hefty amount of baggage during his enlistment. His load included three children, some four-wheelers, dirt bikes, gas guzzling trucks, a decently sized San Diego suburban beach home, and a wife who sat on her ass and collected BAH.

At thirty-four, Queen was merely four years from obligatory retirement. Despite his arrogant demeanor, it was obvious that he was scared shitless of the day when his supply of the Navy's breast milk evaporated.

He took himself way too seriously, expecting the utmost military formality at all times. He was a hypocrite, preaching the Navy's supposed theme of "honor, courage, and commitment," yet he fucked around on his wife with lower ranking females who were enchanted by his E6 rank and tattoos. But I really hated him for only two reasons. The first was that I didn't trust him. He wasn't a good person and I knew that in my heart. The second reason was his obvious hatred towards me.

I can see how the Joe Navy types would have despised me. Young, rebellious, and feverish under the constant regulations the Navy implemented, I did everything I could to push their limits. When regulations required personnel to keep their hair a natural-looking color, I dyed my tresses hot tamale. Because the women's were so ill fitting, I donned men's working uniforms that I tossed in the dryer instead of ironed and creased. I had zero military bearing. My salutes were sloppy and slanted. I giggled and twitched when I was required to stand at attention. I did the minimum about of work it took to get a paycheck.

But Queen's loathing went beyond such annoyances. He hated me because of his own insecurities. Queen and I were opposites. While the Navy revealed the worst version of myself, it brought out the best of his. The Navy was his career and I thought I was better than it. Like most of my lifer superiors at PSD, Queen found great satisfaction in the Navy teaching me a lesson.

Queen led me to the back room where the service records of every enlisted member of the ships on base were kept. It was like a library, full of towering rows of fat paper folders that contained every record of people's careers.

Queen and I were alone.

"Young, you're being transferred out of here today," he said curtly.

He knew everything.

"You're too much of a security risk to work here," he continued. "At least until this NCIS investigation is over. Your Secret security clearance will most likely be removed as well."

By that time I was a timid wreck, weak, without control over my emotions. I began crying.

"Aw, Young," Queen's eyes softened. My breakdown disturbed him. As he dropped his stoic professionalism in to pull me into a comforting hug, I was able to see another side of him. As my salty tears dampened the shoulder of his white uniform, I realized that he was also a loving husband and father. And for that moment, I liked him. I thought I'd misjudged him. That is, until he would later try to screw me over worse than anyone else yet had.

The military soiled my image of pregnancy. Although I'm sure numerous reproductive military couples were well equipped for parenthood, the armed forces does not reward copulation with financial convenience out of wholesome generosity. They lured sailors into procreation with hefty pay increases, cozy base housing, and promises of education, health, and stability for the whole brood. A single sailor is far less likely to take their honorable discharge with a family to support. With stability at stake, of course they'll re-up. But that allure appeals to all candidates, including the overwhelmingly young and irresponsible. I've seen so many girls purposely get pregnant to escape sea duty or to entrap a boyfriend on the brink of leaving. The longer my enlistment, the more untucked maternity shirts seemed to flourish around base. Pregnant sailors are almost immediately removed from sea duty and placed in shore duty positions, working remedial administrative jobs, like the military ID office or the vehicle base decal registration.

Another primary duty for the lower enlisted mommies was picking up trash on base, waddling within the barbed wire gates with a garbage bag in the left hand and a spiked stick on their right.

The day after my NCIS interrogation, fetus free, I became one of them.

Everyone said that the military would force me to grow up. For the first two and a half years of my enlistment, they were wrong. Then, NCIS entered my life and I aged. I have not been the same since. Coke-snorting, musician-fucking, PB-loving Maggie died instantly and an older, damaged, paranoid Maggie fell into a new routine. Knowing I had pushed my luck enough in playing the Navy random drug test shuffle, I forfeited blow for good. I declined invitations to the bars and within weeks, my phone grew silent. My multiple weekend plans ceased and my PB friends disappeared. I was no longer fun.

Drinking gave me little control over my life, so I stopped. I was being held tightly in the Navy's grasp and had been delivered a rude awakening that I was not a free American citizen, but government property. The Navy could do what it wanted with me. But I still had control of my body. Alcohol robbed me of that. It also cost money.

The only thing more terrifying than losing the little control I had was spending money. I joined the Navy to get ahead in life, but instead it was looking like my enlistment wasn't even all for nothing. It was much worse than that. I was on the verge of owing the Navy over thirty thousand dollars. It would be like paying off college loans without a degree or getting a car loan actually having a car.

I was facing deep financial burden, the chances of a negative discharge, the loss of the college money I had joined the Navy to obtain, and possibly brig time. I became afraid of everything, wondering if NCIS was peering through my windows or lurking around my door to spy on me. My heart would spasm when my phone rang, always wondering if it held updates of the punishment that was waiting for me. But I was mostly afraid of losing all of my money. Though it wasn't much, the money I had became precious and I realized how quickly it disappeared. Driving cost money.

Even my friendships required a costly maintenance of cabs, club entry fees, overpriced drinks, sushi dinners, and shopping trips.

I never second-guessed those activities before my NCIS case. I had a stable paycheck. Suddenly, I couldn't trust that or anything associated with the Navy. I became a cheap ass who didn't want to leave my house.

"You can't live your life like this," my friends urged me. "You have to spend money."

I ignored them and retreated to my apartment. My money and my solidarity were the only things that made me feel safe. I existed in a fog. But life went on.

I was issued a Navy Jag lawyer. Her name was Lieutenant Lash. She was a blonde, fair-skinned woman in her early thirties with a serious, but kind face.

I was skeptical of her because she worked for the very force that was prosecuting me. But upon meeting her, I liked her immediately. She was polished, professional, and remarkably intelligent. Lash was what I wanted to be - a strong woman with a successful career.

"I can't believe the Navy is trying to do this," she said, shaking her head.

I watched her from across her desk as she peered down at a large stack of papers that were NCIS documents on my case. She looked puzzled.

"Have you ever dealt with a case like this?" I asked her nervously.

"Sure. I've had two marriage cases before. But those were actually fraudulent. They had fake marriage certificates. Your marriage was real. I just didn't think the Navy would get into this."

Lash wasn't the only person stunned by my case. I had talked to several Navy people of all different ranks.

"Are you legally married?" they'd ask.

"Yes."

"Did you financially support your spouse?"

"Yes, and he's not filing a complaint. He's not even involved in this."

"He lives in San Diego, right? You're not collecting BAH from a better paying location?"

"Nope."

"Do they have proof of adultery?"

"No. And they're not even trying to get me for that."

"Then how the hell can they even punish you for this? Is there some kind of rule that forces you to fuck your husband a certain amount of times per week or something?"

Lash scanned and studied the Navy regulations. She found nothing that incriminated me. Nothing defined a proper marriage.

"If you had researched the Navy rules before you got married, it actually would have been more reason for you to get married for BAH," Lash said. "There were no rules to break."

"Then why are they doing this to me?"

"Hmm," she thought to herself for a moment. "Well, your command initiated this case. You being a woman may have had something to do with it. You stand out. Women are usually more emotional towards marriage. You're also outspoken and articulate. That can be intimidating for military men."

I thought about PS1 Queen and the higher ranking enlisted members at PSD who hated me.

"But I really think this is for moralistic purposes," she continued. "They probably felt what you did was wrong and wanted your punishment to be an example for everyone else. It's not about the money. This case has been going on for six months already. By the time it's complete, the government would have spent a lot more money on prosecuting you than what it collected."

I scoffed at this. It was just typical of the Navy to be so idiotic for the sake of implementing their beliefs on right and wrong.

"What's ironic," Lash said, "Is that they are trying to prosecute you for marrying for financial purposes, but they are the ones putting a price on marriage."

I ended up liking garbage duty. In fact, it turned out to be the best job I would ever have in the Navy. Sure, there was nothing glamorous about spending my days with a spiked stick poking for garbage, but I loved the people I worked with. Garbage duty was for the pregnant chicks that the Navy didn't know what to do with and the troublemakers waiting for a court date or their process out. My bosses were Boatswains Mates serving out their shore duty. Everyone was laid back and kind. My superiors, who worked with all sorts of the Navy's misunderstood stepchildren, were nonjudgmental. When I needed to go to a doctor's appointment, they let me go without a single sarcastic remark. When I needed to meet with my lawyer, I was released without question. When I received the news of Granddaddy's death while I was at work, they were supportive, comforting, and assured me that they had my back if I needed anything.

I couldn't help but notice the dramatic difference in atmosphere between trash duty and PSD. I had to return to PSD to process some paper work in order for me to attend Granddaddy's funeral in South Carolina. I was already shaken up from my NCIS investigation and possibly facing over thirty grand in debt, I was terrified to dip out the cash I needed for my round trip ticket to South Carolina. I knew that I could find that amount of dough in Carl's liquor cabinet, so I gave him a call and asked him for a loan.

"No," he answered condescendingly. "Go take outta loan. You can be in debt for thirdy years insteada twenny years."

After he hung up on me, I lost it. I broke down in front of everyone and not a single person asked me if I was okay. When I was with my new temporary command, I felt like I was in good hands for the first time in the Navy. I trusted those guys and that trust never bit me in the ass. We spent our days driving around in trucks, listening to music. We'd get dropped off around various areas on base, pair up with someone and chat as we walked and cleaned. It wasn't bad.

With my trusty lawyer and better command, I was beginning to realize that the Navy was not entirely evil. But I still had a raging resentment towards it. I hated the uniform I changed into each morning. I hated salutes, crew cuts, and buns. I hated haze grey. I hated the way I could see the ships poking over the horizon when I exited the interstate to go to base. I developed prejudice towards Navy people, rolling my eyes at the military families grocery shopping at the commissary and the local bars infested with crew cut sailors. This is why I was not remotely attracted to Number 18.

It was my first week of trash duty. Since my interrogation, I'd obtained a horrible case of insomnia. At the beginning of my workday at 9 am, which is an abnormally late morning for a military command, I was exhausted. I hopped in the back seat of the truck and passed out as we drove to the other side of base.

"Mornin' sunshine! Get out!" the driver shouted back.

I groggily flopped out, barely balanced on the pavement of a large parking lot by a pier. Rubbing my pink eyes, I looked up to see Number 18 staring at me like a hungry lion staring at a plump, fleshy goat.

He was tall and lanky. He stood at about 6'3" and was so skinny that I'd later be a bit disturbed to see the way his pelvic bones stuck out when he was naked. Maybe he looked at me so scandalously because he was hungry and wanted to eat me. I was shocked to find out that he was twenty-seven because he didn't look a day over twenty-one. His face was young, smooth, and wrinkle free. His hair was a dark blonde and trimmed short. He looked like an all American, church going, country serving boy who belonged on a vintage World War II recruitment billboard.

It was so odd how everything about him looked wholesome except for his eyes. His eyes were a dark, oceanic blue. They made me uncomfortable, as if they could see straight through my clothes.

I was repulsed by anything in coveralls. I wouldn't have been interested in Johnny Depp in uniform. I walked all over base as Number 18 trailed along. He spent the entire day asking me questions about myself. Since I had nothing better to do, I reciprocated the interview process.

The more I got to know Number 18, the more I confirmed my disinterest. At twenty-seven, he had been in the Navy for eight years. Gross. He intended to make it a career and do twenty years before retiring. Yuck. He was an E5 Boatswain's Mate serving shore duty and joined us for trash pickup on his duty days. Ugh.

Besides his huge TV that played thousands of channels, he had no major hobbies. Boring.

He was from a small farm town in the Midwest where his retired military parents raised him. He was an only child and joined the Navy because it was expected of him. He stayed in because he had nothing better to do. At his rank and time in service, his paycheck was fairly hefty and he spent his money on one sports car and another very large truck. I still can't recollect the make or models because, frankly, I didn't care.

We had nothing in common. His interest in me was unreasonable, but apparent. At the end of our workday, he asked me for my number. He called that night and for weeks, I dodged his attempts, only briefly replying when I was lonely or bored.

To most female bystanders, Number 18 would have been attractive. He had those soft blonde hair, blue-eyed Ken doll features. But he was way too persistent. I had grown used to my shallow PB musician types drunk dialing me at 3 am for a few pumps inside of me before practically shoving me out the door. For weeks, Number 18 called, pushing through the excuses I made. He had little to no personality. But most of all, he just reeked of Navy - an entity I'd grown to hate.

Granddaddy's death couldn't have come at a more ironic time.

On October 6th, just a few weeks after my interrogation, I got the call during trash duty's two-hour lunch break. I was lying on one of the dirty couches in the lounge of the old warehouse, watching television with a group of people when my phone rang. When I heard my mom crying on the other end, I knew what had happened.

Granddaddy's death wasn't a shock for anyone. A stubborn chiropractor that didn't trust medicine, he pissed blood for years before even seeing who he considered a "pill dispensing whack job." He suffered from several conditions, some of which are still a mystery to our family because he never spoke of them. But it was the prostate cancer that ultimately got him at the age of seventy-six.

For years, my grandfather had been in denial of his diminishing health. He never retired. He drove long after it was safe for him to, weaving back and forth against the yellow lines on the road at the speed of dripping molasses in January. Up until he was physically incapable, he worked full time at his office, taking on a full rotation of patients every day.

I saw him two months before he passed, knowing it would be the last time.

For the final weeks of his life, hospice came to their tall, log cabin-style home in the woods of Easley, South Carolina. It was the roof I lived under from infancy, until my mother's marriage to Carl. It was a home of hollow, tall ceilings, creaks, and noisy echoes where our huge family gathered for Thanksgivings and Sunday dinners. It was a home that was once saturated with the chaos of squealing little girls, my female-dominated generation, bickering over who got to play with the prettiest Barbie. The house had been havoc for my grouchy, short-tempered granddaddy that never really liked children, but strangely enough, produced five of them. He escaped that house for solidarity, yet it grew eerily silent after his death.

He died in his home surrounded by family. He had months to prepare for it. The past few weekends of his life, our entire family gathered there for cookouts, long talks, and opportunities to repair all the burnt bridges and say the things that were never said when life seemed limitless.

I was the one missing member during those last weeks. My final time speaking with my grandfather was interrupted by an anal retentive chief.

"Get off that cell phone when you're in uniform, shipmate," he barked. "Give me your name and rank!"

He spoke to me with the usual familial roles military society took, the higher in rank the irrational, reprimanding father and the lower, an ill-mannered, rebellious teenager who can only properly function when put in her place.

I was running errands around base on my lunch break. The Navy had just established some rule against walking and talking on your cell phone in uniform, apparently because it prevented us from saluting properly.

Because the last thing I needed was more trouble in my life, I let my grandfather go. I spent the rest of my life regretting not sneaking into a corner and calling him right back.

Since joining the Navy and becoming one with sunny San Diego, my visits to The South always felt a little surreal. They were two different worlds. I'd become so accustomed to one that any reminder of my past always gave my reality a little jolt. As strange as it was to go back home, I was always grateful for that getaway from everything that reminded me of the military. But at Granddaddy's funeral, I couldn't escape it.

"He used to be ashamed of his military service," my grandmother told me. "But as he got older, he became proud of it."

I had just arrived at the house. Along with my parents and a few somber relatives, I was staring at my grandfather's dark wooden casket lying in the middle of the little apartment that had been built on to the bottom floor of the creaky house when my grandparents began having trouble climbing up two flights of stairs to their bedroom. On top of it was an American flag wrapped up in the same triangle that the Higgins flag was folded into after taking it down at dusk.

I had little in common with my grandfather. Our military service was one of the few bonding grounds we had. Though for different reasons, neither of us really talked about that part of our lives. All I'd known was that he fought in the Korean War in his early twenties.

My grandparents hailed from a society that didn't really talk. They took the polite route of keeping raw or negative conversation either heavily sugarcoated or completely under wraps. Wartime trauma was never mentioned.

But once he was gone, it was as if his five-decade-old army days were the center of his life.

"Yoa granddaddy was very good at killin'," my grandmother continued to tell me as my uncles lifted his casket to take it to the hearse parked outside.

"He was too good addit. He rose in rank quickly. They wanted him ta stay in, but the guilt of all the lives he took haunted em'. That's why he became a chirapractor He thought that healin' as many people as possible was the only way he could make up for whad he'd done."

Throughout the morning of riding to the funeral and waiting for services to begin, I listened to one after the next military story from my grandmother, aunts, and uncles.

"He should have died a long time ago," they said. "He was shot a few times in combat."

Not only was I immersed in military chatter. Everyone was suddenly making a big deal out of my enlistment. Suddenly, I wasn't "Maggie, the girl that lives in California," or "Maggie, Annie's daughter." My introductions were, "This is my niece. She's in the Navy," and "This is my cousin, she's the first woman in our family to serve her country."

During the military recognition part of the funeral service, all members and veterans were asked to stand. I was one of three.

"We were so proud of you when you stood up," everyone gushed. "Why didn't you wear your uniform to the funeral?"

The more that people associated me with the military, the angrier I got. Not because of my NCIS case, but because of the way people lumped the military together as one great, big, heroic entity. For the first time since my enlistment, I was realizing that the great American hero, gun in hand, willing to lay down their life, was not a myth fabricated by the media. Despite whatever reason we were at war, because it seems that we never know why we're *really* at war anymore, there have always been and still are people that will voluntarily die for that. My grandfather was one of them. I was not.

There has never been a second of my life that I was willing to die for my country. If for some reason, I had ever been called into combat, I would have broken my leg or run razors up my arm until Navy medical dubbed me too insane to deploy. And though few of them would ever actually admit it, I think most of the people I worked with in the military would react the same way. But because of a contract they signed, these people lapped up that heroic protector image right along with my grandfather. They said their humble thank yous when patriotic Americans congratulated them on Veteran's Day. They copy and pasted big, wordy Facebook posts about how important it was to serve their country and lay their life on the line, when truly, right along with me, the military was nothing but a glorified paycheck with hefty benefits for them. Yet, for the rest of our lives, because of our honorable "service," we'd get the same pats on the back as people dodging bullets and returning home with missing limbs.

To this day, every time someone's eyes widen with admiration when they find out that I'm a veteran, those are the thoughts that cross my mind.

In the midst of the dark chaos of NCIS that consumed me, I'd lost all interest in men. Along with my social life, sex or any kind of intimacy lingered out of bounds of the controlled obsession my life had become. I solely went to work, attended evening college courses, and boxed.

Since my degrading fling with Number 16, boxing class was awkward. But working out made me feel in control of my life. According to the Navy, I was a criminal, but I was being good. I went to school and I exercised. All shenanigans were gone. I went to the boxing club religiously and faced my instructor, watching him hit on every other member with pink boxing gloves.

Then one day, I showed up to the wrong class.

"Its 4:30, not 5:30," Loco, Gia's old flame remarked to me, rolling his eyes.

Although I knew of Loco before joining the boxing club, we never spoke. Looking at him, I understood Gia's attraction. Loco's entire body was flawlessly chiseled. His tattooed legs had bulging muscles from years of Muay Thai training. His right leg bore a large tribal Thai bull tattoo, a symbol of power. His left had an eagle tattoo, representing pride in his Mexican heritage. Loco was handsome with olive skin, dark eyes, and a short, black Mohawk. But I thought he was a prick. He seemed cold, arrogant, and pretentious.

"It's time for Muay Thai," he told me.

In the six months I'd been a gym member, it was the first time Loco had spoken to me.

"Oh," I said, feeling foolish.

My eyes darted away from Loco's.

"I guess I can go run errands for an hour."

"What? Are you scared of my class?" he smirked then rolled his eyes.

I'd heard that Muay Thai was significantly harder than regular boxing. From the glimpses I'd gotten of Loco's class, it did look scary. When I joined the boxing club, I was working at PSD. My shift was from 2 pm to 10 pm, so I boxed in the mornings. I usually took classes with wealthy older, tanned, anorexic cougars. But I worked mornings at trash duty. The evening crowd at the boxing club was filled with young professional nine to five types and there were certainly no PB Boxing cougars in Loco's class. In fact, there was nobody in his class that wasn't under thirty-five and athletic. On Saturdays, I had taken classes before during the same time that Muay Thai was happening. I knew little about the techniques of it, but I did know that moans, groans, and vomiting were often included.

Loco was right. I was scared of his class, but I didn't like his tone. What an asshole. I decided to take stupid Muay Thai class.

When I got into the ring with our small group of eight, my immediate instinct was to laugh at Loco. He wore tiny Muay Thai shorts rolled up to his upper thighs. Then, Loco paired us up. We took turns holding pads for each other and doing repeated routines of punches and kicks. I could almost immediately feel my lungs gasping in for air and my stomach cramping with nausea.

"Come on!" Loco would shout. "Quit being lazy! *Leileileileilei!*"

"What the fuck is '*leilielie*'?" I thought, annoyed at how much Loco was pushing us.

But somehow, Loco's weird little chant made me want to move.

In my mind, "*Leilielie!*" translated into, "Move your fat ass, Maggie! Move, move, move you lazy cunt! Yeah, I know it hurts, FATTY! JAB, RIGHT, JAB, KNEE, UPPERCUT, KICK, KICK, KICK!"

By the end of class, my grey wife beater turned black with sweat. When I limped to my car and realized that I could barely put my keys in the ignition because my hands were so shaky, I knew I'd be back.

I kept myself busy throughout the fall. My life was work, school, and Muay Thai. I knew that the moment I relaxed, fear of the punishment I could be facing would envelop me. So, I never relaxed.

Since the Obsessive Compulsive tendencies I discovered in my adolescence, I had always been wrapped up in addiction. During my teenage years, my greatest obsession was food and I fed into that through my eating disorders. Upon joining the Navy, promiscuity was my kryptonite. But once NCIS dubbed me bad, I just wanted to be good. Whether it was my education or my body, my obsession became bettering myself. I was addicted to productivity.

That mind frame permanently stuck with me. In a way this was good.

I remembered Investigator Brown's words of encouragement after my interrogation and reminded myself that I was a fighter. I knew it would take work, but I told myself daily that death would be the only thing keeping me from becoming a powerful, accomplished person. The downside was that my intense ambition isolated me. By the time I saw some light at the end of my frightening, Navy marriage fraud tunnel, I found myself with nobody to rejoice with.

My first sign of good news came during a sunny, warm San Diego December afternoon on garbage duty. I was riding in the truck headed to some littered area on base. My phone rang and as usual, I felt my gut spasm with panic. And when I saw Lieutenant Lash on my caller I.D., I'm pretty sure I almost had a mild panic attack.

"He-he-hello?" I answered nervously.

"Hi Maggie. It looks like we're making progress in this case," Lash said. "Things might be looking up."

I let out my first sigh of relief in three months.

Lash had been negotiating with NCIS and the rest of the Navy legal system. It was looking like they were going to drop all of my fraud charges if I agreed to pay them a fee of about four thousand bucks. This sum was the difference between married and single BAH during the time that my husband and I weren't living together. I was also looking at Captain's Mast, but my trial would have nothing to do with my marriage.

The second page of a service record, very cleverly called a "Page 2," is the member's address and family information. On my Page 2, I had my husband as my dependent, but instead of his address, I had mine. This had nothing to do with BAH because both of us lived in San Diego. It was just a simple mistake. I was expected to walk away with four thousand dollars less in my savings account and a slap on the wrist. Compared to owing the government over thirty thousand dollars and being kicked out without a dime of my GI Bill, I was more than thrilled to take the compromise.

I got off the phone, overcome with joyous relief. Then, for some reason, I called Number 18.

I spent a few months dodging him, mainly because he reminded me of the organization that was trying to prosecute me. But after a bit of Myspace investigating, I saw trouble. Number 18 had a girlfriend. He failed to mention that during his constant text messages and our hours talking on duty together.

"Ugh, typical Navy guy," I thought to myself.

I added him as a friend on Myspace though, just to show him that I knew.

Number 18 and Paloma had been together four years. They met at their previous duty station in Japan. Because Number 18 never mentioned her, I found out everything I knew through her Myspace page.

Paloma was Hispanic and a good five years older than me. She grew up in New Jersey. She was plain-faced and judging by her photos, her weight frequently fluctuated. Her education and spelling abilities were limited. Both Paloma and Number 18 were career Navy for the same reasons of just not being passionate about anything else. They were probably very good for each other. Paloma had just left for a nine-month deployment, conveniently days before Number 18 and I met.

I have no idea what sprung my urge to contact Number 18 besides the fact I had driven most of my friends out of my life. He had backed off after a month or so of dodging his calls, but he was eagerly responsive when I began making an effort.

Hanging out with Number 18 was one of my oddest experiences with male interaction. He had a girlfriend somewhere in the Persian Gulf, yet it felt as if we were in those awkward, early stages of dating before a first kiss.

Number 18 would drive one of his beloved vehicles across town to pick me up and then take me to his side of town. We'd go to the movies, which he always paid for. Sometimes he would briefly put his hand on the small of my back and then yank it back when he realized what he was doing.

We rarely talked about Paloma. We had a silent understanding to stay away from that, though we refused to admit why. Our conversation was about light and fluffy surface things, like his cars or the way our parents would always eat popcorn every night after dinner. Most of the time, I struggled to keep a conversation going with him.

A friendship with him was impossible, yet Number 18 continued to come around. Together, we spent hours of awkward silence alone in front of his television. Despite our dry, brief dialogue, being around him was never boring. Just as we never talked about Paloma aloud, neither of us verbalized our brewing sexual tension. I have no idea how it happened. We never flirted. Yet, there was something about sitting next to him without even grazing elbows that soaked my panties. I didn't discuss this with anyone. I wouldn't even admit to myself what was happening.

The next time Number 18 was on trash duty with me, our blossoming chemistry was apparent. We said little, but we smiled more. We made subtle jokes. Our eyes lingered on one another a bit longer than usual.

Maybe I was naïve or just lonely, but I was oblivious to how disrespectful we were being to Paloma. I was getting involved with a four-year relationship. They lived together and had professionally taken couple pictures that Paloma posted all over her Myspace page. She considered him the love of her life. He hadn't touched me. I told myself that he was just looking for a friend, but really I knew how badly he wanted to plow me.

I still wonder what exactly Number 18 saw in me. I didn't feel very pretty. Although I was quickly toning up and slimming down from Muay Thai, I was still a lot chubbier than I wanted to be. My skin was broken out from constant stress. My hair was dyed a cheap bottle job red. I had no respect for what Number 18 did for a living. But, I think he liked me because I was absolutely wrong for him on all levels. I was the opposite of Paloma. And I supplied that constant female companionship he was accustomed to.

Then, the mysterious phone calls came. My phone would ring. I'd answer it with a repeated "Hello? Hello?" And then it would cut off. Of course, I knew who was on the other line.

"Paloma hacked into my phone account," Number 18 said.

He called me about an hour after my first hang up.

"She had my password and saw your name on some texts that I sent to you. She's completely freaking out."

"Oh shit. You haven't told her about me?" I asked, panicked.

"No, she'd be pissed if she knew I was hanging out with a girl."

"Why?" I said, sounding like an ignorant child. "We're just friends. It's not like we're fucking or anything."

"That doesn't matter with her. She's the most jealous girl I've ever dated."

Shocked about the whole situation, I went home after work and regrouped my thoughts. I sprawled across my bed, faced my laptop. I began typing and became brutally honest in a way that would scare many men in my future. I admitted all the things that were going on between us that we'd been in denial of. I did what I would do with every man afterward. I made myself vulnerable.

"I like you," I typed. "And I think you like me, too, which is why we have to stop seeing each other. There's something going on with us, but I can't get in the middle of a four-year relationship. I can't compete with that."

I got a response a few minutes later.

"It's over with Paloma," Number 18 wrote. "I saw this coming a long time ago. And I think you and I have a connection. I'd like to see you tonight."

When I was on deployment, I witnessed constant infidelity. Years after my enlistment, I would carry a skewed outlook on Thailand. It was impossible to recognize its natural beauty without visions of the prostitution.

"Cheaters," I thought to myself. "All of them. Men are such pieces of shit."

Just as what happened on deployment stayed on deployment for the sailors, the same rules often applied for the men and women at home. Watching families tearfully see off and greet their beloved sailors was nauseating. Local news crews would film the hugs, kisses, goodbye, and welcome home signs held by little girls in frilly, pink dresses. They'd glorify those brave sailors sacrificing their lives to serve their country, but all I saw was a gigantic lie. I'd look at a pretty young wife with strawberry curls, hugging her new husband with misty eyes, and I'd see her hunched over their bed getting fucked by his best friend. I'd look at a man kissing his wife and kids, envisioning those same lips up a Thai hooker's twat a few months later. Cheating was a norm in the Navy. Few people spoke of this behavior. Deployment was a double life. One had their significant other ashore and aboard. And while that sailor was with their deployment partner, their loved one at home was taking care of their own intimate needs. Number 18 wanted to drag me into that world. And I let him.

Hours into Number 18's newfound singledom, we were sprawled out naked across the king-size bed they shared. Sex with Number 18 was one of the most passionate experiences of my life. I think this was because what we were doing felt so wrong. When Number 18 informed me of his breakup with Paloma, I went against my instincts and pretended to believe him just to relieve the urges built up inside of me.

Deep down, I knew they'd be back together. There were signs of her all over the house. We'd be on his bed, my legs hanging over his scrawny shoulders. Mid thrust, I'd turn to my right and see photo of Number 18 and Paloma on the nightstand. On my knees getting fucked from behind on his couch, girly knick-knacks on the shelves and a pink cloth across the coffee table would interrupt my moans with reality. If I needed to take a shower there, I didn't have to pack an overnight cosmetic bag. The bathroom was stocked with Paloma's girly shampoo, body wash, and her hair dryer.

These bad omens only fueled my desire to fuck the breath out of Number 18 for hours upon hours. He stood for everything I hated. Months of fear, stress, frustration, and nights of solidarity came out in that bed. We couldn't get enough of each other. With occasional water, nap, and bathroom breaks, we spent our entire first night together with my thighs around his neck and his tongue practically scraping my ovaries.

The first time we had sex lasted two hours. Number 18 would rest, rejuvenate, and then go again and again until I felt wheelchair bound. By that point, we quit trying to speak to each other. We never had those nights in bed together that drifted into deep conversations about our hopes and dreams. When we were alone, we fucked around. When we went to the movies, we traded our awkward silence for his hand up my skirt.

Looking back, I wish I'd taken the moral high ground and walked away from that disaster waiting to happen, or at least taken the situation for what it was - an easy opportunity to have the best sex of my life and nothing more. But my NCIS case matured me in more ways than backing off of the party scene and setting my priorities straight. Along with adult obligations came adult emotions. The girl that could fuck a stranger and walk away laughing was gone.

Months of stress, fear, and isolation came crashing down when I got close to him. Suddenly, I needed a security blanket to curl up in.

For weeks while I waited for my Captain's Mast trial, Number 18 and I continued romping around his bedroom. As time passed, I waited to see more signs of their breakup. Her car remained in the driveway. The tacky pink décor she contributed to their home remained on their dressers, walls, and coffee tables. Ignoring the blatant signs that he was still with Paloma and cheating on her with me, we continued having what I still remember as the best sex of my life. However, oddly enough, I couldn't reach a distinct orgasm.

My history with orgasms is complicated. In reality, I began having then when I discovered masturbation at tender age of nine. But at the time, I didn't realize that my urges and what I did to relieve them were sexual. I didn't know that pressure release that told me I was finished was a climax. Then when I began having sex on a regular basis, I'd reach the point of intensity but then I'd make the guy stop whatever he was doing. I didn't know what buildup was, but it made me feel like I was losing control. I didn't want to let go. I was convinced that I never had an orgasm. My vagina destroyed a lot of egos, especially Number 18's. For hours, he'd lie on his stomach with his tongue shoved inside of me, fingers digging in and out and over my clit. He tried everything he could, from focusing on my piercing to putting in his own tongue ring. He tried every combination of oral sex and intercourse in every position.

"I know you've had an orgasm," he'd insist. "You have to have at least one."

"Nope," I'd say with a smirk on my face, challenging him to go at me more. "It's hopeless. I can't have one. I've never had one. There's something wrong with me."

Number 18 refused to give up.

And then, for our final night together, I gave Number 18 something extra special.

We were sitting on his couch drinking a few beers when I kissed him. But as they always did, what meant to be a kiss became the two of us naked in some corner his house with his dogs staring at us in fascination. This time it was his couch.

Moaning, groaning, and nearly hanging off the back of his couch with Number 18 doing me from behind, right when I least expected it was my absolute most humiliating sexual experience.

In the midst of Number 18's vigorous pumping, I began to feel a warm liquid gushing out of my vagina. And this was not the liquid that's in pornographies where the platinum blonde rubs on her clit, and shoots out a quart of liquid like a geyser. I peed on Number 18. It was by far the most uncontrollable, vulnerable ten seconds of my life. This was not a few drops of urine. Once I started, I couldn't stop.

"Oh my God. I am pissing on his dick," I was thinking. "What the fuck do I do? What can I do? I am still pissing on his dick. Oh my God. Fuck. Fuck. Fuck. I shouldn't have drank that much beer. Shit."

If Number 18 and I had been banging it out on any position besides doggie style, he would have seen the severely stunned cringes across my face.

I expected him to immediately pull himself out of me and throw me out the door once he realized what was going on. But instead of a gasp or frustrated yells, Number 18 let out a long, satisfied moan, looked at me, and said, "Wow. That was amazing. I made you cum *sooooo* much."

My suspicions were on the money. That night, I went home to find that Number 18 had uploaded some photos of Paloma. I immediately broke free of my denial, called him and screamed at him for not only cheating on his girlfriend, but getting me involved in the whole mess. Our situation was a typical military soap opera. Number 18 cheated on Paloma with me and was rumored to have been with a couple others.

If there's anything I learned in the Navy, it's that rumors are almost always true and rumors had it that Paloma cheated on him as well. When she found out about me, she called from the Persian Gulf threatening to send her brother's nonexistent gang on me. Although Number 18 continued to call and text me, I ignored him. Three months later, he flew out to Hawaii at the end of her deployment and married her. She immediately got pregnant. They are still in the Navy and now have two children.

Number 18 and Paloma are likely happily together when in port and happily cheating on deployment. From my experience, that unspoken arrangement was the Navy way. Although a boyfriend with an expiration date could have its perks, I wanted no part of it.

But to this day, I'm still glad I pissed all over Number 18.

Number 19

Once I realized that my marriage fraud punishment would probably be less brutal than what I was bracing for, I tried to go back to my pre-NCIS trauma self again.

To an extent, I was successful.

On New Year's Day, I found myself in a Marine barracks room, naked in bed with a young man named Number 19.

My New Years Eve existed in brief, sporadic flickers that I could barely piece together. My friend, Alyssa, invited me to a party up in Oceanside, just forty-five minutes north of San Diego and a few miles from Marine base, Camp Pendleton. Of course Oceanside was the dead center of jarhead mania.

Alyssa was infatuated with Marines and probably destined to marry one. A University of Southern California graduate from a rich, conservative family, Alyssa had never known the ugly side of the military. When she looked at the troops, she never saw the infidelity, the stress, the alcoholism, or the way their enlisted female counterparts were often placed in that class lying just above hookers but below what many of my coworkers called "real women." Alyssa saw the military America wanted to see. To her, Marines were brave, loyal heroes who ventured to the Middle East with the sole, selfless purpose of protecting her freedom. And hopefully her views were a reality in many cases. But while I was jaded, she was enchanted.

I knew that Marines were always included in a night with Alyssa. Although my military prejudice was at an all-time high, my bank account was more important than my standards. A New Year's Eve party in base housing was cheaper than the downtown San Diego clubs my other friends were hitting with fifty-dollar covers. And even though I preferred the company of civilians to military, I preferred Marines to Navy.

Marines were much more of what I envisioned as "real military." They were in remarkable shape. When I drove around Camp Pendleton, I never saw the fat, balding smoker waddling around like on my own base. Instead of spending their days obsessively dusting and polishing like my entire ship had underway, Marines actually did military things. While my weapon training went as far as shooting a gun into the ocean and qualifying for that gun if I hit that ocean, they practiced weapons regularly. If Marines were attacked, they'd know how to defend themselves. If the Higgins had been attacked, we would have retreated indoors to let a handful of people push some buttons and hope all went well.

Just like the Navy, Marines were partiers. Their free nights were spent barhopping and binge drinking. But to me, they didn't seem to have quite the layer of filth the Navy had. They were filled with young, college-aged men, so both branches seemed just as predatorial for the opposite sex. Even more than the Navy, the Marine Corps supported a young, traditional marriage, which usually shattered to pieces because of premature marriages and long, straining deployments. The only difference is that for Marines, it was usually the spouses at home cheating while they got to play the heroic victims.

One with a deployed significant other had a hell of a lot less to worry about if they were in the Marine Corps or Army. While sailors got to play in hooker-infested ports like Thailand, Hong Kong, Japan, and Australia, Marines spent around a year in Iraq or Afghanistan. Meaning, they were in desert or isolated mountain hell, forbidden to touch locals, and rarely even working with women on their own side.

While I was in the military, few women were allowed to venture on the front lines. Usually, in order for a Marine or soldier to cheat on deployment, it had to be either with another man or maybe even the local animal population. Marines had a much more wholesome image.

Because I was not one of their own, they treated me like a real, civilian woman. That is, as long as I kept my opinionated mouth shut.

They had nothing to worry about on New Year's Eve. I left my military rebellion at the front door of the party, right next to my maturity and common sense.

I don't know what inspired me to immediately down a series of tequila shots with a group of muscular, crew cut Marines. The slightest desire to behave that way diminished on the day of my interrogation. My only explanation is that after months of stress, I wanted to go back to those carefree times. And for a night, I did.

I binge drank like the height of my PB days. In the midst of my stupor, I stumbled into the back seat of a truck, my body and tongue intertwined with Number 19.

My tall, blonde-haired, crystal-blue-eyed boyfriend of the night wasn't a complete stranger. We met at a party a couple months before. We were sober and ended up getting into a pretty deep conversation. He was my age. And unlike most Marines I knew, he could verbally hold his own. He too, was impressed with my ability to hold a good conversation and we talked a few days afterwards. Then he got a DUI and was restricted on base with very little communication with the outside world. New Years Eve was a random reunion for us. I guess the tequila helped us discover a mild attraction we never got to explore.

I can't remember how we got to his truck or when we began kissing. I have no recollection of leaving the party, crossing the Camp Pendleton gates, or sneaking into his barracks room. I know that at some point our clothes were off and a few clumsy pumps worth of drunken sex happened. In the middle of the night, I woke up to use the bathroom. With a blanket wrapped around my naked body, I stumbled to the toilet seat, pissed out some tequila, and stumbled back into Number 19's single sized barracks bed.

"Did the ball drop?" I slurred.

"Yeah," he responded, half asleep.

"So it's January?" ·

"Yeah," Number 19 said again before rolling on his side and drifting into a rumbling snore.

I am certainly not the first person to begin my new year with a walk of shame. But that night was a landmark moment in my life. It wasn't my last experience with casual sex or even my last one-night stand. However, as Number 19 drove me to my car on that blurry New Year's morning, instead of feeling a sense of victory for nabbing a guy on the craziest night of the year, I felt regret. I sat in his truck in awkward silence that was occasionally interrupted by forced chit chat and wondered who he was.

"What if we had just gone to dinner?" I thought. "And talked. What if we hadn't seen each other drunk and naked? Would I have liked him or not?"

Sure, a date after a one-night stand is possible. So is a relationship. But I knew I'd never hear from Number 19 again. Maybe he was judging me as a woman for not making him wait. What bothered me is that I would never know. Suddenly, I really truly wanted to *know* the men I slept with. Like an adult, I wanted to *date.*

I went to Captain's Mast three days after I earned my Good Conduct ribbon. All I had to do was complete three years of service without Captain's Mast. I completed three years and three days to be exact. I made sure to wear that ribbon proudly with my dress blues.

I can't remember whether or not I was nervous or calm that day, but I think it was a mixture of both. The formality of it all made me uneasy.

The most awkward thing for me was that I would have to do an "about face" once my Captain was done with me and it was my time to leave the room. I hadn't done that since boot camp and even then I hated the tricky, swift, spin-around gesture that always made me feel like I was going to fall on my ass.

However, since any marriage fraud charges were out the window and I was going to mast for some paperwork malfunction, I was expecting a slap on the wrist and nothing more.

Since I was stationed at a shore command, my "Captain" didn't even work in my building. She didn't come to our office and give speeches. She was a stranger. My Higgins Captain and I knew each other. I liked and respected him. In the end of my time there, he seemed almost fond of my outspoken, very un-military personality. I would have hated to go to his mast, facing him like a reprimanding father. My shore Captain was so far removed that I didn't care what she thought of me as long as I didn't leave her too banged up.

Two of my supervisors from PSD Afloat, my official shore duty command, were there, including PS1 Queen. To even things out, two of my supervisors from trash duty were there, too.

There was this random, fenced-in base bordering downtown San Diego. Like every other base, it was haze grey, industrial, and depressing. Among the classy, trendy Gaslight District, the decorative palm trees, and the postcard worthy view of the blue, Pacific Ocean, that base was like a fat, hairy mole smack dab in the middle of a beautiful face.

My mast was in a building on that base. Ironically, the same building I'd taken many of PSD's surprise drug tests in. Anxiously pacing outside of the room where my mast would be, I thought about how less than a year before I was often doing the same thing. Except back then I was nervous about cocaine showing up in my urine.

Standing outside the room beside me was a young, enlisted man in his dress blues. His sole purpose was to coach me through the whole thing.

"The Captain's going to call you in," he warned. "You're going to walk to the front desk where she is. Then immediately stand at attention until she orders you to stand at parade rest."

Parade rest was a formal, yet more relaxed, stance where you put your hands behind your back and spread your feet apart a bit. It was how the military stood at events because if they stood at attention the whole time, they'd likely pass out from the lack of blood flow through their legs.

"Make sure you answer her questions with "yes Captain" and "no Captain."

Suddenly, I heard a stern, female voice from inside the room.

"SEAMAN YOUNG, YOU MAY ENTER," she boomed.

Although I was nervous, I wasn't terrified. I managed to follow through all the necessary steps without tripping or jittering. I answered her questions with confidence and with all the traditional formality that was asked of me. My marriage wasn't mentioned. Compared to my NCIS interrogation, Captain's Mast was kindergarten.

My Captain reminded me of my Higgins Master Chief. She was middle-aged, blonde, and shrewd looking. Like most military career females, she probably had to be.

"Seaman Young," she continued after a series of basic questions about my rank, how long I'd been in, and where I worked. "I understand that you have your address on your Page 2 instead of your husband's."

"Yes, ma'am," I answered.

"Do you understand how important a Page 2 is? In case of an emergency situation it's how your spouse is contacted."

"Yes ma'am."

"I also understand that you worked at PSD Afloat West. Your job was handling service records. You should have known better. Why did you put your address instead of your husband's?"

At that point I had nothing to hide. I was guiltless for something so petty. Only a sailor with a command out to get them would go to mast for such a thing.

"Honestly, ma'am, I didn't know. I should have, but I didn't. It was just a careless mistake on my part."

She looked at me expressionless and I truly wondered if she felt like she was wasting her time as much as I was.

"What a stupid reason to go to mast," she was probably thinking. "I've got better things to do with my life. Okay, let me do the disciplinary charade."

Barely looking at me as if fighting her urge to roll her eyes, she delivered my punishment.

"Reduction in rank," she said, frankly. "Go fix your Page 2. You may leave."

I let out a long sigh of relief. Off balance, but without tripping, I awkwardly about faced right out of that room.

"That's it?" I thought to myself happily. "My pay grade will get pushed down to an E2. I'll get paid just a little less and in six months I'll be right back up to E3 again. I'll never advance more than that, but who gives a shit? I'm getting out in a year anyway. One more year of being good and I'm free. It's all over."

Little did I know, my command wasn't finished. PSD Afloat, and especially PS1 Queen weren't about to let me show my whole command that they could get away with what I did.

"You're lucky you said what you said in there," my mast guide told me right after he came out of the room. I was still waiting outside for everything to wrap up. "After what you told her, she realized that you just made a little mistake. Before that, your guys from PSD were trying really hard to get you kicked out. They don't seem too happy with you getting off so easy."

We chuckled for a bit as I imagined the vicious snarl PS1 Queen was holding in.

I rode back to base with PS1 Queen and the other PSD first class that came with us. They'd escorted me to my mast with the PSD fancy company vehicle. I rode in the back seat like a criminal in a cop car.

I made an effort to be extra cheery, just to annoy Queen.

"Wow, that wasn't that bad at all!" I practically sang. "The Captain seems super nice, actually. "

As I watched Queen's eyebrows crinkle with frustration in the rear view mirror, I rambled on merrily while he replied with mumbles and one-worded answers.

"Oh no PS1, you know what this means?" I chimed, knowing he wouldn't respond. "You get to work with me for one more year! I know you're excited!"

When we returned to the PSD, I waited around for my Master Chief to either tell me to stay there or return to trash duty. In the mean time, I pranced around the building to brag about my Captain's Mast triumph.

Gossip certainly did not die down with shore commands. The second I entered the building; my coworkers could barely keep their eyes in their sockets. Everyone had been eagerly following my case step by step from the day I was interrogated. Some were on team Queen and wanted me to pay for defacing the sanctity of marriage. Others were on my side and thought the Navy was ridiculous for trying to punish me. Ironically, in their thorough six-month investigation, they probably spent far more money trying to bring me down than any of the BAH I ever would have pocketed.

"What happened?" one after another eagerly whispered.

Gleaming, I bragged about my pain-free wrist slap.

"Wow. That's it?" some asked shocked. "See, I told you, if you're legally married you can't get in trouble for it," others said.

But in the midst of our hushed, rapid chatter, my Command Master Chief broke it up.

"Seaman Young!" he barked, barely restraining a fuming yell. "Can you please step in my office?"

"You're being sent back to trash duty," he informed me.

"Really?" I asked.

I halfway expected that to happen. Ever since my interrogation, I'd been considered a security risk, hence why I was sent to garbage duty in the first place. Since it was viewed as some kind of punishment, it would look better for the PSD's image that I spent my last year enlisted there. At least I'd be paying for something some how. But I was actually delighted to go back. I had no desire to return to PSD among the stacks of service records and the snooty, egocentric first classes I couldn't trust.

"I get to go back for the rest of my enlistment?" I asked like a kid finding out they were getting a puppy for Christmas.

"You sure do," he said with a sly smile that I shrugged off my shoulders. "You're free to leave."

When I first got to boot camp, I didn't see the point of marching. It seemed like a silly, outdated ritual. Not to mention, it was a pain in the ass. As if I wasn't on edge enough, every time I went anywhere, it was in tight ranks. I had no individuality in boot camp. Even my footsteps were one with my entire division. When they put their right foot forward, I had to, also. If I stepped too soon, I scraped someone's ankle. If I stepped too late, I got stomped on. If I didn't stop exactly when everyone else did, I ran into the person in front of me and we all tumbled onto the frozen ground like dominos. But after a few weeks, marching became second nature. By the time we graduated and got liberty, every time we walked anywhere together, our footsteps were perfectly in sync without even realizing it. Our RDCs told us that marching, like everything else we did in boot camp, was about teamwork. We relied on our "shipmates" to step, turn, about face, and stop accordingly so that we could move as one. When someone was falling behind on a step, we had to help him or her just to walk a block.

Your ship, or any command you end up going to, will be the same way," our RDCs informed us. "You all have to work as a team to get anything done. But you'll find that because of this, your command will be your family. You have to trust your shipmates more than anyone else because in some cases, your life may depend on it. "

Oddly enough, of all the lessons I learned in the Navy, one of the most valuable was how *not* to trust.

The familial camaraderie I was told I'd get in my enlistment was nothing but a tall tale - at least in my experience. I saw it in certain divisions on the Higgins, like the engineers. That support wasn't in deck, but PSD made me truly appreciate it. As much as I loathed my days of chipping paint in the beating sun, I labored away knowing that my supervisors did not want to harm me. No matter how much I cursed, how lazy I got, how rebellious I became, nobody in deck, including my temperamental chief, was outright malicious.

My PSD Command Master Chief, a grown man who probably had children close to my age, did not even have the decency to tell me that they were kicking me out of the Navy in a matter of days. It turns out that after any Captain's Mast, a sailor's command has the choice to discharge them. I never knew about that little rule because it was so rarely done. During my three years in, I saw sailors go to mast for DUIs, domestic violence, and even child pornography possession and their commands still didn't try to kick them out. Because they could not get me for marriage fraud, they were getting me for not updating an address on my service record. I found out about this from my trash duty supervisors. Dumbstruck, I immediately rushed back to the PSD.

"Yes, you're getting discharged," my Master Chief, said sternly.

Once again, I was in front of his desk like a misbehaving child who routinely ends up in the principal's office.

"When?" I asked, shocked and wide-eyed.

"Probably in the next few days. Your paperwork is getting set up right now."

"This is will be an Other Than Honorable Discharge," he began explaining to me. "It won't look bad on your record. You'll still get all of your veteran's benefits, like medical care."

"Will I still get my GI Bill?" I asked him.

College money was my ultimate reason for enlisting in the first place. If I didn't get that, then the last three years of my life would have been completely wasted.

"Yes, you'll still get all of your GI Bill," he said, making direct eye contact with me.   "Actually, I think your paperwork may be ready. Go check in the separations section."

The PSD building was one big room with cubicles all over. Its areas were divided and organized by their functions. There was a Transfers section to process the paperwork that transferred sailors out of their ships to other places. There was a section that processed pay. There was a section that took over the paperwork for people arriving at their command. And there was a separations section that discharged sailors from the Navy.

Although the walk from my Master Chief's office to the separations section was about five hundred feet, I had enough fluctuating emotions for a walk across Brazil.

At first I was shocked. I was getting out of prison an entire year early. Although I didn't like the shackles that had been tying me down, I was so used to them. Then, fear came over me.

"Am I ready to be a civilian?" I wondered. "What will I do? Where will I go? Will I stay here in San Diego? Will I go to school? I haven't even enrolled into this semester."

I had zero time to prepare for the freedom that was so rapidly approaching me.

But after fear came exhilarating joy for those same reasons. I had no idea what to do, but suddenly, I had so many options. I could go to Tennessee. I could stay in San Diego and go to school. I could move somewhere else and go to school. I could just skip the semester and go backpacking in South America. For the first time in three years, I could do anything that I wanted.

"Wow, I can't believe I got away with all of this," I thought. "Not only did I just pull out of this marriage fraud thing, I get out of the Navy a whole year early. I'll still get everything I would have gotten if I'd stayed in another year. I'm walking away with *everything*."

Then came skepticism. It was all too good to be true.

A First Class Petty Officer from separations handed me my discharge paperwork and a pen.

"All we need is your autograph and you're free," he said with a smile, pointing at the bottom of the page.

I looked at him and then back down at my files to freedom.

"Um, actually," I replied. "I think I'll take these to my lawyer."

"No. You won't get a dime of your GI Bill if you sign these papers," Lieutenant Lash said as she looked down at the papers and shook her head. "God, you'd think they'd leave you alone after the mast and everything. Your Master Chief told you that you were getting all of your education benefits?"

"Yeah, that's what he said."

"Well, he was lying to you."

"Do you think he knew?"

"Well, considering he's in charge of a command whose job is to separate people from the Navy, I'd say so."

Fuming, I struggled to suppress a stream of curse words ready to erupt from my throat.

"You don't have to sign these papers," she told me. "You can fight it. If I were you, I'd request Captain's Mast. I bet she doesn't even know about this."

Nobody *ever* requested Captain's Mast. It was something someone was ordered to attend when they were in trouble. If a sailor wasted a Captain's time, they could be reprimanded horribly. There is no stricter structure than the military's chain of command. Imagine that it's a food chain. A command's Captain is a vicious carnivore that eats everything, like a lion. A command's Master Chief or Officer in Charge is like a snake, where a First Class Petty Officer like PS1 Queen is a toad. I am a Seaman. I am the lowest species on the food chain. I am something necessary to the functioning of the food chain, but not very respected - like a maggot. When a maggot has an issue, they go to the toad, which goes to the snake, which then goes to the lion. A maggot *never* goes directly to the lion. If they dare to actually summon the lion, the toad and the snake are livid, especially if the maggot is exposing their sneaky, conniving behavior.

When I requested Captain's Mast, I rattled PSD. I couldn't see it. I couldn't hear it. But I could *feel* it. The higher ups knew they were in trouble. They thought

I'd be naïve. They thought I would assume that anything they told me was true, and that I'd slip under the radar forever. My Captain would never know I was gone. But I knew that she would not approve of them discharging me for a next to nothing offense. They knew it, too. They *knew* that what they were doing was wrong. So, I prepared a lovely speech for my Captain. I was ready to stand in front of her again and burn PS1 Queen, my master chief, and our command's Officer in Charge at the stake. I may not have been the most well behaved sailor, but I was a damn good public speaker and they knew it.

Days before I was scheduled to stand at mast, the PSD's officer in charge called me to his office. Our officer in charge was the highest-ranking person in the building. He was hardly there, but much more involved than our Captain. He was the only official in charge of our master chief. Entering the building from trash duty, I walked to his office, relishing in the fact that I knew I probably made those jerks shit themselves.

"Seaman Young," he began, and proceeded to lecture me about my behavior as if I was the one in trouble.

After a few minutes of listening to his rambling and struggling to nod instead of roll my eyes, he asked me, "If I let you stay here, do you promise to behave yourself?"

Number 20

Almost every woman, at one point or another, has had a Number 20.

He's average looking, certainly not anyone she would eye from across a room. He isn't any good in bed. If he has a job, it's a service or construction job - whatever gig some relative was able to snag him. If he doesn't live with his mother, his "curtains" are sheets nailed to his windows. He is funny and that humor is his most attractive quality. He is nice enough, but fails to keep his dates with her. He never puts forth any acts of romance.

He is mediocre at best. Yet, for some illogical reason, she is blindly and almost obsessively infatuated with him.

There is no formula for spotting a good quality guy. My mom always told me to go for the nerdy, chubby types because they would be humble and grateful for my affection.

"You can always whip em' in shape," she'd say. "Men can change." Romantic comedies like to sway towards the less handsome, buddy types that are usually best friends with the hot guy that charms the girl in the beginning. Once the hot guy breaks her heart, the less sexy but golden-hearted underdog steps in to save the day. Those little lessons are meant to teach women to not be shallow. But in my experience, they only teach us to settle. And that's exactly what I did when I became addicted to Number 20.

It was my final year in the Navy and my discharge date was practically stabbing me in the eye. In the meantime, I had to behave myself. I said goodbye to the only trusting atmosphere I would know in the Navy and somberly left trash duty. When I returned to PSD, I actually worked. I was taken out of the service record room and to our mutual relief, out of PS1 Queen's department. I was placed in the Transfers section. I was given my own cubicle, which I decorated with a few photos of myself with friends. My new boss was PS1 Perez. He was young for his rank - a twenty-eight-year-old who didn't look a day over sixteen, Mexican, and a tad bit nerdy. Although he still had that high and mighty attitude that most first classes at PSD acquired, I almost always liked him.

My hatred for the Navy faded into a mild irritation. I still cringed when I left the base in uniform, even if it was only for an hour. But, I went to lunch with coworkers and occasionally even showed up at parties they invited me to.

My main focus was Muay Thai. My job was just a waiting game and a college fund to me. I lost desire to get shit faced and play "who is willing to fuck me" every weekend. Muay Thai felt like my own way of reinventing myself. I put all of my energy into being fit, strong, and fierce. Every day after work, I drove to PB, ran five miles along the coast, and kick boxed. I sparred every Thursday.

I was always so proud of the fresh bruises I earned. My worst injuries were a concussion and a sprained ankle, but I usually just showed up on base with black eyes or blue spots all over my body from getting punched, slapped, kneed, or kicked. Muay Thai was a healthy way to channel all my time and energy while I waited to start my post-Navy life.

I became remarkably productive without a man in the picture. I worked, I exercised, and I studied. I began thinking about what I wanted to do after the Navy. Getting my degree was definitely my first priority, but I also wanted to travel. I thought about backpacking through Europe or South America.

I moved into my own studio in Ocean Beach. OB was a more mature version of Pacific Beach. Just south of PB, it was much calmer. There were still partiers all around, but they weren't screaming, shirtless frat boys hanging out of the windows of moving vehicles. PB was cocaine with a Fireball shot. OB was a joint and a beer.

I loved where I lived. My studio was directly across the street from a nice, calm beach with the perfect west coast view of the sunset. I was walking distance from a small strip of restaurants and a handful of pubs. I'd take sunny strolls down the road and pass by dreadlocked hippies, getting a whiff of marijuana every other block. There was nightlife in OB, but it consisted of retiring from the bars to a backyard campfire serenaded by somebody's acoustic guitar and bongo drums. The area perfectly suited that period of my life.

I lived in a building of six studios. People left their doors wide open while they were home so they could feel the ocean breeze and occasionally peep their heads out to chat with their neighbors. I remember my first night there, among the piles of my stuff with so much organizing ahead of me and thinking, "Wow, this is *my* place. *Just mine. All mine.*" I felt such a sense of accomplishment. I had come so far in a matter of months.

"Just enjoy it. Be young," I should have told myself. "Now is the time for you to be single and free to get somewhere in your life. Get educated. Get fit. Make plans to travel after the Navy. Love can come later."

But I still felt like finding a good guy was the missing puzzle piece. I wanted a man, but vowed to do things differently that time. I decided not to choose a man based off of looks or what instrument he played in whatever band. I would not pursue a man based on the drugs he carried or the size of his penis. No, I was searching for a diamond in the rough. I couldn't tell that Number 20 was synthetic.

It still amazes me how social media has opened up a whole new dating ground for Millennials. In my most promiscuous days, Myspace was my most successful dick fishing tool. But once I decided to tone it down, I had no idea I would become the bait.

When a man you've never met finds you on a site like Myspace or Facebook, he's not contacting you because he wants a new friend. Maybe he's lonely. Maybe he does want a meaningful relationship. Maybe your photo seems special or your "about me" paragraph really did touch his heart. Maybe he thinks that because you both love Led Zeppelin or that your astrology signs are compatible, that you could possibly be soul mates. Call me cynical, but probably not.

He's most likely contacting a woman because he's hoping at some point, at the very least, he'll get his dick in her mouth. And it's only common sense to assume that if he's trying to maneuver a digital pick-up line, he's already tried it on many, many other women. In fact, it's probably a nightly ritual, which he will follow with busting his nut on his laptop screen.

The day I found Number 20's "message" in my "inbox," I hadn't reached this adult enlightenment.

His typed words were generic.

"Hey! How are you? I'm a friend of Murphy's. I thought your profile looked cool so I wanted to say hi."

Of course this was code for, "Hi. I'm a creep that Myspace stalks a guy I met for like five minutes to see if he knows any decent looking chicks."

Murphy was a San Diego State student about my age who bought weed from my previous roommate. I actually wanted Murphy pretty badly when I first met him the year before. He wasn't interested, though. Murphy awkwardly laughed off the hints I was practically screaming until I lost interest as well. We became friendly acquaintances. Number 20 knew less about Murphy than I did. They met at a bar once through mutual friends. Number 20 mentioned him because he knew that I'd be more at ease talking to a friend of a friend rather than a stranger.

I sifted through Number 20's profile pictures before I responded to him. Number 20 was decent looking - even cute - in some photos. His profile picture was a close-up black and white. He was wearing sunglasses, a plaid, short-sleeved shirt, and had a wide, open-mouthed smile that showed a top set of flawlessly straight, white teeth. I continued to browse through his photos. He looked tall. At least six feet with a medium build and ash brown hair. He wasn't fat, but didn't look like he worked out.

I could tell he liked to play with cameras and Photoshop because a lot of his pictures were black and white, faded, brightened, or taken with fisheye lenses. He seemed very friend-oriented. Most of his photos were of him smiling and laughing with his buddies, some on road trips, others by a pool, slightly flushed, with beers in their hands. He was average looking, but his smile was wide, genuine, and warm. He looked like he'd be everyone's best friend.

I continued my Myspace investigation. He was twenty-eight years old from Ramona, California, a small town about forty minutes northeast of San Diego. He looked better in sunglasses because he had a few wrinkles around his eyes that were premature for his age. He graduated from Cal State San Marcos with a bachelor's in communications. He wasn't in a band or in the military. From what I could tell, he was a nice, *normal* guy.

"Maybe this is someone I could actually date," I thought.

"He's cool," Murphy told me after I asked about him.

At the time, I had no idea that they'd been around each other for about ten minutes.

"*Really* funny, too," he added.

Number 20 and I messaged back and forth for a few days, then escalated to phone calls. I liked his voice. It completely suited his appearance: casual, humorous, easygoing, and full of personality. Oddly enough, he was one of the most familiar strangers I ever met.

My belief in soul mates has always been like my belief in God. Sure, it was a romantic, comforting idea. I *wanted* to believe in it, but its existence went against all rationality. I really think that there are numerous people out there for everyone. A lot of marriages and relationships form because the timing seems right. I fell so hard for Number 20 because I was twenty-two years old, tired of sleeping around, and had been single for a few years. It felt like the right time to have a boyfriend and Number 20 seemed like a good fit.

By the time he picked me up for our first date on a sunny, spring weekend, we already had a few late night phone conversations. I knew about his two younger siblings, the marriage of his brother, and the Heroin addiction of his sister. His mother was a fifth grade teacher and his father a contractor. His parents had been separated for about ten years, but oddly enough, never divorced and occasionally went to the movies together. As far as he knew, neither of them dated other people. He grew up on a large chunk of land with horses. He owned a kayak. He liked Hawaiian pizza and IPA's.

I could mentally recite the chime in his voice when he answered the phone. Number 20 had revealed a bit of the man behind his photos, so our first date didn't feel so blind. He seemed like a country boy, unlike most PB guys. He drove a red Chevy he called "Big Red" and spoke of as if she were his horse, occasionally patting her before hopping in his saddle. He wore a plain white t-shirt with jeans and his signature sunglasses. And just as I expected, he greeted me with a big smile and open, strong embrace as if we were old classmates reuniting.

Within ten minutes of riding in his truck, I was convinced that Number 20 was cozily resting in the palm of my hand.

Number 20 had a gift. He made me feel more beautiful than any man ever had.

Sure, he would slip in the typical flattery like, "I usually don't like red heads, but you seriously pull it off so well. I think you're stunning." But what was really enchanting was the *way* he looked at me. Sitting in the passenger's seat, I was terrified that he'd steer Big Red off a bridge. He kept turning his head right to watch me while we talked. These were long, intense stares for operating a vehicle. And as long as his eyes were on me, they remained lit and in awe.

Since he was a San Diego lifer, Number 20 played tour guide. As he drove Big Red through the rolling, palm tree-covered hills, he recited random facts about the city, like its oldest sandwich shop and beach mileage.

"When it comes to completely pointless, out of left field facts, I am a genius," he smirked. "Unfortunately, I'm not a genius in anything useful, but at least I can keep you entertained."

He was pleasant and amusing to listen to as he talked about his childhood growing up in the country, his best friends since elementary school, and poking fun at his odd family dynamics.

Number 20 had this subtle, but captivating, charm so powerful that I never saw how distracting it was until he was long out of my life. I never once noticed how Number 20 would talk about the big wheels he played with as a kid, but never mentioned what he did for a living, where he lived, or who he lived with. Those details slipped out little by little. By the time I found out that he lived in Ramona with his mother, had been fired from his previous job, and could only hold a job as a construction worker for his daddy, I was already hooked.

I didn't even notice that he never asked a thing about me. Number 20 never knew that I wanted to be a journalist or that my mom's name was Annie. He couldn't even remember what state I was from.

"Where you from? West Virginia?" He'd ask.

"Oh, yeah, I knew it was somewhere out in the middle of nowhere full of inbreeds," he'd respond after I reminded him, yet again.

After a few rounds of this, I gave up on telling him that Chattanooga was a city of over half a million.

Despite a few stumbles, he said all the right things and made all of the perfect, gentlemanly gestures at the appropriate times.

He took me to Mount Soledad, a small mountain near Pacific Beach where some of San Diego's wealthiest resided. From there, we could see all of San Diego and a bit of Mexico. It was a pretty and very typical scene for a date. It was good people-watching. I leaned against a railing on the side of the mountain, my face in the sun, staring off into the distance as Number 20 rambled on about the European discovery of San Diego. By the time he dropped me off that night, my tongue was shoved halfway down his throat.

I still wonder if intuition exists. There are times where my judgment is right on the money with people, but it seems like there are no rules in dating. Of all the men I've been with, the ones who felt the safest had the scariest skeletons.

Number 20, my country, useless fact knowing, Big Red driving boy next-door, was a meth addict. Although I never would have pegged him with the habit at first glance, when I reflect on our relationship, that's exactly what being with him felt like - the unhealthy, dehydrating, emotional tornado that is a meth addiction.

The guy who made me feel like a supermodel by his intense stares, as if the smell of my perfume alone made him climax in his jeans, the man who nose dove across the bar to grab my water bottle cap after I dropped it, the man who gave me vivid images of his elementary school teacher mother, camping with his childhood buddies, and teaching his brother how to build Lego forts was that first hit that I was willing to drain my savings account to get more of.

My Number 20 high drifted into the day after our date. I giddily downloaded, listened, and hummed to his favorite music as I cleaned my apartment and visualized our future together.

But trouble in paradise came quickly.

Number 20 had a pattern of dropping off the face of the earth. Although he swore that his meth habit was in the past and that he was getting help, I later found out that his addiction had everything to do with his behavior.

In the beginning, I told myself that he was just from San Diego. Never following through with plans was part of that beachy, laid-back culture. I was just an outsider from an old-fashioned land of plan making and calling before canceling. I had to adjust to the environment I chose to live in. I assumed that the way Number 20 acted was normal southern California dating behavior. I was supposed to be cool and not care, so while massively suffering inside, I pretended not to.

I was cool with everything.

When I did show the slightest inkling of any emotion, like stress or frustration, whether it was towards him or not, Number 20 seemed afraid of it.

"Shh… settle down," is what he'd say, covering my mouth with his fingers as if he were calming down a hyperactive puppy jumping in his face.

In person, Number 20 was full of promises and plans of the fun things we'd do together.

"I have to take you out in my kayak sometime," he'd say. "Oh, and we'll have to take Big Red off roading out in Ramona."

One of Number 20s first promises was to help me get some of my furniture out of storage, which he eagerly volunteered for.

I had a bad feeling he wouldn't go through with his word, so I made sure to double check on his plans the night before. When he told me that things were still good to go, I convinced myself to ease up.

"Relax, Maggie," I said to myself. "He's not like most people around here. He's a good guy."

"Settle down," I'd repeat Number 20's constant phrase in my head. "Settle down, Maggie."

But the next day, Number 20 was mysteriously M.I.A.

"I'm so, so sorry Maggie," he stammered oh-so-genuinely a few days later. "I had pneumonia and took these strong sleeping pills. I was completely passed out. I'll make it up to you, I swear."

"Oh, it's totally fine," I lied. "I understand. It's cool."

The weeks passed after our missed date and Number 20 never made anything up to me.

My twenty-second birthday came and went without so much as a phone call. Though I got the occasional Myspace message or drunken text, I assumed things were over when June came along and we'd yet to go on a second date. I never called him, demanding some kind of apology or explanation. Instead, I chose to use another drug. Though it was less satisfying than my Number 20 high, it held me over for a bit.

Ty was the front man of a local band - surprise, surprise. Despite the band thing, on paper, he seemed like a legitimate adult. He was thirty-two, an entire decade older than me, but he was attractive, standing tall with black hair and tan skin. He had his master's in computer science and worked as an exchange engineer. He lived in his own bachelor pad, conveniently five blocks away from me.

Our normal routine was meeting about halfway between our apartments on warm, breezy nights, and then heading back to his place. Our relationship was passionless. When he kissed me, his tongue laid limply in my mouth like a dead limb attached to his face. Then, a month passed and I began to realize that I had never seen him sober. Another month went by and we'd yet to have sex because he was always too drunk for his dick to function.

No reality beyond intoxication existed for Ty. No matter how many conversations I tried to have with him, he never knew me. He often mumbled about his wishes for me to move in with him and to romp around his apartment in high heels with dinner cooked. In return, he offered to pay all the rent and my college fees. When he told me that he loved me, yet couldn't remember my last name, I knew it was time to cut the cord. But Ty refused to accept it. After a stumble of denial to my apartment, I downed two bottles of wine just to drown him out. Somehow I ended up at his place, vomiting in his bathroom while he returned to the bars. I drunk dialed Number 20, dumped Ty via text message the next dehydrated, hung-over morning, and before I knew it, Number 20 and I were back on track.

During my life on San Diego's beaches, I dated little and fucked often. But it turns out that there wasn't much of a difference. Actual dates only lasted until I put out, which was pretty quick, since I was never good at giving men a "chase." There was no talk of the future, and "girlfriend" or "boyfriend" titles were dangerous territory. There was no age limit for "not being ready to get tied down." There were no rules, boundaries, or structure for appropriateness.

During my second go with Number 20, there was one date. It was the first time a man took me to dinner. That night, we had sex, then it was back to me making sandwiches for him whenever he decided to drop by.

We were always in bed within minutes of seeing each other. He fucked me with no skill, but instead, wildly flopping his naked body on mine. He was an incredibly creepy lover. We were almost always missionary with his face about an inch from mine, and he got fussy every time I drifted from eye contact. He called me things like "good little girl," cooing at me in a tone that a man would only use when he softly raped his five-year-old niece.

In many ways, my world was anything but traditional. Southern California beach life was wild and free. It was the norm for women to strut outdoors in bikinis under the continuously blazing sun. Everyone kept their sexuality out in the open like liberated flower children. Men weren't expected to court women, pay for things, or even keep their plans. Monogamy was practiced by few. But for some reason, the beach girls craved commitment.

I was one of many who willingly and repeatedly were treated like shit. In fact, this behavior was such a norm that we didn't even know how to spot it. Sure, my man never had his wallet, would disappear for weeks, and then show up randomly for an entire weekend, but when he was with me, he was just so sweet.

No matter how deep in shit Number 20 buried me, that initial boyishly innocent charm was always going strong. Number 20 and I never fought, not because I never wanted to. It was just hard to argue with his finger over my lips.

"Settle down," he'd always say, petting me until I curled beside him like the loyal mutt.

Afraid of being cut off from my drug, I hid all the bad and sketchy things about him with denial, and clung to the good. And when things were good, they were great. There were weekends that Number 20 and I ditched reality, spent days making out on the beach, mixing cocktails, and having sex with the front door open while we let the ocean breeze cool off my apartment.

He was always making me laugh. Because he ignored the hardships of his life, I forgot about the hardships in mine, too. When Number 20 was around, everything else dissolved. I wasn't in the Navy. I had no cares of the future and there was no need to prepare for it. I was perfect the way I was, so there was no need to work out or eat healthy. When he was around, I didn't need anything else. Number 20 was a drug that kept me in a blissful fog and the second he went away- every time- I came down.

And Number 20 went away often.

Though I never took it seriously back then, I'd often heard the phrase, "once an addict, always an addict."

Number 20 was definitely an addict. He covered it up well, but he was very much addicted to meth. So, just like Ty, there was no logic, structure, or reality in his life. He worked for his father, so he took off on benders without getting fired. When he was high, there was no getting in touch with him. Number 20 would be gone for weeks. When he was with me, he was my boyfriend and our affectionate connection was undeniable. But, every time he left, I wondered if I'd ever see him again.

And I suppose just like Number 20, I was an addict, too.

I'd had a problem since high school, but Number 20 made it blatantly obvious that I had an unhealthy addiction to men.

When I was with him, I was high. The moment he left, I came down. The longer I went without a phone call, text, Myspace message, or any kind of Number 20 fix, I became depressed, paranoid, and erratic. I would call my friends, elaborating on and analyzing the fuck out of every word Number 20 said and each detail I noticed about him. I don't know whether they were too nice to be honest with me or bowed down to the same standards, but together, we made excuses for him.

And the numerous excuses usually boiled down to one big one: He was a San Diego boy. Dating there was different than other geographic locations. It was laid back. Commitment took months, even years to happen. Men settled down later in life. It was nonchalant and I had to mask my emotions in order to blend in with my culture.

"Be patient," they told me. "He'll come around eventually."

But, like any addiction, the longer I fed it, the worse things got.

I rarely slept. I ate little. The nervous cramps I had in my stomach kept me nauseous. Although I functioned at work and school, my ambitions faded. I was constantly distracted. When I showed up to Muay Thai, I got my ass beaten by a girl I'd once been able to obliterate. I realized that I hadn't fought in weeks. I had taken all that passion I once put into boxing and channeled it into Number 20.

I knew Number 20 was still on meth. I knew it when he'd camp at my apartment for several days at a time, phone off, and furiously scrub every inch of my abode while I was at work. I knew it when the months passed and he never introduced me to his family or friends. And it was more obvious than ever after I let him stay at my place while I went to my cousin's wedding in South Carolina.

"It's a lot closer than your mom's," I said before I left. "You can do a lot more apartment searching from here."

When I arrived home after a long day of airplane hopping, I had high hopes in coming home to a clean place and something to eat. I was exhausted and ready to shower and pass out. Then, I opened my door. Half of Number 20's possessions were stuffed inside my modest studio leaving only a tiny path to cautiously meander from my bed to the bathroom and kitchen.

"Oh, yeah," he said, seeing my dismayed expression. "I needed some of my stuff here. You're cool with that, right?"

There were boxes and boxes of notebooks and papers. There were storage containers filled with his clothes and other random objects like photos, a baseball glove, and files, all pouring out of my closet to where the door could not be shut.

A Mac desktop was lying in the center of the apartment. The server, speakers, and mouse pad were all balanced and placed on the cardboard boxes he brought in. My studio was small, so I kept it neat. Everything had its place, but with all of Number 20s belongings invading the space, I couldn't pee in the middle of the night without tripping over a box of his childhood memorabilia.

My kitchen was even worse. Dirty dishes were piled in the sink.

"I was going to do those tonight," he said.

With the exception of some of Number 20's beer, only some ketchup and half a stick of margarine were left in the fridge.

"Yeah, I was so broke," Number 20 chuckled, not bothering to make eye contact with me. "I even ate that creamed corn in your pantry straight out of the can."

"What are these?" I asked, in confusion with what was poking out of the space between my fridge and the wall. "Is that…. lumber?"

"Yeah," he said casually, as if storing thin sticks of lumber behind your fridge was as common as dishwashing liquid.

"You brought *lumber* home from work?"

"Yeah."

"Uh. Why?"

"I don't know. For projects."

"Projects?"

"Yeah. Projects."

The next day, Number 20 took off to his best friend's place in Long Beach, leaving my apartment cluttered with his stuff. Even when I was rummaging through all of the evidence, nothing registered with me. As I sifted through sheets and sheets of chicken scratch, scribbles, and drawings, I didn't remember being seventeen and my sleepless nights with Number 3, sketching, crafting, *tweaking* and busying myself with "projects."

Nobody ever barged through my front door, demanding that I go to rehab for Number 20. My intervention was my drug himself, slipping through my apartment and taking all of his things back while I was at work. The meth paranoia had set in and he was convinced that I did something I hadn't. I had no clue what I was being accused of. Besides a few mean texts and snarls about me being a liar, he refused to communicate with me. My drug was snatched out of my grasp.

My withdrawal from Number 20 was painful. I spent an entire weekend in bed, hysterically sobbing. I cried myself asleep and I cried myself awake. For weeks, I existed in a fog. Some days were better than others. And even months later, brutal, emotional pain overwhelmed me. Slowly, I sobered up and I eventually recovered. Number 20 wouldn't be my last hit, but he hit me the hardest.

Emotionally exhausted, I ended my Number 20 inebriation and faced sobriety as a civilian.

Number 21

Anyone who knew me in the Navy never would have guessed what I'd become after it.

As a sailor, I was underestimated. I was a dim-witted fat girl. If I played my cards right, I might have a shot at life in a doublewide trailer.

In many ways, this was my fault. I was a lazy sailor. I quickly realized that putting any energy into the Higgins or PSD was meaningless exhaustion. I felt that, at best, if I worked *really* hard, I could acquire a decent reputation among a group of people I planned to surpass. So, I didn't really try.

But every time someone said I was dumb or ditsy, it hurt. I used it as motivation. I knew that within a few years of my freedom, they'd be choking on their own tongues.

Every young veteran takes on civilian life differently. Many were worn out from the wild ways of the Navy and were eager to settle down. Several of my shipmates got married, had children, and moved away to raise their families. A few went from being the hated military women to the jealous military wives. Plenty that seemed all too eager to crawl out of the Navy womb jumped right back in. I knew a couple that reenlisted or joined the reserves and deployed even more than they did in full service. Many made better sailors than civilians. I've seen numerous go from Navy to mall security guards or even drug dealers. But not many of them thrived.

We were like fresh high school grads with a choice of either using the lessons we were taught or not. Suddenly, unprotected, some of us sank, and some of us swam.

After four years, I felt like a rattled champagne bottle. When the Navy released me, the cork popped.

Kevin Cox changed everything.

My journalism professor was my first positive male influence. It only took a few minutes in his class to know that he would become my life long mentor.

Two thousand and eight was truly a new year for me.

When the midnight clocks chimed, I was a month and five days away from my official discharge, but I had thirty days of leave saved up, called "terminal leave." I technically wasn't completely out of the Navy's grasp.

"You still have to behave yourself," my master chief scolded me on my last day.

He was bitter. Instead of teaching my command a lesson about the wrongs of marrying for the money, I was getting out honorably. To top it off, the Navy was paying for my college, my health care, and full access to the VA loans and all other lofty benefits.

"We can still pull you in for a drug test," he muttered.

Although it was tempting, a big, fat bong hit was not on the top of my to-do list.

College was my motivation for joining the Navy and the only thing that kept me in it.

I envied my childhood peers as they zipped to their degrees and the California kids who seemed to take it for granted. I spent four miserable years working for something that was handed to so many.

Talked down to and degraded in the Navy, I considered college students a much higher class of young adults. As I strolled through the sunny, outdoor campus of San Diego Mesa Community College, I felt like I had landed on planet earth after four years in haze-grey hell.

Cox's Introduction to Journalism class was an ideal start because he fed my overwhelming urge to push forward in life.

Unlike the PhD career intellectuals who usually have reign of universities, Cox was just a community college teacher. He had enough intellect for a bachelor's from Stanford, but he was a worker. Cox was a journalism veteran who started teaching after a few decades of the media hustle and bustle.

Reporting is a hectic, low-paying, unstable career for only the most passionate news junkies. The switch into education with a side of freelancing was a common path for old newsies. Cox still wrote and occasionally picked up jobs for Hollywood tabloids.

With a background in television and writing, Cox immediately put us to work.

"If you want to *study* journalism, you might as well leave this classroom right now," he said up front. "In my class, you *do* journalism."

Cox was a small man, maybe an inch or two taller than me. He was in his early fifties, but had aged well and was trim with few signs of grey in his hair. His dark eyebrows were sharp, often highlighting the strong tones of attitude, humor, and sarcasm that kept our class alive.

"Are you bored yet?" he'd ask us every half hour or so. "Really. Let me know if I'm boring you."

We never were bored. Cox was lively, animated, and actively walked around the class, talking into our faces when he felt like it. His looks and humor reminded us of actor, Steve Carell.

He spoke conversationally and to the point, unlike most teachers who taught as if they were giving a grand speech to a crowd of a million. He fed our inattentive age group, which I've always called an ADHD generation. Unlimited access to smart phones and social media has stripped our attention spans. So, Cox juggled about a half dozen of our activities. One minute we were fabricating creative deaths for obituary writing, the next we were watching a documentary on a murder case that Cox helped crack.

Cox spoke candidly about the harsh, unstable world of print and television journalism. He had dipped in both.

"If you want to be a journalist, you have to surrender to the idea that you'll have no job security," he lectured. "The media is changing. Technology is emerging - budgets are being cut. And you'll get laid off," he said up front as our eyes popped.

"Oh yeah, just like that," he said, reading our startled expressions. "I've been laid off before. You can't be bitter about it. That's the way the business goes. *Never burn bridges*." He elaborated constantly. "You never know when you're going to need those professional connections. Just play it cool and leave gracefully. And when it happens, don't feel bad. In the media, advancement is *never* based off talent, merit, or work ethic. It just isn't."

"Hmm, sounds like the Navy," I thought.

Unlike most in his field, Cox did not ramble on about journalistic pioneers like Nelly Bly or Edward R. Murrow. We never had a single lesson on the birth of Yellow journalism or the achievements of William Randolph Hearst. Although we were expected to read the morning paper and got quizzed on it, Cox preferred less prestigious media outlets.

"I like the Hollywood tabloids," he admitted. "They are just so much more fun to work for. They pay better, too. And I believe it or not, they're usually more honest."

I loved class. I was sent on assignments that intrigued me. For my midterm essay, I had to put myself in a place completely out of my element and write about it. As a white agnostic with a traumatic, Baha'i and Bible-Belted upbringing, I attended a gospel Baptist Church service. I had a blast and I got an A.

Then the time came to write our final papers.

"You're all going to write a magazine article. If you want to, you can even submit it to a real magazine. Who knows? Maybe you'll get published. Write down some ideas. What are you hobbies? What are some of your favorite family stories?"

Scribbling about Tennessee and Muay Thai, I knew I could do better. Though it was risky, the thought felt like sharp object nudging my brain.

"Professor Cox," I approached him. "Can I write about something… different?"

"Sure. Pitch me some ideas."

"Well, you know how I was in the Navy?" I started.

He looked intrigued. As he nodded I continued.

"Well, I was married," I started, pausing for a bit. "For the money."

I went into *everything*. I divulged the details of the Mexico fling and arrest with my future husband who I would never have sex with. I talked about deployment, the infidelity, the hookers, and the fact that a twenty-minute courtroom session, awkward peck kiss, and marriage certificate doubled a Navy salary. And as I told him all about my NCIS investigation, my humiliating interrogation, and how I barely but successfully got away with it all, I couldn't help but notice the way Cox's eyes bugged out as if he'd stumbled on a sack of diamonds.

"Brilliant," he said with a gasp. "Write *that*."

I submitted my article to the *San Diego Reader* the day I was officially and *honorably* discharged from the United States Navy. Three months later, I was on the cover.

The *Reader* was and still is the largest press paper in San Diego County.

Merely months into my civilian life, an image of me with chopped black hair in an open dress blue uniform blatantly displaying my cleavage and chest tattoo was plastered throughout one of the world's largest military towns. I even sported the good conduct medal that I earned a couple days before my Captain's Mast.

"Confessions of a Phony Navy Wife" was a labor of love for Cox and me. We stayed after class every day. I wrote, he edited, shaking his head at the sensationally controversial juiciness of it all.

"This is going to piss some officers off," he'd say every now and then with the devilish smile a kid gets after peeking into their gifts before Christmas morning.

Cox sure as hell saw it coming. I was a local celebrity for a few weeks.

I would go to a party and see my magazine on the kitchen table.

"Hey, I know you!" people would point out, automatically recognizing me by my tattoo. "That was a damn good read!"

The owner of the San Diego Reader told me that *Confessions of a Phony Navy Wife* was by far their most popular article. The web post alone got over forty comments and the office was apparently flooded with both love and hate mail.

There are reasons that certain military things are supposed to remain unspoken. Inability to keep things quiet is why women were not allowed in the military for so long, God forbid we end up with one as a president...

It is a disgrace that this would get published, let alone get a cover story.

I say BULL. This is a matter of ethics. The "everyone else is doing it so why shouldn't I?" defense doesn't fly.

The author only succeeded in portraying herself as a complete trash bag with no talent for writing.

Great story, well written and honest, about a real-life issue.

I have to tell you that I have never read something so TRUE!!

Wow, that's stunningly good!

Thank you for such a well-written article, and I hope to see more of Maggie Young's publications in the near future.

That article was a groundbreaking step for me, but not for the expected reasons. I was officially a published writer. I followed that article up with another attention grabber. It was the first stepping-stone to a series of prestigious journalism internships to follow. But I was oblivious to the most important part of my achievement. *Confessions of a Phony Navy Wife* was the foundation for the only life I could happily exist in.

I was meant to be a target. Something about making myself the image of corruption and splattering it in the world's face gave me a certain type of high that no drug could ever reach.

I don't know whether it was some sick form of self-loathing or self-worship that made me that way. But the shock-and-awe impact of my work's release gave me a sense of purpose. And for a bit, it filled every single void in my life.

The success of my first publication did not miraculously jet set me into a feminist independence. Finishing my spring semester and getting ready to transfer to San Diego State University, my attention was not a hundred percent devoted to my goals. Although feverous, my daily motions of writing and studying were robotic. As the months without Number 20 rolled along, I remained in a period of mourning.

"Has he read the article?" I wondered what his reaction would be to see my face on the newsstands. "Will he call me once he sees it?"

I thought of him often, jumping at every chime of my cell while reciting a secret prayer that he had seen the error of his ways and was in the midst begging for my forgiveness.

And one night, I got my wish - sort of.

Three months after our falling out, Number 20 drunk dialed me.

"You were a baaaaddd guuurrrlll," he slurred. "You are suuucch a good liar. But I missshh you. Pleasee just say that you liieeedd so I can fuck you again."

After struggling to bring him to some level of comprehensive logic, we agreed to talk it out once he sobered up the next day. But when I called, it was business as usual. I was desperate and he was out of reach.

Consciously, I told myself to move on. That decision was evident when I took Cox's advice for a location change.

"There's not much media going on in San Diego," he told me. "If you really want to get into it, you could always move up to L.A. Instead of San Diego State, you could transfer to Cal State Long Beach or Northridge."

Although it felt like a risky step out of my comfort zone, I was ready to leave San Diego. The *Reader* was asking for more material. They wanted me to be a regular contributor. I could have established a decent life there, but the town reeked of Navy. Hanging around past my discharge was beginning to feel like I was overstaying my welcome.

Unconsciously, men were still a heavy influence. That decision was evident when I made Number 20s best friend my Number 21.

"He's a player," I remembered Number 20 saying of his buddy.

We were never properly introduced, but 20 often told me about his best friend's antics. "I always hated going out with him because he got all the women and I was usually the wingman. But, at least I had the nice guy thing going for me."

It was easy to see why Number 21 got all the pussy. Although Number 20 was tall, his b-f-f stood 6'4" with a lean, muscular physique. He had a pretty, boyish face with chocolate brown eyes against his tanned, southern California-born face. With thick, shaggy, brown hair that curled into wavy ringlets behind his face, he looked just like a younger and hotter version of actor, John Corbett who played Aiden on Sex and the City.

While I was dating 20, I wasn't a fan of his friend. I'd heard way too many stories of how he'd bang whatever woman 20 was interested in and brag about it the next day.

"He had to take one girl to get an abortion," he told me.

Despite that Number 20 may have treated me badly, I saw somewhat of a hero worship in him.

Number 20 was a meth head, pushing thirty, and living with his mother. His employment status was a charity case from his dad.

Number 21 was everything that 20 was not.

Even with a splotchy romantic track record, Number 21 had his shit together. His tall, athletic frame scored him a basketball scholarship to the California Maritime Academy in San Francisco right after high school. At twenty-nine years old, he was the operation's manager at the Port of Long Beach. Although I had absolutely no idea what that meant, I knew that he had no problem dropping a couple grand at Neiman Marcus on any given Tuesday.

Although twenty-one smoked, drank, and occasionally dabbled in a line of cocaine or two, he was an overall healthy guy. He worked out on a regular basis and was always in a basketball or football league.

While dating Number 20, I did plenty of Number 21 Myspace stalking. Although I resented what I knew of him, I was infatuated. He was a southern California poster boy. His lean, smoldering body was almost always sharply dressed, with dark blazers and designer jeans or khaki shorts with white cotton shirts that hung open for a breezy day at the beach. In the rest of his photos, he was shirtless with brooding, intense facial expressions and smirks. From what I could tell, Number 21 was composed, arrogant, and fucking beautiful.

We didn't like each other as people. There was little to no real sexual tension between us and we didn't have much to say to each other. He thought I was loud and obnoxious. I thought he was boring. He was physically and materialistically out of my league. I was still hung up on the average-looking loser with the fun personality.

Number 20 was the only thing that united us. Number 21 wanted to piss on his territory. I wanted revenge.

Once again, Myspace had gotten me into trouble with boys. My first contact with Number 21 was while 20 and I were still dating. After months of occasionally scoping out 21's profile, I was caught off-guard when I saw his friend request pop up on my screen.

My belly jumped. I immediately pressed, "accept" and proceeded to examine every inch of his profile.

"Hey," he messaged me that day. "I love your photos. I really appreciate a woman with some curves, especially when she shows them off!"

"Oh thanks! I've heard a lot about you," I replied.

We chatted. He was boldly flirtatious. I was friendly, but subtle enough to declare my innocence in case Number 20 caught wind of the conversation.

Number 21 proceeded to tell me more about himself, his life in Long Beach, his job, and his desires to move back to San Diego to be closer to family.

"My big sister has twins and is about to have her third baby," he told me. "Even though I'm only a two-hour drive away, it doesn't seem close enough."

I never asked what compelled him to contact me. For a short while, I got a thrill out of conversing with my neglectful boyfriend's best friend.

But, in the midst of my Number 20 breakup delirium, I deleted my Myspace account.

Because of the California State Universities in the Los Angeles area, my choice was to either move to Long Beach or Northridge. Although I was convinced that I had kicked my Number 20 addiction, moving to the same town as his best friend was not a coincidence. As fucked up as it may seem, I saw it as the perfect opportunity to contact him again and give him the whole "I don't know anyone here and I'm looking for friends" spiel. The scheme of getting some sort of payback for Number 20 was not my only reason for the Long Beach relocation, but it was a major factor. Plus, I'd sort of always wanted to fuck him.

My French bulldog, Dasher, and I moved into a house full of hippies. The chunky, big-eared canine that looked like a mix between a bat and a pig, was given to me right after I got out of the Navy.

For five years, Dasher was my mother's. He clung to her, following her around incessantly and snarled at anyone who came near her if he was in his guardian position atop her lap. Although he loved everyone during puppyhood, my little brother began to tease and torture him, eventually making Dasher unpredictably aggressive. He especially hated men and growled like a dragon at any sign of testosterone.

Then my parents bought a large American Bulldog puppy. The two alpha breeds clashed, snapping and attacking one another on a daily basis. Once the American Bulldog grew into fifty-pound maturity, Dasher's life was on the line. I took Dasher in with a scarred ear, scratched body, and bruised emotions. I was his person.

Dasher's days were spent dozing on my bed and I grew used to his frumpy gallops whenever I arrived home. He began letting people approach him on our walks and eventually rubbed his head against random strangers for pats.

The two of us bonded as fellow debris from my parents' impulse decisions. He came into my life at the beginning of my period of isolation. In the years following my enlistment, my world would become cramped studio apartments among books and my laptop. Often, it was Dasher's warm, snoring body curled against mine that prevented chronic loneliness. He wasn't a high maintenance dog. He didn't require long walks and his hefty, stubby body had little energy for fetch. But he craved my company. His happiest days would be spent in my college apartment with me on my laptop, him sunbathing in front of my wide open door and occasionally getting up to munch on the basil planted along the outside walkway.

Dasher left my parents in the same condition I was in when I escaped. He'd gone from my mother's beloved pet to the baggage dulled by the shiny and new.

He'd been teased, tested, tainted, and rejected for reacting. We were angry and jaded, but healed by each other.

Dasher fulfilled so many emotional voids. He provided me the protection that Carl never had and the affection that I had always sought in casual sex. He gave me responsibility and kept me in my own bed each night. I learned to nurture and care for something more than myself. Dasher would be the only constant thing in my life. Ambition is lonely and hard work is isolating. I've never belonged anywhere, but he belonged with me.

I picked up a restaurant job and began the process of researching the next step in my education. It wasn't the most comfortable life, but it was my own. I felt truly separated from the Navy.

When I messaged Number 21 to tell him about my new location, he sent me his number right away. That night, I was in his apartment.

Long Beach is a small community outside of LA with a wide distribution of wealth. Downtown Long Beach has a few nice, tourist spots, but also has a cheap grimy feel. There are parts of Long Beach that are artistic, with tattooed, starving musicians in vintage get-ups. Of course, Long Beach has the sketchy, ghetto areas bordering Compton that Snoop Dogg rapped about. But as you head south near Orange County's borders, the houses get large, the people get white, and rent inflates dramatically.

Number 21's apartment was on Belmont Shores, just a few blocks away from the beach boardwalk and a trendy shopping strip that leads to Orange County. Walking in after he buzzed me through security, I spotted his apartment immediately from the San Diego Chargers sticker on his window. I remembered that Number 20 was helping him move in when we first began talking. It was the place that Number 20 escaped to so many times during his random weeks of absence.

Approaching the door, I began to get nervous. I realized what a bold move this was. I was going to the apartment of my ex-boyfriend's best friend, whom I'd never met before, and I was pretty sure he planned on nailing me.

He greeted me at the door wearing basketball shorts and a white wife beater. My chest jumped a bit when I realized that he was just as gorgeous in person. His curls had been cut short and he was sporting a rugged five o'clock shadow that I suddenly wanted to run my tongue against.

"Hi," he said, with that smirk I recognized from his photos.

He didn't hug me or do anything to express enthusiasm. He just stepped back for me to enter his domain.

His brown, mischievous eyes scanned my face with an intensity that wasn't strong enough to make me feel uncomfortable, but assured me that it would only be a matter of time before he got me naked.

Number 21 went through the motions of touring me through his one-bedroom apartment. It was nice, basic, but expensive because of the area's cost of living. It was immaculately clean. To this day, I wonder what kind of fabric softener he used.

Number 21's home very much reflected him. It was attractive, sleek, and well put together, but lacked any hint of uniqueness. His walls, carpets, and much of the furniture were white. The rest of it was black. The bit of artwork on his walls was black and white. When he handed me a beer, I was afraid I would spill it.

I sat down on his couch and he sat in a small loveseat just a couple feet away. We almost immediately began talking about Number 20 as I hashed out the details of what happened.

"He's a compulsive liar," he told me, and right away I could see that there was a genuine bitterness in his expression. "And he is a very good one. I've been friends with him since middle school, but he still lives this whole double life that I don't know about."

We began talking about his drug habit.

"You two seemed pretty close," I said. "He was always coming up here."

"Yeah, he'd stay here to come down," he told me. "Every time he went to Long Beach, he was recovering. His brain was always so scattered. I remember him taking newspapers that had been outside and were soaked from the rain and spreading them right over this coffee table," he said as his eyes gestured to the glass coffee table in front of his seats. "He would lay them out and say that they were for me to read. Like, what the fuck would I do with wet newspapers?"

"I came back from the airport to find lumber behind my fridge," I laughed. "He said they were for 'projects.'"

Both of us began laughing, but then 21 snapped out of it and his expression got serious.

"Why'd you put up with it?" he asked me.

"I don't know. Why do you put up with it?"

Neither of us had an answer, so we awkwardly switched subjects.

I enjoyed Number 21's company. We weren't in tune with each other, but it was nice to have some male companionship, even if it wasn't meant to last.

And Number 21 was blunt about the fact that his female relationships were fleeting.

"I'm usually done with a woman as soon as I sleep with her," he admitted.

Since I didn't have feelings for 21, I didn't care. I think that from the get-go, there was an unspoken understanding that we were using each other.

"Oh! This is my favorite show!" he said, as *Two and a Half Men* popped on his TV screen.

Although *Two and a Half Men* is definitely a rough blow to the female gender, I was a fan. I had to write a paper on the sitcom for a media class. It's about two brothers, Charlie and Allen. Allen is a freshly divorced father who ends up having to live with his wealthy, playboy brother. While Allen has lived his life as a faithful, devoted husband and father, he gets screwed over by his domineering ex-wife. Allen is perceived as dorky, weak, and almost always the butt of all jokes. Charlie, on the other hand, is a successful music writer who barely works. He's usually sipping margaritas all day in his Malibu beach house and banging an ungodly amount of idiotic women. Nearly every female character is either a raging cunt or borderline retarded. Two and a Half Men is obviously a male fantasy. Charlie is the hero that most viewers, including Number 21, idolize.

"I'm going to be just like that guy when I'm forty," Number 21 laughed.

Number 21 was exceptionally open with me about his skirt chasing victories.

"Oh my God," he huffed after checking his phone. "This bitch will *not* leave me alone."

Holding his cell out to my line of vision, he flipped through photos of a firm, bare ass with a black, laced thong running up her crack.

"I've been ignoring this chick for a week, but she can't take a hint."

I once heard a girlfriend of mine say that the men in southern California had "Peter Pan Syndrome."

"They don't want to grow up," she told me. "And the So-cal's sunny beaches stacked with gorgeous, insecure women is their Never-never Land."

We were drinking cocktails and bitching about men. At the time, I was seeing Number 20 and stressing the fuck out over one of his disappearing stints.

"He says that he's not ready for a relationship," I said, rolling my eyes. "He's twenty-fucking-nine years old and not that good looking. What the hell is he holding out for?"

"Funny how they always give you the 'I'm not ready for a serious relationship' line *after* they have sex with you. Never before," she scoffed.

My friend's theory for Peter Pan Syndrome was that, because southern California was so full of beautiful women, beauty has become a dime a dozen. Women are held at a much higher physical standard and have significantly steeper competition than in other areas of the country. Their self-esteem takes a blow because of it.

And since there are so many beautiful women in So-cal, the men are spoiled. They can toss one aside knowing that another will come right along. Already insecure, the ladies tolerate it. Men rarely feel the need to work for a monogamous relationship. They get bored easily. They want *more*.

And more is always at their fingertips.

Sexy, athletic, and successful, Number 21 was treacherous territory to any women who dared to care.

But, I still sensed emptiness in his heart. Why did he bother to have me, a woman significantly less stunning than his regulars, as his flavor of the week?

With me on the couch, 21 on the chair, we drank beer and watched Two and a Half Men as he took my hand and held it. His palm was warm and rough from the calluses of weight lifting. Puzzled by this simple, intimate gesture, I realized that he was just going through the motions of the inevitable.

I strung Number 21 along for about a week. I didn't want or expect any kind of relationship with him, but I knew that it would be a while before I established any friendships in Long Beach. He was my last piece of Number 20 that I wasn't eager to forfeit.

I began to realize that, despite his Peter Pan syndrome, he was a pretty nice guy.

He let me sleep in his bed and use his shower when he had to leave for work early in the morning. I got a phone call from Carl just before he had to bolt out the door. Though it turned out to be nothing, he remembered my serious tone and made sure to ask me if everything was okay later that afternoon.

He remembered little things, like the highlights I was planning to get in my hair and would ask me how they turned out. He thanked me for the food I brought him from work. And, when he wanted to get me drunk and naked, he did it with a bottle of Patron.

By my second visit to his place, Number 21 called me out for sitting in the chair away from him.

"Come sit here," he ordered, motioning me to the couch with him.

The whole process was like acting out a movie scene. We were supposed to get it on so we were required to take a certain number of steps to get there. First was the hand holding and then sitting close to each other on the couch.

While I kept my eyes glued to the television, unsure of what to do next, he began kissing my neck. He smelled of clean, sweet cologne and soap from the shower he took right before my arrival. His lips were soft and felt good behind my ear. But all I could think was, "Um. I guess I better kiss him now."

I'll admit that Number 21 was fun for a night of fooling around. We took shot after shot of Patron. The drunker we got, the more our opposing personalities could harmonize. We spent the majority of the night in a drunken stupor, dry humping each other on his fluffy, queen-sized bed that sat next to an entire wall of mirrors.

"Holy shit, I *love those!*" I slurred.

It was my first time watching myself fool around and it was unexpectedly hot. The lighting was dim and all of my physical insecurities vanished as I watched myself half naked, sprawled out under Number 21's lean, chiseled body. Watching him kiss my neck, I was quite proud of my conquest.

Wanting one more night of fun, I held out from sex. I knew exactly how Number 21 operated.

"I just jerked off while thinking of you," he texted me the next day.

"How romantic," I replied. "But seriously, I am truly flattered."

"You know that the sex is going to be amazing with us, right?"

Women often think there is some sort of formula to predicting the size of a man's penis.

"You have to look at their feet," is the common theory. "And their hands. The bigger the hands, the better."

I've heard that both tall and short guys are heavier hung. And I've heard that race is usually a determining factor, with black guys being a guaranteed magnum, Asians hung like pencils, and every other race a complete surprise package.

"He definitely isn't packing much," they'd say. "You can tell from his stature."

In my experience, there is no rhyme, reason, formula, or mechanism to knowing how big a dick is until you *know*.

Standing at 6'4", I had high hopes for Number 21. Although I've never been able to stick to a specific type, a common pattern I'm drawn to is the tall, lanky build. I've seen the best pricks of my sexual career hanging from those frames.

But when 21's boyhood slipped into my eager vagina, I was utterly devastated. I literally had my first "oh wait, it's already in?" moment. My pussy has had more gratification during pap smears.

Number 21 and I fucked like it was our fifty-year anniversary.

"Pull my hair," I demanded.

"No."

"Can you at least slap me around or something?"

"No. And stop scratching my back."

"Quit being such a pussy."

"I don't want other chicks to see me covered in back scratches."

"Well, go faster and harder!"

"I already came. I'm tired."

The first night we spent together, we had fallen asleep in a tight, cuddly spoon, which lasted throughout the entire night. I awoke from my second morning with his arm draped around my body and my head against his chest. By the morning after sex, we were on opposite sides of the bed.

I was grateful for Number 21 pretending to be asleep that morning. I left in silence and opened the door to the bright, California sunshine.

"You look like you're headed to the beach," an old man said to me on the elevator down.

His smile was friendly as his eyes gestured to my flip-flops.

"Yeah," I said, returning his smile and appreciating his oblivion to my walk of shame.

Once I got out of the Navy, my life changed entirely. Nearly every second of my day was devoted to my career. I had a vivid, precise vision of what I wanted to become. I was determined to be one of the most successful journalists in history. I was going to make the world forget Diane Sawyer. I would rise so far above my fellow sailors that the mention of my name would feel like a blunt kick to their teeth.

The Navy was my rock bottom and I was willing to forfeit my life to claw my way to the top. I spent my military freedom imprisoned in my room, buried in my writing and studies. I only went out when my friends dragged me and even then, I was in a mental panic from wasting an entire evening. I continued with Muay Thai to my final days in San Diego, but lost my passion for it. All of my energy went into becoming my ideal self.

I became even more isolated in Long Beach. I picked up a waitressing gig and never replaced my San Diego friends. I had no desire to down vodka shots into the wee hours of dawn. That was all it took to socially oust me from my coworkers.

At first, I moved into a small house full of hippies, including a fire dancer with a shaved head and her four-year-old daughter. They never put flea medication on their cat because they thought it was unnatural, so nothing was strong enough to keep the fleas off Dasher. They rarely worked and blew the little money they had on surfboards and tattoos.

When they didn't have the cash for Internet service, I decided it was time to drop the roommate thing. Dasher and I moved into our own shabby studio in downtown Long Beach. The rickety, hollow building was dark, depressing, and came with its own fleas. Even with the best locks, two of my bikes were stolen. My wallet was even snatched off my bed while I was in the shower. But despite a less than ideal living situation, I was happy to have my own domain. I had my dog, my awesome gay neighbor across the hall, and my future.

College didn't work out quite as planned. After I withdrew from San Diego State University, I was going to transfer to Cal State Long Beach for the spring semester. The switch would only set back my graduation date a few months, but as soon as I made the move, I found out that they were not accepting new students until the following year. Panicked by the delay, I enrolled in Long Beach City Community College. I figured I could at least get some extra classes in while raking in some Montgomery GI Bill cash.

"Wow, you've got some pretty impressive grades," said Long Beach City College's career counselor.

The thin, middle-aged African American woman with librarian glasses was helping me set up my class schedule. She stared down at my transcripts with a pleased look on her face.

The news about Cal State Long Beach set me in a panicked frenzy, but her encouraging tone was comforting and made me chatty. I began rattling on about my career aspirations and my *Reader* article. My second *Reader* article was in the process of publication.

"My, my, you've had an interesting life, young lady," she said with a smile. "You know," she continued, looking down at my transcripts again," With your resume, if you got straight A's this semester, did some volunteer work, and completed our honor's program, I bet you could get into something better than Cal State Long Beach. I bet you could get into Stanford or Berkeley."

"*Berkeley,*" the name echoed in my brain. "Did she just imply the idea of me actually being accepted into one of the most prestigious universities in the world?" I wondered in utter dismay.

Growing up, I always heard the names of top schools like Harvard, Princeton, and Yale. Universities like Duke, Stanford, and Berkeley were not technically the "Ivy leagues" of the North East, but they were always lumped in with all the legendary education facilities that I thought were only reserved for the rich and brilliant.

I knew Berkeley's name before I knew the rest of its details. Berkeley is located on the east side of the San Francisco Bay. Of all those big name schools, it was the only one that was public. Known as "Cal" to Californians, it was the first university in the state and has had an intense rivalry with its Palo Alto neighbor, Stanford, since the 1800s.

I loved Berkeley's rebellious reputation. It was notorious for not only its academic prestige, but its liberal, outspoken antics during the Vietnam War and Civil Rights movement. Berkeley students were known to protest *everything* and I loved a good protest.

"You really think I have a shot at Berkeley?" I asked.

There was no way in hell anyone who knew me in the Navy would have believed it.

"Absolutely," she said. "You not only have good grades. You've got writing talent and most of all, you've got life experience. You have truly *lived* and that means something to Berkeley. They don't just want brains. They want their students to be unique and you are certainly that."

It was true that my grades were decent. I had mostly A's splotched with a few B's from classes like economics and sciences that I could never comprehend. I didn't so much doubt my academic abilities, but my overall intelligence.

"Young, you're book smart, but you have no common sense," all of my shipmates were constantly telling me throughout my enlistment.

Bambi nicknamed me "Crayola" because she said I wasn't the brightest crayon in the box. This was, in her eyes, with love. Bambi was my friend, so my enemies were often much harsher. But I had already exceeded her expectations.

"I'm so impressed with what you're doing with your life. You really surprised me," she told me when I decided to move to Long Beach. "Here you are making these big moves in your life when I thought you'd end up in a trailer with a few abortions."

With a UC Berkeley degree, *nobody* could justifiably call me stupid again. On top of all that, it was a facility that would not only accept me, but would appreciate me. Feeling included - actually wanted for who I was - was something I couldn't even get from my own parents. I fantasized about my admission. Seaman Young attending UC Berkeley would be a hot, satisfying slap in the face to the Navy. That was motivation enough.

Though I had good grades, they never came easily. I had never been a flawless, straight-A student. I had one year to complete the honor's program, meaning that at least three honor's classes per semester would be more strenuous than the average course load. My schedule was packed with all the qualifications I needed. I had a heavy, concentrated schedule that needed to be tackled with flying colors. Unless I was at work or the gym, I studied and researched all day, every day.

After hearing those words of encouragement from my college career counselor, I developed tunnel vision. With Berkeley in my direct line of sight, everything else faded. Hobbies, fun, friendships, and even sex were no longer on my agenda.

In hindsight, I can spot a lot of things that made an impact during my twenties. The Navy, college, travel, friendships, fuck buddies, and lovers are on that list. But it was social media that molded those years sneakily, unexpectedly, and overwhelmingly.

I was first sucked into that world when I got my Myspace account. I was fresh from deployment and pushing twenty-one. I lived in Pacific Beach, the dead center of the party scene. Myspace was still in its infancy. The majority of my fuck buddies, casual hookups, fleeting, dysfunctional boyfriends, and sporadic dates of my earliest twenties originated from Myspace. And then Facebook took over.

I got a Facebook right around the time that I moved to Long Beach. I found an overwhelming amount of people from the depths of my past. I added childhood friends, Baha'i youth I hadn't seen since my teens, high school friends, and distant relatives.

I began corresponding with my grandfather's little sister. I stalked old classmates, browsing photos of their spouses, children, and lives. I saw who had gotten fat, bloomed and prospered in adulthood, remained in their hometowns, and who left. Facebook gave me a glimpse into the faiths, rituals, passions, and accomplishments of these random characters that barely flickered in my most distant recollections.

While I retreated back into the depths of my dark apartment and shielded myself from the real world, Facebook's virtual one sucked me right in. It was my main and sometimes my only connection with other human beings. Facebook became my imaginary friend.

As a kid, my mother's attempts to get me involved in sports were a lost cause. I always found myself with my head in the clouds and face on the concrete. My greatest safety hazard was my own feet.

I was notorious among my family for dramatic displays of clumsiness during the holidays, like when I ran straight into a glass door at Thanksgiving. I ended up flat on my back on the wooden deck. My plate of food remained smashed against the glass door.

Balls were smacking me in the face long before my sex life. Years of failed attempts at ballet, soccer, and softball left me with concussions, black eyes, and an array of bruises that Maggie wouldn't be Maggie without.

After all that, for some odd reason, my parents thought basketball would be a good idea. In eighth grade, they signed me up for our local YMCA basketball league. To my relief, there was another girl on the team just as clumsy. The rest were boys who were surprisingly considerate. They laughed along with us rather than at us. However, my teammate, Number 22, was the only one who actually seemed happy to see me there.

Even then, he was a nice-looking boy. At thirteen, he was already tall and lanky with a build that would make him a natural athlete throughout high school. His skin was a medium dark with eyes so dark brown that they were almost black. Though the details of his face faded in my memory through years of drug use, teenage rebellion, and military shenanigans, I never forgot his smile. Number 22 smiled big and often. And when he did, that smile dominated all things around him. Young and innocent, he hadn't yet discovered his natural gift. When the finesse was turned on and combined with that smile, he molded everyone into putty in his clever hands. But at thirteen, long before he discovered his craft, the charm let loose, endearingly and uncontrolled. We weren't yet jaded by lust and broken hearts. There were no lines or mind games between us. There was only that smile constantly directed towards me returned with a flush on my thirteen-year-old cheeks.

Number 22 and I went to rival high schools. We had a few mutual friends, so here and there, I heard about him. He was popular and athletic. Unlike me, he blended right into that world. I ran into him once at a football game sophomore year. He was on the sidelines waiting to play when I approached him. We chatted for a bit, a gate between us, with the same smiles and light flirtation we had two years before. That time, the mutual attraction was not hidden behind shyness.

"Maggie has gotten really pretty over the years," he told my friend in class the next week.

But, before driver's licenses and social media, different high schools seemed worlds away. He had a girlfriend anyway. So, we lost touch and grew up.

I forgot all about Number 22 until Facebook. His message came a few hours after I added him.

Number 22: How have you been? It's been a long time.
Me: Good! Yeah. I live in California now. What have you been doing over the years?
Number 22: Well, I just graduated from Tennessee State University with a major in biology pre-med and a minor in chemistry and psychology. Right now, I'm just preparing to enter medical school.

I was interested.

After years of uneducated drug addicts in and out of jail, so "above" the waste of a college education, or guys who were simply waiting for their bands to take off, I was burnt out from burnouts.

I was changing. I was starting to respect myself. I was rigorously pursuing my education and career. I only had interest in someone who understood that and was right there with me.

I sifted through Number 22's profile. As a Facebook newbie, I was completely unaware of its power of self-promotion. Number 22 had mastered it.

"Well, *you* have developed quite nicely," I thought to myself as I shuffled through his photos. And he had *many* of them.

Though he traded high school football for his all black, step dancing, bow-tie wearing fraternity, Number 22 had kept his athletic physique. He'd grown to a solid height of 6'1" and replaced his teenage lankiness with lean muscle and broad shoulders. His eyes were still that dark almond brown and his skin a clear, light chocolate. His hair was cut short with neat sideburns. His full, brown lips were now outlined with a neatly groomed goatee.

Number 22 was pretty, but his entire image went far beyond natural features alone. His photos presented someone who belonged on the cover of *GQ*. Number 22 had hundreds upon hundreds of self-portraits. Several digital albums appeared to be modeling shots that I later discovered were actually taken by friends upon request. The rest were of him either indulging in Nashville's nightlife or at events with his fraternity brothers. There was not a single photo where he was not sharply dressed. He was usually decked out in tailored suits of dark blue with light, thin pinstriped matching dress shirts and vests, corresponding hats, bow ties, and Gucci shoes. He was almost always perfectly accessorized with watches and even dark-rimmed glasses that made him look like a young Malcolm X.

"They're nonprescription," he later confessed. "I actually have 20/20 vision."

Whether he was staring off into the horizon, seemingly deep in thought in an airbrushed "modeling" shot or shaking hands with a fellow brother in a crowded room, he appeared sharp, intellectual, and important. There were even some images of him holding children, joyfully greeting them with a bright, open-mouthed smile. I imagined any political official or celebrity would post similar photos. There was no doubt that they were very strategically selected.

I continued to click through one image after another of the grown up version of the boy I once knew. I searched for the one thing I clearly remembered about him. That bright smile was still there. But as the boy grew up, it shined less often. That smile revealed his sole physical flaw of slightly crooked teeth. It revealed the human being behind the deity. That smile was the one and only thing about Number 22 that was truly genuine.

Me: That's great. What kind of doctor do you want to be?
Number 22: A pediatrician. I want to specialize in treating autistic children.

I was impressed. I realized that I had never been involved with a man who had ambition. My mind crept back to all my Numbers. A few didn't even have high school diplomas. Some completed military enlistments, but their civilian endeavors were unimpressive. Number 20 had a college degree he did nothing with, not to mention the drug problems he juggled and his resting place in mommy's home. Number 21 was making a great life for himself, but our passionless one-nighter could hardly be considered a relationship. No wonder I was drawn to Number 22.

"I'm a very self-motivated, cool, laid back person," he described himself in his Facebook biography. "My main focus in life is to heal the children of the next generation."

I had no interest in children, but I couldn't help but find his self-proclaimed compassion for them endearing. Number 22 had an image he wanted to portray and I hungrily gulped it all down. I saw brains, success, money, and power. I saw the perfect match for the ideal Maggie.

"I smile quite often," it continued.

I realized that I was smiling back as I read.

"Life is entirely too short to allow unfortunate mishaps to break my spirit. You never know how smiling at someone and giving them a kind 'hello' may affect their lives. I try to keep an open mind and heart in order to stay mindful of new experiences that may occur."

He used big words, making sure to clearly project his maturity and intellect.

"Last, I am a very focused individual when it comes to my endeavors and dreams, but I don't allow it to consume me. Balance is key!"

We continued chatting back and forth. Between graduating from Middle Tennessee State University and entering medical school at Vanderbilt, Number 22 was juggling serving jobs in Nashville. He remained close to his fraternity brothers. Although he kept an avid social life, he said that his center focus was his career.

"I won't get married until I'm at least thirty," he said. "I want to obtain all my goals before I establish a family."

Our friendship quickly escalated from Facebook chatting to long phone conversations and emails. We got into the serious discussions I never had with men before. We were able to talk about our futures because Number 22 actually had one. It didn't take long for our friendly chemistry to develop a flirtatious tone.

Conveniently, Number 22 never mentioned his girlfriend.

"The women out here just don't do it for me," he said, coolly. "Maybe I need an intelligent, beautiful southern California woman. How about you conduct the interviews and when I come visit you, we will do a speed date?"

We began talking about love, our relationship history, and the qualities we were looking for in a partner.

I presented myself with a combination of my traditional gender roles and feminist progressiveness. Knowing his future plan to procreating, I tossed aside my opposing lack of desire to reproduce.

"I like to cook and clean like crazy," I told him. "But my future husband better not expect me to be the full-time mother with dinner on the stove every night at 6."

He presented himself as the man who saw beyond all things shallow.

"Intelligence and ambition are the things that attract me the most to a woman," he told me. "Her looks may get her in the door, but her drive and insight on life is what really keeps my attention."

"I want a man who's not ashamed to rock one of those baby belly packs."

"I want a unique woman."

As I familiarized myself with Facebook, I developed Number 22's technique of self-promotion.

I began interning for Inside Edition in Los Angeles. I had the privilege of attending several red carpet events in Hollywood. I made sure to gussy myself up with side-do's, smoky eyes, and vintage black dresses. I took countless photos of the anorexic, Adderall snorting celebrities, exemplifying how unbelievably close I was to them. I was damn determined to show everyone that I could have licked the cocaine out of their nostrils.

I had my supervisor snap shots of me holding the Inside Edition microphone with the blood-red carpet in my background. Though I was merely an unpaid, community college intern, to my Facebook viewers, I appeared to be something so much more. Number 22 and I inhaled each other, dazzled like infants with wide-eyes gazing at shiny, sparkly objects.

One day at a time, our attraction bloomed. We were both dreamers who were so certain of the people we wanted to become. I, the iron-woman who graced the media's airwaves, Number 22, his Facebook image with the title of "Doctor." While I mistook Number 22's ego for his reality, he did the same for mine

I wasn't a fan of Long Beach. It was a dingy suburb of Los Angeles desperately trying to be like San Diego. It was almost always too hot, with incessant sunny weather lacking the ocean breeze that would have made it enjoyable. Just south of Compton and north of Orange County, both ghetto hood and hoity-toity beach money littered the area with no in-between.

There were probably many better areas around Los Angeles to venture, but that city only further justified my brilliant idea to lace the water with birth control. In LA, it's impossible to sneeze without spewing snot into a stranger's eyeball, let alone drive ten miles without wasting a day and a lung full of exhaust. It took me four years to get over San Diego. It took me four weeks to get over Long Beach.

Long Beach City Community College was the only good thing that the town had going for it. For some reason, that campus was a different world. It was flooded with bunnies that somehow procreated and flourished there. The college staff fed them. It was routine to see cute little fur balls scurrying across the sidewalks on the way to class.

My teachers actually had a passion for educating and an interest in the futures of their students. Many had their own spin on their craft. My philosophy teacher based his entire course on The Matrix trilogy. My California wildlife biology instructor had us crawling through local parks, trapping and executing bugs. My art history teacher let me complete my final project on ancient Roman sexuality. I got to venture into the perverted and shockingly nonchalant, bisexual lifestyles of our ancestors. I was earning straight A's for turning in images of penises and vaginas.

I liked my classmates. Since I was in the Honor's program, most of them were hard-working and had bright futures. Though I found some companionship in their company, they had their own lives in Long Beach and I had little time for one of my own.

Number 22 was such a strong motivation that it's tough to tell whether I was persevering so forcefully for me or for him.

"I am so proud of you," he'd tell me. "I am seriously your biggest fan."

My phone was always flooded with his words of encouragement.

"Look at you. You made it all the way to California. Your writing got you on the cover of a magazine. Now you're on the Hollywood red carpets with Inside Edition. The next thing you know, you'll be attending UC Berkeley. I brag about you all the time. You have no idea, Maggie," he continuously informed me.

Whenever my brain felt weak or thoughts turned to mush from cramming, I thought about the things he told me. I frequently fantasized about a life with Number 22. We were a highly accomplished, barrier-breaking power couple conquering the world one day at a time. Having an infatuation with such a driven, intelligent man pushed me to keep up to par with him.

Whenever he was off living his life, unavailable for his endearing motivational coaching, I had his Facebook page.

Every day, often multiple times, Number 22 posted his very own inspirational Facebook statuses, usually quoting himself.

Smile today. You have your health, a sane mind, and most of all breath. Don't take advantage of the things that flow so freely.

Never underestimate the power of your inner mindset and mentality. A lot of times issues that we face can simply be resolved by taking a deeper look at one's self rather than placing the blame on others.

L-I-V-E, Learning Increases Vortex Energy, Vortex Energy drastically influences your environment which overall influences your Happiness. L-I-V-E life freely.

God's Power: I'm in Kroger and a gentleman and I make eye contact, immediately I feel a certain way. I then felt lead by the Spirit of God to approach him to let him know that God wanted me to tell him that everything would be okay and He has everything under control.

"Uh oh," I thought.

In so many ways, Number 22 was new to me. There was his ambition, work ethic, and then the whole black guy thing. But he also ignited a bit of melancholic déjà vu.

After four years of absence, I was beginning to miss pieces of The South. The salt, sand, palm trees, and deafening, consistent sunlight beaming into my face were getting old. More and more often, I began catching myself longing for humidity-soaked summers with lightning bugs shimmering through the woods that outlined so many roads and the crisp, crunch of colorful autumn leaves beneath my feet.

However, I did not miss the Bible Belt.

To this day, I don't know or care about my California friends' religious beliefs. We just didn't discuss it. I love sushi. I could give a fuck less whether my friends love it, so why would I care if they loved the Bible, too?

But the significance of one's religion still heavily infiltrates my homeland. Religious conflicts run deep in my ancestry.

It was quite the scandal when my grandmother, Adele, a southern Baptist of Irish descent, married my grandfather, Everett. My granddaddy was an Army veteran and witty, sharp, up-and-coming young chiropractor. But to my grandmother's family, he was just a Jew. She was a proper Christian woman with an outstanding IQ and also a certified chiropractor. He was interested in a wife he could build a practice with. They seemed like a great match, but both families were fiercely against it.

"You have to stop that marriage from happening!" my great-grandmother ordered Granddaddy's little sister.

They had a quickie, courthouse wedding, without their parents' blessing. Then they ditched both religions for the Baha'i Faith. One would think this would make them a bit more tolerant to other religions, but it did the opposite.

My grandparents saw the Faith as the ultimate truth and couldn't understand why anyone introduced to it would look away from it. When my grandparents fell into the Faith full force, a rift grew throughout the family. They were broken hearted when their siblings refused to convert.

"They must be ashamed of us because we're Baha'is," my grandmother still scoffs when speaking of them.

Some of my aunts and uncles remained devoted Baha'is. Others were Baha'is on the surface to prevent hell from breaking loose.

My grandmother had me memorizing prayers as toddler. When I was four, she convinced me to donate my entire piggy bank to the Baha'i Faith's fund. But Baha'is were condemned from the things I enjoyed most as a teen, like booze and premarital sex.

I initially ditched the Faith out of teenage rebellion. As I got older and began giving spirituality some real thought, my belief in God became fickle. I didn't like the rules that religion enforced. I also had a hard time trusting any spiritual text, whether it was the Bible or Baha'i writings. Scriptures written hundreds to thousands of years ago by people whose bones were now dust in the soil was not solid enough evidence for my devotion. I couldn't assume that a book could map out my existence.

For a long time, I carried bitterness towards religion. In a society where it was so significant, I could do no right. As a Baha'i child, I constantly had to explain myself to my predominantly Christian society. I was the only kid who did not come back from winter break to brag about the Christmas gifts I had acquired.

"I'm a Baha'i. We celebrate Ayyam-i-ha in February," I'd have to tell everyone in our sharing circles.

"Ayami- what?" the southern kids would ask with a little twang, puzzled by the bizarre Middle Eastern wording.

Ayyam-i-ha was lame. There was no sparkly, sweet smelling pine tree, no Santa Clause, and no commercialized carols. For gifts, my extended family threw our names in a bowl and did an anonymous gift drawing. We would each get one present with a twenty-dollar spending limit. Unless we were lucky enough to get picked by my mother, we usually ended up with something awkward, like a reptile book from an uncle.

I wasn't a big fan of Christianity either. I went to my fair share of Sunday services and church lock-ins with friends. I walked on eggshells because if I dared to mention that I didn't buy into their preaching, I was apparently going to hell. After bringing a number of Sunday school teachers to tears with my sinful questioning, I avoided the whole Jesus show altogether. That was fine by me. But what I didn't like were the alliances religion formed. Something that was meant to unite divided so many. Popular girls who hardly spoke to me suddenly became concerned with my soul's fate once they found out I wasn't saved. They wouldn't invite me to their birthday parties, yet were suddenly holding my hands, praying for my change of heart as salty, sympathetic tears streamed down their cheeks. Many of my best Baha'i friends also distanced themselves from me once I began sneaking swigs of liquor and kissing boys. Damn my teenage curiosity.

Until Facebook came along, I had long forgotten the culture clashes of my youth. Suddenly, former cheerleaders, present stay-at-home suburban mommies were messaging me about accepting Christ as my savior. Although they said they wanted a lunch date with me, I had a feeling that the meal ticket they were really looking for was into heaven.

"GOD supplied me with not only new car, but at a great price," read Number 22's Facebook status.

"Psalms 37:13: The steps of a righteous man are ordered by the Lord. When you have a relationship with Him and trust Him, He will never let you down."

Number 22 was, indeed, a southern man.

I left The South because I was young, curious, and eager to explore the world. I needed to escape a life of meth and food stamps with my boyfriend. I was fiercely independent and craved adventure. But the primary, underlying reason of my great escape was that my spirit has always been instinctively wild. I left Tennessee as a child who didn't know how to curb myself for my surroundings. When I wanted to curse the world, I spat out profanities loudly. When I wanted to defy the feminine, ladylike composure I was raised to have, I fucked whom I chose and bragged about it to everyone in earshot. When I disagreed with faith and rules that my family and peers held sacred, I laughed aloud at them and made sure my defiance was clearly heard.

There is an air of grace and tradition The South takes pride in upholding. When all hell is breaking loose, southerners face the world with a smile. All anger, resentment, and feelings of hierarchy only flutter in bits of passive aggressive, light-hearted gossip. In southern culture, it is a cardinal sin to utter a single word without a sweet layer of sugarcoating.

I was a meek child who bloomed into something untamed and out of place. Just as I never mastered the skill of walking on my own two feet, I never acquired southern social etiquette. Whenever I was at a family gathering, tension surrounded me. Everyone always wondered, "What the hell is Maggie going to say next?" My mother cleverly masked her true feelings with her pretty, young face and consistent, bright smile. I, as her daughter, was a representation of her. And she was carrying a time bomb in a nursery. In a world where it was impolite to air one's dirty laundry, I wore my most ragged, period-stained panties as a trendy accessory.

As far as southerners went, the younger generations were easier to relate to. Though they weren't as raw as I was, they would usually tell you what was on their mind if you asked them directly. I could understand my cousins and some of my aunts and uncles perfectly well. But the layer of southern politeness was so thick around my grandparents that my only understanding of them was from careful observation. If I asked my grandmother something as simple as, "Did that make you angry? How do you feel about that? How are things with you?" I could never hope for *real* and *direct* response.

Perhaps I could have understood my grandmother better if she had a Facebook account.

As Number 22 and I continued to talk, I began to realize how much he was like my grandparents. He only gave me his best face. He was always pursuing his dreams. His life was constantly wonderful and the slightest sign of conflict was simply "God's obstacle." I couldn't decide whether I wanted to praise or rattle him. Then I began picking through the seeping holes in his barricade.

Facebook has a funny way of making or breaking a reputation. Just as Number 22 was able to create the man he wanted the world to see, his page was still occasionally littered with fragments of his real life.

Tagged photos are a jealous woman's assault rifle. When a pretty young lady who is sleeping with Number 22 goes out drinking with him, she makes sure her friends snap plenty of images of the two of them intimately leaning together with bright smiles on their faces. She then uploads that picture to her Facebook page, clicks on it and types Number 22's name on his image. Suddenly, every single one of his Facebook friends can view that photo of the two of them together.

This move seems nonchalant. The girl can write off that she is just posting photos of a fun night out. But it can also be a move to obtain possession over that man and to show all the other females on his Facebook page that he belongs to her.

After enough stalking, I realized that Number 22's Facebook page was one big estrogen-fused, pissing contest. The alpha dog was Lana West.

There were others, but Lana was by far the strongest female presence on his page. And I wished with all my heart that she was ugly.

After enough photos of Lana and Number 22 together popped up night after night, I couldn't resist diving into every single accessible image. Lana was, in fact, gorgeous, with clear, sparkling blue eyes, an auburn brown bob that was longer in the front than the back, and a blemish-free, sun-kissed complexion. She had the body of the stereotype of every black man's perfect ten, with a slim waist, very thick thighs, and a plump ass. Her physique was curvaceous, but firm. She worked out often, which was clearly displayed in the abdominal muscles that showed when she wore teeny bathing suits.

Lana knew she was attractive. She also came from money, which was displayed in several shots of her showing her suntan beneath sundresses in front of the family yacht.

She was twenty-two, a year my junior, and loved to party. She was at a club, teetering on stilettos in a short skirt and had a drink in her hand in all of her photos.

She also made sure to post comments on his wall like, "I can't wait for this weekend!" or tidbits of inside jokes they had.

Facebook was a great threshold for reading relationship dynamics. While she was all too eager to display photos of them together and publicize their association, he never reciprocated. Number 22 did not post a single photo of himself with Lana or any other women that he wasn't directly related to or in a large group with. He never remarked on Lana's posts. He seemingly ignored them and showed zero communication back. There was an array of miscommunications between them. To Lana, they were together. To Number 22, he was a single man. I could only imagine the series of exhausted attempts to cup her hands together to prevent him from fluttering away.

Granting me instant access into the lives of so many people at once, I developed an array of emotions. I praised and admired others through their pages. I judged. I compared. I developed attractions. And I also learned how to loathe complete strangers.

I deeply envied Lana for reasons beyond Number 22. She was everything I was not. My days were spent confined behind books, while she was lively and carefree. She had a solid group of girlfriends, whom I saw in all of her photos. I would often go to work, serving food for groups of friends with cocktails in hands or observe the guarded, but giddy mannerisms of first dates. I knew I was missing out on life. And while I obsessed over the lives of others three thousand miles away, Lana lived hers.

I picked through all of her photos, desperate to find the ones where her makeup was too heavy, skin was overly bronzed, or thighs were too fat.

"She's a spoiled, rich brat," I thought to myself, making a series of premature and unnecessary judgments. "She's been handed everything."

I assured myself that she was just something for Number 22 to play around with. Of course he had his share of women. He was an attractive twenty-three-year-old male. But she didn't have that goal-oriented drive he admired in me.

I fabricated as many irrational rationalizations as it took for me to tolerate it all and cusped them tight. As more curvaceous, white women appeared on Number 22's page, I went through the mental charade over and over again.

As the fall months rolled along, my visit home for Thanksgiving was swiftly approaching. Number 22 and I would both be in Chattanooga. Our realities were finally set to intertwine. Number 22 and I spoke less and less about religion, spirituality, and career aspirations and more about sex.

"I had the absolute most boring sex earlier this summer," I told him of my awkward night with Number 21.

"Too bad it wasn't with me. I would have put you a wheelchair," he assured me.

He slowly slipped in random facts that praised his performance.

"I've made women collapse," he filled me in. "Just from being overwhelmed by pleasure. At least that's what they said."

"So, I have to ask," I texted, finally with enough courage to pursue my curiosity. "Is it true what they say about black guys?"

My phone chimed a few minutes later. I picked it up with a little rush down my spine once I saw that Number 22 had sent me a picture message.

Stereotype confirmed.

I got to know Number 22 when I had no social life of my own. As a result, I turned him into a supplement for everything I was missing out on. He became my motivation. I used the rewards of his approval to keep me pushing through study sessions, lonely Saturday nights in my dark apartment buried in my laptop, and intense gym sessions. But as sexual tension developed, he supplemented that aspect of my mind as well. Somewhere along the way, every one of my self-induced orgasms were inspired by a pair of thick, black lips massaging my clit. I found myself constantly looking at my phone, just to catch a glimpse of that photo of his thick, black dick.

"Regular condoms don't fit me," he mentioned more than once. "I always have to use the Magnum XLs."

The closer November came, the more I found myself breaking from my midterm studies, my legs spread, back against the wall, sweat glands moist, exhausting my vibrator with thoughts of him yanking my hair back as he tore my insides apart. I began to have vivid dreams of Number 22 fucking me senseless.

By the time I arrived in Tennessee, my expectations of Number 22 were an entity of their own.

Thanksgiving was my favorite holiday with my extended relatives because it was one that both Christians and Baha'is got fully involved in. Having been a dedicated dieter since age eleven, it was the one holiday I allowed myself to consume as many fatty calories as my stomach could hold.

That year was my first Thanksgiving home since joining the Navy. As Mom, Carl, Grandmother, and all of my distant relatives gathered in the living room, holding hands and saying a blessing, it felt incredibly bizarre to be thrown back into a world I'd almost forgotten. The South and California were two different planets. When one clashed with the other, I was always a little thrown off. Number 22 was a piece of my past and part of my present. Our correspondence had been familiar and fun when I was out west, but suddenly, I felt uneasy with him being in geographical range.

For months, Number 22 made me excited about coming home. His tradition, his faith, and even his strategically controlled, graceful demeanor reminded me of the beauty of The South. In his own way, Number 22 was the sugar-sweet southern accent, the crisp, fall leaves, and the comforts that I caught myself homesick for. But suddenly, I was there and I was scared.

I was afraid of Number 22 because he had to act on his promises to see me. We had made plans for months. When it was a far-fetched idea, it was impossible to face disappointment. But once we were both in our hometowns, it had to happen. If it didn't, I'd have no choice but to be angry and disappointed. We weren't on Facebook anymore. I had to face Number 22's reality. Somehow I knew that I would prefer the mask to the man.

I had high hopes for my night with Number 22. We had talked up our evening of passion so much that I expected just that - a full night and possibly day of incessantly banging it out until our genitals felt like they were going to fall off. But first, he had to meet Carl.

As a little girl, I assumed that dating was in my future. The thought of my earliest courting sessions both excited me and frightened me with the anticipation of how Carl would handle it. Whether it was in television, movies, friends, or relatives, everything I knew about the way fathers handed their daughters off to the care of another man was an embarrassing process of the dad evaluating, interrogating, and subtly threatening new suitors.

"What's yer name, son?" I imagined Dad asking, throwing a scrutinizing glare in the face of an awkward teenage boy who was fighting an internal battle of hiding his skittishness behind good manners and a firm handshake.

"How old are ya?" Dad would continue. "Do ya have a job? What's yer family do? What are yer plans for yer future? *What are yer plans with ma daughter?*"

After ordering the boy to have his precious little girl home by 10 pm sharp, Dad would grudgingly release him, then spend the evening pacing by the front window and looking at his watch every twenty minutes until his daughter's safe return.

In southern society, a father was nauseated and infuriated at the idea of his daughter being sexually appealing to any man. A father resented her boyfriends until they earned his respect. A father's daughter was a princess who deserved nothing less than a prince. It was socially acceptable for a southern father to spend his daughter's prom night on his front porch with his rifle. But Carl never adopted that behavior.

Shortly after my first dramatic anorexia weight drop at age twelve, men started telling me that I was pretty. I was 4'10", seventy pounds from starvation, wearing a kids size ten denim shorts. I was blonde and tan from a summer of boating with Carl when I started to sense the mild flirtation and lingering eyes from his red, country-accented, forty-something marina companions after a few shots of Jack and a six-pack of Bud Light.

"Ah, fur one, don't care if ya go out with sum guy," Carl told me when I asked him if I could go out on my first date at age fifteen. "But yer mother's oudda town, so have 'em come in and shake ma hand real quick, just so she don't give me shit when she finds out."

Mom established dating rules. I had to be sixteen to have a boyfriend and I was not allowed in my room alone with him unless my door was wide open. But when she was gone, I had free rein. Although I loved my vacations from adolescence, a part of me was always waiting for the dad to come out of Carl. But when Carl encountered my statutory courtship with Number 1, he passed him a joint. When police called my parents after finding Number 3 and I drugged out and camped in his Blazer by the highway, he bitched about getting woken up in the middle of the night and later joked about meeting my boyfriend in Hamilton County handcuffs. And when my parents drunk dialed me in California, Carl chuckled along when his best friend slurred that he'd always wanted to "fuck me sideways."

During family gatherings, my relatives usually disperse into two crowds. The majority are the religious ones who do not drink and turn into bed early. The handful of rebels remained on Carl's boat to consume hefty amounts of booze. Number 22 would be meeting the latter crowd.

He was expected to arrive at the marina around ten o'clock Thanksgiving night. They were just there to party, but I was playing a game of make-believe. I pretended to be a young woman who young doctors desired and fathers loved.

I mentioned to Carl that Number 22 was black. In typical white, republican baby-boomer fashion, he expected a thug with cornrows, baggy pants, and gold teeth, spouting out rap lyrics.

Number 22 was running fashionably late. Eleven o'clock rolled around, then midnight.

"Is this guy coming?" my cousin asked impatiently.

"I'm about to hit the sack," Carl slurred, face flushed red.

I was already humiliated from the chance of being stood up. I continued to take shot after shot of Patron. It was useless. I was too anxious to get drunk.

At almost 1 am, my phone chimed. Number 22 was rolling up the marina drive. I scurried up the dock to meet him.

As I practically skipped to his beat up car he'd owned since high school, I felt an unexpected sensation. Nothing.

I tried to tune into my intoxication. I opened the passenger side of his door and there he was, wearing dark designer jeans, a pale pink dress shirt, a light-grey vest, and a tie with hints of pink to match his shirt. He'd forgotten my request to wear his glasses. I love men in glasses. But none-the-less, he looked as flawless as his photos.

"Hi," I said awkwardly, climbing into the passenger side of his car and searching inward for an emotion.

"Hey!" he said, pulling me in for an "old classmate I haven't seen in a while" hug. "It's so good to see you!"

This would have been the perfectly appropriate reunion, had we not spent months talking it up with sexts and dick pics. I was immediately disappointed. My little fantasies that pushed me through so many rigorous study sessions were being devoured by reality. I had to do something, so I leaned in and kissed him.

He was a good kisser. His tongue massaged mine perfectly with my preferred combination of intimacy and aggression. His plump, Chap Stick coated lips felt pleasantly different on mine. I reached my hand behind his neck and felt his hairline. Although I couldn't seem to summon up bursts of lust and passion for him, I was enjoying the shapes and textures of a black man. His hair felt like groomed Velcro.

Carl was an instant fan of Number 22.

As I watched the two of them sip on Jack and Cokes, the signature drink of choice for both of them, I couldn't help but notice their unlikely similarity. Both Carl and Number 22 were manipulative, smooth-talking salesmen. Both could sell baking soda in a room of premium cocaine. While Carl decorated himself with material items like yachts and fancy stereos, Number 22 did the same with intricately accessorized clothing. Both men knew how to carry themselves in an inviting demeanor. Carl and Number 22 naturally carried out the polite, graceful, but not always completely *real* social norms of The South.

I sat back on the yacht with my vodka soda and watched Number 22 destroy every racial stereotype Carl ever conceived. I couldn't follow his words. I was too distracted by his movements. He practically floated. He spoke, smiled, nodded, and laughed with so much flawless grace. I suddenly felt an urge to push him over. I wanted him to fall on his ass just so he could seem human. I wanted him to laugh, open-mouthed and uncontrolled.

Three in the morning crept up on us. Though we were exhausted, Number 22 and I had no choice but face our preplanned night of passion. I stashed a bottle of tequila in my pack, knowing that we were going to need it. From there, everything felt forced. We were on a time crunch for our great hookup. We drove into town, eventually finding a Holiday Inn to hook up.

All events up to banging it out with Number 22 were disappointingly robotic. We awkwardly paid for the hotel room, splitting the cost down the middle and stood in the elevator side by side. Our encounter felt like old friends who happened to be traveling together with sole intentions to sleep and only sleep. But once we got in our single room with our king-sized bed, we opened my backpack, busted out the booze, and took a few swigs each. We might as well have just taken a deep breath and said, "Well, this is it. I guess we have to fuck now."

However, once we got started, it was an entirely different scenario.

Number 22 immediately shoved me on the bed, yanking down my jeans and thrusting his tongue and thick, black guy lips inside me. The pussy eating session didn't last long before I ripped off his designer jeans. With most casual fucks, I had always been a pillow princess, but Number 22 was an old childhood friend. Though our encounter felt awkward, it didn't feel so random. Plus, I needed to take a look at the first completely black dick I ever had contact with.

Quite honestly, I wasn't keen on the unfamiliar dark color, but I had no complaints about the size. In Number 22's case, the big black dick theory rang true. It had to measure up to at least nine, possibly ten inches, but its girth was what impressed me. He was going to make me feel like I was getting foot fucked. Staring at what was beginning to seem like a threatening dark monster, I was terrified at tackling a blowjob.

"Can my gag reflex handle this thing?" I wondered. "What if I vomit all over his penis?"

I opened my mouth as wide as I could, making sure to warm up the tip and run my tongue around everything else. The more slippery I could get that baseball bat with my saliva, the less it would feel like a punch in the throat.

"At least his balls don't have that musty hair gel smell, too," I thought.

I went for it, literally pushing him as far down my throat as it would go. Suddenly, deep-throating him became a feat I had to conquer. My stomach clenched in pain as I struggled to keep from hurling. I couldn't help but think how useful this would have been during my bulimia days.

After going as far down as I could, I sucked, lifted my head back up and took in a breath. I repeated this a few times. But after I was satisfied by the few moans he unleashed, I stopped. His sexual pleasure was not worth suffocating for.

Sex with Number 22 was good, but could have been better. He fully met up to the stamina he bragged about and in return, I was able to enjoy it more than my previous partners. Something about me was changing. I was getting older and more in tune with what stimulated my body. Number 22 liked variety, switching positions constantly. He was rough by nature, slapping me around, pulling my hair, handling me without much care for my pain tolerance. But I held back from demanding my needs for making things rougher, crazier, and possibly a bit more degrading. However, at one point he broke a barrier that permanently changed my sex life.

Although I've been getting myself off since I was nine years old, it took twenty-two men for me to recognize the true, full intensity of an orgasm. I always identified my urges as sexual. I knew that I had a built up pressure inside of me and knew how to release it.

When I began having sex, men claimed to see me cum, but my orgasms were so faint that I never knew when I had them. When a guy asked me if I got off, I truly didn't know how to answer him.

Number 22 flipped me on my side, my legs twisted into an awkward bend that had my knees almost against my cheeks. From there, he gave me penetration so rough and deep that it felt like reverse childbirth. And there it was.

I felt like I was seizing and suddenly, I remembered all the times I'd felt that way before except before, I was so terrified of losing control of my body that I stopped myself from letting it take me over. For some reason, I let it happen. My entire body convulsed. Letting go of all composure, I screamed at the top of my lungs. At the age of twenty-three, fourteen years of masturbation and twenty-two sexual partners later, I had my first full-fledged, maximum-intensity orgasm.

It took me *that* long to learn what the fuss was all about.

Number 23

I still have a handful of vivid toddler memories. I'm two years old in my first one. I'm standing in my grandmother's kitchen, holding a sippy cup, and watching my shadow as the afternoon sunlight shines through the surrounding woods behind my tiny, wobbling stature. I have another where I'm being rolled in a hospital bed just after having foot surgery. My eyes are covered with cloth. I can clearly recall my third birthday party. My mom, aunts, uncles, grandparents, and cousins are standing around the dining room table. Uncle Dave scoops a stray chunk of chocolate frosting from my kitty cake and licks it off his finger.

"Uncle Dave!" Mom shrieks.

Another flashback comes from a few weeks later. I'm standing in the hallway outside my mother's bedroom. It was the second floor of my grandparents' house where Mom and I lived. Grandmother was telling me about the birth of Number 23.

I think that love is, by far, the most complicated emotion ever felt. Sure, there were times when I thought I was in love. But I inevitably became far removed from those emotions that once flipped my insides out.

Have I been really, truly in love before?

I have no idea.

But if I loved any of my Numbers, I loved 23 the most.

Number 23 had all the ingredients for a bona fide romance. He was charming and handsome. He opened doors for strangers and addressed elders with "sir's" and "ma'am's." He paid his mother's rent and grandmother's cable. He was intelligent and sensitive. He was polite and chivalrous. He was considered a gentleman and a hero.

I wish I could say that Number 23 had been *my* hero - that he left roses on my doorstep and awoke me at dawn to drive me to pristine mountainside sunrises. I would have liked to part ways on a bittersweet note, with a tear in my eye and gratitude in my heart for the man who showed me what true love was.

Perhaps Number 23 was indeed a knight in shining armor. But rather than his damsel, he saw me as the dragon he needed to slay. A lot of blood was shed during our saga.

The morning after the earth-shattering orgasm that Number 22 provided was less than earth shattering. We had a decent morning wall banging competition with our hotel neighbors. And then he took me back to my parents' house. There was no profound pillow talk to connect us on some higher level. There was no breakfast beyond our body parts. And although we both had a few more days left in Chattanooga, we never met up for a second round.

At the time, I wouldn't admit to myself that my expectation for the greatness of that meet-up was one big, beautiful delusion. I created him to keep me company with my books. But the image unfolded rather quickly.

Number 22 dropped out of medical school less than a year into it to pursue his real dreams. It turns out that he didn't want to help the children of America by healing their diseases. Instead, he wanted to help the children of America as a model, giving them the gift of staring at his immaculate beauty.

We remained superficial friends, but he made it very clear that he saw no relationship potential with us. I later found out that once he discovered that I was not Christian, he decided to do the Christian deed and just make a sinner like me his live pocket pussy. But for a long time, I got what I needed from him. The one thing that was real about our friendship was his support for my ambition.

"No matter how much of a bitch you may be," he said during one of our most heated fights, "There's no denying your talent and work ethic. You're going places, Maggie."

His words got me through a lot.

I called Number 22 immediately after receiving my UC Berkeley acceptance letter.

Number 22 wasn't the first person to believe in me, but he was the first to truly invest in those dreams *with* me. Whether most of his presence was real or in my imagination, he remained right by my side.

Even with an unobtainable, nonexistent romance looming over me, I was becoming my own person. I spent my first year as a civilian separating myself from the military. I pushed away everyone who reminded me of that world. My visit home for Thanksgiving left me with a bitter, uneasy taste.

But when I returned to California, I got in touch with my urge to travel - the one thing that was truly mine. That Christmas, I backpacked through Guatemala.

I may have inherited my nomadic tendencies from my grandmother. As a wealthy housewife with an intellect that left her stifled in her role, Grandmother was always venturing through the southeast for Baha'i teaching trips, pottery camps, meditation retreats, and visits to various relatives, friends, and acquaintances. While Granddaddy's escape from his unhappy marriage was long hours at his chiropractic offices, Grandmother's was constant movement. As her favorite granddaughter, she often hauled me with her.

Even from the beginning of Mom's marriage, I felt unexplainable tension when my stepfather was around. No matter how many scented candles or how much fabric softener Mom sprinkled, home was never a source of comfort.

My grandparents had been on their share of Baha'i pilgrimages to Israel and teaching trips to China and Australia, but they weren't big travel buffs beyond their religion. In fact, there was nobody in my life who had a burning desire to venture through Europe or move to Bali on a whim. Even my Navy friends were traveled out from deployments.

Navy port visits provided some overseas adventure, but the stunted adventures with rules and liberty buddies were just a tease. I wanted more.

Since puberty, my obsession with men influenced almost my entire identity. They inspired my taste in music, hobbies, goals, and even opinions. I altered my life plans, personality, and even deep-seated beliefs to suit what they wanted. I had almost zero identity without them. Traveling was the only part of me that they hadn't inspired.

I left my world behind to spend sixteen days in a tropical country with villages where English wasn't spoken and residents hadn't stepped ten miles outside their homes. I swam through caves, holding a candle over my head as my only source of light. I crawled up steep, damp stairs to the top of Mayan ruins that towered over rainforest trees.

I surrounded myself with people who prioritized traveling. There was the Canadian professional who always used her vacation days to venture somewhere exotic. One of her favorite trips was hiking Mount Kilimanjaro. I traveled with a Kiwi and his teenage son. Every time one of his kids turned sixteen, he took them on a trip around the world. I even met an old Canadian rancher who, in his mid seventies, realized how fleeting life was.

There were so many reasons to fall in love with traveling. It pushed me outside my boundaries. I did things I'd never do in the states, like clumsily attempt to salsa dance or eat cantaloupe that had fallen off a truck. I slept deeply and peacefully. I was constantly learning.

Travelers are eternally curious with an insatiable desire to try and see new things. But my favorite part was that it showed me the world through a wider lens. How could the Facebook photos of Lana and Number 22 together bother me on New Year's Eve when I was hiking an active volcano? I was doing and seeing bigger and better things than all the petty crap that gripped my heart in the states.

I returned to my dark, empty apartment in Long Beach, suntanned and covered with mosquito bites. I was rested and refreshed. I vowed for my Guatemala trip to not be my last.

With much relief, I left southern California for the San Francisco Bay that summer to join the ranks of UC Berkeley.

Northern California was significantly different than its southern region. It was pricier and classier. Trends changed from bug-eyed sunglasses to patterned panty hose under shorts and an array of tacky rain boots from plaid to rubber ducky yellow.

Berkeley is just north of Oakland and a few miles east of the city across the San Francisco Bay. Though still California, Nor Cal was a step down to earth for me. There were hills, trees, and rain. Though there weren't really specific seasons, I didn't have to deal with the constant arid sunlight scorching my eyes.

My dog, Dasher, and I took up residence in a tiny studio a couple miles off campus. Strolling through my new university, old enough to have educated Civil War veterans, I gazed at the tall, brick buildings, the library that looked like it belonged in the prime of ancient Rome, and Berkeley's signature campanile towering over fountains and grassy areas where hippies and Asians lounged, knowing that I had come a long way from my Higgins haze grey days.

"Seaman Young attending UC Berkeley!" my former shipmates had exclaimed. "Who the hell would have guessed? I bet that was a slap in the face to the Navy!"

Everyone knew where I was. I had Facebook to showcase my life achievements.

As my digital life continued to blend with my real one, I stumbled across the profile of one of my oldest childhood friends.

"Joshua!" I exclaimed to myself, excited to see his familiar name across my laptop screen.

The last time Joshua Robinson and I had crossed paths was in seventh grade. I was visiting my grandmother in Greenville and we all had to attend a picnic with the local Baha'is at the park in front of the zoo. We older kids drifted away as we always did. Joshua, his little brother, and I were being rebels, running off and sloshing through a nearby stream. I was twelve and though Joshua was eleven, he was skinny and towered over me. He had his pants rolled high to prevent as much damage as possible from our mud stomping. I called him Huckleberry Finn.

I smothered a few faint giggles when I browsed through his photos. Joshua looked exactly as I remembered him. He was tall and skinny with round, blue eyes, a soft, cheerful face, big smile, and a head full of angelic, chestnut ringlets with a pair of thick eyebrows to match.

He was a Georgia Tech graduate and still harbored his childhood comic and video game obsessions. But over the years, his intellectual goofball persona evolved into a type of nerd-chic that I imagined appealed to a lot of women. I was proud to see that Joshua had made something of himself. He had a nine to five developing smartphone apps.

We hadn't been close as children. We were just forced playmates in certain situations. But reunited as adults, Joshua and I clicked. Our bond was naturally platonic with a nostalgic, sibling feel.

The Robinson's and the Young's have long history that keeps intertwining.

The relationship began with my grandparents and Joshua's grandmother, Janice.

At some point during the 1970s, Janice's husband left her for his secretary. As a single mom, Janice took a position with the Greenville, South Carolina Baha'i community. Granddaddy also placed her in his chiropractic office and set her and her daughter up with a place to live.

Number 23's mom, who was my mom's age, grew up with my aunts and uncles. My aunt was even her college roommate and key witness to all the drama of Number 23's parents' shotgun wedding. There are photos of Joshua and me together, me over a year old with a head full of blonde hair and Joshua, premature and pint-sized, barely able to sit up. In a classic shot of the two of us, he is pushing me with his baby hand on my undeveloped breast as I return the action with a smoldering glare.

I sifted through Joshua's pictures to catch up on everything I missed. I saw his transition from scrawny video game nerd to savvy young professional, prom photos, awkward facial hair phases and all. Then I stumbled across one from way back, laughing aloud at the sight of the kid I remembered. He was about seven, his ringlets slightly lighter and features softer. He was on a bike next to a little boy with big, blue eyes and shaggy blonde hair.

"Oh yeah!" my memory snapped back. "I totally forgot about Joshua's little brother."

I scrolled my mouse over his photo where there was a link to his Facebook profile. There he was, the younger Robinson - my Number 23.

Without giving it a second thought, I clicked on his profile and added him.

Number 23 was a blank spot in my memory of the Robinsons.

When I was six, Joshua five, and Number 23 only three years old, the Robinson's divorced and the Young's were tangled up in the drama. After the divorce, my family played an active role in matchmaking. My aunt and uncle eventually introduced him to wife number two. I heard that before all of that, Benjamin actually had a crush on my mom.

"He used to come visit me at my dog grooming shop," she once told me. "I think he was on the verge of asking me out right before Carl came along."

Benjamin was a Carl contradiction. While Carl was an Odessa Community College dropout, Benjamin was a Georgia Tech Engineering alum. Carl's family upbringing was volatile and abusive and Benjamin hailed from South Carolina's wealthy white collars that summered in lake houses. Carl's drink of choice was a liter of Jack and Coke, while Benjamin's was O'Doul's nonalcoholic beer.

Benjamin was slim and handsome with the head of curly brown hair and the thick lashes his eldest son inherited. There was nothing flamboyant or flashy about the humble Benjamin, but his eyes served as a telescope to his mind. I have seen a series of Benjamin's emotions throughout my life, ranging from happy, melancholic, awkward, concerned, and sympathetic. But those eyes never emulated a hint of threat. I could not fathom Benjamin concocting so much as a scrutinizing glare.

Benjamin was ironically the type of man Mom urged me to go for.

"Be with the smart guy - a little nerdy, but cute, sweet," she advised. "Be with the man who will never deceive you - who will love you forever, unconditionally."

But Carl, making all around him the collateral damage of his demons, was the type I always ended up with.

Yet Mom wasn't interested in the safe, soft-eyed Benjamin.

"He probably just wanted me to raise his kids," she said once, rolling her eyes.

Mom wanted the salesman, the charming master manipulator who cursed, slung whiskey, and showed zero interest in fatherhood. She wanted the rebel willing to yank her out of the mundane, wholesome protection of family life. Never mind the bloody cuts and scrapes her little girl would obtain from being drug behind.

Benjamin gained full custody of his boys after his divorce, which was a rarity in the state of South Carolina. Watching Mom and Carl's wedding video during adulthood, I caught a glimpse of Benjamin with his sons mingling through the crowd during the reception. I watched Benjamin hold Number 23 with one arm, Joshua's hand with the other, smiling, patiently acknowledging both wedding attendees and his boys with balanced sincerity.

"Benjamin is the only reason those boys turned out as well as they did," Janice often said.

I didn't see much of Number 23 once I moved to Chattanooga. He was rarely around during my visits to Greenville and when he was, I hardly acknowledged him. Our three-year age difference seemed like a generation gap back then. When he was around, Joshua and I, along with the other kids wrote him off when he tried to tag along.

Number 23 was someone I knew existed, but never thought about. He, on the other hand, didn't remember me at all. He was caught off guard when he received a Facebook friend request from a twenty-three-year-old blonde with a very familiar last name. But, he gladly accepted the new encounter. The twenty-year-old soldier was open to anything that could keep him occupied in Iraq.

Joshua and Number 23 took completely different paths. While Joshua was scholastic and zipped straight through college, the classroom setting wasn't really Number 23's thing. His whole family had always regarded him as the kid with ADHD, so when he dropped out of college his freshman year, they thought the Army would be a suitable route for him. At nineteen years old, he became a part of the Airborne Infantry. He was trained to jump out of planes, and shoot guns.

I didn't really regard Number 23 when we first began communicating.

He was just another beer-guzzling, tobacco chewing recruit. When I envisioned what he was like in person, I pictured the Marines I used to party with in San Diego who took turns throwing things across the room and breaking each other's noses.

I sifted through his photos. He looked nothing like his brother. While Joshua was a younger version of his father, Number 23 inherited his mother's pale blue eyes, ash blonde hair, and olive skin. While Joshua's hair was packed with unruly curls, Number 23's was straight and sharply groomed to Army regulations. At 6'1", he was slightly shorter than his big brother.

Number 23's face was endearingly boyish and always clean-shaven because, to his utter devastation, he couldn't grow a beard. In his camouflage uniform and military-issued sunglasses, he looked just like an Army Ken doll.

He was the only person from my childhood to join the military, so that was what spurred our first conversation. I also discovered via Facebook that he and his girlfriend had just broken up. Although they vowed to tough out the year, in good military tradition, she cheated and dumped him a month into his deployment.

I pitied him. Deployment was probably the worst place to go through a breakup because one didn't have the means to do fun, distracting things to recover. And Number 23 was in the Army. Navy deployments were tough. I thought about my days as a Deck Seaman, standing watch for hours on end with nothing to do but stare off at the horizon. With my mentally paralyzing tasks, I was forced to think and over think. But I at least got breaks with booze and party port visits.

My deployment was only six months long. Number 23 was sentenced to an entire year of patrolling ravaged, poverty-stricken desert communities and thinking his life to death. While his ex-girlfriend was moving on, Number 23 was stuck in a military time capsule.

We were a part of each other's distant past, but experienced something the rest of them hadn't. With him deployed and me, constantly studying, we were a distraction for each other. I understood his life better than everyone else he knew outside of the Army. Because of that, we became fast friends.

At first, I talked to him like I was an elder who had seen the world, dealt with the drama, and informed him of the evils of the military. When we began communicating, he was fresh into deployment. He left the previous Thanksgiving and was expected to be home for Thanksgiving. Number 23 was stationed in Fort Bragg, just a few driving hours from our birthplace of Greenville, South Carolina. Still fresh in the game, he was a spirited young buck caught up in the glamour of being a war hero.

Number 23: So, you used to be in the Navy? Small world.
Me: Yup. Four years incarcerated. I've been out for year now! How's Iraq?
Number 23: It's pretty boring. We just do a lot of patrolling. I just enlisted for another eight years though.
Me: You're joking! You're going to regret it, dude!
Number 23: Oh, you wouldn't be saying that if you knew what my bonus was.
Me: That money won't matter a few years down the road. Just wait. I bet you're going to hit the bar as soon as you return, huh?
Number 23: Well, I can't hit the bars just yet.
Me: Oh yeah! You're only twenty! You are just a baby!
Number 23: Babies don't fight wars.

Our banter began like that, casual and sporadic, for a good bit of that year. I was wrapping up my final semester at Long Beach and preparing for my transfer to Berkeley. Every now and then I would be logged into Facebook when I'd hear the chime of an instant message.
Number 23 would be on break in need of an escape.

We talked about my internship at Inside Edition, my admission to Berkeley, and my journalism aspirations. He'd talk about his family, his desire to travel, the love for the outdoors that we shared, and his constantly changing plans for the future.

His ambitions were fickle. Sometimes he wanted to be a park ranger, then a pilot, business owner, and then a military lifer.

As I got to know him, I started to see two versions of Number 23: the man he wanted to be and the man he was. Since my discharge, I had gone out of my way to immerse myself in the military opposite. UC Berkeley's progressive culture of intellect sharpening, authority challenging, government criticizing, and peace protests were a much welcomed culture shock.

Number 23's enlistment alone made me hesitate getting too chummy. But I quickly saw that Number 23 just didn't fit the soldier stereotype. He was intelligent, sensitive, and free spirited. His inner battle with the army was transparent. His personal email address included his military rank. The majority of his Facebook photos were of him in uniform with comments like, "That's the face of a guy who loves the Army," and praise for his bravery for defending "our great nation." His statuses detailed his excitement about his Iraq deployment, his thrill for destroying the bad guys, and his drive to achieve weapons training qualifications. But once he began calling me from Baghdad, he didn't talk about deployment unless I brought it up. When he did, a shadow seemed to loom over his voice.

"Only a few more years until I'm out," he'd say with exasperated hope.

I remembered the way career sailors spoke of their enlistment like they were serving a prison sentence. Everything was a countdown in the military.

"Five months and twelve days until the end of deployment. Three weeks until leave. Seven years, three months, five days, thirteen hours, and three seconds until I'm free from Uncle Sam's shackles."

"Why'd you reenlist?" I asked.

"Ugh," Number 23 would grunt as if scolding himself. "Because I was dumb. They got me at the beginning of deployment before it was awful - when I was pumped up and excited about it. They threw a bunch of money in my face. It seemed like a good idea at the time."

"Do you regret it?"

The line was silent for a moment as if he were deciding on whether or not to tell me a dark secret.

"Yes," he said.

"Gosh, he turned out to be so handsome," Mom remarked

I was using Facebook like a photo album when she came to visit me just a couple months after I reconnected with the Robinsons.

"Yeah, he's alright," I shrugged.

In the beginning, I would have never considered Number 23 as anything beyond a friendly acquaintance. He channeled juvenile innocence. Hell, he wasn't even old enough to buy me a beer. He was on the other side of the planet and even when he returned, he would still be on the other side of the country.

College kept me geographically tied, but his knot was even tighter. As government property, Number 23 couldn't even plan vacations a month in advance, let alone visit a long distance girlfriend during her university breaks.

Number 23 absolutely was not even an option. Then one tiny gesture changed everything.

Number 23: We should go on a date…. you know… if we're ever in town at the same time.

The phrase was so simple and for most women, so generic. Any other female would have laughed off such a question from a boy she had no interest in. But in my case, it was a landmark moment in my life. Number 23 had gone where no other man had gone before.

Until then, my history with men had been volatile. Instead of a boyfriend or even a drunken prom date, my virginity was forfeited to a very disturbed, grown man while I was unconscious on a bathroom floor. The remnants of what could be considered high school relationships were blurry and drug infused. Even the one long-lasting courtship I held with Number 3 went without traditional dating rituals like Valentine's Day, birthdays, anniversary gifts, or even dinner.

Into young adulthood, I was never the girl who men asked on dates. I was asked on many fucks. I was a pair of tits to cum on, a mouth to force a cock down, and even a playmate to spice up a marriage.

At twenty-four, I had slept with twenty-two men, gotten lustfully heated with countless more, but had never once been given flowers. With less than a handful of dates in my past, romance was something I accepted as not being in the cards for me. My personality was too strong, my language too foul, and my opinions too outspoken. No, I was not the girl who got asked out on dates and though that made me sad at times, I buried myself too deeply in productivity to dwell on it.

But, that day, Number 23 sparked a fuse. That question showed a glimmer of a simplistic sweetness that men never gave me. Suddenly he went from being some Army kid to the boyfriend I never had.

In the months approaching the end of his deployment and my Christmas trip to The South, we grew closer.

We made cracks about our family history, and cringed a bit at the "what ifs" when it came to his dad's old crush on my mom.

Me: Well I guess the two of us going on a date would make an interesting combo. My gene pool basically owes your gene pool since my mom never gave your dad a piece! Hahaha!
Number 23: Or my dad was just too shy to try and get some! Oh well. We will have to make up for our parent's inaction. ;)

Our chats became a daily ritual. I started leaving myself logged onto Facebook so I would be sure to catch him whenever he was online. We found ourselves on the phone for hours.

The dialogue flowed naturally. Because of our family ties, we were familiar with each other. But since we didn't directly connect each other with those memories, the sibling bond that he had with my cousins and I had with his brother was absent with us. Our flirtatious tone also gradually flourished.

He told me more about his childhood and caught me up on his family dynamic. Though long divorced, his parents still struggled with swallowing their hostility and rarely communicated. They both remarried and had more children.

Once I started to pay attention, Number 23 and I were magnetic. Over emails, over phone, over Skype, I fell in love with him. I fell in love through devices, through screens, through surfaces that my nails would tap against if I reached out to touch him. I often thought about being with him. I imagined the details like the scent of his skin, the warmth of his neck, and the softness of his lips. Those thoughts kept me company during my hectic academic deadlines, dense reading assignments, and one after another brain cramming session. They stood as an unsatisfying substitute.

Number 23 had plenty of redeeming qualities that made falling for him a justifiable accident. But our connection had nothing to do with our similarities, our differences, our aesthetic attractions, or our emotional and physical needs. When we spoke, he was truly *with* me. Our egos, our personas, expected social cues, the facades that everyone builds around them that are supposed to sculpt the way the world sees us, were stripped with Number 23 and I. He was immediately my best friend, familiar and safe - an epiphany that I had been spending my life alone in crowded rooms.

Our souls were naked. We initially curled into the warmth of that connection. But once we knew how real it was, we felt exposed, vulnerable, and raw. While his defense was his fearful recoil, mine was dictation.

Neither of us were what the other had in mind. I considered him an emotional fluke. His life experience contained the grit of an infant compared to mine. He was accustomed to the type of girls who said "ya'll," called everybody "hun," wore sundresses to church, baked lemon bars for their sorority fundraisers, and vowed to be wives by their early twenties.

Number 23 was the type of guy who took girls to movies and made small talk with their fathers at July 4th picnics. He seemed so perfectly wholesome, like something that should have been delivered to my doorstep wrapped in a plaid bow. Number 23 represented The South, my family, and the military.

It seems quite bizarre how much I loved one big bundle of all of my demons, but that may have been his core appeal. If he could embrace me, there was a chance I could become tolerable, even passable in those worlds that considered me a plague.

I snuck up on him, too. I'm sure Number 23 looked over my photos and saw a cute blonde, merely a twenty-something version of the girl who roamed his high school halls. Sure, I was attending a fancy school on the west coast, was obviously smart and a bit more cultured than cliché southern belles, but I was harmless enough. But as we unfolded our personalities, he got to know a woman with a past, a woman who'd been through drug use, eating disorders, military scandal, world travel, and a significantly heftier sexual history. Number 23 was just beginning to set foot on the paths I'd been trekking for years.

At first, he marveled in my stories, my unapologetically bold personality, and my profane dialogue. He gradually indulged in pushing his conversational limits.

Number 23: So, uh, I had an interesting experience yesterday.

Me: Oh? What was that?

Number 23: Well, when I whack off, it's usually in the shower. It's the only place I can get privacy out here.

Me: Okay…

Number 23: And the last time I did it, I kind of brought you into the fantasy.

The gentlemanly Number 23 would have never made such a crude statement to a lady. But I was not a lady. Sure, I was intelligent and strong, but I dared to be wide open. I was Maggie Young, chaser of boys, writer of scandal, dropper of f-bombs, tits on a stick.

Number 23 was enamored when I was the truest version of myself. It was evident in the way his eyes seemed to dance in fascination during our Skype conversations.

"This is amazing," he would say every now and then, halting our conversation like a runner who needed to catch his breath. "This is perfect. These talks. I love them so much. You're ADD like me. You can keep up with me. We bounce around and it never gets boring. I've never had conversations like this with anyone in my life."

But everything that he liked about me suddenly made me the female of steel - the mutant. Without precautions and considerations that were a requirement with anyone else, Number 23 loosely flung details of other women at me.

He elaborated on his 4'10", ninety-pound ex girlfriend and the blonde, high school sweetheart who wanted to become an actress who he still harbored feelings for. The grandiose look he got in his eye when he spoke of both of them made me flinch, but Sheryl was by far the most gruesome of the monsters. When he returned to our homeland for the holidays, she would be waiting.

"She's the best friend of Joshua's girlfriend," he informed me. "We clicked right away and had amazing conversation. We had sex a few hours after we met, which is crazy because I was only the second guy she had sex with."

That stung, especially when I remembered Number 23's judgmental grimace when we dished our Numbers: his four against my twenty-two.

I understood why Number 23 felt at ease with mentioning other women. I came off as the casual "cool girl" who was far too busy with my ambitions to give heed to pointless emotions like jealousy. But was it necessary for him to tell me about their romantic weekend when he snuck her away to his family's lake house? Did he have to glorify her value in introducing him to his love of the outdoors? Was he obligated to inform me about the bush between her thighs and their premeditated hookup I would be scraping off leftovers from?

His unfiltered conversation topics reminded me of my female sailor status: More than a hooker, less than a woman. I was a brick wall he could chuck rocks at all day and not feel a thing. But they hurt. God, they hurt.

I studied Sheryl's Facebook page like it was my midterm.

I believe that social media has become a treacherous platform for love interests. Before the Internet invaded our lives, I'm sure that each single person liked a lot of people at one time. Before falling into a committed relationship, there are steps taken to get there. Often, this involves talking to and even dating a few people at once. That's logical. But with Facebook, your competition is suddenly splattered in your face.

All I had to do was click onto Number 23's profile and scan one after another wall post from ladies who may or may not be his mating potentials or mating pasts. I see their names and faces. When I click onto their photos, I open a Pandora's box into their lives. I see their friends, professions, achievements, hobbies, and bodies. I evaluate, I compare, and when I'm insecure, I tear apart. I copy, paste, email, and text the images to my friends, so that they can assure me that I'm prettier, smarter, have bigger breasts, clearer skin, have something that would make him a fool to want her over me. Suddenly, I am stalking, letting fits of rage overcome me with violent hatred for these women who I've never met.

Sheryl wasn't beautiful. She was actually quite plain. Her hair was a long, fine dirty blonde. Her eyebrows were dark and too thick for her fair complexion. She didn't wear a spot of makeup. She was rail thin with A-cup boobs at best. And though I used her figure as a means to cut her down, I secretly envied it. It was obvious that her physique came from a super high metabolism, when I hit the gym six days a week to obtain curvy.

She was four years younger than me and went to Stanford straight out of high school. She had her shit together early on. From her photos, I could tell that she had a lot of fun with a solid group of friends. Sheryl was comfortable in her own skin. Nearly every photo was of her backpacking a mountain or jumping in a lake with her tie-dyed hippie dorm mates, smiling wide and carefree.

To make matters worse, she was brilliant. She ironically went to Stanford, my rival university less than an hour from my campus. On top of our outdoorsy, wanderlust natures, we were both members of the west coast's academic elite. She planned on being a world-traveling doctor.

I spent months brooding over her, allowing my shortcomings to eat me alive. Both of us would be boarding flights from the San Francisco Airport to spend our holidays in The South. Though we would be sharing Number 23, I was determined to win full custody.

For years I painted a beautiful picture of my homeland. I smudged the bigotry, ostracism, and narrow-mindedness of the Bible Belt and brightened it with colorful glasses of sweet tea, fresh, country hillsides, and southern hospitality. I erased the whiskey, the vitamin force-feeding, and the screaming fights that sent me crying and fleeing. I replaced them with sketches of a loving daddy who charitably tolerated me. I plastered tough love atop emotional indifference and neglect. I painted Mom with the unconditional nurturing that would wash away with the first light rainfall. Distance indeed made my heart grow fonder and Number 23 was an ideal addition to my dreamy abstraction.

But I had to become worthy of him. I was everything The South loathed - strong, bold, boisterous, brutally honest, fiercely unapologetic, raw and quite visible after destroying the walls that southerners kept so sturdy. Berkeley and the Navy were charms they could jingle in my absence to make up for their cringes in my presence. Berkeley was my apology. A punishment to my family, a flight risk for Number 23, I needed to be a good girl.

Me: I'm not as slutty as I sound. I'm going on a year of celibacy right now.

Truthfully, my sex free year was accidental. After Number 22 had been my Guatemala trip. Then I was plugging away at my 4.0 GPA and waiting tables in the little free time I had. Then I was transferring to Berkeley. I was just too busy for men. But Number 23 didn't need to know that.

I thought a celibacy stint was dynamite. I would become a reformed bad girl that Number 23 could adopt, romance, and de-virginize. I was pulling an old southern belle trick on Number 23 that had worked for centuries of matrimonial entrapment. I was emulating a girlish innocence, weakening myself to boost his ego, while coquettishly flashing bits of sexual innuendo to preview his rewards for commitment.

Number 23: I'm kinda on a year of celibacy too, but I have no choice. We aren't allowed near Iraqi women for good reason.
Me: Yeah, the celibacy thing is strange for me. I'm not doing it for God or Jesus or anything. I've had opportunities, but I just can't bring myself to do it.
Number 23: You don't have to have a reason to be celibate. I wish I could control my smoking habits like you can control your urge for sex.

I gradually heated our conversation.

Me: It's physically difficult for me. It's like going through drug withdrawals. Like today, I'm fine. The other day, I almost had an orgasm in spin class.
Number 23: Wow. How did that happen?
Me: You know. You're moving at a fast pace, you're sweating; you have this hard bike seat rubbing up against your clit as you bounce up and down from peddling.
Number 23: Ha. Just put a vibrator on the seat and you'll be set.
Me: That's a brilliant idea!

We steadily dove deeper into our risqué tone. We began asking each other the male and female anatomy questions that normal conversation didn't allow. I asked him how often his penis got caught in his zipper. He wanted to know what a Brazilian wax was. I made sure to let it "slip" that I got them regularly, subtly including the details that my clean, bare lady parts were also accessorized with a clit piercing. I picked up a few hints that Number 23 was a Magnum XL condom user. I wondered if Army Ken would be legitimate competition for his predecessor.

Number 23: What do your waxers think of the piercing?

Me: I once had a young, male gynecologist call it my "hardware." He was in his early twenties and I think he was actually turned on by it. I wonder if he enjoyed sticking that cold clamp inside me.

When I went home for Christmas, I behaved more like Mom than ever before. Number 23 was my happy pill. I hopped around Chattanooga to visit every high school friend I could contact. I eagerly jumped in front of Mom's digital camera for a rigorous family photo shoot in front of the fireplace - Mom and I smiling, brother squinting, and Carl glaring. I bounced around the kitchen giddily, ditching my vegetarianism for Carl's greasy sausage balls and breakfast burritos for our early holiday celebration. I didn't complain when my parents ditched us for Christmas for their couple's getaway. I took my brother, who'd turned numb to them at puberty, to the movies and a buffet. I saturated the environment with the bouncy enthusiasm Mom forced our whole lives.

Number 23 and I connected the day after Christmas in Atlanta. I spent months sweet talking his mother and had made her adore me, so I was invited to stay with her and his brothers that night. The next day, Number 23 and I were set to head north to Greenville to do some hiking. Though we spent months avidly communicating through every form of technology available, nothing replaced being in his physical presence. Seeing him walk up my cousin's driveway was awkward at first. He looked a bit gawky and even more boyish, but still handsome with his light blue eyes and peach fuzz face. He'd warned me that he was growing a beard on leave.

"Oh, you decided to shave the beard!" I exclaimed when I saw him.

"No," he said, sheepishly darting his eyes down for a second. "I've been growing it out for a week."

But once he got to me, his arms swallowed me in a hug that lifted me off the ground.

It only took ten minutes for our first spat.

"So," he started, looking a bit awkward.

He was driving his clunky 1986 stick shift Toyota pickup with me in the passenger's seat. We were heading to the movies to meet his family.

"Sheryl is leaving for South Africa tomorrow," he continued, getting more comfortable as if remembering how honest he was always able to be with me. "She's spending a whole semester there. I told her I'd say goodbye to her tonight. It'll just take an hour or so. And," he laughed a bit, "It may be the last time I'll have sex for a while."

Ouch.

"*That?*" I thought. "*That* was what I'd been waiting for? *That* was the golden boy I put on this godly pedestal? *That* was were all the flirtation, three-hour Skype conversations, all of that anticipation of being in the same room, the schedule coordination, the flights, the layovers, the drives, the pain in the ass obstacles led up to? *Really*? Sheryl? FUCKING SHERYL?"

Again and again she kept festering back, no matter what I did to exterminate her. I was done. I was ready to slice her off with or without Number 23.

"Wow. FUCK YOU!" I snarled, watching him jolt back a bit in shock. "TURN THE CAR AROUND!" I demanded. "I AM DONE WITH THIS *SHERYL* BITCH. DONE. TURN THE CAR AROUND *NOW*!"

"No," he said, looking a little scared.

"Turn the goddamn truck around right *now*!" I demanded.

"No," he said again. "Forget it. I won't go."

"Seriously *bro*, I don't want to keep you from rubbing one more out on Sheryl's thumb tack tits!" I continued. "God forbid little 'ole me prevents you from getting laid. It's fine. Take me back."

"No," he said a bit more confidently, steadying his ground. "Forget I said anything, Maggie. Really. I want to be with you tonight."

He smiled, playfully, soothing our stiff tension. Breathing a sigh of relief, we both let out a few loose laughs. I took the last bits of my aggression and playfully, but firmly punched his arm.

I won the battle but was facing a war.

With the two of us together, competition, jealousy, Skype, Facebook, the Army, Berkeley, all the things that stood in our way before vanished. It was just *us* - purely and organically.

Number 23 and I spent three days together. They were probably some of the best of my life. There was no sex. I planned on saving myself for the real deal- a committed relationship when the time came as if somehow giving Number 23 the honor of taking my imaginary virginity would make me a woman he could handle.

So, we embarked on a vacation back in time. We were teenagers, sneaking around his mom's house, playing grab ass in the kitchen when she and his younger brothers weren't looking. We spent entire nights furiously sucking face and dry humping, his fingers lodged deep enough inside of me to draw blood.

I couldn't even brush my teeth without being shoved onto a bathroom sink, Number 23's hand in my hair, lips pressed against mine.

We headed to Greenville, my birth city, where I saw his dad for the first time in a decade. Benjamin Robinson had the same kind eyes I remembered, only with a few extra wrinkles under them. They widened when I got out of the car.

"Maggie! You look exactly like you did when you were five!" Benjamin exclaimed before pulling me into a big hug.

Benjamin was exactly how I remembered - warm, calm, and effortlessly genuine. He seemed like an illustration of a father, created just for that very role. Number 23 idolized him.

"My dad is the strongest man I know," he told me once. "He's been through so much. He dealt with my mom's craziness. Then she took off and he had to practically raise Joshua and me himself. His wife now has her own issues and he's got to hold that on his shoulders. But you know, the man never complains. He never looks bitter or angry. He never takes his shit out on anyone. He never even lets you know what he's going through."

That was the Robinson anthem. Stay positive. Focus on the good. Don't talk about the bad. Do your best to forget about the bad. Bury the bad.

"I hate gossip," Number 23 told me. "That's one of the biggest lessons I took from my childhood. Dad always told us to never talk badly about people."

But when I looked, when I really paid attention, I realized their eyes told all of their darkest secrets.

When we went inside, Benjamin, Number 23, and I rummaged through all of their old family albums. It was all bizarre déjà vu, as if I were finding out that the man in my present was a boy in my earliest past. My affection for Number 23 was a different dimension than any warm fuzzies I'd felt before. Gazing at the images of the blue eyed, shaggy blonde toddler, boy, awkward preteen, I longed to be there with him to absorb every second of his life. I wanted every second from then on.

We visited my aunt, uncle, and cousins. We sat around in circles, and talked about all of our lives and dreams. We cracked jokes about the mud holes we found as children, sinking in while playing spa, and then transforming into swamp monsters up to our necks in goop, growling and prancing to our horrified mothers.

We busted out retro family photos of my toddler cousin lifting her skirt and flashing the photographer her panties. The experience was wonderful - almost euphoric because it was the first time in so long I'd felt like I was truly *in* a family. We were all *together*. Holidays with my parents were sitting on the couch while Mom and Carl plowed through one after another television shows.

After, Number 23 and I drove around Greenville, drank pints of beer, made out in bathrooms, and fooled around in my mom's SUV. I even accidentally ripped Number 23's jeans.

I felt young and innocent for the first time since the Numbers. Though the temptation was overwhelming, there was something marvelously alluring about going to the edge and not crossing the line that would take us all the way.

Benjamin arranged for Number 23 to sleep in his thirteen-year-old brother's room, while I was bunking in his little sister's. The kids were away for the night. But just like heathen adolescents, we ended up naked in his brother's bottom bunk bed. And no, he wasn't kidding about his ample endowment. With the 6'1" Army Ken on top of me, we were dangerously close to juvenile, just-the-tip sex.

Afterwards, Number 23 tucked me into his sister's pink, pony-littered bed. He wrapped the blankets securely under me, set a few of her stuffed animals near my cheek, and kissed me goodnight.

Those three days went beyond our habit of feeling each other up every five seconds. With no technology separating us, we didn't have to fill our voids with conversation. We quickly fell into a natural bond. We laughed a lot. We took long drives, blasting Number 23's stereo system with Queen, as he sang off-key and played air-guitar to Bohemian Rhapsody.

We fell into a pattern of me lying in his lap while he drove. Sometimes he slipped his fingers inside of me. Other times, I napped while he ran his spare hand through my hair and rubbed the back of my neck.

He took me on some of the few dates I've had. We ate sushi. We drank beer. We hiked Table Rock. The park was one of my favorite childhood spots, but nobody was ever willing to trek to the top with me. So we went. I watched his every move that day as he took my hand, holding it while we walked the trail, like a boyfriend would. Other times, he darted off the path to climb on every rock like a hyperactive seven-year-old playing Indiana Jones.

I was myself around him. Always the klutz, I stumbled on every rock and root, eventually falling head first into a pile of leaves. Rolling onto my back, he bent down to help me up. Both of us laughed hysterically. I observed the way he watched my every step, terrified that I'd fall off the mountain. He stopped to offer his hand to every stranger struggling up the hills. I think, even then, I knew I loved him.

"I'm really wondering what's going to happen to us," he told me.

It was our last full night together. We were in a bar, our bodies facing each other, our eyes in fixed contact. With a shot of whiskey in his system, Number 23 had just enough liquid courage to show me a glimpse of his unfiltered thoughts.

"If you end up getting that CNN internship in Atlanta this summer," he continued. "And if you move to Atlanta after college...."

His eyes drifted off for a second and then returned to me with a sharpness that was intimate enough to scare me.

"For some reason," he continued. "I'm just so captivated by you."

His mouth curled into a smile as effortless as a heartbeat.

We put off separating as long as possible. It was past dark and I had a plane to catch the next morning. In the South Carolina December night, he walked me down Benjamin's driveway. Just before I put the car in drive, with the window rolled down, he took my hand, looked me dead in the eye, and kissed it.

As I drove through the black, dry winter countryside to my grandmother's house, I sobbed.

I fell in love with a sniper - a man whose basic training instills psychopathic tendencies. I loved a professional dehumanizer. I loved a man who lived in a world where empathy was suicide. I loved a man who had to be ready to put a bullet through a toddler's skull if necessary. I loved a man highly skilled in burying his emotions, resurrecting them *if* and when he chose. I loved a man who saw me as his enemy. I loved a man I was disposable to.

I knew Number 23 so well that his secret thoughts might as well have been carved on his face. His mission: to be the Army hero, the southern Republican, the head of his wholesome household who comes home from a day of fighting bad guys to a meatloaf cooked by his homely, submissive wife.

The real Number 23 was not that man. The real Number 23 cried during sad movies, loathed the military's rigid confines, dreaded war and violence. The real Number 23 seeped through when his mind wandered into dreams of hopping in his truck and disappearing into the horizon. The real Number 23's haven lies deep in the Rockies where he can climb ledges, pounce in streams, and frolic through the earth like his everlasting childhood playground.

His real war was within himself. He was a boy dressed as a soldier, pumping his chest, slinging his gun, and fleeing in horror at a glimpse of his own reflection. I was a terrorist, set on obliterating the image that he fought to convey. I didn't need to voice my threat. My existence was enough. I was awful at disguise.

No celibacy vow could tone me down to the dowdy, womanly charm he was comfortable with. I failed in committing Number 23 to me the same way I failed as a southern belle. I didn't know how to fake my way into a dumbed down, watery version of my most pleasant face.

After we met, things became real. I think there were times after that he'd watch me carry on about sexism in the media, military corruption, my nineteenth birthday trip to Mexican jail, and my desire to eat Peruvian rat out of morbid curiosity and think, "Oh, no. No. No. Not *her*. I wasn't supposed to love *this* kind of girl, this wild, bold, outspoken, *crazy* girl. No. This wasn't the plan. She hates the Army. She bosses me around. She will never follow me. No. No. Not her. Fuck."

I think he's been mad at me ever since.

I fought like a Viking, with filthy, bloody perseverance. I fought to beat three thousand applicants for an internship in Atlanta, driving distance from Number 23. I fought to keep our fire going with a continent between us. I made sure we talked constantly, taking full control and initiating communication almost every day. I fought to keep the passion alive with a man I couldn't touch. I would spread my legs across my desk, laptop camera pointed down at my snatch while shoving my vibrator inside me and trying to mumble all the dirty things I wanted to do to him until his desk was salty and wet.

Number 23 fought back. He cut me with the make out photos of his military ball date that popped up on Facebook. He punched me with slut shames.

"You whored around a lot more when you were my age and you know it," he'd say. "I will never, *ever* in my entire life reach the Number you're at now."

He lured me with propositions of being together over the summer. He stabbed me with the information that he'd be escorting a friend to her sorority ball, warning me that he "might fuck her." And when I cried, when I pleaded, when I begged for him to wait for me, he reacted like a true soldier. He buried me.

I used to think that distance was our greatest barrier, that if the masses of land between us melted away we would just cave into each other and be happy. The nightmares began when I was under that misconception, but just kept going after they came true.

The details always vary and shuffle around. Sometimes we are among his family, my family, random friends, or the ex girlfriends of Number 23. I remember Facebook stalking, or even my current lovers. We are anywhere and everywhere, familiar and uncharted. But the same theme remains in every single dream. Number 23 and I are close. We are in the same city, the same building, or the same room. In those dreams, we have *finally* conquered the obstacle of distance. But I can't reach him. If I call him, he won't pick up. I find myself running around and around in every room, on every street, flagging down every pedestrian to ask if they've seen him. Sometimes I'll catch a glimpse of him driving by me on a street or walking several blocks ahead of me on a sidewalk. But if I call, he just glances back and quickly turns away. If he's right in front of me, I talk to him. If he responds, it's with distant, sarcastic rejection.

He didn't care. He doesn't care. He buried me a long time ago.

I got my summer internship. I sped east immediately after taking my last final. I remember feeling desperate to kick the miles behind me, as if Number 23 would explode if I didn't get to him in time.

I followed the signs to Fayetteville. It was an ugly town - quaint, colorless, void of any aesthetic beauties like mountains, rivers, or oceans. It was the type of town that forced people to convince themselves it was pleasant enough so they wouldn't feel guilty for staying there.

I imagined its nightlife as a gang of soldiers flooding into its handful of bars and strip clubs, flirting with aging bartenders with cigarettes hanging out of their lips and exotic dancers crisp from the tanning bed oven. Fort Bragg had the prison aura of most military bases with steel gates and square concrete buildings that boycotted creativity. As I drove up to the gate and waited at the congested traffic line to be checked and approved by security, I had a hard time shaking the grime of Navy déjà vu. Entering felt like slipping in quicksand.

I'd been fantasizing about my reunion with Number 23 for months. I spent dull points in class, jogs, and bike rides imagining scenarios of the bear hug he'd pull me into, the hours on end we would spend rolling around in bed, and the effortless chemistry that would only amplify and solidify in person.

That's why I was aghast at his reaction when I jumped out of my car, wrapped my arms around him and planted a kiss on his lips. He was a brick wall - hard and absent. He pushed me away, mumbling something about his issues with public displays of affection. After eighteen months of celibacy and waiting on Number 23 like an obedient Girl Scout, our big bang in the cheap motel room was a devastating disappointment.

"I swear, this never happens to me," he said after about five minutes of exasperated pumping before complete deflation. "I mean, my ex girlfriend and I went at it for hours. I had no problem keeping it up for her."

He took me to a family gathering, instructing my expected behavior in the car.

"No kissing, no cuddling, no handholding in front of them," he cautioned. "I'm not ready to introduce us as a couple. Also, watch what you say. Don't be controversial. Don't curse. Make sure you cover your boobs. I don't want to watch my little brother go through puberty."

We didn't last. No amount of his mother's dishes I washed, relatives I charmed, or road head I gave him was enough. He dumped me during a camping trip I'd driven seven hours to attend. I arrived to a group of soldiers who seemed to resent me immediately like the foreigner they'd been instructed to hate. I wandered through the woods alone, stuck in West Virginia without my car while he rock climbed with the boys. I buried my head in books. I occasionally threw myself on him in the tent as a pathetic cry for attention.

I remember departing his barracks at 4 am that Monday. I was sleep deprived, but told to leave before his workday. As I veered through the eerily silent town, I wondered if my whole reunion with Number 23 had been just another one of my nightmares.

This was our two-year cycle. He would want me. He would chase me. He would get me.

Then he would do everything in his power to push me away. He'd invite me into his world, then completely ignore me once I was got there.

He would have a one-night stand or begin sleeping with an ex girlfriend, making sure to fill me in on the details. I would get angry. I would lash back. We would fight.

He would criticize my body, claiming he was used to girls he could "pick up with one hand."

I would remind him of his malfunctioning dick. He would blame me for his sexual impotence.

I wasn't good enough. I wasn't thin enough. I wasn't quiet or delicate enough. I needed to be trained and scolded, and rejected when I didn't obey. I would get furious. He would dump me. I would cry. I would mourn. We would distance ourselves. I would recover. I would lose interest. He would call. He would keep calling. We would become friends. We would become *best* friends. He would promise that we would always be best friends, no matter how hellacious our bond got. He would always be there for me. He would never leave me. He would pursue me. He would get me. We'd be incredibly happy. Then, he would bury me.

I've witnessed all sorts of addiction. Whether it was cocaine, whiskey, or fried chicken, they all seem to have the same effect. Addictions take over lives, haunt emotions, manipulate minds, and alter some of life's biggest decisions.

I once knew a recovering alcoholic in his forties who began drinking at sixteen. His therapist told him that since his alcoholism began at that age, he was at sixteen-year-old maturity level. If this is the case, my behavior with all of my Numbers makes complete sense. My addiction to men began in my teens. Over the years, I matured. I was confident and even cocky. In nearly every aspect of my life, I was a woman of steel. But once I felt something for a man, I became a weak, irrational child.

Number 23 loved me as an image on a screen and a voice in his ear. He wanted his finger to tap on a flat surface when he reached out to touch me. He wanted to keep me stuffed in the mental attic with the rest of his neglected dreams so he could feel safe in his mundane daily grind.

"You'd leave me in six months," he joked. "You would be so bored if we ever did buckle down."

Sometimes I tell myself that Number 23 was an idea, a fabrication I created to be that heroic male figure who compensates for all the awful ones in my life, an unhealthy fix for my desperation for love. Reducing him to nothing but a reflection of my insecurities comforts me. It makes me feel like I have the power to vaporize him. But if I have that power, I haven't found it.

From a young age, I was taught to be sexually appealing. As a preteen, my stepfather described two categories of women- the ones like my mother, who are pure enough to be worthy of marriage, but are sexually prudent, intellectually inferior, and bound to a life to antidepressants and a dominant husband who mocks her flaws behind her back. Then there were the sluts made for bedding and never wedding.

My grandparents loved what they could dictate and did so with their money, creating a vicious cycle of codependent children who loved from need and not want. Love came with terms, agreements, strings, and compromises I was not willing to make. So, I chose to go my own way. I was lambasted, shunned, and forgotten.

I decided to be the woman no man would ever love. I chose my rules, ego, independence, agenda, sexual freedom, and pride. Loving somebody is my greatest humiliation. Telling someone I love them feels like stripping down naked on my period under bright, fluorescent spotlight for millions to view my scars, wrinkles, bloated belly, and blood dripping down my thighs. What distinctly separated Number 23 was that I was willing to embrace that humiliation for him.

And essentially I did. I humiliated myself by sending him care packages of scratch-baked cookies, stuffed animals, books, and random paraphernalia from our inside jokes. I humiliated myself by altering my life for him. I humiliated myself by submitting to emotional destruction again and again, rebounding back for more. I humiliated myself by not only just swallowing the pain. I longed for it.

The Army transferred Number 23 to Anchorage, Alaska. College graduation was approaching. I suddenly stopped hating cold weather. We were in one of our "best friend" phases.

I had a slew of logical motives to move to Alaska that made it easy to lie to myself. I wanted to be a television reporter. Alaska was a small market with little competition. Its culture loves independent women. I would acquire a lot of fascinating stories of avalanches, mushers, and reindeer that were impossible to obtain in The Lower 48. I loved the outdoors. I loved an adventure. I custom crafted Alaska to make sense. I was due to take a trip up there and check it out.

Me: Are you comfortable with the idea of me moving to Alaska? Or would that be weird?
Number 23: NO! Of course I would love for you to live here! I couldn't imagine anything more badass than having my best friend up here. We could go hiking every day. OH! I could teach you how to hunt!
Me: But…we do have a history…
Number 23: But that's history.
Me: Look, I think we need to be more honest before I come up there to visit. Just so we can know how to conduct ourselves.
Number 23: Honest with ourselves?
Me: I think there's still something going on between us.
Number 23: No, there isn't. We're just best friends. That's it.

Me: Come on. We talk every day…all day. We're incredibly close. You know that a male and female with a romantic history that remain that close most likely have something going on. I'm not saying that we should be together. I'm saying that we should just own up to how we really feel and put all of our cards on the table. I just want to figure this out.

Number 23: Yes, there was a time I had those feelings for you. It happened. But, I don't know. They just went away. I don't know why. I only see you as a friend. A good friend, but JUST a friend. I'm sorry, but I just don't feel the same way you do.

Me: I don't believe you. But that's fine. TOTALLY fine. Give me some space and I will have you friend zoned by the time I get up there. :)

A few weeks of Number 23 detoxing worked wonders. His boyish awkwardness seemed to amplify when his truck approached the airport terminal. I felt so indifferent to him. I questioned what had hooked me for so long.

"I'm confused about my feelings for you," he confessed that evening.

I shrugged. I was indifferent. I felt like I'd won.

By the next morning, we were tangled in a naked pretzel.

Number 23 was indeed confused about his feelings. For a weekend, we were ecstatically in love. Then, he practically ignored me my last day there. He said that was his way of emotionally preparing for my departure.

He bought a ticket to meet me in Italy during my summer European backpacking trip. Despite my crying pleas, he fucked another girl on my birthday. I met that girl years later. She had a baby. She worked retail. She lived in her South Carolina hometown. She was the cliché of what happens to small town women. I couldn't imagine the mentally complicated Number 23 connecting with her. She was just a girl.

"*This* is who he broke my heart for?" I wondered.

His appendix ruptured the week before he was supposed to fly to Rome. The army wouldn't let him leave the country, so he went to The South and fucked her again.

By the time I moved to Alaska, Number 23 felt like a traumatic accident. He'd haunted me throughout Paris, Ireland, England, and Italy. Although I shrugged his memory off during the days of busy exploring, the handful of drunken stupors I drank myself into resulted in crying over him. By the end of my journey, I was done. Even while driving to Alaska, I was done.

"We can be friends, but *just* friends," I told him. "But no sex. No cuddling. None of that."

At first, he respected my boundaries. He was always around. We cooked dinner together. He walked my dog. He came to my studio and watched me do newscasts. We went to carnivals and beer festivals. But then, the lingering glances started, the longing in his blue eyes that he got when I was out of reach, and the constant compliments on how beautiful I looked that day.

"So, my brigade is having a military ball," he mentioned. "I'd really like you to be my date, you know, if you don't mind buying your own ticket."

I shrugged off the sting of his last remark. This was a big deal. I'd never been a date on somebody's arm at a lavish event, escorted into a ballroom in a beautiful gown.

As much as I tried to express distaste for feminine clichés, part of me felt sad for missing out on that girly princess treatment. I'd certainly never been a daddy's princess. I didn't go to prom. If I ever did get married, I'd never have the heart to deal with Carl awkwardly walking me down the aisle, struggling to fake some emotional investment in the whole charade.

I was shocked that Number 23 was even considering showing me off among soldiers. Whenever I met his friends, Number 23 always acted like a little boy brushing off his mommy to impress the cool kids. But he assured me he wanted me there.

I bought a multicolored purple and green gown with a long train that dragged in psychedelic swirls. It was elegant enough for ball standards, but I would definitely be the most unique.

"It's perfect," Number 23 told me, eyes glowing, when I tried it on.

But once I gave into his compliments, our close friendship evolving to mild flirtation, evolving to nighttime cuddles, evolving to sex as it always did, my value dropped like a new car driven off the dealership lot. It wasn't long before Number 23 had me, grew interested in other women, divulged that information, and snapped at me for reacting.

"We're not in a relationship," he scoffed. "I owe you nothing. I'm too young for this shit."

The military ball came in the thick of our tension. As I applied my makeup at the station Number 23 was due to pick me up at, I found myself acting unexpectedly like my mom again.

"Plaster concealer over those dark circles. Curl your hair. Apply your lipstick. Look pretty. Don't drop that smile. Don't you dare ruin that mascara. FUCKING SMILE, BITCH."

"Watch what you say around these people," Number 23 warned me on the way there.

We were back to my usual obedience training for public appearances.

"Not a word about the Navy. No politics. Nothing controversial."

"I got it," I growled.

"Do you, really? Because you've never gotten it before and I have to work with these people. This is my fucking career. And you should have picked a dress that doesn't show so much skin."

I tried to have a grand time.

I tried to shrug off Number 23's opting out of escorting me on his arm, his hesitance to even stand on the escalator beside me on our way to the ballroom, and his habit of disappearing for long periods of time to wander through crowds of strangers.

I tried to make nice with the Army wives and their plastic smiles on the brink of exploding a flood of catty comments. I tried to find charm in the sharply dressed soldiers, the fancy pledge, their ceremonial prayers for the safety of service members overseas, and the toast to the women in the room followed by the boys hollering with their fists in the air. And for a moment, I was able to gaze around the ballroom and find gallantry in it all as if to manifest my own fairytale.

But then I looked around the room and noticed the structure of male and female interactions. The women only talked to each other. They clustered like hens in little circles. None of them talked to me. I drank wine.

Once dinner was served, I had the chance to force conversation with several couples around the table. Number 23 had little to say to me beyond how my dress showed too much cleavage. One guy made a funny remark. The second I jumped in to tease him, all of the men verbally burnt holes in my face.

"Girls aren't supposed to give guys shit," Number 23 gritted through his teeth. "Just keep quiet, okay?"

I drank more wine.

"Weren't these shitheads just toasting to their women?" I hissed back.

"That's different." he snapped. "This is the Army. There's a role and place for them. You know that."

I drank more wine.

The last glimpse I caught of Number 23 was his back turned to me, walking into the distance towards his truck parked a few blocks from my apartment.

It was an October Alaska day, weeks before the fall of the first flakes that would become its snowiest winter in recorded history. The air was frigid and dry. The vegetation was colorless and dead. The brown grass crunched underneath my boots. Number 23's eyes were to the ground and shoulders limp with his hands in his pockets in a sorrowful slump of a cowboy who'd lost the heart to watch his favorite horse's execution.

I knelt on the concrete to scratch my dog's large, pointy ears, more for my comfort than his. There was eeriness in Number 23's house call. We'd been weird for the past few days since the ball, but beyond our usual weird of fighting, hashing, detailing, dissecting the tumultuous us. His blue eyes had faded into grey and cheeks drooped. I couldn't remember the last time I'd heard him laugh. He'd become the walking dead.

There was no purpose for his visit. He didn't want to apologize for his distance at the military ball, grab lunch, vent over family conflicts back home or any anxiety from the Afghanistan deployment he was leaving for the next month. He just sat on my bed, small talked for ten minutes, and left.

His voice was a lifeless monotone when I called that night.

"I need to know what's going on," I demanded. "You're different. Something's off."

"Aren't you tired, Maggie?"

"Tired?"

"Yes, *tired,*" the temperature in his voice rose. "Tired of *this*, tired of fighting, tired of yelling, tired of this runaround of hating each other. Fucking *tired*! I know I am. Aren't you?"

I began to cry. I felt panicked, my eyes tiny waterfalls, with air suddenly unable to suck into my lungs without desperate gulps.

"Maggie, I can't do this anymore. *You* can't do this anymore. We cannot be in each other's lives."

"You're supposed to be my best friend, you asshole!"

"But you are always threatening to cut me off when I fuck up. And I *always* fuck up. Always. Why not just do it? Cut it? Because we can't live like this."

I can't remember what I said in response. I was drunk on two shots of panic and three shots of despair. I just know that I was face to face with the death of my one truly intimate connection. And when our two-year union flashed before my eyes, I only saw the wonderful parts. I saw the jokes, that first gravity defying, body swallowing hug, the boy who tucked me into a pink bed of stuffed animals and kissed me on the cheek, his arms lifting me off the ground after a trail tumble, burrowing in our universe of blankets and pillows. For every good, there was bad. But for a fleeting moment, there was only love.

"I don't understand," he continued. "Of all the shit we've been through, of all the crap that I've done to you, why do you still keep me in your life?"

I paused for a second, my wits long gone. In shaky sobs, I muttered the only answer I could think of.

"There was nobody else."

I wish I could say that I let things die with dignity, that I told him that although I would miss him, that he was absolutely right about our relationship being bad for both of us.

I wish I could have said, "Yes, we made a mistake by keeping things going for so long" and that I hoped for nothing but happiness for him.

Instead, I screamed a slew of curses, completing my verbal fire with a cliché, "FUCK YOU," before hanging up. And that wasn't enough. I had rage that needed unleashing.

I sent him a series of texts and emails about what a despicable human being he was. I took a photo of my face, cheeks slick with watercolor stripes of black mascara flowing from my lashes, eyes red and puffy, hair matted with a caption saying something along the lines of, "THIS IS WHAT YOU DID. I HATE YOU."

The amount of times I called him that night could have guaranteed him an airtight restraining order. But by dawn, I was ill from the sound of his voicemail greeting. I spent the weekend paralyzed by grief, making my sheets my own chamber of sorrow.

I didn't leave my room the rest of that weekend. On Monday, I went to work carrying a heavy layer of despair. I channeled my depression into productivity. I became obsessed with it. I worked fifty-five-hour weeks. I went to the gym religiously. I met a CrossFit trainer who guaranteed me the skeletal physique Number 23 belittled me for lacking. I did hard workouts six days a week. I lived on an eight hundred-calorie diet. My life was trudging in the snow before dawn, beating myself at the gym, starving myself, working, and collapsing every evening. I spent Sundays in bed. I retreated into antisocial recoil. Men disgusted me. I went on another long celibacy stint. And then I snapped. Through it all, I cursed Number 23's name.

It's not the sickness that Number 23 reduced me to that frightens me. It's how long I willingly ingested it. The last time I heard Number 23's voice, he was telling me that I had a dependency on men, that I'd made him my life raft, that the only reason I put up with him was because I was broken inside. It was the truest thing I've ever been told. Although it was my life's greatest detriment, I was unconscious of it. Unconscious male dependency was the fuel to my Number 23 rebound, a rebound that sent me back to my preteen anorexia, driving me to the vulnerable weakness that sent me crawling back to The South.

My Number 23 withdrawal came in phases. First there was rage and then despair and then oblivion. Once he gained enough distance in my memory, my mind did the deceptive artistry it had done for The South. My fuzzy image of him allowed room for imagination. So, I painted him to be a pure, golden-hearted soldier who rescued me from that male dependency, and me the harlot who poisoned him with rage.

My rude awakening came when I returned to my homeland. I saw my girlfriends' dedication to men who incessantly cheated, spent days on the couch with their eyes plastered to PlayStations while she slaved for their rent, or stole her jewelry to score his heroin fix. I saw it in my grandmother, blind and bitter, glued to her recliner, anticipating the end of the world through the news while holding back scowls fueled from regrets of surrendering her career in the name of 1950s barefoot and pregnant expectations. But the cruelest awakening was losing Mom. Thanks to good old-fashioned patriarchy, as always, Carl won.

The end of Number 23 gave me my first taste of the most somber realization I will ever come to. We can deeply love our poison. We can love the taste of it, the scent of it, the comforting weight of it in our belly and find ourselves woken in the night with stabbing cramps, arms around porcelain toilet bowls, hurling every last bit until collapsing on bathroom tile, limp from dehydration. Sometimes parting with love is essential for survival. I've found the most tragic aspect of losing loved ones wasn't the big boom of the fallout, but realizing later how much healthier I was without them.

I still wonder if Number 23 ever thinks about his catacombs.

Though the process was lonely and grueling, I somehow kicked my kryptonite and began living by days instead of Numbers.

ACKNOWLEDGMENTS

I owe my first token of gratitude to my former journalism professor, Kevin Foster Cox. Thank you for introducing me to this craft that became my life, my heart and my greatest salvation. Thank you for recognizing my talent, and for encouraging me to write from my gut. Thank you for showing me how to spot the larger themes in my stories. Thank you for all of your time and dedication in reading, evaluating, and editing this book in its infancy - especially for soldiering through those dreadfully awkward graphic sections. Your mentorship, support, and most of all, friendship is priceless. Every word I write is in your honor.

To my editor, Ashley Taborsky: Thank you for your utterly selfless time and dedication. Gracefully walking the fine line between allowing my creative freedom and calling me out on my shit is a rare and precious gift that I will never take for granted. This book would not be half what it was if it weren't for you. You are magnificent.

To my best friend, Nathan Bridges: You have coached me through some of the hardest and saddest times. Without your support, your friendship, and your guidance, I would have never found the strength to see things in the real perspective necessary to write this book and completely *be* its author. A true doctor, you have kept my spirit vital through famine.

To my talented cover designer, Cole Sweeton: A book is indeed judged by its cover. Any success *Just Another Number achieves* will be highly accredited to you. I love your work so much.

Thank you, Chelsey Ashford, for donating your talents to our fun graffiti photo shoot.

To my brother, Jordan, cousin, Ashley, and Aunt April: Thank you for listening, for empathizing, for understanding, for supporting, and most of all, for loving me during the times I thought I was unlovable.

To Chris Henderson: Despite your efforts to remain humble, your kind heart, patience, morality, and devotion to your loved ones are transparent. Thank you for being my friend through all of this and reminding me of the beauty in burdens.

To Nancy Markovich: Thank you for your constant love, support, and appreciation for my unfiltered self. I will forever and always be your spiritual granddaughter.

To Jessica Wood, Brooke Binkowski, Corey Denig, and Dustin Mullins: Thank you for always assuring me of the achievements behind and ahead of me. Your encouragement and faith in my future brought me comfort when I was the most frightened.

Grandmother: Thank you for passing on your ambition, your brashness, your intelligence, and most of all, instilling my self-confidence. Though it lay dormant for many years, it kept me alive and blossomed when ready.

Granddaddy: Thank you for passing on your determination, your ferocity, your humor, and your rebellion. I'm vowing to use the combined attributes of you and Grandmother to defeat the secrets, the facades, and the charades that have haunted us all for far too long.

To my military brothers and sisters: It has astounded me how many of you have been so incredibly loving and supportive over this past decade. Even when we don't always agree on things, including morality issues in publishing this book, your loyalty has remained unconditional. Thank you for showing me what a family truly is.

To my UC Berkeley professors: Thank you for teaching me how to think critically.

To Number 23: Thank you for showing me how to channel turmoil into art.

To my parents: I may have become a strong swimmer, but you will never get my praise, gratitude, or respect for shoving me into the roaring river.

I owe infinite appreciation for the feminists who came before me, who fought towards gender equality, who were unapologetically smart, gritty, fierce, and bravely willing to brace for the collateral damage that comes along with fighting for what they believe in. You are all my heroes.

The final years of this book's production have been some of the hardest of my life. Thank you to the friends who helped me survive it, whether it was giving me a place to stay, connecting me to readers, buying me lunch, or even just listening to me cry. I have a special place in my heart for every single one of you and promise to pay it forward.

Most of all, I owe my eternal appreciation to my readers. I don't know how I became an author. Writing an entire book seems like a great effort to humor the college professor that suggested it. But I do know that it was all of you who kept me going. What started as positive feedback from a few copy and paste slaps for whatever opinions I could scrape together transformed into emails, outpouring the connection you felt with my writing, our similar experiences, and your faith in the positive changes my voice could make. I want all of you to know that it's not the writing itself that truly fulfills me, but the connections I make with all of you through it. Every day, I will remember how blessed I am that all of you have showed me why I exist.

24436936R00206

Made in the USA
San Bernardino, CA
27 September 2015